1002
N. Cent.
Expy
Suite
579

Repubic
Cabinets in
Garland
972-484-8899

Media
Management
In the age of GIANTS

Business
Dynamics of
Journalism

Media Management

In the age of GIANTS

Business Dynamics of Journalism

Dennis F. Herrick

DENNIS F. HERRICK is a former owner and publisher of newspapers in Iowa and a former reporter on dailies in Michigan. He is on the journalism faculty at the University of New Mexico, and he is a member of the Executive Board of the Media Management and Economics Division of the Association for Education in Journalism and Mass Communication.

© 2003 Iowa State Press
A Blackwell Publishing Company
All rights reserved

Blackwell Publishing Professional
2121 State Avenue, Ames, Iowa 50014, USA

Orders: 1-800-862-6657
Office: 1-515-292-0140
Fax: 1-515-292-3348
Web site: www.blackwellprofessional.com

Printed on acid-free paper in the United States of America. Produced directly from camera-ready copy provided by the author.

Cover design by Justin Eccles

First edition, 2003

Library of Congress Cataloging-in-Publication Data

Herrick, Dennis F.
  Media management in the age of giants : business dynamics of journalism /
Dennis F. Herrick.
    p. cm.
  Includes bibliographical references and index.
  ISBN-13: 978-0-8138-1699-9
  ISBN-10: 0-8138-1699-8 (alk. paper)
  1. Journalism—Management. 2. Journalism—Economic aspects. I. Title.

  PN4784.M34H47 2003
  070.4'068—dc22

                                                                      2003061997

The last digit is the print number: 9 8 7 6 5 4 3 2

TO BEATRICE

"Our liberty depends on the freedom of the press,
and that cannot be limited without being lost."

—Thomas Jefferson

TABLE OF CONTENTS

PREFACE: *XV*

CHAPTER 1:   Responsibilities of Media and Journalism   3

    Historical perspective on the media   5
    Public (stockholder) ownership of media   10
    The biggest story in American journalism   13
    Preparing for a new media world   14
    Conglomerates aren't all bad—are they?   19
    A new media world of convergence   23
    The difference the First Amendment makes   26

CHAPTER 2:   Preparing Yourself for Management   39

    First, get the right job   40
    Getting discovered and climbing to the top   42
    Your first management position   48
    Surviving in the cross-fire   51
    Managing yourself—handling time   52
    Not just anyone can be a manager   55
    Journalists becoming managers   57
    The indispensable management resource   59
    The quick way to the top   59

CHAPTER 3:   Motivation and the Work Force   67

    Unionism in media companies   68
    Layoffs in hard times   75
    When you must fire or lay off someone   82
    Approaches to managing employees   84
        Scientific (or classical) management   84
        Humanistic (or behaviorist) management   86
    Theories of management   88
    Maslow's Hierarchy of Needs   90
    Management by Objectives (MBO)—it's everywhere   92
    Employees need to feel they're being treated fairly   95

ix

Contents

CHAPTER 4:   Qualities of Leadership and Management   105

The sources of power   105
Leadership practices   109
 Model the way   110
 Inspire a shared vision   111
 Challenge the process   111
 Enable others to act   113
 Encourage the heart   114
Characteristics of leaders   115
The immeasurable value of optimism   119
Pointers on being an effective leader   122
The MBAs arrive in media companies   124
Being an effective manager of others   126
Jerks and vampires don't see themselves in the mirror   128

CHAPTER 5:   Decision-Making   135

What is decision-making?   136
The steps to making decisions   138
Risk-taking in the decision process   140
Categorizing decisions   143
Analytical decision-making tools   144
 The basic tool   145
 Critical Path Method (CPM) and
  Performance and Evaluation Technique (PERT)   145
 The Decision Tree   149
 The pay-off matrix   151
 The computer spreadsheet   152
Hidden traps of decision-making   153
Who are the decision-makers?   157
 Individual decision-making styles   158
 Group decision-making styles   159

CHAPTER 6:   Media Ethics, Regulation and Laws   167

Do the right thing   168
Government and the press   172
Legal issues in media businesses   176

CHAPTER 7:   Operations and Structure of News Media Companies   189

The ethics of the media profit chase   192
The decline of local news coverage   195
Influence of stockholder interests   199
Uncommon types of ownership   204

CONTENTS

Three main kinds of ownership 209
    Sole proprietorship 209
    Partnership 210
    Corporation 210
The functional parts of any business 214
Structure of media companies 217

CHAPTER 8: **Budgeting and Financial Management** 227

The profitability dilemma of media managers 228
Profit maximization and responsibility 233
Budgeting and planning 237
Gantt and milestone charts 240
The balance sheet 241
The income statement 245
Financial analysis ratios 247
Cash flow and cost-control 249
Time value of money 251
Investment criteria 254
    Net present value 254
    Internal rate of return 256
    Payback period 256
The never-ending conflict 258

CHAPTER 9: **Sales, Marketing and Market Analysis** 263

Traditional wall between business and news 264
The 4 P's of marketing 268
Market penetration and pricing 273
Pricing and marketing decision tools 276
    Pricing analytical tools 276
    Marketing analytical tools 278
Total market coverage 283
Market analysis 285
Market-driven journalism 288
The power of the cluster 292

CHAPTER 10: **Consolidation and Convergence** 303

There's some safety in large size 307
Monopoly, oligopoly and joint operating agreements 309
Combining forces and news roles 319
Going international 328
Fragmentation of media markets 329

Contents

CHAPTER 11:   Entrepreneurship   341

  Entrepreneurs and managers   342
  Traits of an entrepreneur   344
  Promotion or ownership?   346
  Trying repeatedly is what brings 'luck'   347
  Tips for entrepreneurs   348
  Starting up a business   350
  Seeking success with a business plan   352
  The necessity of money   354
  Ten secrets of business success   359

CHAPTER 12:   Technology Creates New Media   363

  Newspapers and technology   366
  Television and technology   371
  Media business and new technology   373
  21st-century electronic and digital media   377

INDEX   389

From the conclusion to Geneva Overholser's acceptance speech as Gannett "Editor of the Year" in 1990:

"Here's my dream for the next risk-taking, history-making endeavor: Let Gannett show how corporate journalism can serve all its constituencies in hard times. As we sweat out the end of the ever-increasing quarterly earnings, as we necessarily attend to the needs and wishes of our stockholders and our advertisers, are we worrying enough about the other three? About our employees, our readers, and our communities? I'll answer that: no way. And we're not being honest about it.

Geneva Overholser

"Too often by far, being an editor in America today feels like holding up an avalanche of pressure to do away with this piece of excellence, that piece of quality, so as to squeeze out just a little bit more money."[1]

This portion of her speech was omitted from the Gannett magazine. Overholser resigned in 1995 as editor of the Des Moines Register.

PREFACE

THIS book introduces basic business concepts, terminology and management theories for a course that was called "Media Management" in some semesters and "Business Aspects of Journalism" in others (depending on what a university secretary typed for the catalog).

Rather than writing for professionals already experienced in management, this text is oriented instead toward professionals being promoted to their very first management position and toward students whose first management jobs might be some years in the future. This book is intended as a broad overview and is only introductory at best. Entire semesters of courses and thick volumes of books are available for what is covered here in each chapter, or even portions of chapters. The text is an overview of the business dynamics of journalism and of the current media industry.

> "The things taught in schools and colleges are not an education, but a means to an education."[2]
>
> —*Ralph Waldo Emerson*
> *Journal, 1831*

This book will necessarily always be trailing behind the current situation because of the major changes taking place so rapidly in the media industry through mergers and acquisitions, the cyclical nature of the economy, technology, and the changing personalities of leadership—the latter being often the most important component of all. To try to alleviate that problem, a complementary Web site is maintained at <www.mediatextbook.com>.

For those wanting more information on a point, endnotes are provided for each chapter. Case studies and suggested Web sites for additional information also are at the end of each chapter.

Students and beginning managers say they need an introduction to broad concepts. Students want information they can come back to in a few years when they actually have an opportunity at management, and beginners do not need detailed explanations better suited for experienced managers. This book is oriented to students and beginning managers.

The business dynamics of journalism are rapidly changing. As Loren Ghiglione of the Medill School of Journalism pointed out, "Trends within journalism—the push for ever-larger profits, the dominance of ratings-driven, crime-laden local TV news, the decline of local radio news, the rise of infotainment, the disappearance of news bureaus abroad, the refusal of broadcast outlets to pay interns—all deserve continuing examination."[3]

This book's goal is to provide that examination. It focuses on the management only of news-oriented media companies. That includes newspapers, magazines, television and radio, along with their constant companions of the advertising and public relations firms.

Regardless of what field of the media you enter, a background in business basics will help you to succeed. And having some grounding in business perspectives will give you an advantage over most of your peers in taking steps toward advancement. Nearly all careers in journalism and communications are fulfilling. If one also wants to be paid well, however, that usually is accomplished best through management positions.

Unless students take courses available in a business administration curriculum (often not very accessible to non-business majors), there is little opportunity for communication and journalism majors to be exposed to basic business management principles. This book addresses both managerial and entrepreneurial issues while it also builds a foundation of knowledge in business basics.

A University of Iowa journalism professor, Carolyn Stewart Dyer, wrote in a 1992 essay about the difficulties of researching business facts on newspapers. (The same difficulty lies in trying to research the business side of other media companies.) The natural consequence of those difficulties has been relatively few books written about the financial and operational aspects of journalism.[4] Most of the books concerning themselves with the business practices of journalism have been biographies and autobiographies, fiction, and press critic viewpoints.

Business greed has been the theme of many books, even up to the present. Their main focus has been more on the effects of business practices on the dissemination of news, however, rather than on the business aspects themselves, which this book addresses.

A handful of books, plus articles in current periodicals, have marked the beginning of a new direction in the study and understanding of "the business of journalism," which has opened the way for media management courses in colleges, universities and private institutes. Until these later works focusing on the business side, media management courses were not offered at the undergraduate level to students of journalism and communication studies.

Partly, this was because journalism educators had not deemed the business of media companies relevant to their academic goal of preparing new graduates for the job market.

The immediate goal of nearly all journalism education is the grooming of undergraduate students to, in essence, be good employees. Our communication and journalism schools do this by teaching the skills needed to be a news reporter, headline writer, publications designer, copy editor, photographer, videographer, editor, writer, anchorperson, advertising and public relations expert, and now even an HTML or XML programmer. The schools round out the student's education with classes in the practical, historical, legal, ethical, sociological and theoretical impacts of mass communications in the United States and the world. Despite the condescending criticism of some media executives, the communication and journalism schools excel in annually providing a skilled, knowledgeable and motivated group of entry-level recruits to the work force.

These new journalists are entering an industry very changed from the one that existed just a generation ago. Most would declare that circumstances are worse than even in the bad old days.

Even when discounting the somewhat different complaints about the excesses of the early political press, the penny press, and the yellow press, alarms have been raised about the effects of rapacious business practices by the nation's daily newspapers for more than 100 years. First there were the union activists in the late 1800s, followed by novelists like Upton Sinclair in 1920; government officials as high as President Franklin D. Roosevelt in 1934; and press critics, including George Seldes in the 1930s and A.J. Liebling throughout the 1940s, '50s and '60s. Several government studies have addressed media business—especially the 1947 U.S. Senate committee report titled *Survival of a Free, Competitive Press* and Canada's studies of concentrated newspaper ownership by the Davey Committee (1970) and in the Kent Report (1981), all to be discussed later.

This book focuses much of its attention on the effects that stockholder ownership and giganticism have on the business conduct of media companies.

The media conglomerates that dominate news and information everywhere today cause innumerable conflicts of interest for virtually all media analysts, educators and journalists themselves in reporting and evaluating media mergers and buyouts. These conglomerates are so large and diversified that nearly everyone who has any pension or 401(k) retirement fund owns investments in some of them. Therefore, the maximization of profits by these conglomerates directly benefits those of us who comment on the transactions.

I believe readers have a right to know when those conflicts exist. Then they are able to judge for themselves whether the conflict has affected the way in which the transaction has been explained or presented.

It is appropriate to report, therefore, that my wife and I have IRA, 401(k), and Iowa and New Mexico state pension plans that undoubtedly contain shares of media conglomerates in different amounts at different times. In addition, we also jointly own the stock of several media companies. As of the end of 2003, we owned shares of stock in the following media or communications conglomerates: Gannett Co., AT&T, Bell South and SBC Communications Inc. We also then owned a media brokerage firm, Newspaper Associates, that specialized in the acquisition and sale of weeklies. Now you know.

The goal of this text is to make readers aware of the good and bad points of the current media industry, explain what changes have occurred, and explore why they exist—all with historical, economic and operational perspectives. In this way, readers going into media management should be able to better cope and adapt to current and future developments. That will enable them to enjoy satisfying careers as media managers or entrepreneurs—and move into a position to make the positive changes they believe are needed.

I have touched more lightly than some texts on subjects such as legal, ethical and news reporting issues because most curricula include separate courses on such topics. Rather than restate those efforts, I have tried instead to concentrate the book's emphasis on business issues that are not generally available for study by aspiring journalists.

As noted by Cynthia Tucker, editorial pages editor of the *Atlanta Constitution*, "How can those of us who are managers in news/editorial do our jobs well if we have so little knowledge of the basic (business) issues that confront newspapers?"[5]

Acknowledgements

SEVERAL PEOPLE examined the book's manuscript and made valuable suggestions directly resulting in its improvement. My heartfelt thanks for those at Iowa State Press who offered encouragement and guidance—especially Mark Barrett, acquisitions editor; Cheryl Garton, publishing assistant; and Judi Brown, project manager/editor. I am grateful for the careful review of the manuscript and many excellent suggestions for improvement offered by Leslie-Jean Thornton of the State University of New York–New Paltz, and Thomas L. Beell of Iowa State University. Special mention goes to the support and encouragement I received from all the faculty and staff in the Department of Communication and Journalism at the University of New Mexico.

Professionals who provided valuable advice on the manuscript include: Raymond L. Gover, my 1960s–70s city editor and now retired president and publisher of the *Harrisburg (Pa.) Patriot-News*; Bill Kezziah, a former weekly

> A glossary of more than 1,000 business terms is available at:
>
> http://www.washingtonpost.com/wp-srv/business/longterm/glossary

publisher now teaching media management at the University of Nebraska; and Roger Van Noord, an author and former managing editor of *The Flint (Mich.) Journal.*

I am indebted not only to the sources referenced throughout this text but also to the students I have had the privilege of meeting and learning from while teaching journalism and mass communications classes at the University of New Mexico, the University of Iowa and Kirkwood Community College and while advising the student newspaper at Cornell College in Mount Vernon, Iowa.

Students in my spring 2002 and spring 2003 media management classes at the University of New Mexico were guinea pigs for preliminary drafts of this book. They offered many helpful suggestions from the students' point of view.

Special thanks to the following UNM students: Wendy Apkarian, Sky Atkins, Marisol Avilés, Jeff Becke, Ben Berger, James Bledsoe, Heidi Brown, Maeghan Bruce, Amanda Cannedy, Michael Carlson, Kim Coffman, Ryann Collard, Tonya Crossley-Paulette, Antoinette Davis, Derek Davis, Colin Darby, Kristen Ferris, Tim Fish, Karen Francis, Mary Franklin, Darise Gallegos, Deidre Gallegos, Cyndi Garcia, Shannon Jackson, Shauna Kastle, Dan Koski, Ana Lucero, Tabitha Medvedik, Kristy O'Malley, Kendra Oden, Will Potts-Gorham, Clare Russell, Courtney Smith, Oscar Solis, Chris Valencia, Emily Williams, Ivan Wilson, Leland Wyman and Susan Yara.

The greatest thanks goes to my wife, Beatrice. Her patience and encouragement over three years of research and writing made this book possible.

—*Dennis F. Herrick*
University of New Mexico

 *Suggested Web sites:*

www.poynter.org—The Poynter Institute
www.spj.org—Society of Professional Journalists
www.americanpressinstitute.org—American Press Institute
www.miami.edu/com/mme—Media Management and Economics, AEJMC
www.journalism.org—Project for Excellence in Journalism, Committee of Concerned Journalists

Endnotes to Preface

[1] Text reprinted with permission of Geneva Overholser. A more extensive quote of her remarks is by Gilbert Cranberg in "A swan song in Des Moines," *Columbia Journalism Review* (May–June, 1995). Photograph is by permission of Geneva Overholser

[2] Lewis C. Henry, *Best Quotations for All Occasions* (Greenwich, Conn.: Fawcett Publications Inc., 5th ed., 1962), 65.

[3] Loren Ghiglione, "The splendor of our failures," *Journalism & Mass Communication Educator* (Autumn 2001): 16.

[4] Carolyn Stewart Dyer and Carol Smith, "Taking stock, placing orders: A historiographic essay on the business history of the newspaper," *Journalism Monographs* (April 1992).

[5] Cynthia Tucker, "Newsrooms need to learn about the business of journalism," Journalism and Business Values, Poynter Institute <www.poynterextra.org/centerpiece/jbv/tucker.htm>, accessed May 15, 2001.

Media Management

In the age of GIANTS

Business
Dynamics of
Journalism

CHAPTER 1
RESPONSIBILITIES OF
MEDIA AND JOURNALISM

SOME journalists achieve management positions, and others have management thrust upon them—often sooner than they expect. One day you're covering your beat, and then suddenly one of the editors asks you to head up a three-reporter team on a special project. Now you are "management," at least in the eyes of the team's other reporters who are now looking to you for leadership.

Taking a course on business management principles while still in college is wise preparation for such an eventuality, which might come earlier than you expect in your career.

The commercial side of media companies is necessarily a blending of two separate disciplines: business and journalism. Those using this book will learn the inner workings about the business of news-oriented journalism companies. Frankly, the companies are not very cooperative in revealing such information.

Let's face it. Newspapers, TV and radio broadcast stations, magazines, and even Internet sites are quick to tell us about the business practices of every business in town—except their own. As early press critic A.J. Liebling observed, on those rare occasions when the media do report on themselves, or on each other, the result is a generally uninformative account filled with circumspection, deference and awe.[2] Press critic George Seldes noted, "The press publishes the news, true or false or half-way, about everything in the world except itself."[3]

> "Most editors have had little management training. We got our jobs because we were good at something else—reporting, copy editing, photography. Then one day we became managers, and were asked to master an entirely different discipline."[1]
>
> —*Edward D. Miller*
> *Newsroom Leadership Group*

Some things never change. In 1999, *Brill's* magazine asked why *The New York Times* never explained to readers the reason its legendary editor Abe Rosenthal was leaving. The apologetic reply of executive editor Joseph Lelyveld was, "It's very hard to cover yourself aggressively."[4]

One quick example of this phenomenon could be seen in Iowa City, Iowa. The nation's hottest newspaper war was conducted there from September of 1999 to early 2003, with three daily newspapers in a town of only 60,000. But the din of battle was reduced to a mere whisper in the newspapers on the battleground. There were articles about that war only in places such as the national trade magazine *Editor & Publisher* or in the *Chicago Tribune*. When editors of Gannett's *Iowa City Press-Citizen* received a press release about the startup of the rival *Iowa City Gazette*, their reaction was to ask each other—like interns encountering their first news story—"What do we do with this?" [5] They decided on a two-paragraph business brief and nothing much afterward on the biggest business story in town. Not even the third paper, *The Daily Iowan* at the University of Iowa, ventured to take a close look at the city's newspaper war. The war tapered off after three and a half years. The *Iowa City Gazette* was restructured as another zoned edition of its privately owned parent, the *Gazette*, published 20 miles away in Cedar Rapids.

Ironically, the very rarity of this head-to-head competition leads to the heart of what this book is about, which is, What is going on with the media in today's society. Just what are, as this chapter's title states, the responsibilities of the media and journalism?

The Ford Foundation raised the following questions in a summer 2003 forum on media diversity and the public interest.

Regarding the responsibility of media

• The current media system in the United States and other Western nations is manifested by giant cross-platform conglomerates dominating the printed, spoken and viewed news. Does this system promote the diversity of perspectives and viewpoints (the "marketplace of ideas") essential for citizens to function in an informed way within their participatory government and social environment?

Regarding the responsibility of journalism

• Modern media corporations seem far more interested in profits than they are in news dissemination. Because of this, or in spite of this, do they provide sufficient content and services to adequately address the local news and information needs of citizens and communities?

These are two momentous questions. They have never had to be asked before in quite this way.

The rest of this book will deal with these questions and their many ancillary ones, debating if the present conglomerates are meeting the responsibilities of both the media and journalism and, if not, whether anything can be done about it.

These questions frame the idea a little differently than most books grappling with the issues of media conglomerates and their role in society today. Usually the questions are asked about whether the profit chase is resulting in poorer, more superficial and less informative journalism; whether good journalism can co-exist with good business; whether convergence, market-driven news, consolidation and other facts of modern newsroom life are producing better journalism; or whether some kind of balance needs to be struck between the way journalism used to be done and the way it is going to be done.

All of those also are part of the debate. But overlying all of these issues are the basic questions about responsibility of the media and responsibility of journalism.

Historical perspective on the media

EARLY JOURNALIST Lincoln Steffens warned about the corporatization of newspapers as early as 1897, declaring, "The magnitude of financial operations of the newspaper is turning journalism upside down. Big business was doing two things in general to journalism: it was completing the erection of the industrial institution upon what was once a personal organ; and it was buttressing and steadying the structure with financial conservatism."[6]

Former *Des Moines Register* editor and *Washington Post* ombudsman Geneva Overholser sees a weakening of journalism under most chain ownership. "In an era that cries out for entrepreneurialism and a belief in the future," she wrote, "newspapering is risk-averse and dispirited, cowed by the over-emphasis on short-term profits, and steadily bleeding the commitment to public service that animates us."[7]

Numerous legal actions alleging anticompetitive practices were brought against newspapers over the years until the Newspaper Preservation Act was passed by Congress and signed in 1970 by President Richard Nixon. The new law uniquely exempted newspapers allied in Joint Operating Agreements (JOAs) from antitrust action.

Many feel not enough was known about the business end of journalism then, or now.

In a 1992 media business issue of *Journalism History*, editor Barbara Cloud contended there was not enough research on the operational and financial aspects of media companies. She observed, "To understand the roots of the mass media and the course of their development, we must pay attention to their economic dimension."[8]

Today, information on the business side of journalism seems more important than ever.

A new era has suddenly come upon us with the emergence of giant media corporations, with more than half of the 30 largest newspaper chains publicly traded on the stock market, as are the corporations owning most broadcast stations and magazines. These huge firms now dominate daily newspapers, many weeklies and shoppers, as well as magazines, radio and television. They also are increasing their presence in advertising and public relations. Their influence is growing stronger by the year—by the month even.

Stock-market journalism is a relatively new business phenomenon.

It has occurred in newspapers only since the early 1960s with the emergence of the first publicly traded U.S. publishing entities, Booth Newspapers of Michigan and Dow Jones & Co. in New York, both by 1963, when they became stockholder-owned companies. They were followed by Times Mirror Co., then publisher of the *Los Angeles Times*. Most American media companies have gotten in bed with Wall Street since then.

Ownership of radio stations by national publicly traded corporations was not common in the United States until the Telecommunications Act of 1996. That law was passed ostensibly to foster competition, but it had the opposite effect, creating today's giant radio companies instead.

In TV, legislation and other factors led to gargantuan mergers, allowing publicly traded conglomerates to take over all of the U.S. television networks in the 1980s and 1990s.

The final major factors limiting U.S. conglomerates, a ban on cross-ownership and a limit on broadcast market ownership, were eliminated or loosened by the Federal Communications Commission (FCC) in 2003.

This new age of giants, many publicly traded and with an obsession for the bottom line to satisfy stockholders—who in turn are increasingly dominated by huge multi-billion-dollar institutional investors—has suddenly made awareness of business and financial issues more critical for both new and continuing employees of such enterprises.

However, only trade journals, a few books and some Web sites report on the factors that are making it possible for conglomerates to grow and seize even more control over all kinds of media companies. The biggest are only going to get bigger, but as noted, you generally won't hear that from the media.

In all, the FCC eliminated or loosened six ownership regulations in 2003 that had served to limit media conglomerates—though the 3–2 vote that year was only a culmination to a pattern of deregulation concessions to giant media corporations that federal policy, courts and FCC decisions had been building up to for several years.

The accompanying editorial cartoon,[9] depicting cross-ownership as an octopus outside the consumer's view, is by John Trever, editorial cartoonist for the *Albuquerque Journal*. It very likely would never have been acceptable for printing in most newspapers, but the *Journal* is one of the few remaining family-owned dailies over 100,000 circulation left in the United States.

—Reprinted with permission of John Trever

In broadcast, the 1996 telecommunications bill had eliminated caps on radio station ownership, resulting in three corporations gaining control of nearly 1,700 of the nation's radio stations over the next six years. And a 1999 court ruling ended the "duopoly" prohibition that had prevented one company from owning two TV stations in the same market. Within four years, the nation had 90 TV duopolies.[10] The local ownership limit was further raised from two to three TV stations in 2003, which was expected to set off another buying spree. The cap of eight radio stations in a single market was maintained, but will come up for review again in 2005.

Also ended in 2003 were regulations preventing TV stations from owning cable companies in the same city and the FCC prohibition against any conglomerate being allowed to reach more than 35 percent of American households. (The FCC had allowed Viacom and News Corp. [Fox TV] to both grow over that limit, to about 40 percent each, so raising the cap to 45 percent of the total U.S. market was only a bow to what the FCC already was allowing.)[11]

In newspapering, there was a ban from 1975 to 2003 against the same company owning both a newspaper and a TV station in the same city, but it was a ban in name only. About 40 jointly owned operations predating the ban were allowed to continue, and the FCC granted waivers that created several others over the years.

Finally, in 2003, even the bureaucratic ambivalence against cross-ownership ended. The FCC decided to keep the ban in place only in small markets with three or fewer stations. But the cross-ownership ban was loosened for mid-sized markets. And in the large cities where the competition is the most fierce, the ban was eliminated altogether.[12]

U.S. major media groups with holdings in both newspapers and TV in 2003[13]

Elimination of cross-ownership ban will lead to further consolidation

Chain	Dailies	TV	Other major holdings
Gannett Co. Inc.	100	22	400 non-dailies, USA Weekend
Tribune Co.	12	26	WGN, cable, non-dailies, radio
Dow Jones & Co. (with Ottaway)	16	*1	24 non-dailies, WSJ Sunday
The New York Times Co.	19	8	2 radio
News Corp.	^1	35	Fox, DirecTV
MediaNews Group	45	~1	121 non-dailies
Hearst Corp.	12	27	magazines, radio
E.W. Scripps Company	21	10	cable, shopping network
Cox Enterprises Inc.	17	15	cable, 25 non-dailies, radio
Freedom Communications Inc.	28	8	37 non-dailies
Belo	4	19	cable
Media General	25	26	100 non-dailies
Washington Post Co.	2	6	cable, non-dailies, Newsweek
Journal Communications (Milwaukee)	1	6	nondailies, 36 radio, fiber optic
Block Communications	2	5	cable
Dispatch Printing Co. (Columbus)	1	2	radio, cable
Gray Television Inc. (Atlanta)	4	29	misc.
Mormon Church	1	1	radio
Gazette (Cedar Rapids, Iowa)	1	1	radio, shoppers
The World Company (Lawrence, Kan.)	2	1	8 non-dailies
Landmark Communications Inc.	7	2	cable, 100 non-dailies Weather Channel, magazines

* - In partnership on CNBC; also numerous international joint ventures in print
^ - Many other newspapers owned overseas
~ - Announced intentions to buy at least four more TV stations
` - TV operation is a local cable franchise

The biggest beneficiaries from ending the cross-ownership rule are expected to be newspaper chains. Many chains already owned TV stations as well as newspapers, and some quickly announced plans to buy more in 2003 as a result of the FCC's action. The press time for this book was in mid-summer 2003. By the time it reaches readers, several newspaper purchases of TV stations in their market are expected to be consummated. Many companies had entered negotiations even before the ban was lifted because the outcome was so certain.

Why will newspaper companies buy TV stations, rather than broadcast companies buy newspapers? It is because TV properties are as a rule much more profitable than newspapers, so broadcast properties will be attractive to newspapers, but not vice versa.

It might be illuminating to compare this book's chart of media companies that own joint newspaper and TV holdings to a similar record that is updated a couple of years later.

All of this consolidation has gone largely unreported by newspapers and TV networks because most of their owners have a huge financial interest in getting all barriers to greater media concentration removed.

Is lack of coverage why there is so little public reaction to the consolidation of media companies into ever-larger conglomerates, or to the FCC's moves that are bound to result in even more control of media by mega-corporations?

Consider the field hearings that FCC Commissioner Michael J. Copps single-handedly conducted in 2002–2003 concerning the FCC's proposed repeal of ownership rules. Copps convened field hearings because the FCC would agree to hold only one official public hearing during the entire hearings process.

Copps said the FCC was able to get away with ignoring public hearings on such an important issue because no public interest was being expressed. Copps blamed that lack of public interest on the refusal of the press to cover the story. A field hearing attended by Copps and former ABC anchor Hugh Downs in Phoenix was typical. None of the newspapers or commercial TV stations covered the hearing. About 150 citizens attended, many notified by e-mail messages from the sponsoring Benton Foundation. There was no notice about the hearing in the Phoenix area press, one audience member noted, and the only reason he found out about the hearing was because he had heard it publicized on a BBC cable broadcast.[14]

Afterward, Copps was quoted in *Editor & Publisher* magazine taking the press to task for refusing to cover such an important issue as the ownership changes.[15]

He accused newspapers and TV of denying the public any information on the issue. It did little good. Media companies continued to treat the ownership changes that would enable them to grow larger and exert greater dominance in their cities as un-newsworthy.

FCC Commissioner Jonathan S. Adelstein also conducted some field hearings on his own. Like Copps, Adelstein felt that the proposed changes to cross-ownership and the ownership caps needed to be brought to the public's attention. However, their opinion was a losing minority on the five-member FCC.

Eventually, in the final days of the final week before the FCC's vote on June 2, 2003, TV networks and newspapers ran stories about the FCC being about to abandon the cross-ownership ban. Unless citizens had listened to National Public Radio or the Public Broadcasting System, both of which did provide regular coverage, those last-minute stories marked the first time that most people had ever heard about the ownership changes.[16] Congressional opposition was not voiced until afterward.

"It is possible that large corporations are gaining control of the American media because the public wants it that way," Ben Bagdikian writes in *The Media Monopoly*. "But there is another possibility: the public, almost totally dependent on the media for such things, has seldom seen in their newspapers, magazines or broadcasts anything to suggest the political and economic dangers of concentrated corporate control."[17]

Public (stockholder) ownership of media

IT STILL IS rare to be able to obtain detailed financial information on media companies, with the notable exception of the annual reports now issued by publicly traded media conglomerates. The first comprehensive study of media companies' financial operations, made possible by exploiting the availability of financials and other inside information found in annual reports to stockholders, was conducted at the University of Iowa in 1999–2000 by professors Gilbert Cranberg, Randall Bezanson and John Soloski. They researched corporate finances, media ownership by outside investors, and the effect that shareholder-driven ownership structures have on the mission of journalism.

The three professors published a book in May 2001 detailing the results of their study, titled *Taking Stock: Journalism and the Publicly Traded Newspaper Company*, published by Iowa State Press.[18]

"The manuscript represents a study of the 17 largest publicly traded newspaper companies in the United States," Soloski explained, "with a specific emphasis on ownership structure . . . and ultimately the consequences of the large-scale publicly traded form of organization for the newspapers owned and published by these companies. The 17 firms account for over 50 percent of daily newspapers in circulation in the United States."[19]

The *Taking Stock* authors believe the effect of corporate ownership on journalism today should be considered differently than corporate ownership of other companies. "It's commonplace, but accurate, to observe that while newspapers are a business, they are a different kind of business, with certain constitutional protections," they point out.[20] The authors' concern over the influence of security markets on the newsroom drives their book.

AT A GLANCE

Who Controls Media?

A rapid decline to fewer companies

1983	50 companies
1990	23 companies
1997	10 companies
2002	6 companies

The number of companies that own more than half of all U.S. media outlets

Adapted from editions of *The Media Monopoly* by Ben H. Bagdikian

"Publicly traded media companies are in a vicious circle they can't break out of," Soloski said in a 1998 interview with *Columbia Journalism Review*, referring to the relentless fiduciary obligation of executives in these companies to produce constantly rising profits for stockholders.[21] (In 2001, Soloski was named the director of the Grady School of Journalism and Mass Communication at the University of Georgia.)

Newspaper companies began selling stock in the early 1960s in an effort to raise large sums of money for acquisition, reduce their direct borrowings, and gain national exposure. They were followed in turn by other media companies, as detailed in this book's preface.

"In the late 20th century, the financial markets expanded rapidly, making capital easily available to larger and successful enterprises," the authors of *Taking Stock* note. "For the newspaper business, the bargain struck was a Faustian one: capital was available for the newspaper industry, but with it came a new set of expectations. An investing market demanded returns on its investment."[22]

Arthur O. Sulzberger Jr., publisher of *The New York Times,* is one of those who is concerned about the changes to journalism wrought by the financial expectations of investors. "The pressures are growing," Sulzberger said. "Wall Street is demanding of newspaper companies what it is demanding of auto companies or airline companies or any other companies: an increasing profitability year after year that some might say is long-term unachievable."[23]

Echoing Sulzberger is Debbie Goldman of the Communication Workers of America union, who said, "Wall Street is driving already very profitable newspapers and broadcast outlets to reach even higher profit margins, resulting in job loss and a lower quality product."[24]

Certainly, the need for profit always has been important in journalism. It's impossible for even the best companies to fight for truth, justice and the American way if they lose money for too long. As bluntly stated by Terry Quinn, senior vice president of the bottom-line Thomson Newspapers in a speech to the New England Press Association, "The average journalist squirms at the concept of newspapers as a business, but no profits mean no salaries."[25]

The very first sentence in William Serrin's book, *The Business of Journalism*, says much the same thing: "A nasty, unreported truth about journalism is this: Journalism is a business. Journalists like to pretend this is not so, but it is."[26] Serrin also concedes, "I have worked at newspapers with money, and newspapers without money, and the former is the place to be."[27]

Jim Bellows, editor of the now defunct *Washington Star* and *Los Angeles Herald Examiner*, observed, "In the real world, it's bottom-line journalism."[28]

Any business without profits is like a high-flying airplane that stalls and then spins into a downward spiral that crashes it to the ground. So there definitely is a need for media companies to be profitable.

But the demand for consistent profit margins comparable to the best investment opportunities in the stock market is a new development that Soloski first examined in a 1996 article "The New Media Lords," co-authored with Robert G. Picard. It explains the emerging influence of huge institutional investors—such as insurance companies, pension funds, universities and investment banks—with their demands for unprecedented profit margins from media companies that are traded on the stock market.[29]

The predictable result of investors' influence over the publicly traded companies is to also create a higher profit threshold for all media companies. Even privately owned newspapers and broadcast stations are now boosting their margins to remain competitive against the threat of the stockholder-owned conglomerates around them. Cash, and plenty of it, is needed to remain competitive.

Partly as a result of this heightened financial emphasis, the study of the business of journalism is growing. From the outside, there are more curriculum additions of university journalism courses on media management and media economics. From the inside, study of management principles now includes the formality of the four-year Executive Intern Program at Harris Enterprises, and the informal on-the-job-training that comes from revolving-door editorships at newspapers owned by various chains. There also is the Advanced Executive Program for established media managers whose companies pay $19,800 plus wages, transportation and expense allowance to send a manager for four weeks to the Media Management Center (MMC, formerly known as the Newspaper Management Center) at Northwestern University.[30]

The biggest story in American journalism

FOR THE PAST few years, MMC has been a leading proponent of the multi-faceted neologism of market-driven journalism. MMC Director John M. Lavine, a former publisher of a newspaper chain, told the 1997 convention of the International Newspaper Marketing Association that a market-driven newspaper "changes the rules" by redefining both its market and its medium with new strategies and alliances. He said editorial departments must get on the marketing team with the rest of the paper and help build profit margins.[31]

In its practice, this still-evolving concept of market-driven journalism is driven itself by geographic cluster ownership; coordination of news and advertising staffs on marketing; deep cost-cutting usually at the expense of news staffs and news coverage; increasing reliance on information-entertainment known as "infotainment," which includes celebrity news; extensive use of wire copy over locally written news stories; market segmentation in place of mass circulation; substitution of younger reporters for more expensive veterans; increased profit margins and shrunken news holes; homogenization of papers and stations under common ownership; and consolidation of ownership—not only for newspapers and broadcast but also for public relations firms and advertising agencies.

The ever-broadening ramifications of all that MMC teaches about market-driven journalism have perhaps forever altered the relationship between journalists and the public.

In *Market-Driven Journalism: Let The Citizen Beware?* John McManus contends that print and broadcast journalism are both compromised, writing, "Market journalism values the attention of the wealthy and the young over the poor and the old because news selection must satisfy advertisers' preferences. In fact, rational market journalism must serve the market for investors, advertisers and powerful sources before—and often at the expense of—the public market for readers and viewers."[32]

As the media come to be operated like any other business, with news only a commodity rather than a responsibility with some, one wonders if the public perception toward the media might also be affected. The media have been granted major sheltering under the First Amendment since ratification of the Bill of Rights in 1791. It is conceivable that these protections could be chipped away if media companies come to be considered as just profit-maximizing businesses, rather than the quasi-public institutions they generally have been seen as being in the past.[33]

"It's the biggest story in American journalism," former *Time* magazine editor Ray Cave declared in a comprehensive 1998 article written by Neil Hickey in the *Columbia Journalism Review* about media companies' money lust. He added, "Regrettably, it's also the least reported story in American journalism."[34]

Sounds like Seldes and Liebling were right, as well as Lelyveld.

In the same article, an unnamed *New York Times* editor describes this as a new era in journalism with its hallmark being "a massively increased sensitivity to all things financial."[35]

William Ketter, a former president of the American Society of Newspaper Editors, pointed out in the same article what he sees as an underlying factor for the cost-cutting and news-hole diminishment. "I'm concerned about the prices being paid for newspapers and the need for greater profit margins to meet those financial obligations," Ketter said, referring to the debt loads incurred by the buyers. "The squeezing of editorial budgets is a short-sighted way of dealing with that need."[36]

This problem is not limited only to newspapers, however, because premium prices also are being paid for radio and television stations, advertising agencies, and public relations firms. Consolidation and heavy debt loads are being imposed on them, too.

Preparing for a new media world

THE QUESTION very soon becomes clear. How can journalism schools properly prepare their graduates for a job market that seems to fulfill the chilling perception of management expert Peter F. Drucker, who believes today's jobs are "dangerous liaisons" for employees?

This book is an attempt to answer that question. Introducing under-graduates to at least the principles of management is beneficial in at least six ways.

(1) Students will be even better entry-level and developing employees if they have an understanding of why managers make the decisions they do and if they understand the managers' problems and goals.

(2) Introducing students to basic management principles might help

many to realize that eventual ownership opportunities are within their ability. That in turn will motivate them to set such a goal early on and to use their first years in the work force to the best advantage so more of them ultimately will become entrepreneurs or managers.

(3) Students with a basic understanding of some management perspectives will hold a competitive advantage for quicker advancement over students without such education.

(4) If nothing else, as new employees they will have improved survival skills for coping with the challenges of working under managers—both good ones and bad ones.

(5) Students who study media management will be more knowledgeable as reporters covering complex business operating and financial stories. Some editors see this skill-building benefit for reporters as the most important reason for developing an understanding about business.

(6) I am disturbed as I see, more and more frequently, how newspaper publishers, station managers, and public relations directors are being selected from the business and advertising ranks rather than from the editorial side. Perhaps a more conscious attempt to instill awareness of business and advertising principles in at least some journalism courses will improve chances for young reporters to rise in the ranks toward decision-making leadership positions in the media.

A major challenge for new employees and students as they ready themselves to enter the work force is to understand how the positive and negative influences in today's mass media industry should be made to co-exist in a sustainable environment of responsible journalism in all media companies.

All journalists must be aware of the changes and be motivated to adjust to these new business dynamics and still be professionals—not be discouraged and left with a sense of hopelessness and frustration, nor driven away from a career in the media. The vast majority of students are well aware of the problems of inequitable pay and declining morale across much of the industry, but they have decided they want to enter one journalism field or another regardless. It should be the paramount goal of journalism schools to prepare students to be able to do the best they can once they enter this new and sometimes frustrating media industry of the 21st century.

Many of the negative points raised about today's practice of journalism are detailed in the article "Journalism Education: A Lost Cause?" in *The Chronicle of Higher Education* by journalism educator Neil Henry.[37] In the article, he deplores the unprofessional wages paid to reporters, the greed driving some media owners to seek ever-higher profits at the expense of news coverage, and the decline in journalistic

15

quality resulting from the attendant rise of infotainment journalism. He also wonders if journalism professors could justify encouraging students to enter what he considers an irresponsible industry.[38] As author Graham Greene once observed, "Media is a word that has come to mean bad journalism."[39]

I am not as pessimistic nor as discouraged as Henry or Greene, however, for I believe cyclical circumstances could coalesce in some way to improve the mass media.

For one thing, as one media critic admitted, "Good journalism has a way of being there when we need it."[40] There have been two recent and harsh examples. The terrorist strikes of Sept. 11, 2001, restored international news coverage, which had been dropping precipitously in the years up to that fateful day. One estimate is that national newscasts had reduced foreign coverage by 65 percent in the preceding decade alone. In the months after Sept. 11, international news coverage in all media climbed back toward previous levels—at least temporarily. Then, when war ignited against Iraq in March 2003, the news networks ran round-the-clock commercial-free coverage, and many local newspapers and TV stations spent lavishly to send reporters, photographers and videographers to the war zone.

Even without earth-shaking stories, there is much excellent journalism on a daily basis today despite publicly traded media companies.

At the same time, there is a lot of journalism being performed by overworked, underpaid reporters and editors, resulting in many of the best people abandoning news positions after a few years for less stressful careers. Corporate executives like to say they do not interfere with their companies' news operations, but their influence is felt, even if it is through a culture of subtle employee subordination. Many reporters admit to self-censorship, hesitating to tackle stories that might conflict with their company's investments or the owner's friends.

Here is a hopeful note: There might finally be some recognition that too much of the media companies' news gathering and reporting function has been sacrificed to golden calves. MediaNews Group CEO William Dean Singleton said he thinks the cost-cutting reductions in newsrooms probably have gone too far and need to be reversed. Mike Reed, CEO of Community Newspaper Holdings Inc., believes profit margins must come down if newspapers are going to keep their market share—although he also acknowledges that many media companies that are traded on the stock market are "probably scared" to even voice such a concept.[41]

The Media Monopoly's early concerns about consolidation and bottom-line journalism, derided by many as alarmist through the earliest editions of the book, now seem prescient instead. Thoughtful people are starting to speak out about the downward spiral they perceive—the first step toward other people listening to them.

Geneva Overholser was once a Gannett establishment insider who rose through the ranks to become editor of *The Des Moines Register*. She now is corporate journalism's gadfly with columns and a weblog at <www.poynter.org/geneva>. In one column, she lambasted the newspaper chains for their "emphasis on profitability" over news.

"I'm hoping the profit-pressure pendulum has swung so far that the return to excellence is coming," Overholser wrote. She urges news companies' bean-counters to set aside a percentage of profits each year to improve news coverage in a fund she called "The News Trust."[42]

The Aspen Institute called in several newspaper leaders from the editorial and business sides—including Overholser—for a two-day spirited discussion in 2002 on whether great journalism can continue to co-exist with today's business demands. A conclusion was that "the challenge to journalism is preeminently commercial rather than ideological, and is coming not from the usual antagonists of the press, but rather from media owners and managers purporting to be friends."[43]

Alex Jones, a Pulitzer Prize–winning reporter and former host of National Public Radio's "On the Media" program, sums up the rising dissatisfaction on the editorial side in this way:

"Journalists are among the most idealistic and driven people in American society. There's a real crisis of confidence and in morale among journalists now because they feel they're not being led right. They're simply not being told that they're doing something really important, and they're not being allowed to do many of the things that brought them into journalism in the first place."[44]

We are starting to hear from others who are in managerial positions enabling them to make a difference, such as Tom Johnson. He retired in 2001 as CEO and chairman of CNN television but continues as a CNN consultant and adviser.

Johnson attributes the dissatisfaction of editors and reporters to the realization that "their owners and managers haven't shown the same commitment to them that they did to profits, or that they did to the market." He adds, "They didn't find the quality of the newspaper they were putting out as important as answering the needs of their shareholders."[45]

Many others are concerned that the bottom-line emphasis is solving the media companies' short-term problems, but setting up the industry for greater problems in the long run. Some of these long-range problems might include lessened public respect for an industry already low in rankings of public esteem, a rise in competition from the Internet, wireless, and technologies we are not aware of yet, and increasing difficulty in attracting quality employees.

Media owners feel that competition is greater than ever before. They are concerned about a rapidly increasing number of choices competing for customers' time, fragmentation of markets, declining daily newspaper and TV audiences, rising costs, and changing public tastes.

Increasingly, personnel of news-oriented media companies are concluding in companies large and small that their industry's prosperity requires a commitment to cooperation between all departments of their newspaper, TV or radio station, or magazine. Such cooperation is internal, leading to a tearing down of the traditional walls between the newsroom and the rest of the company's departments.

As one editor at a 2003 Gannett management seminar observed, "If the news department is going one direction, advertising another, circulation a third, market development a fourth—and on-line is an afterthought—you can count on failure. You may have some strong individual departmental performances, but you will not have a success-ful, coordinated effort in which the whole is greater than the sum of its parts."[46]

Another chain's editor noted that editors have a lot of responsi-bilities, and one of them is to use resources effectively, which sometimes can mean newsroom cuts. He added that the challenge always has been to put out a quality newspaper within a certain set of financial goals and that continues today.[47]

Cooperation also is external. It leads to convergence of newsrooms between a company's own newspaper, TV and Internet outlets. It also leads to degrees of cooperation even with the news, circulation, production and ad departments of nearby competitors.

Executives of stockholder-owned media companies often are accused of focusing more on the bottom line than on product quality, but there are powerful financial incentives for executives at these investor-backed companies to do that.

"Increasingly," the trade magazine *American Journalism Review* noted in mid-2001, "newspaper CEOs are compensated based on stock prices and how well their companies perform financially—not for high quality, public service journalism."[48]

That's also true, by the way, of other media CEOs, and it equally applies to nearly all editors, publishers and station managers.

The magazine reported that the CEOs of 12 of the largest publicly traded newspaper companies took home an average of $3.6 million in compensation, bonuses and stock options in 2000, quoting one as admitting he never thought he would ever be making so much money as he is now.

In turn, the "average operating profit margin" for those companies was 22.7 percent that year, according to the magazine.[49] ("Operating profit" is pre-tax revenue, as opposed to "net profit," which is what is left after all expenses are paid.)

Some editors question whether accepting stock options—and thus buying into the over-riding concern for profits that such acceptance requires—is a betrayal of their commitment to journalistic responsibility. To make money from a stock option, the recipient must benefit from a rising stock price that usually is powered by increased profits.

"It is a way of reminding me that part of my salary is tied to the performance of the company," retired *Los Angeles Times* editor John Arthur said, referring to stock options. "I don't think it is an appropriate way to compensate editors, frankly."[50]

Robert H. Giles, curator of the Nieman Foundation and a former editor and publisher of *The Detroit News*, observed that executives of publicly traded newspaper companies (and the top officers of other publicly traded media companies) woo Wall Street investors with glowing reports of market share, circulation, advertising sales and profits.

"They hardly ever talk about news content or investment in staff training or the knowledge base in the newsroom," he said, criticizing the profits mentality brought by stock options and fat salaries. "So analysts come away thinking this is like any other bottom-line industry and that there's no difference between newspapers and making widgets."[51]

Conglomerates aren't all bad—are they?

BY PRESENTING the business of journalism, it is not the intention of this book to go about corporate-bashing. There is no question that the newspaper chains, broadcast giants and other media conglomerates have many advantages to offer, or they would not prosper. There's even the argument that in this day of a greatly fragmented audience the conglomerates are essential.

Media author Benjamin M. Compaine notes, "There is no compelling evidence that newspaper readers have been ill served by the trend toward groups. There are at least as many documented cases in which a newspaper purchased by a group was substantially improved as there are cases in which a paper was weakened."[52]

While I might argue that the 50–50 split is over-stated, I must nevertheless concede that I know of newspapers that were undeniably improved by chain ownership.

The strengths of such large companies, and the key points made by their defenders, are frequently and succinctly put forth by David Demers of Washington State University. He maintains that "most of the criticism against the corporate newspaper is more myth than fact."[53]

For years, Demers has conducted voluminous research on the operations of "corporate newspapers," which he defines as large companies with complex organizational structures—as opposed to the "entrepreneurial newspaper," which he defines as family owned and managed. (*Editor & Publisher* magazine estimated that only 20 percent of the nation's dailies were still in family hands in 2001,[54] and virtually all of those were under 100,000 circulation.)

In a *Newspaper Research Journal* article, Demers maintains that "critics have vastly overstated the adverse consequences of the corporate form of organization."[55] His research concludes, "Although structurally organized to maximize profits, the corporate newspaper actually places more emphasis on quality journalism and much less emphasis on profits than its entrepreneurial counterpart."[56]

In another example, Demers presents research in the *Journal of Media Economics* from surveys he conducted whose "findings do support a growing body of research that suggests that corporate newspapers, even though they are more profitable, place more emphasis on quality and other goals."[57] In other words, greater profits do not necessarily mean that corporate newspapers are inherently bad.

AT A GLANCE

Who Owns Major Media?

You might be surprised

Media outlet	Owner
CBS	Viacom
ABC	Walt Disney Co.
NBC	General Electric
CNN	AOL Time Warner
Fox	News Corp.
New York Post	News Corp.
USA Today	Gannett
Detroit Free Press	Gannett
Detroit News	Knight Ridder
Los Angeles Times	Tribune Co.
Chicago Tribune	Tribune Co.
Denver Post	MediaNews Group
Boston Globe	New York Times Co.
Newsweek	Washington Post Co.
Time	AOL Time Warner
Telemundo	General Electric
KTNN-AM	The Navajo Nation
Deseret News	Mormon Church

Gerald Stone, another educator, conducted a study on newspaper ownership from a different angle, concluding, "There is no consistent documentation that group ownership of newspapers is inherently bad."

He noted that, "Chains have a distinct economic advantage derived from their experience and expertise in management, marketing and use of the economies of scale. Evidence is that this financial planning sophistication can make newspapers more profitable businesses without debasing the journalistic product."[58]

Compaine notes that not one of the top 10 individual media companies of 1986, based on revenue, was among the top 10 just 11 years later—at least not as the same company.[59]

Robert G. Picard, who has headed media management institutes in Finland and Sweden, points out that nothing lasts forever.

"Although media magnates have existed since the commercialization of newspapers in the 19th century," Picard writes, "the rapid and seemingly unending expansion of communication conglomerates at the end of the 20th century has fueled rhetoric that taken uncritically might lead some to believe that such conglomerates are self-sustaining, continually expanding, nearly immortal organizations . . . . The empires are portrayed as . . . . creating their own rules, acting at will, constantly expanding, and having limitless potential to grow even larger."[60]

Picard points out that the fortunes of media companies rise and fall in response to a wide range of market forces, some of which are so dramatic that they can even affect any one media giant's existence.[61]

One reason for this impermanence might be in the very size that conglomerates reach and the far-ranging diversity of their holdings. Most media conglomerates today have divisions in several fields that include most or all of the following: newspapers; magazines; Internet; television; radio; movies; music; cable; real estate; and various retail, wholesale and manufacturing enterprises.

In his book, *The Economics and Financing of Media Companies*, Picard wonders if a company can get too large and complex. "Size can provide strength and economies of scale, but it can also make enterprises difficult to manage," Picard wrote.[62] Executives of the largest media company, AOL Time Warner, came to rue the huge size of that company in 2003, with some of them urging that the corporation be scaled down in size because they believe it has become too large to manage effectively.[63]

Sometimes we see a vulnerability brought on by financial strain, such as with Community Newspaper Holdings Inc. Established in 1999, CNHI bought up hundreds of small and mid-sized dailies, weeklies and shoppers in just two years. But during the economic downturn of early 2001, it began selling off some of its large clusters in Iowa, Texas and other states. By 2003 CNHI adopted a new business strategy that included selling all of its dailies that are under 10,000 circulation.[64]

Other times the big change can take longer, as when Canada's then-largest media power, Conrad Black, his Hollinger International Inc. empire strapped for cash because of huge debt obligations for his acquisitions, sold most of his Canadian and U.S. papers in late 2000—keeping the *Chicago Sun-Times*, the *Jerusalem Post* and the London *Telegraph*—a total of 77 dailies and 302 community papers.[65] Hollinger's Canadian holdings alone brought $2.4 billion in U.S. dollars.[66]

Times change quickly. By May 2001, Black, by then a newly appointed British Lord, said Hollinger was flush with cash and he was thinking of making a major acquisition in the United States.[67] Hollinger became one of the major investors in April 2002 in the start-up of the daily *New York Sun*.[68]

Crushing debt loads brought on by too-rapid growth holds portents for other media companies, whose growth projections used to pay for the debt can be deeply compromised by recessions.

Clear Channel Communications Inc., which saw its sales jump in a decade from $74 million to $8.4 billion by 2002, could be one example. That 100-fold increase in gross revenue was made possible by buying about 1,200 radio stations, 19 television stations and 770,000 billboards across America, as well as becoming the nation's largest live-concert promotions firm—and all in only six years, after the deregulation brought on by the Telecommunications Act of 1996.[69] When the 2001 recession hit, however, Clear Channel was burdened with $9 billion in debt in the face of suddenly diminished revenue. Clear Channel went on to record four consecutive quarters of massive hemorrhaging that totaled $366 million for just the fourth quarter of 2001.[70] The company ended up losing more than $1.14 billion in 2001. Everything finally turned around in 2002, when Clear Channel posted a net profit of 8.63 percent, clearing $725 million.[71]

In 2002, French media giant Vivendi Universal SA began selling several of its properties to reduce debt after firing Jean-Marie Messier, who had almost bankrupted Vivendi in an acquisition spree that had swallowed up several American and European media rivals. Naturally, the prospective buyers were other media conglomerates.[72]

Some companies sorted out tough economic times by changing direction. Thomson Newspapers, now known as Thomson Corporation, had been one of the largest newspaper chains in the United States and Canada. But in 2000, Thomson sold all but a minority interest in one of its 130 U.S. and Canadian daily and weekly newspapers to other chains after deciding to re-focus on its other communications properties.[73]

In 2003, the family owners of America's 14th largest newspaper chain, Freedom Communications Inc., decided to put their 28 dailies, 37 weeklies and 8 TV stations across the country on the market. That set off numerous rumors on who might be interested, with the front-runner being America's largest chain, Gannett.

So, is it all just swapping Monopoly® cards?

Conglomerates come and go, perhaps, but isn't it a fact that they usually sell to each other, so that conglomerates are here to stay, but just with different names and bigger asset lists?

It is an indisputable fact that one large company's divestiture becomes by necessity another larger company's acquisition. Frankly, many daily newspapers and television stations have just grown to be too mega-expensive for individuals to be able to afford to buy them. The conglomerate with its deep pockets has become a necessity. At times, an investor like Warren Buffet decides to diversify and buys a *Buffalo News*. Even more rare is when a local resident can buy the hometown daily from a chain, as wealthy businesswoman Wendy P. McCaw did in 2000 by outbidding at least three chains to buy the *Santa Barbara News-Press* from The New York Times Co.[74] Media broker Thomas C. Bolitho remarked afterward, "That is so unusual it just doesn't happen."[75]

A new media world of convergence

IT WILL COME AS NO SURPRISE to journalists or to journalism students that the current business practices of media companies have distressed and even angered many employees on the news side. Numerous books have come out in recent years attacking the rapid changes brought on by consolidation, stockholder influence and the newest trend—convergence—where broadcast and print newsrooms are merged.

Go to any gathering of publishers or high-level media managers and you will surely hear the same mantra. Consolidation is needed because only the strong survive, they will say. Journalism is important, they always will be sure to say, and it can be made better by running media companies as lean business operations with high profit margins. The first duty of at least the higher ranks of managers is to the stockholders, they say, and, like the previous argument, if the stockholders are happy the media companies can better serve the public. Reducing staffs, merging newsrooms and getting reporters to cover stories for all of a company's media outlets through convergence is essential, they insist, so as to cut wasteful duplication and increase readership and viewership.

News side employees hear these recitations, often couched in desperate terms of necessity and impending doom, but they often remain unconvinced.

Publishers have been talking poor-mouth for generations, but newsroom staffers now realize that the print and broadcast media companies are among the nation's most profitable businesses—even in bad times.

Convergence (combining newsrooms) is becoming increasingly used by companies with more than one media outlet. At a recent journalism seminar, a roomful of journalism educators and editors listened rather skeptically to a plea for convergence from a former executive with the Tribune Co., which they all knew enjoys 20 percent-plus operating profit margins. L. John Haile, who now runs a consulting business to help companies achieve convergence, asserted that costs would be reduced and better journalism would naturally result if newspapers and TV stations would converge newsrooms.

Reprinted by permission of *Quill* magazine
The mobile reporter of the future under convergence?[77]

In rebuttal, one editor scoffed: "Convergence is not a gift for journalism. It's a way of doing things on the cheap—trying to get more production out of the same people, without hiring more people."[76]

In the first study of its kind on convergence, educator Jane B. Singer of the University of Iowa visited Tampa, Sarasota, Dallas and Lawrence, Kan., in 2003. In each city, one owner had both the daily and a TV station and had implemented converged newsrooms. The 120 journalists she interviewed felt that working in a converged print-TV-Internet newsroom was good for their career and overall a good idea, but they also feared that convergence could lead to reduced staffing. They described their combined newspaper-TV-Internet news duties as "more time-consuming than they believe their bosses realize."[78]

It was estimated in 2002 that 15 to 20 newsrooms were in "serious convergence," with scores of others doing at least some degree of convergence.[79] The move to convergence is rapid. By mid-2003, companies reported 51 convergence newsrooms, 22 convergence advertising combinations, and 11 projects listed as joint "outreach" efforts between print and broadcast.[80]

More on convergence and how it also relates to consolidation will be discussed in chapter 10.

It is not necessary to organize a combined newspaper-TV-Internet newsroom for today's reporters to experience convergence.

Some newspapers, even those that do not own a TV station, field a mobile journalist—what reporters call a "one-man band" or "one-woman band"—where reporters carry a backpack or briefcase containing a wireless laptop, a digital camera and a digital camcorder.

"As journalists, we are stewards of information," said Andy Cutraro, a photojournalist with the St. Louis Post-Dispatch who covered the war in Iraq. "As the medium changes, we are duty-bound to master those changes. If we fail, those less qualified may replace us. If we adhere to our basic journalistic principles and story-telling techniques, we should have nothing to fear (from all-in-one mobile journalists)."[81]

Whether new journalists face full-blown newsroom convergence or the mobile journalist concept of reporting, all must become comfortable with the efficiencies their managers see in having only one journalist writing a story, taking a still photo, and shooting and perhaps even editing video. Cutraro worries about the traditional team of a reporter and a photographer being reduced to a single person, thus losing the advantage of an extra pair of ears and eyes on a story. But the fact remains, he said, that more reporters are going to be required to master two or three journalism skills instead of only one as in the past.

Frankly, journalists at many weeklies and small dailies always have operated like this in needing to cover all aspects of a story.

The desire for efficiency and profits is driving convergence in all its forms. But don't make the mistake of thinking there was some elysian time when media magnates did not concern themselves about efficiency or the profits that result. The first thing students need to be reminded of on the first day of class is that "profit" is not a dirty word. No commercial newspaper, TV or radio station, magazine, advertising company, public relations firm or other media company can survive if there is no profit.

The question is the degree of the profit. Do media companies really need double, triple or more the profit margins that most national retail, service and manufacturing companies attain? (See chart on page 191.)

What complicates the question for media companies is that they make up an industry with an unusual dichotomy of dual markets.

Newsroom staffers think the customers are the reading and viewing public. But managers tend to think the customers are the advertisers. (Some critics go so far as to say that the CEOs and boards of directors of publicly traded conglomerates even seem to believe in a third market, with the stockholders as the main customers.)

The newsroom wants to inform the public, while an increasing number of managers see the public as a lure for advertising so they can grow as large as possible and achieve high profit levels for the owners.

The modern-day heavy reliance by media companies on advertising—and also the creation of chain newspapers and broadcast conglomerates—is due to the controversial legacy of Frank A. Munsey.[82]

Munsey became king of the pulp magazines when he reduced the newsstand price of his magazines in 1893, marking a permanent shift by nearly all print publishers to advertising sales for meeting the cost of their publications.[83]

A businessman with little respect for journalism, Munsey then began buying newspapers at the turn of the century and combining them into a chain. That was contrary to that era's predominant thinking in which a publisher would own a single newspaper and build it into an economic force that drove out lesser rivals one by one. Despite some setbacks, Munsey proved the competitive advantage of using the combined power of several papers owned by one individual to crush all rivals. Media critic A.J. Liebling disparaged Munsey as a "mass murderer of newspapers" because of Munsey's consolidation of several papers in New York City. Munsey justified his actions as simply eliminating "an oversupply of evening newspapers."[84]

In a brutally candid appraisal of Munsey's tactics, William Allen White expressed the opinion held of Munsey by many independent publishers when he wrote in his *Emporia* (Kan.) *Gazette* in 1925:

"Frank Munsey, the great publisher, is dead. Frank Munsey contributed to the journalism of his day the great talent of a meat-packer, the morals of a money-changer, and the manners of an undertaker. He and his kind have about succeeded in transforming a once noble profession into an 8 percent security. May he rest in trust."[85]

The difference the First Amendment makes

REGARDLESS OF THE scorn heaped on him by early critics, Munsey has become an exemplar for many media conglomerates to this day.[86] Munsey's turn toward overwhelming dependence on advertising by media companies, however, has created a troublesome business model.

On the one hand, the First Amendment extends protections to news media unavailable to any other business. *New York Times* publisher Arthur O. Sulzberger Jr. says the First Amendment "ought to make you responsible and it ought to make you brave."[87]

On the other hand, there also is the awkwardness of Munsey's business model that combines idealistic journalism values with the financial bonanza of advertising.

As the famous TV news broadcaster Edward R. Murrow put it, "One of the basic troubles with radio and television news is that both instruments have grown up as an incompatible combination of show business, advertising and news. Each of the three is a rather demanding profession. And when you get all three under one roof, the dust never settles." [88] Minus only the show business, newspapers have the same kind of in-company conflict.

What news-oriented media managers should keep in mind even in the heat of business is Sulzberger's reminder of special responsibility that should result from the First Amendment. Special protection is provided to the news. It is a protection extended to no other business.

> "Congress shall make no law respecting an establishment of religion, or prohibiting the free exercise thereof; or abridging the freedom of speech, or of the press; or the right of the people peaceably to assemble, and to petition the government for a redress of grievances."
>
> —*First Amendment to the U.S. Constitution*

The nation's founders added the First Amendment, thereby making Americans the world's first citizenry to enjoy a guaranteed free press. The First Amendment was needed because free flow of information and news is essential for people to be able to wisely govern themselves in a participatory government.

This constitutionally conveyed power often is abused by individuals and companies. But so far it has survived as a distinct hallmark of empowered citizenry that has since been copied by some other nations. The implied contract for the First Amendment's protection of the press is that the press in return should pledge responsibility and public service.

Such a lofty obligation is often subjugated to capitalism's need to turn news media into profitable operations, which is best accomplished through efficient operations, large size and relentless expansion.

The competitive advantages that Munsey pioneered of being more efficient, larger and more expansionist than your opponent are so obvious to business success that they don't need explanation here. But those very attributes that guarantee the success of capitalism often are at odds with the ideals envisioned in the First Amendment's guardianship of a free press within a system of self-governance.

Large size alone does not necessarily lead to abuse of press responsibility. In fact, it could be said that larger size actually has the potential of enhancing responsible journalism by making more resources available, enabling the news media to stand up to government and commercial pressures, and allowing more opportunity for printing or airing more news and information. Some of the most respected journalism is provided by large organizations, such as the Associated Press, The New York Times Co. and the Washington Post Co. Interestingly, responsible journalism also can be provided by even much smaller companies, such as *The Eagle-Tribune* of Lawrence, Mass., which won its second Pulitzer Prize in 2003.

Resources can be used to improve the journalism mission, or they can be used to expand the business mission. Most companies recognize there is a need to do both, but where the emphasis is placed varies considerably between media companies large and small alike. Larger size often is used primarily for the business mission—to satisfy stockholders, increase company value and drive out competing smaller companies.

The eternal advice to smaller companies facing a giant competitor is to fight back by being more creative, working harder, providing better customer service, and exploiting niche opportunities. Doing so has enabled a few companies to survive their David and Goliath match-ups. However, the smart money is usually still bet on Goliath.

One of the best accounts of what happens in many of these mis-matches between a large company and a smaller one is in Richard McCord's book, *The Chain Gang: One Newspaper versus the Gannett Empire*. Actually, the book tells of two small papers that went up against Gannett—a weekly in Santa Fe, N.M., and a daily in Green Bay, Wis.[89]

Many tactics that McCord ascribed to Gannett are typical of what you could expect from any large company intent on dominating its market and driving out smaller competitors. If you have the misfortune of becoming a manager at the smaller company in such a situation, McCord's book presents useful advice on what tactics to expect and how to counter them. The book makes it clear that success is possible, but it is by no means necessarily probable, and that winning will take heroic efforts, sacrifice, and probably a bit of luck as well.

In the end, all of the issues in this chapter come down to money.

Today's "gold standard" of the quarterly profit,[90] which seems to obsess the stockholders and the higher-ranking executives of media conglomerates, contrasts sharply with the public service mindset of the typical print or broadcast newsroom employee.

Is that gold standard outshining the news and information roles of the media? Are the large newspaper chains and broadcast conglomerates sacrificing the news content envisioned as their responsibility when America's founders passed the First Amendment, trading it for the glittering satisfaction of profits instead? If many of the large media companies are putting too much emphasis on profits, and too little emphasis on news and information, what consequences does that hold for the public's perception of the role of the press in society? These are some of the questions explored in this book, as it examines Edward R. Murrow's uneasy co-existence of capitalism and journalism.

The media conglomerates are here to stay. The debate rages on whether these huge corporations, most of them beholden to institutional and individual stockholders, are capable of serving the public interest for news and information in a socially responsible way that answers the ethical code of the Society of Professional Journalists to (1) seek truth and report it (2) minimize harm (3) act independently, and (4) be accountable.[91]

30 largest U.S. chains by circulation

Based on a 2002 Boston Globe study and updated to mid-2003 for this book[92]

Rank	Chain	# of dailies	Circulation	Headquarters
1.	Gannett Co. Inc.	100	7,646,732	McLean, Va.
2.	Knight Ridder	31	3,807,608	San Jose, Calif.
3.	Tribune Co.	12	3,374,273	Chicago, Ill.
4.	*Advance Publications Inc.	26	2,694,669	Newark, N.J.
5.	Dow Jones & Co. (with Ottaway)	16	2,322,960	New York, N.Y.
6.	**The New York Times Co.	19	2,277,601	New York, N.Y.
7.	*MediaNews Group	45	1,741,877	Denver, Colo.
8.	*Hearst Corp.	12	1,655,431	New York, N.Y.
9.	E.W. Scripps Co.	21	1,376,148	Cincinnati, Ohio
10.	**The McClatchy Company	11	1,369,494	Sacramento, Calif.
11.	Cox Enterprises Inc.	17	1,170,052	Atlanta, Ga.
12.	Lee Enterprises	43	1,029,206	Davenport, Iowa
13.	*Community Newspaper Holdings Inc.	95	1,006,145	Birmingham, Ala.
14.	*Freedom Communications Inc.	28	993,377	Irvine, Calif.
15.	Belo	4	900,561	Dallas, Texas
16.	Media General	25	863,574	Richmond, Va.
17.	**Washington Post Co.	2	801,497	Washington, D.C.
18.	*Morris Communications Corp.	26	695,585	Augusta, Ga.
19.	The Copley Press	9	684,047	La Jolla, Calif.
20.	Hollinger International Inc.	7	669,461	New York, N.Y.
21.	Pulitzer Newspapers Inc.	14	578,810	St. Louis, Mo.
22.	Journal Register Company	23	542,544	Trenton, N.J.
23.	*Ogden Newspapers Inc.	38	503,082	Wheeling, W.Va.
24.	*Landmark Communications Inc.	7	456,462	Norfolk, Va.
25.	*Seattle Times	6	383,840	Seattle, Wash.
26.	Block Communications	2	380,897	Pittsburgh, Pa.
27.	Stephens Media Group	11	375,145	Las Vegas, Nev.
28.	**Omaha World-Herald Co.	8	342,401	Omaha, Neb.
29.	*Wehco Media	7	325,475	Little Rock, Ark.
30.	*Liberty Group Publishing	66	320,732	Northbrook, Ill.

* *Privately owned*
** *Closely-held voting stock not available to the general public*

Chapter 1

CASE STUDY   *A Question of Judgment*

by BILL KEZZIAH
University of Nebraska

You're the publisher of a medium-sized newspaper that covers the town's local news.

Your editorial page comments on local, state and national events as you try to place events into perspective. Often, your editorial page is a vehicle for town/county boosterism, offering congratulatory editorials for jobs well done to businesses and to residents.

On the advertising pages and in promotions, your paper boosts local businesses' new products, expansions, etc., even sponsoring a children's fair and events that both bring people to the community and increase the newspaper's advertising revenue.

One such promotion involves a national pizza company that offers an all-expense paid trip to the Rose Bowl to watch the state's team on New Year's Day. The contest offers plane fare, hotel accommodations and two tickets. All a customer has to do is register and place a slip into a box. Contest rules prohibit only company employees from winning. The newspaper publisher's 12-year-old son enters the contest and wins. The announcement of his prize is made in the news pages with a picture.

Because he is a youth, he chooses his father-publisher after the story to accompany him on the trip.

ASSIGNMENT:

In groups representing the paper's editorial board, a group of readers chosen at random, and members of the advertising staff, consider these questions:

• What perceptions are either implied, or explicitly stated by the acceptance of the prize by the publisher and his son?

• If the publisher sees nothing wrong with accepting the prize, should the paper consider an ethics code?

AUTHOR:

Bill Kezziah is former weekly newspaper publisher who now teaches journalism courses, including media management, at the University of Nebraska in Kearney.

CASE STUDY *Convergence Newsroom—Ready or Not*

by JANE B. SINGER, Ph.D.
University of Iowa

You are the executive editor of a 200,000-circulation newspaper, along with its associated Web site, in a mid-sized U.S. city. Yours is one of about 30 papers owned by the Day-Kidder chain. Although the state's largest metro newspaper staffs a bureau in your city, your main news competitors for the past quarter-century have been the local affiliates of the TV networks.

But in June 2003, the Federal Communications Commission lifted most of the rules that had prevented newspapers from owning a TV or radio station in the same city. Day-Kidder now is ready to finalize a multi-city deal that includes purchase of the local CBS affiliate, the top-rated network in your market. The corporate office is about to launch a full-scale advertising and public relations campaign, stressing the benefits of combining the news resources of the print, broadcast and online newsrooms.

Ads touting the wonders of what the media industry calls "convergence" will start running in your city next week, the day the purchase is publicly announced, in a pre-emptive marketing move intended to head off consumer concerns about the implications of a local information monopoly.

Your job is to make such a "converged" news operation work, meaning your print journalists will need to share information with their TV counterparts and potentially even produce content for television. It has to work fast, to fulfill the promise of the imminent marketing campaign. It has to work without significant financial resources for salaries or anything else because Day-Kidder has less than nothing to spare after its purchasing spree. And if you try to micro-manage it, as your predecessor did with the change from traditional beats to "topic clusters," you know it will be an absolute disaster.

Somehow, you have to get the entire newspaper newsroom on board—right away. They're a skeptical lot and as fond of complaining as any other group of journalists you've ever known.

But your goal is for them to **want** to cooperate with their competitors, change their entrenched work routines, and maybe even put on a clean, ironed shirt (in a solid color) so on television they don't look quite so much like the ink-stained scribblers that they are. All while still

31

maintaining the quality of the newspaper that, after all, they are paid to produce every day of the year.

This is not going to be easy. You gaze out your glass window overlooking the cubicles and cluttered desks, observing the motley assortment of journalists who make up your staff. You reminisce, less than fondly, about the year from hell that followed the last major newsroom change, the conversion to a pagination system almost a decade ago. You sigh, then turn to your keyboard to e-mail notice of a staff meeting this very afternoon to discuss how your paper will take advantage of this tremendous opportunity to better serve the public.

Being a firm believer in open communication, you invite people to send you any questions in advance so you can try to address them at the meeting. You brace yourself. As well you should. Your inbox floods almost instantly. Don't these people have stories they should be working on?

Here are just a few of the responses you get:

• One of your award-winning photographers suggests that when people are asked to be jacks-of-all-trades, it generally means they can be masters of none. The result, she predicts, will be mediocre journalism all around. How will you guard against this?

• Your K-12 education reporter fires off a detailed and lengthy list of the stories he currently is working on, another list of those he wants to work on but doesn't have time for, and a third list of tips he has received but has not yet been able to check out. He asks how you can possibly expect him to find time to produce stories for television as well, on top of all this!

• Your star investigative reporter says that surely you don't think she is going to work with those "blow-dried airheads" over at the TV station. Maybe some of the junior reporters won't mind, but she personally has always considered television to be a "subspecies" of journalism and has no intention of having anything to do with it. Ever.

• Speaking of junior reporters, one enthusiastically volunteers to be the chief city government reporter for CBS (which already has its own city hall reporter, who recently won a prestigious duPont award for a piece exposing a prime bit of local corruption—a story your investigative reporter should have had but didn't). You're grateful to get at least one positive response, but unfortunately, this particular reporter is struggling just to cover the small and placid suburban community to which she has been assigned. Her bureau chief has been working with her diligently but reports that she still has a long way to go.

• Your day-side cops reporter reminds you that he has been busting his butt to beat CBS (and the other TV news stations) on crime coverage for the past two years, and now you want him to suddenly stop competing and start working WITH the TV guys on stories! He thinks not. And besides, the "trend stories and analytical pieces that work in the newspaper" aren't suited to television, where "if it bleeds, it leads." Let them cover the fires and film stand-ups in front of the crime scene tape—but he wants no part of that sort of "quote-unquote journalism."

• A features writer wants to be sure he understands correctly that you are talking about expecting journalists to do additional work for no additional pay. "As you know," he adds, "I was a Newspaper Guild officer at the last paper I worked for, and I'm sure my friends in the Guild would be very interested in this proposal." Your newsroom staff does not currently have union representation, and you are quite certain that Day-Kidder would like it to stay that way.

• Your reporter who covers the TV industry thanks you very much for instantly eliminating her credibility as a journalist. How can she cover television if she is part of television herself?

• The sports columnist who writes mainly about the local university's teams declares that he has spent years—years!—building up his sources in the athletic department and he will be damned if he's about to share them and/or any tips they give him with "that ex-jock muscle boy who reads the sports on Channel 4."

• An assistant city editor, recently promoted from the reporting ranks, worries about "scooping ourselves" if the television station airs "one of our good stories" during the 6 p.m. newscast, in time for the metro paper's bureau reporters to put together their own version for the next day. The Web site is bad enough, but it generally doesn't have many details—and few if any visuals. Putting a story out on the top-rated news show, though . . . .

• A veteran business writer, who required no less than seven months and the nearly full-time assistance of a research librarian with apparently unlimited patience to figure out how to locate information on the Internet, wonders what sort of technical training the company will provide to help people "learn how to do television."

• Your copy desk chief reminds you that she has 16 vacation days coming to her this year, counting the overtime she put in last Christmas, and she wants to take them all. Starting next week.

You sigh again and wonder if it's too late to accept that job offer to write news releases for the state's Nature Conservancy chapter. It didn't pay much, but a little fresh air sounds really, really good at the moment.

CHAPTER 1

Well, in the meantime, it's sure to be an interesting meeting. You turn back to your computer to jot down some ideas about addressing these concerns.

SCENARIO:

The author recently completed a set of case studies of "converged" newsrooms around the United States. The concerns expressed by the fictional journalists in this case study echo just some of what she heard. (To be fair, though, she also heard positive comments about convergence, even from the curmudgeons.)

AUTHOR:

Jane B. Singer teaches online journalism, media ethics and other courses in the School of Journalism and Mass Communication at the University of Iowa. She has 15 years of professional experience as a print and online journalist, much of it as a newsroom editor and manager.

🖵 Suggested Web sites:

www.poynter.org—The Poynter Institute
www.spj.org—Society of Professional Journalists
www.journalism.org—Project for Excellence in Journalism
www.americanpressinstitute.org—American Press Institute
www.miami.edu/com/mme—Media Management and Economics, AEJMC
www.freedomforum.org—The Freedom Forum
www.washingtonpost.com/wp-dyn/photo—Camera•Works convergence media site
www.grady.uga.edu/annualsurveys—Annual surveys of Journalism and Mass Communication

---

Endnotes to Chapter 1:

[1] Edward D. Miller, "Newsroom leadership," at <www.newsroomleadership.com>, accessed December 7, 2001.

[2] A.J. Liebling, *The Press* (New York: Ballantine Books, 1961), 35.

[3] George Seldes, *Lords of the Press* (New York: Julian Messner, 1938).

[4] Michael Gartner, "A thousand voices bloom: Brill's Content," *Columbia Journalism Review,* (March–April 2000): 38.

[5] Tricia Birt, assignment editor of *The Iowa City Press-Citizen,* interview by author on June 13, 2000.

[6] Frank Luther Mott, *American Journalism* (New York: Macmillan, 1947), 547.

[7] Geneva Overholser, "Newspapers are languishing as the Net speeds up," *Columbia Journalism Review* (March–April 2000): 60.

[8] Barbara Cloud, ed. "Special issue: The media business," *Journalism History,* Vol. 18 (1992).

[9] Editorial cartoon by John Trever, *Albuquerque Journal,* June 6, 2003, A14.

[10] Stuart Overbey, "Free speech for sale: FCC's media give-away," *Crosswinds Weekly,* (May 29–June 5): 2003, 6.

[11] Michael Liedtke of The Associated Press, as published in, "Media shake-up looms: FCC may loosen ownership rules," *Albuquerque Journal,* May 31, 2003, C-4.

[12] Kenneth N. Gilpin, "F.C.C. votes to relax rules limiting media ownership," *The New York Times,* June 2, 2003.

[13] Various sources, including "23rd annual 100 leading media companies," *Advertising Age,* August 19, 2002, S1-2; newspaper articles; and corporate Web sites.

[14] Michael Copps and Hugh Downs appeared at a field hearing about the FCC rule changes that was sponsored by the Benton Foundation and held April 7, 2003, at Arizona State University in Phoenix.

[15] Mark Fitzgerald, "M. Copps: A plea for news coverage," *Editor & Publisher* (April 14, 2003): 5.

[16] Al Tompkins, "Can PBS and NPR save the democracy?" The Poynter Institute, <www.poynter.org/content/content_view.asp?id=35942>, accessed June 2, 2003. A Pew Research Center survey shortly before the FCC decision reported that 72 percent of Americans knew nothing about the proposed rule changes. Even *Editor & Publisher* criticized the press for ignoring the issue.

[17] Ben H. Bagdikian, *The Media Monopoly* (Boston: Beacon Press, 6th ed., 2000), 15.

[18] Gilbert Cranberg, Randy Bezanson, and John Soloski, *Taking Stock: Journalism and the Publicly Traded Newspaper* (Ames: Iowa State Press, 2001).

[19] John Soloski, letter to publishers for manuscript, July 18, 2000.

[20] Cranberg, Bezanson, and Soloski, *Taking Stock: Journalism and the Publicly Traded Newspaper*, 109.

[21] Neil Hickey, "Money lust: How pressure for profit is perverting journalism," *Columbia Journalism Review* (July–August 1998): 30.

[22] Cranberg, Bezanson and Soloski, *Taking Stock: Journalism and the Publicly Traded Newspaper*, 109.

[23] Arthur Sulzberger, as quoted by Marty Linsky in *The View From The Top* (St. Petersburg, Fla.: The Poynter Institute for Media Studies, 1997), 35.

[24] Janelle Hartman, "Media convergence hot convention item," *The Guild Reporter*, July 12, 2002, 6.

[25] Bill Kirtz, "Newspapers as a business," *Publishers' Auxiliary*, March 6, 2000, 1.

[26] William Serrin, ed., *The Business of Journalism* (New York: The New Press, 2000), vi.

[27] Ibid.

[28] Doug Underwood, *When MBAs Rule the Newsroom* (New York: Columbia University Press, 1993), xi.

[29] John Soloski and Robert G. Picard, "The new media lords: Why institutional investors call the shots," *Columbia Journalism Review* (September–October 1996), 11-12.

[30] Newspaper Management Center, <www.MediaManagementCenter.org/center/>, accessed August 5, 2003.

[31] M.L. Stein, "Get with the program," *Presstime* (May 17, 1997), 18.

[32] John H. McManus, *Market-Driven Journalism: Let the Citizen Beware?* (Thousand Oaks, Calif.: Sage Publications, 1994), 197.

[33] Aaron Moore, quoting Dennis F. Herrick in "Small links, big chain: Community Newspaper Holdings and the power of the cluster," *Columbia Journalism Review* (July–August, 1999): 14.

[34] Hickey, "Money lust," 29.

[35] Ibid., 29.

[36] Ibid., 35.

[37] Neil Henry, "Journalism education: A lost cause?" *The Chronicle of Higher Education*, September 25, 1998, B8–B9.

[38] Ibid.

[39] Graham Greene, as quoted by Ted Gup in "Media means so much, it means nothing," *The Chronicle of Higher Education*, November 23, 2001, B12.

[40] William A. Hachten, *The Troubles of Journalism: A Critical Look at What's Right and Wrong with the Press* (Mahwah, N.J.: Erlbaum, 2nd ed., 2001), 187.

[41] Lucia Moses, "Profiting from experience," *Editor & Publisher* (February 3, 2003): 22.

[42] Geneva Overholser, "The Newsroom Trust and other novel ideas," *Columbia Journalism Review* (May–June 2000): 65.

[43] Neal Shister, *Journalism and Commercial Success: Expanding the Business Case for Quality News and Information* (Washington, D.C.: The Aspen Institute, 2002), 2.

[44] Marty Linsky, *The View From The Top*, in The Poynter Papers: No. 10 (St. Petersburg, Fla.: The Poynter Institute for Media Studies, 1997), 1.

[45] Ibid., 33.

[46] "Gannett newspaper management conference stresses efforts across departments; excellence resounds as a theme, too," at <http://www.gannett.com/go/newswatch/2002/august/nw0816-1.htm>, accessed August 19, 2003

[47] Editor of a chain-owned daily in a personal letter to the author, August 15, 2003.

[48] Alicia G. Shepard, "Moguls' Millions," *American Journalism Review* (July–August 2001): 22.

[49] Ibid., 21.

[50] Brent Cunningham, "Two brothers, two worlds," *Columbia Journalism Review* (July–August 2001): 38.

[51] Ibid., 21.

[52] Benjamin M. Compaine, "The expanding base of media competition," *Journal of Communications* (Summer 1985): 88.

[53] David Demers, "Corporate newspaper bashing: Is it justified?" *Newspaper Research Journal* (Winter 1999): 84.

[54] "Death to the estate tax," *Editor & Publisher* (April 16, 2001): 11.

[55] Demers, "Corporate newspaper bashing," 95.

[56] Ibid., 84.

[57] David Demers, "Corporate newspaper structure, profits and organizational goals," *The Journal of Media Economics* 9, 2 (1996): 20.

[58] Gerald Stone, *Examining newspapers: What research reveals about America's newspapers* (Newbury Park, Calif.: Sage, 1987), 103–104.

[59] Benjamin M. Compaine, "Mergers, divestitures and the Internet: Is ownership of the media industry becoming too concentrated?" Telecommunications Policy Research Conference (September 26, 1999) and recounted in summary of the final chapter of *Who Owns the Media?* at <users.primushost.com/~bcompain/WOTM/tprc99.htm>, accessed January 18, 2002.

[60] Robert G. Picard, "The rise and fall of communication empires," *The Journal of Media Economics*, 9, 4 (1996): 23–24.

[61] Ibid., 24.

[62] Robert G. Picard, *The Economics and Financing of Media Companies* (New York: Fordham University Press, 2002), 192–193.

[63] Martin Peers, "After deep wounds, AOL ponders radical surgery," *Wall Street Journal,* Rocket e-book, January 31, 2003, 16.

[64] "CNHI sells operations in a dozen cities," NewsInc., Web subscription site, May 26, 2003.

[65] Elena Cherney, "Debt catches up with media mogul: Canada's Black dismantles part of his empire," *Wall Street Journal,* August 1, 2000, A17.

[66] Mark Fitzgerald, "Chain reactions," *Editor & Publisher* (January 1, 2001): 20.

[67] Mark Fitzgerald, "Peer pressure on 'Post,'" *Editor & Publisher* (June 4, 2001):10.

[68] Lucia Moses, " 'Sun': It shines for some," *Editor & Publisher* (January 21, 2002): 12.

[69] Jeff Leeds, for the *Los Angeles Times,* as published in "Numbers give radio big clout: Clear Channel's growth prompts allegations of bullying," *Albuquerque Journal*, March 3, 2002, C-1.

[70] T.A. Badger, of The Associated Press, as published in "Radio chain's loss nearly double: Clear Channel misses expectations," *Albuquerque Journal,* March 1, 2002, B7.

[71] The Associated Press, as published in "Clear Channel beats the street," *Albuquerque Journal,* January 15, 2003, D5.

[72] Martin Peers and Robin Sidel, "Five bidders vie for some assets of Vivendi in U.S.," *Wall Street Journal,* June 24, 2003, A2.

[73] Fitzgerald, "Chain reactions," 20.

[74] Joel Davis, "Billionaire to buy News-Press: Wendy McCaw makes the call in purchasing hometown paper," *Editor & Publisher* (July 17, 2000): 11.

[75] Associated Press, "Santa Barbara News-Press to be sold to Wendy McCaw," July 9, 2000.

[76] Editor, whose identity is being withheld, in comment volunteered in June 2002 to author and other journalism educators.

[77] *Quill* magazine cover art, issue of July/August 2002, reprinted with permission of the Society of Professional Journalists.

[78] Jane B. Singer, "Strange Bedfellows: The diffusion of convergence in four news

organizations," unpublished paper presented at the August 2003 convention of the Media Management and Economics Division of the Association for Education in Journalism and Mass Communication, Kansas City, Mo.

[79] James K. Gentry, dean of the William Allen White School of Journalism at the University of Kansas, in response to question, June 10, 2002.

[80] "Convergence tracker search page," maintained by James K. Gentry and graduate students at the William Allen White School of Journalism at the University of Kansas, <www.americanpress institute.org/convergencetracker>, accessed June 12, 2003.

[81] Andrew Cutraro, of the *St. Louis Post-Dispatch,* personal e-mail to author (June 23, 2003).

[82] Priscilla Prijatel and Sammye Johnson, "The renegade and the rules: New ASME guidelines are a response to new media developments," *Journal of Magazine and New Media Research,* 9, 2 (Fall 1999).

[83] Ibid.

[84] A.J. Liebling, *The Press* (New York: Ballantine Books, revised ed.,1964) 10 and 58.

[85] William Allen White, *The Autobiography of William Allen White* (New York: Macmillan, 1946), 629. Also quoted in slightly different form in *Journal of Magazine and New Media Research,* 1, 2 (Fall 1999).

[86] George Fox Mott, et. al., *New Survey of Journalism* (New York: Barnes & Noble, 4th ed., 1958) 35.

[87] Arthur O. Sulzberger Jr., speaking in the video "The Art of Leadership in News Organizations," 2002, The Freedom Foundation, Arlington, Va.

[88] Ann M. Sperber, *Murrow: His Life and Times* (New York: Freundlich, 1986), xvi.

[89] Richard McCord, *The Chain Gang: One Newspaper versus the Gannett Empire* (Columbia, Mo.: University of Missouri Press, 1996, and reprinted in 2001).

[90] Jim Naughton of The Poynter Institute used the "gold standard" expression about quarterly profit statements in his Message from the President column titled "Mob Rule," *Poynter Report* (Summer 2002): 13.

[91] Society of Professional Journalists, Code of Ethics, version adopted in 1996.

[92] "Groups by circulation," *Boston Globe* Web site at <www.boston.com/asne/groups_by_ circulation.htm>, accessed November 17, 2002, and updated in places by the author where new properties were acquired or divested after the *Boston Globe* study.

CHAPTER 2
PREPARING YOURSELF
FOR MANAGEMENT

L EADERS SOMETIMES are not good managers. This is often seen in people who start up a business or who work by themselves in their own business. The best managers, however, need to be leaders as well. Warren Bennis, whose study of leadership is often quoted in business circles, defined the distinction, saying, "Leaders are people who do the right thing; managers are people who do things right."[1]

Doing the right thing, by providing an ethical and financial plan to operate a company, and doing things right are both essential to a company's success. Business consultant Peter F. Drucker knew that leaders and managers (for all the faults of many of them) are needed by corporations because of his one unalterable, undeniable law of business:

"The only things that evolve by themselves in an organization are disorder, friction and malperformance."[2]

Managers see those dysfunctions as their personal enemy—to be conquered and controlled so production and sales can resume, paychecks can be met, and customers can be satisfied. Good managers know what Drucker knows: that to do nothing results only in more disorder, friction and malperformance.

Drucker's law of business is really just a commercial variation on entropy, which is the second law of thermodynamics, stating that all physical matter deteriorates when there is no attempt to preserve or conserve.[3] So, too, with business.

A manager can be the owner, but as we think of the term in this book a manager will be a ranking employee who works for someone else. Using this definition, there are three ranks to managers: (1) senior management, sometimes referred to as executive management; (2) middle level management, often in the roles of heading up departments or divisions; and (3) lower level management, who are people supervising the rank-and-file employees and usually are so well experienced that they could do the work of one of the employees as well or better than the employee.

Each rank reports to the rank above it in the hierarchy. In fact, even the senior managers are not the ultimate authorities that they sometimes seem to be. They also must report higher, to the owner in some companies and to the board of directors of major corporations.

This is, of course, the simplest form of organization. In large corporations there are several layers of each of these three principal management types.

A manager accomplishes his or her tasks by planning, coordinating and supervising the work done by others. Unless you're the owner's kid, you start somewhere else and work your way up to management.

First, get the right job

EVERYTHING STARTS with finding the right job in which to launch a career. In the book *Peter Drucker: Shaping the Managerial Mind,* author John E. Flaherty recounts some of Drucker's thoughts on why he considered a job as a way of achieving growth and self-development. As you think about applying for your next job, or your first "real job" after college graduation, consider Drucker's advice as recounted by Flaherty:

"Drucker was astonished that executives (make that read "anyone") failed to realize the importance of job selection and to analyze potential jobs. He observed that many chose a job for such superficial reasons as slightly higher salary, convenient commuting, or the promise of rapid advancement and other attractive perks."[4]

Drucker always tried to emphasize a person's own capacities so tht each person would took responsibility toward managing oneself. "Management texts stress managing others. Few talk of managing oneself," Drucker noted. "But managing others is always iffy. Does it really work? One can, however, always manage oneself, or at least try."[5]

You really are, as poet W.E. Henley noted, the master of your fate, the captain of your soul. Whether as an employee starting out, or as someone who has recently been promoted and now has employees answering to you, it is critical to get off to a good start.

Unless you are desperate and will settle for anything with a paycheck attached, you should carefully research companies before you even apply. There are major differences between different media companies. Some media chains are horrors, and others are respected for their excellent journalism. The same is true of independent media companies.

To paraphrase an early press critic from the days of horses, some media companies make you pull a plow all day, whip you and skimp on the oats and hay, while other media companies take you into a warm stable after a hard day of work, feed you and treat you like a member of the family. The list of which company fits which of these alternatives changes from year to year. But the personalities of the different companies can be sorted out by asking employees at the company that interests you.

Good journalism is produced consistently at the best newspaper, magazine, television and radio companies, but it also can emerge at lousy companies because of the determined professionalism of people. It was once believed, and believed so strongly that the phrase became a business cliché, that happy workers are productive workers. A closer examination of human nature brought about the realization that some lazy workers were happy because they did not need to be productive, while at the same time some conscientious workers were among the most productive even when they were unhappy.

It is now believed that the most consistently productive workers are those who are motivated to do well. Consequently, those who are motivated have a sense of responsibility about their jobs, see opportunity for growth and advancement, and enjoy feelings of achievement. These ideas make up the concept known as "job enrichment."[6] If you want a good start, look for job openings that promise those kinds of dynamics.

Of course, despite Drucker's disdain for basing decisions on salaries, anyone considering a job wants to know if the salary being offered is a fair one for the industry. Salaries are always unknown territory to people who are starting out. The figures in the accompanying chart[7] are from the annual survey of journalism and mass communication graduates conducted by the Grady College at the University of Georgia. They show the average starting U.S. salaries by industry for non-management positions. These figures are averages for graduates hired into their first full-time jobs.

The traditional cynical humor is that nobody pursues a career in journalism for the money. Though they certainly rank below salaries offered graduates in many other programs, media salaries have been going up in recent years after stagnating for four years in 1990–93. Media

AT A GLANCE

Salaries for graduates
Getting started in media companies

	1999	2000
Online	28,000	30,004
Magazines	26,494	28,236
Newsletters	26,000	27,976
P.R.	25,012	28,964
Ad agencies	25,000	26,988
Dailies	24,960	26,000
Radio	22,500	23,400
Weeklies	21,000	22,800
Broadcast TV	19,968	21,840
Cable TV	14,693	15,159

salaries have been especially boosted by the competition for top graduates from online companies, which began being tracked by Grady's survey in 1996. And, of course, some media companies pay more than the averages cited in the Grady study.

Getting discovered and climbing to the top

UNLESS YOUR PARENTS or other close relatives own the business, the likelihood is that you will need to become successful the hard way—by first becoming someone else's employee on one of the lowest rungs of someone else's ladder. The very first rule of distinguishing yourself is simply becoming the most reliable and dependable person in the firm.

As Woody Allen observed, "Eighty percent of success is showing up."

And while you're there, do the best job you can—and then do even more. Never shirk additional responsibility. It is incredible how many people do only enough to get by. "That's not my job," is an attitude that has killed innumerable chances for advancement.

This book will repeatedly emphasize that you should not sell yourself short. You must instill confidence—but not braggadocio—in yourself. Make sure your confidence is grounded in experience and knowledge. We are well aware when others are trying to persuade us that they know more than they really do. Even if we do not challenge such a person publicly, all but the gullible among us can distinguish between facts and opinions. Everyone is entitled to his or her opinion, of course, but make sure that facts back up those opinions.

Do not accept—or worse yet, invent—limitations to hinder your progress. The most common limitation used as an excuse is youth, but even relatively young executives who are talented, confident and visionary have been given strong positions of leadership and authority. One of the best examples is William Paley, who took over a nearly bankrupt and insignificant CBS in 1928 when he was only 27 years old and built it into a broadcast powerhouse over the next 40 years.[8]

Acquiring a mentor as early as possible in your career is one of the most promising things you can do to improve your chances of moving up in the organization. Pick someone you admire, perhaps even someone outside the company you work for, and seek them out for advice and direction. Most people are pleased to be treated as someone whose advice is valued, and they undoubtedly all had mentors themselves and therefore can appreciate you approaching them wanting to be their protégé. In fact, mentoring relationships often are initiated by the mentor, who begins to show interest in a staffer who they think has unusual potential. Mentoring works only when there is mutual respect and mutual agreement to giving and receiving advice.

In *Best Practices: The Art of Leadership in News Organizations,* an entire chapter is devoted to reminiscences by leading media figures such as Arthur O. Sulzberger Jr. and William Hearst III about some of the mentors they have had in their careers.[9]

Closely related to mentoring is simply showing respect for the people above you. Even a strong personality like Gannett's former CEO Allan H. Neuharth knew how to show respect and learn from most of those who outranked him.

In his autobiographical *Confessions of an S.O.B.,* Neuharth clearly illustrates how the top ranks of many businesses are often dominated by persons with less than lovable personalities. Like many an S.O.B., Neuharth would be ruthless with those he could dominate, but he also could be charming and gracious with those who merited a more conciliatory approach. He knew whom he could intimidate and push around, and whom he couldn't. Though always a bit flashy and even eccentric, Neuharth did not rise through Gannett's ranks by treating his bosses and mentors shabbily—at least, not unless he knew he could beat them.

Most up-and-comers nurture a personality that shows them to be likeable, knowledgeable, sensible and competent—but also tough when they need to be.

They often are people who are specialists in what they do best but also have many other interests in which they also are conversant. Such a broad range of knowledge enables them to quickly find common ground for non-business talk with their bosses when they come into contact with them, effectively dodging the career-killing bullet of not being able to engage in "small talk." Their bosses like them because they can carry on a conversation (or at least know how to show genuine interest) in the personal interests or topics that the boss brings up. "I have a lot of interests," one news executive commented, "so whenever I had a chance to meet one of my bosses, I was never tongue-tied. I could talk about subjects outside the office that my boss also was interested in."[10]

Jealous fellow workers not capable of talking about anything other than their work have some rather derogatory terms for describing such competitors for the attention of the boss. A more productive attitude, however, would be to become more interesting persons themselves.

Unfortunately, many people are promoted for insufficient reasons that appear to be good ones on the surface. For example, many are promoted only because the boss likes them, or only because they have been the best performer in their department. Neither asset, alone or in combination with the other, necessarily means that such a person is the best one for the promotion—even if that person is you.

Nevertheless, if your boss respects you as a competent, aggressive and ambitious manager or employee, you certainly hold an advantage for promotion over your peers who have not earned such exalted recognition. Up to a point at least, that might be all that is necessary to merit a promotion. However, if your boss knows you well enough to also like you as a person, you are suddenly on the fast track.

Conversely, if the boss plainly dislikes you, regardless of your competence, your best option almost certainly is to resign and find a different boss with whom you are more compatible.

This concept of the boss liking you personally is not spoken out loud by the leadership. No one wants to admit that their promotion of an individual is for anything other than the highest professional reasons. But we're talking about human beings here, and most executives want their managers to be people with whom they can get along.

What is the stated point of view for executives as they decide whom to promote? Here's the thought process of Tom Johnson, former publisher of the *Los Angeles Times* and former chairman and CEO of CNN News:

"Rule one, integrity. I want people in leadership positions who have integrity. Rule two, a passion for their work. I want people who love it and who are committed to it . . . . You must be able to understand, in this world that we're living in, economics, history, political science and at least one international language . . . . I don't want anybody in my newsroom who doesn't read the daily papers, read books—nonfiction especially . . . . How can you be in the field of current events and not be reading each day?"[11]

Jack Fuller, president of Tribune Co., said he looks for people to promote who are "comfortable with the person they are" because they understand their own strengths and weaknesses. "They are less likely to behave irrationally or emotionally," Fuller explained. "They're going to have better judgment. They're going to be able to deal with other people better because they're not (thinking) every exchange is a test of themselves."[12]

Lou Boccardi, who retired in 2003 as president and CEO of The Associated Press, said that choosing whom to promote into leadership positions is a blend of quality attributes, saying, "It's brain, it's character, it's ability to work with people, ability to get things done, this overworked thing called vision—call it creativity."[13]

Those are some executives' attitudes and the qualities they are looking for when they check you out for possible promotion. You might be able to glean from the preceding comments that expertise in your current job is important, but the real reason an executive usually settles on someone for promotion is because an aptitude or strong potential for leadership has been spotted.

One of the cruelest myths is that if you work hard and are a valued employee, you will inevitably rise to the top. I have too many friends who are outstanding in their jobs and did not get promoted to jobs they desired to ever believe in that, or try to get you to believe in it. There are too few opportunities and too many people chasing them. There are no guarantees. But working hard and being a valued employee will make it more likely that you will be promoted—a lot more likely anyway, than if you just wait for Lady Luck to smile on you.

Though it pains me to admit it, Lady Luck still is not smiling much on women and minorities in media companies. Both women and minorities have a difficult time advancing into management ranks and onto boards of directors of major entertainment, telecommunications, cable and publishing industries.

African American males have made the most progress. In fact, the nation's largest media company, AOL Time Warner, is headed by Richard Parsons, a highly experienced African American executive who took over as CEO in May 2002. Robert Johnson founded Black Entertainment Television in 1980 and became the nation's first African American billionaire when he sold it to Viacom in 2001.[14] One of America's most visible African American media leaders is Jay T. Harris, former publisher of the San Jose *Mercury News* and executive editor of the *Philadelphia Daily News*, who now is a journalism professor and founding director of the Center for the Study of Journalism and Democracy at the University of Southern California.

Hispanics have become America's largest minority, but they are just starting to move into leadership positions with mainstream media companies. Leadership positions tend to be concentrated in the West and Southwest. There are several Hispanic editors of both TV and newspaper outlets and there also are major organizations, including the National Association of Hispanic Publications, which represents about 180 Hispanic-owned newspapers and magazines across the United States.

Some people have overcome both race and gender to head media companies or divisions. Cathy Hughes, who was turned down by 32 banks before she received a loan to buy her first radio station, became the first African American woman CEO of a publicly traded company when her 65-station Radio One group went public in 2000.[15] Pamela

45

Thomas-Graham is an African American woman who became CEO and president of CNBC at the age of 38.

A woman also heads up a major newspaper company—Mary E. Junck of Lee Enterprises, Inc. Some women head up corporate divisions, including Beverly Jackson, former senior vice president of the Ottaway Newspapers unit of Dow Jones & Co. and now president and publisher of the ANG Newspapers unit of MediaNews Group; Mary P. Stier, president of Gannett's Midwest Newspaper Group; Ann Moore, chairman and CEO of Time, Inc.; Janet Robinson, senior vice president of newspaper operations for The New York Times Co.; Cathleen Black, president of Hearst Magazines; and Anne Sweeney, president of ABC Cable Networks.

A small minority of publishers and general managers are women, including *Editor & Publisher* magazine's "Publisher of the Year" for 2003, Virginia F. Moorhouse of *The Bakersfield Californian.* In 2003, there were at least two dailies where the top two positions were held by women—the *Sarasota Herald-Tribune,* headed by Diane McFarlin and Janet Weaver as publisher and executive editor, and the *Record Searchlight* in Redding, Calif., with Deborah Smiddy as publisher and Kelly Brewer as editor.

One of the companies with the best overall representation by women in its highest positions is Gannett, which in 2003 had three women on its eight-member board of directors and six women among its 21 officers and divisional heads. *Fortune* magazine included Knight Ridder in its 2002 list of the best 50 companies for minorities.

However, it is still mainly a Caucasian man's media world. A gender study released in September 2002 reported that women make up only about 14 percent of top executives in media companies.[16]

"With few exceptions, we have not moved beyond tokenism in the number of women in top leadership positions or serving on the boards of communication companies," explained Susan Ness, former FCC commissioner and a director for the Annenberg Public Policy Center of the University of Pennsylvania, which conducted the study.[17]

Whether it is gender, race or something else, everyone has personal or professional obstacles to overcome before they can be considered for promotion. One aspect they all need to make sure they build their knowledge on is the business itself. If you really want to become a manager, you absolutely must understand your company's business.

"Generations to come are going to be challenged even more than we have been with technology, with business concerns," the AP's Boccardi pointed out. "So if you want to rise toward the top of a media company, you're going to have a pretty good business understanding acquired either on the job or in school."[18]

Never stop educating yourself. Some of the ways new managers can grow in their career are continuing education classes at the university, company-sponsored seminars, programs at industry conventions, and "walk-around management" where you can talk to and learn from employees. It seems to be obvious advice. But many new managers fail to accept the challenge of continual learning, and as a result their careers stall far lower in the hierarchy of command than they expected.

In addition to taking a media management class, former Gannett editor Barclay Jameson recommends that aspiring managers should also take basic courses in accounting and marketing. To be a manager, you need to understand accounting, because you will be constantly working with budgets, and you should understand marketing, because your company's success depends on managers coming up with strategies that will result in robust sales.[19] Students who aspire to management ranks should consider carrying at least a minor in business. If you already have graduated, accounting and marketing courses and other business classes are available to part-time students at community colleges and the continuing education programs of colleges and universities.

You should be a voracious reader, as Tom Johnson pointed out earlier. No matter how much you learned in school or in previous jobs, you need to keep up with what is going on in your company and in the industry if you want to be knowledgeable enough to merit a managerial position. To do that, read books, magazines and newspapers and watch TV broadcasts, regardless of which industry you are in. As an aspiring news media manager, you need to be more aware than your peers about what is going on. Studies have shown how top business executives devote much of their leisure time to reading the advice-for-success books of other business people. They favor autobiographies and biographies of current and past corporate leaders, as well as any books about business. You should follow their lead.

Read the leading trade journals of your industry. If you are in newspapers, you should be reading *Editor & Publisher* every week. A quick look at the endnotes of this book involving the many references from *E&P* should quickly convince you of the trove of information about both daily and weekly newspapers in that magazine. It is primarily manager oriented, as most trade journals are, but that is an advantage to building your perspective, too. If you are in the broadcast industry, you should be reading *Broadcasting & Cable* magazine. If your interest is in advertising in either industry, then surely you will want to be a regular reader of *Advertising Age*. A trade journal that covers the managerial aspects of both the news and the entertainment industries is *MediaWeek.* There are many other trade journals. Pick the ones that are right for you. There also are journals or newsletters for nearly every key position in media industries published by organizations such as the American Society of Newspaper Editors and the Radio-Television News Directors Association.

If you are looking for an early start and are still in school, many industry journals are available at your institution's library. Most colleges and universities will carry a subscription to any trade journal requested by a professor, though you still might need to buy a subscription for the first year. The libraries are cooperative, but not fast.

Most of these publications are available partly or entirely on the Web, so there really is no excuse for not reading them. The Poynter Institute's Web site is an excellent resource for any kind of news-oriented media company. Web site addresses of several industry trade journals are listed at the end of this chapter.

These print and Web publications not only carry general information on their respective industries, but all of them also cover aspects on the critical skill of managing others.

The importance of being able to get along with others and learning how to work with them and to motivate them is probably the single most important business skill for the aspiring manager to master.

An insight into just how highly executives prize the ability of a new manager to be able to lead others was succinctly put forth a hundred years ago by John D. Rockefeller, founder of the Standard Oil Company, when he declared, "I will pay more for the ability to deal with people than any other ability under the sun."[20]

Work hard, be a conscientious and competent employee, volunteer for more than is expected of you, know the business, and show that you are a leader of others. The combination of behavior, skills and initiative will make you a prime candidate for promotion.

If you are promoted into the management ranks—for valid or arbitrary reasons—you will find your work life changed forever. From that point on, you no longer are responsible for just your own performance.

Your first management position

PROUDLY YOU clean out your old desk, perhaps under the envying eyes of people with whom you've worked side by side for many years. Or perhaps you're the quiet sort who comes in after hours or on the weekend to make the big move. And a big move it is, as you transfer your belongings to a specifically designated desk that automatically confers authority upon you, or even into an office of your own separated by a doorway from the employees who once were your peers but now have become your subordinates.

Like others before you, once you are promoted into your first management job you immediately are confronted with some mixed emotions. Loren B. Belker points out in *The First-Time Manager* that people achieving their first management position usually are "absolutely delighted with the promotion and absolutely panic-stricken with the realization that from now on they'll be judged by how well their subordinates perform."[21]

Probably the first thing you will discover after your promotion is that not everyone is pleased with your selection. You will be subjected to early tests of your leadership by some, so be prepared to deal with such challenges wisely.

In "The first-time manager's survival guide" in *Presstime* magazine, new managers promoted from within are warned: "Younger people with less experience think they can carry forward personal relationships, and that's not possible. Those people you worked intimately with will have a different connection to you; it will not be cold, but cool."[22]

The first advice usually given to any new manager is to not implement major changes too quickly. Make sure you understand the present situation before you start your revolution. Even if you were certain of changes that needed to be made when you were a staffer, give yourself time enough to discover if a manager's greater access to information either changes or reinforces your earlier conviction. Instead of immediately instituting changes, open up the lines of communication first with your subordinates.

"You're going to be judged by how well your section or department functions," Belker notes, "so the people who now work for you are the most important in your business life . . . . Your goal in these early conversations is to let your subordinates know you care about them as individuals and you're there to help them achieve their goals."[23]

Even with the arrival of MBA degree executives in major media companies, the promotion of non-business-trained employees into the management ranks still is common. Such people are promoted as a result of them having been good at their previous jobs, leaving them with the formidable task of learning management while they're doing it.

Two management co-authors note that media managers become members of two often-conflicting worlds. "Increasingly, in the climb up the corporate ladder, media managers need to expand their knowledge in a different direction from the focus of a production journalist," say management authors James Redmond and Robert Trager. "As a manager, daily tasks include budgeting and conveying the journalist's point of view to corporate executives who don't always understand the greater purpose of 'informing the public,' a philosophy to which many working journalists subscribe. Thus the media manager has a foot in each of two worlds . . . . The result can be a tremendous sense of achievement and great personal reward for those who do it well."[24]

The complexities of media management are rooted in the very essence of the American model of media business. With very few exceptions, American news media companies are mostly supported by advertising sales. As A.J. Liebling put it, "The function of the press in society is to inform, but its role is to make money."[25] This can lead to a lot of pressure on media managers, making their personal stress management skills as important as their ability to manage others.

Most lower and middle managers in media companies are as devoted to the ideals of informing the public and serving the public interest as the creative professionals under them. As members of the corporate world as well, however, they also must strive to build audiences for advertisers so they can increase profits for the company. That second role often leads to conflicts with working journalists.

Nowhere is this more difficult than in television, where infotainment and superficial news coverage have become a norm. Matters only worsen with contrived features and programs every February, May, July and November when A.C. Nielsen conducts television ratings in every market to determine advertising rates. There are up to three additional sweeps months in some of the largest markets,[26] resulting in an unending cycle of pressure for TV managers to gain viewers and sell advertising.

Media managers face a constant tug-of-war between their mission of informing society and their need to pay for that mission.

It is a very difficult job, but there are things newly promoted media managers can do to be as successful as possible.

Building communication with both subordinates and superiors should be one of a new manager's highest priorities if he or she hopes to keep moving up in the ranks. Numerous management studies have concluded that the managers who go the highest in an organization are those who get along with others, can command respect of both their subordinates and their superiors, and are able to consider the opinions and perspectives of others—all skills used in working with people.[27]

In *Newsroom Management,* Robert H. Giles notes that a great deal of management is simply learning how to encourage, modify and strengthen the behavior of other people. His advice to new managers on how to establish and maintain effective supervision of others is based on what he calls five behavioral science principles that managers should keep foremost in their minds:[28]

(1) All people are different

(2) There is no one best way

(3) Personalities cannot be changed

(4) Perfection with people is impossible

(5) Natural motivations are more powerful than artificial ones.

Despite their awareness of these five principles, many new managers still make the mistake of trying to micromanage their new subordinates. "Give reporters room to write their own stories," advises Deanna Mascle, managing editor of the *Mt. Sterling* (Ky.) *Advocate*. "Just because it's not exactly what you envisioned does not mean it's wrong."[29]

At the same time, warns Ron Sawyer, publisher of *The Tuscaloosa* (Ala.) *News*, "Don't settle for poor performance. Poor performers are contagious and set the acceptable performance-level bar too low. By accepting poor performance, you communicate that poor performers are OK."[30]

Giles' five key principles about managing other people must sink in even before promotion, because your understanding and appreciation of their truths will signal to your boss that you just might be ready for a position in which you manage others. Develop and perfect your job skills as well. Often it is the mastering of those skills that first attracts the attention of supervisors, if only because they are easier to see, However, it is your people skills that will keep you in the management position.

Surviving in the cross fire

PRUDENT PARANOIA. That's how a *Harvard Business Review* article referred to the state of mind described by Intel Chairman Andrew S. Grove, who turned his favorite saying into the business book title of *Only the Paranoid Survive*.[31]

Grove's sense of paranoia is mostly pointed outward, like defensive artillery toward the enemy—his competitors. He maintains in his book that paranoia is an effective counter to the dangerous complacency and overconfidence that can settle into established companies.[32] Grove values paranoia for its help in anticipating and recognizing what he calls "crisis points" that threaten companies.

"When it comes to business, I believe in the value of paranoia," he explains. "Business success contains the seeds of its own destruction. The more successful you are, the more people want a chunk of your business . . . . I believe that the prime responsibility of a manager is to guard constantly against other people's attacks and to inculcate this guardian attitude in the people under his or her management."[33]

While Grove watches his competitors, Roderick M. Kramer's article in *Harvard Business Review* describes the value of paranoia in protecting yourself against executives, colleagues and staffers inside your own company. It is well and good to count on other people, trust them to do their jobs and to cooperate with you. But sometimes, alas, there is betrayal, sabotage and hidden agendas. To survive in the executive ranks, you need to expect the best but always be prepared for the worst.

Kramer advocates "prudent paranoia" in the workplace, based on his conclusion that, "there is room in the workplace for healthy distrust, for constructive suspicion about people's actions, motives and intentions . . . (and it) is healthy, a kind of early warning system to let you know, say, that your power is being threatened or you need more information about your situation."[34]

In his article, Kramer notes that people often are too trusting of others with whom they work. "Contrary to popular expectations, colleagues and bosses may not have our well-being at heart," Kramer states. "Many are often indifferent to us or see us as competitors."[35] In talking with hundreds of executives, Kramer reported that about 80 percent said they had made a major mistake by trusting someone they shouldn't have trusted. Odds like that should give anyone pause.

The balance, which no one can define exactly, is finding that point between the sensible level of prudent paranoia and the clinically pathological level of full-blown paranoia. Falling over into the latter is every bit as damaging to a career, if not more, than a lack of the former. As in everything else, moderation is the key.

Managing yourself—handling time

IT ALL STARTS NOW—if not sooner. Future managers need to start managing their own lives, for no one will respect your efforts to manage their beleaguered lives if you are out of control yourself. Your first priority? Drucker declares nothing is more important to executives and managers than time management, stating: "Time is the scarcest resource, and unless it is managed, nothing else can be managed."[36]

Or, in a more humorous vein, Malcolm Forbes Sr. pointed out, "There is never enough time, unless you're serving it."[37]

John Flaherty wrote how Drucker emphasized the importance of time management because it is "a unique resource that a company cannot buy, create or invent. Everybody is allocated only a certain share, which is irretrievable, ephemeral, irreversible and unstorable."[38]

In *The Effective Executive*, Drucker noted, "The supply of time is totally inelastic. No matter how high the demand, the supply will not go up. There is no price for it and no marginal utility curve for it. Moreover, time is totally perishable and cannot be stored. Yesterday's time is gone forever and will never come back. Time is, therefore, always in exceedingly short supply."[39]

Managers manage their own time by using the following steps:[40]

(1) Prioritize and plan.

(2) Think in terms of reaching a goal.

(3) Keep the main thing the main thing.

(4) Keep your vision intact.

(5) Plan short range and long range.

(6) Always use integrity in the moment of choice.

Remember, **time is not on your side**. All of us are busy in our jobs and our lives, but a great many people are not as productive as they could be because they do not follow the six steps above, Most people stumble over the very first step of prioritizing and its equal partner of planning on how they will use either their time or the delegated time of subordinates to meet priorities.

One of the greatest time-wasting practices of anyone is the human tendency to want to tackle the easy tasks first. There can be times when this is a smart tactic, such as when you need to clear your desk, calendar, mind, etc. so you can truly focus on a major task before you without distractions.

Usually, however, doing the easy tasks first is an unconscious way to avoid prioritizing—by delaying or ignoring the difficult or unpleasant task.

Picture yourself entering your office in the morning after worrying all night about how to resolve a particularly unpleasant situation facing you—like firing someone. You sit down, but then get up for a cup of coffee and visit with others in the office. You fret some more about the confrontation coming up, and then decide to make some phone calls on some routine matters. Maybe you even call your spouse and chat a bit. You find other things to do, making it appear that you are very busy, but in fact you are busy doing tasks that are either not important or that could be delayed without penalty. Hey, now it is lunch time. You take a longer lunch than usual, talking to a customer or business associate, and wander back into the office. Some other simple, non-immediate tasks capture your attention, and the day goes on. You cannot relax, of course, because you know that sooner or later you must do the dreadable. You are haunted all day by the specter of the big problem.

Instead of all this dancing around, management experts recommend you make it a practice to do the most unpleasant task of the day as soon as you arrive in the office. Fire the employee, cancel the contract, argue with the lawyer, solve the production crisis, increase the price, or whatever else it is that you have picked out as the day's monster challenge. Do it first. This is called "eating the frog."

After you have dispatched the worst problem of the day, swallowing anything else will be easy by comparison. You have prioritized by doing the most difficult, or the most important, task first.

A key concept of time management is to get the most important things done first. Business consultant Tom Gorman advises, "If you accomplish the insignificant at the expense of the essential, you will not be around long—even if you did it at your boss's direction . . . . It's not easy to refuse to take on work, especially from your boss, but it pays to let her know how much you and your people are doing, and to warn of what projects might fall through the cracks . . . . If you and your people get the most important tasks done, you will be OK."[41]

Brian Tracy wrote a book titled *Eat That Frog!* and he says much the same thing, writing, "Time management is really life management, personal management. It is really taking control of the sequence of events. Time management is control over what you do next."[42]

When you take on new tasks, or re-address old ones, you must start by assessing their importance relative to everything else you do. Will the new task create revenue or reduce costs? Does it fit the goals of the company in an ethical sense as well as a business sense? What will happen if the task does not get done, and how will your own priorities shift as you take on the new task?[43]

In every line of work, you will repeatedly hear others tell how they worked until late into the night, put in 70 hours a week, and have not been on a vacation in years. It's an easy trap to fall into, especially if you love what you are doing.

Ken Blum, who writes a regular business column for *Publishers' Auxiliary*, gives the following opinion: "No job is worth a 70- or 80-hour work week and/or five or ten years without a vacation. Hours that lengthy are a symptom of addiction, not dedication. They send a strong signal that an otherwise intelligent publisher is letting the business run him or her, instead of vice versa. And the irony is that the business probably would be better off if the publisher was working less, not more."[44]

So don't think telling someone how overworked you are will win sympathy. It probably only means that you are unorganized and not managing your time well.

Time management depends on your approaching tasks in a systematic and planned way.

Staffers who thought they did all the work while their managers sat around twiddling thumbs will be in for a shock when they start their first management job. Managers, at least the best ones, are among the busiest people in the office, with an incredible variety of time-consuming problems and challenges facing them every day. They must actively and even creatively find ways to get as much done as possible in their new position while also maintaining a semblance of family life and personal free time at home.[45] It is not easy, and it can be frustrating and disturbing. But you need to start the habit of organizing your time before you start a management position—the earlier the better.

The simple tactic of the "to-do list" is effectively used by countless people who face the challenge of having too much to do and too little time to do it in. Immediately start the habit of composing a list of tasks and priorities. Every morning you should get into your office early enough so you can write down on a paper pad or on your computer every task you need or want to accomplish that day. Then cross each one off as it is accomplished. Transfer any uncompleted tasks to the next day's list. Some people separate their tasks into long-term and short-term lists. More people are turning to pocket-sized personal digital assistants to organize their activities and keep resources such as telephone numbers and memos with them. Some PDAs come combined with cell phones and infrared transmitters. Cell phones can include digital cameras as well as telephone directories and Internet access for checking e-mail.

Another helpful organizational tool is the telephone log. Managers often must make scores of telephone contacts each day. One way to keep track of them is to keep a daily log next to your phone, writing notes while you talk that record when you talked with whom and what was discussed. If you keep such a log, you will find yourself referring back to it repeatedly to refresh your memory on details that were discussed, promises that were made and who said what and when.

Very importantly, accept the fact that you do not have time to do everything and use your managerial authority to delegate some tasks to qualified subordinates.

Not just anyone can be a manager

JOE SULENTIC, who teaches Entrepreneurship and New Venture Formation in the business school at the University of Iowa, is an example of the type of resource that could open up new perspectives for journalists when they enroll in some business classes. In his classes, Sulentic emphasizes that it takes a particular kind of person to succeed in management.

What many working journalists seem to lack is the business training, experience, and attitude that media companies now are drawing on for their managerial ranks. The result is that media executives are frequently pulled from the circulation, accounting and advertising departments instead of the newsroom.

Interestingly, however, the best journalists share some of the same traits as a good manager, though they often do not understand how to transfer those traits to a management role. For example, journalists in print and broadcast newsrooms tend to be tenacious, scornful of a 9-to-5 mentality, creative in thought and deed, goal-driven, deadline conscious, and energetic. All of these traits are typical of successful managers.

Sulentic says the most effective manager-leaders prominently display the following six characteristics.

(1) **High energy.** This includes a concern for one's own physical health, through exercise and healthy living, as well as for one's own psychological health, achieved by molding what Sulentic calls "psychological armor." More on the latter later.

(2) **Vision.** This will be discussed in the chapter on leadership. Vision is essential for a manager to be able to move the company forward in growth and prosperity.

(3) **Calculated risk-taking aptitude.** Neither managers nor entrepreneurs are reckless. They do not roll the dice and risk everything—that is, not unless they have looked at everything closely and feel they can win. Many people cannot accept even minimal risk, and others are afflicted with "analysis paralysis" in trying to decide whether a risk is worth taking. To succeed as a manager or entrepreneur, you need analytic skills, confidence, indomitable character, and willingness to risk making decisions despite a degree of uncertainty.

(4) **Team-building ability.** The true test of a leader is whether that person can build a teamwork approach with others to solve problems and accomplish goals. Loners are effective in some intensely personal professions such as science, academia and the arts. But most business goals can best be reached, and often only can be reached, through several people working together as a team headed by an effective leader.

(5) **Ability to deal with ambiguity.** Uncertainty is the only thing certain in decision-making, and people who lack confidence or still have not progressed from the black-and-white cognitive processes to the gray will find it impossible to make the complex decisions needed in business.

(6) **Resources, especially time.** Managers are busy people, regardless of what their subordinates think, and to get the work done and to get it done right takes wise use of both personal and delegated time.

In summary, the three most critical management skills that must be developed to succeed in running a company are:[46]

(1) Management of cash flow through accounting and marketing,

(2) Management of people through interpersonal skills, and

(3) Management of time, both your own and your subordinates'.

Out of these three basic managerial skill fields come all of the supporting actions—such as marketing, sales, planning, operations, product development, financial accounting and investment, goal-setting, decision-making, budgeting, productivity, quality control, adaptability, promotion, succession, communication, and perseverance.

Managing media employees is more challenging than managing employees of many other types of businesses. That is because reporters, editors, photographers, videographers, writers and designers all tend to be creative people well known for their independent and strong-willed personalities. But Francis Dale, who was an editor at the old *Los Angeles Herald Examiner*, says the differences are not as great as many people make them out to be. "A manager is a manager," he said. "Modern professional managerial techniques apply to whatever the product is."[47]

Journalists becoming managers

AS THE PROFITABILITY of the press has become better appreciated by business leaders and investors, news organizations are being increasingly led by business managers from outside the newsroom. Many publishers of daily newspapers today, to whom editors must ultimately answer, rose to that position through marketing, management, financial and advertising careers—not from the news side. Historian William McKeen observes that in the past several years the emphasis in news organizations has shifted "from the newsroom to the board room."[48]

Surveys of media companies show that most publishers today originated somewhere besides the newsroom. Ironically, if news side employees made the effort, they could better understand the creative people in the news and advertising departments than could a rising accountant, lawyer or professional manager.

A realization is building that reporters and editors must develop their business skills as well as their news-handling skills if they ever want to gain influential leadership roles in their media company. Slowly, and despite a great deal of opposition from many journalists, some editors are replacing the impenetrable walls isolating the newsroom from the rest of their company with walls at least made of glass, which enables them to see and communicate with other departments.

The Poynter Institute, which hosted a 2000 conference on Journalism and Business Values; the American Press Institute; the Media Management Center mentioned in Chapter 1; and some journalism schools are beginning to stress more cross-training in both news and business for those in newsrooms.

Many complain about a negative influence on journalism's public interest duties in the newsroom by managers who hold MBA degrees instead of journalism degrees and by advertising directors, accountants and corporate front-office executives heading newsrooms. But reporters and editors cannot simply beat back these irrepressible forces caused by today's competitive pressures. A more useful response is that newsroom folks need to learn how to participate instead, thus having a say in the decisions to be made. As the Borg in Star Trek's "Next Generation" would say, resistance is futile. Education could be the solution.

One of the pioneers in the concept that journalism students should learn about the corporate culture is the University of Illinois, which offers a joint master's degree in journalism and business administration. A combination is needed, the university states, because:

"Many media executives have expressed the regret that most journalists are inadequately prepared for advancement to positions of leadership in management. All too often journalism graduates are told that capable individuals in the news-editorial operation lack an understanding of the special problems of marketing, personnel relations, organizational behavior, etc. In order to prepare journalism graduates for positions of professional leadership beyond entry-level jobs, a joint master's degree seems an appropriate and logical approach."[49]

Regardless of where you get your education, you can accomplish the same goal by taking the initiative to include useful business courses in your formal education or afterward.

Too many times, talented reporters are promoted into positions of more responsibility where they become quickly frustrated and unhappy because they have no idea how to manage others. They neither understand nor care to understand their company's business operations. There has to be a better and more effective way to prepare people than just giving them news coverage awards and then kicking them upstairs to an uncertain fate in the radically different world of management.

The indispensable management resource

UNFORTUNATELY, none of these qualities, principles, skills and habits will work if, as Sulentic says, you do not mold your psychological armor for the difficulties and travails of being a manager. Though it might be satisfying and rewarding to be at the top, it is not easy. You are a scapegoat for disgruntled workers, and when things go wrong you can give yourself a real guilt trip when you are forced to realize it **really** was all your fault. A lot of people are depending for their livelihood on you not making fatal mistakes, and the pressure can be intense as you make complicated decisions. Your self-worth is always on the line. People will expect you to reassure and advise them when they are having difficulties, but who is going to do that for you?

It has a lot to do with what I think of as optimistic perseverance; "persistence" was the word favored by President Calvin Coolidge. Though best known as Silent Cal, this taciturn man is the source of a famous quote about the value for a strong leader to, as the line from the movie spoof "Galaxy Quest" so aptly put it, "Never give up. Never surrender."[50]

Coolidge, though more humorlessly than that movie's script writers, put the same concept forth quite well in the 1920s when he observed, "Nothing in the world can take the place of persistence. Talent will not; nothing is more common than unsuccessful men with talent. Genius will not; unrewarded genius is almost a proverb. Education will not; the world is full of educated derelicts. Persistence and determination alone are omnipotent. The slogan 'Press On' has solved and always will solve the problems of the human race."[51]

But all of that is easier said than done for some people. You need to toughen yourself so you can persist in the face of negativity, opposing odds, and setbacks. **Management is not for the faint of heart.** Stress vanquishes both managers and the people they supervise in media companies. This is especially true in the newsrooms, where everyone must work on deadline while always remaining vigilant about accuracy, fairness and balance—and libel and slander. Who wouldn't be stressed?

Molding your psychological armor simply is about bracing yourself mentally—to make a conscious effort to create a compelling future, prepare to enjoy battle daily, stay positive, enjoy work, and live healthily.

The quick way to the top

LIFE CAN BE UNFAIR. Or it can be more than fair. Put another way, no amount of skill, hard work and planning can replace dumb luck. That's especially true about business in general and in media companies in particular, where family dynasties can and do run their corporations for three or more generations and success can be based on what family the new executive was born into.

It leads to situations like the owner of *The New York Times* designating his son Arthur Ochs Sulzberger to be publisher of one of the nation's largest dailies in 1963 at the age of only 37, despite his having little executive experience. "It can be truly said," said Arthur Hays Sulzberger, who was himself appointed publisher by his father before him, in announcing his son's promotion, "that *The Times* is a family enterprise."[52]

Similarly, in 2002 Rupert Murdoch named his 31-year-old son, Lachlan, as publisher of the nation's 15th largest and fastest growing daily, the *New York Post*. Before that, Lachlan Murdoch had been deputy chief operating officer for News Corp. since he was in his 20s.[53]

Nepotism is a long-honored tradition throughout business, at least partly because it often turns out to be successful. Whether it be genes, connections or just the pressure to prove you deserve the position, such "born" leaders often turn out to be thoroughly capable.

There is resentment to such appointments by those outside the hereditary loop, as epitomized by columnist Steve Lopez, who wrote the quintessential insider-envy insult. As a former Knight Ridder reporter, Lopez was offended by the ease with which Tony Ridder was given the CEO position at his eponymous company. "It's a little like the case of George W. Bush with Tony," Lopez wrote in the *Los Angeles Times*. "He was born on third base and thought he hit a triple . . . . If not for his family, would Tony be in the position he's in?"[54]

Well, probably not. So what? Focus on your own abilities; that will keep you busy enough.

Or, you could even consider the issue from the other point of view. Christopher B. Galvin, grandson of Motorola's founder and its CEO since 1997, responded to charges against him of nepotism by noting: "No one gets to choose to whom or where they are born. My situation has extraordinary benefits, and it has its challenges and burdens."[55]

The most unthinkable scenario is what happened to poor Ted Fang on Oct. 27, 2001. Editor and publisher of the *San Francisco Examiner* since his family bought it a year earlier, Fang was fired by the company's board chairwoman—his mother.

In a terse statement, Florence Fang said her son would "continue to have the opportunity to consult and advise us on strengthening our business, and at the same time be free to pursue other interests."[56]

And you thought your mom was tough on you sometimes.

CASE STUDY   *Learning To Think Like a Manager*

by THOMAS L. BEELL
Iowa State University

You've just been promoted to managing editor of a small town newspaper. The other three reporters are glad there's going to be a change in leadership because the previous editor had made all of them unhappy for one reason or another.

First, he played favorites. He gave the good story assignments to the people who kissed up to him and never argued with him nor complained.

Next, he kept the best stories for himself and submitted those to regional and national news competitions. The rest of the staff reporters were never honored with awards, and thus had a harder time asking for pay raises.

Third, he gave orders, and wasn't interested in hearing comments from his staff.

You're determined not to make your predecessor's mistakes.

You decline to move into the managing editor's private office, deciding to stay at your old desk in the middle of the newsroom.

You refuse to take sides in arguments between the reporters. "Work it out for yourself," you tell them. You don't want them to hate you the way they hated the previous manager.

You encourage them to give you feedback, unlike your predecessor. But you don't want to upset them by telling them what you think.

You don't think it's fair to shove your work off on your old friends. So you work long hours to cover the city council meeting and your other news beats, in addition to the budget and reports required of you as managing editor. Unfortunately, you've gotten behind now and your bosses are beginning to get upset with you.

Both of these examples illustrate common mistakes that managers—especially new managers—make.

Identify as many things as you can that both you and your predecessor are doing wrong **before** looking at the analysis of the solutions on the following page.

ANALYSIS. The previous managing editor:

1. Wasn't even-handed in dealing with his subordinates. That built up resentment.

2. Rewarded people who were currying his favor. That meant he wasn't given the information he needed to prevent problems from happening and to fix them when they did.

3. Is a perfect example of a manager who engages in one-way communication. He issued orders, but refused to listen.

ANALYSIS. Your mistakes:

1. You desperately want to be liked. You forgot that being promoted to manager means that you are no longer one of the gang. You now have responsibility over your friends. You must make decisions that will affect their jobs, perhaps negatively.

2. The key to your success as a manager is to be fair and reasonable. But you might be forced to make an arbitrary decision at some point. If you have a reputation for being fair and even handed, your subordinates will accept your decisions without undue resistance.

3. You should move into the managing editor's office. You need the privacy to discuss things with your subordinates and your superiors. The office also lends gravitas to your position, with the result that your decisions will be more readily accepted.

4. Leaving problems for your reporters to work out abrogates your duty as a manager. Managers must make decisions, and subordinates expect them to do so.

5. Your communication problem is the opposite of your predecessor. It is still one-way communication, but this time in your direction. Communication, to be effective, must be two-way.

6. You refused to delegate work. Managers aren't required to do everything themselves. In fact, good managers get things done through others. You are making a major mistake in not delegating some of your work.

AUTHOR:

Thomas L. Beell is an experienced newspaper reporter, radio reporter and TV news producer. He is a professor of journalism and mass communication at Iowa State University in Ames.

CASE STUDY *Entrepreneurship,*
or a Management Career?

by HUGH S. FULLERTON, Ph.D.
Sam Houston State University

(First in a series of five related case studies)

Jerry Anthony is a copy editor on *The Daily Record,* a paper of 60,000 circulation in a city of 150,000. Jerry is 33, supports his family reasonably well on his salary, and has been in the newspaper business for a decade as reporter and copy editor. The Record is a well-established but not innovative paper, and promotion is slow because of low turnover at the top. Jerry is in line to become assistant managing editor in a few years when the executive editor retires and others move up. His future there seems secure, if unexciting.

Jerry has long nurtured a dream of owning his own newspaper, so he could "be his own boss." He has ideas—lots of them—that he thinks could offer more to the readers and advertisers, and he thinks he could make more money as a business owner, rather than by remaining just an employee. So he does a little shopping with newspaper broker Bill Bostwick.

Jerry does not have a lot of capital, but Bostwick sends him information on the *Jamestown Call,* a small weekly available at what seems to be a reasonable price, and the retiring owner will finance most of the purchase cost.

Jerry is excited, but after talking to his wife and his lawyer, he starts to have doubts. Is he cut out to be an entrepreneur? Can he afford to gamble what little assets the family has been able to accumulate? Should he leave the apparent security of *The Record?*

Help Jerry to determine whether he is cut out to be an entrepreneur, or whether he should remain at *The Record* and work toward promotion there. What questions should he be asking himself at this fork in the road?

AUTHOR:

Hugh S. Fullerton was a daily newspaper reporter and also publisher of a group of weekly newspapers in Michigan for several years. He teaches journalism at Sam Houston State University in Huntsville, Texas.

CHAPTER 2

🖳 Suggested Web sites:

www.editorandpublisher.com—*Editor & Publisher* magazine
www.nieman.Harvard.edu—*Nieman Reports* magazine
www.cjr.org—*Columbia Journalism Review*
www.ajr.org—*American Journalism Review*
www.foliomag.com—*Folio Magazine Management*
www.broadcastingcable.com—*Broadcasting and Cable* magazine
www.asne.org/kiosk/editor/tae.htm—*American Editor* magazine
www.naa.org/presstime/index.html—*Presstime* magazine
www.adage.com—*Advertising Age* magazine
www.prweekus.com—*PR Week* magazine
www.magazine.org—News of the magazine industry
www.colegroup.com/newsinc—News Inc. webzine
www.mediaweek.com—*Media Week* magazine
www.poynter.org—Poynter Institue
www.freep.com/jobspage/links—Journalism jobs site
www.poynter.org/medianews—Jim Romenesko's media news
www.mediaed.org—Media Education Foundation
www.newsroomleadership.com—Edward Miller's reflections on leadership
www.scripps.ohiou.edu/jh/jh.htm—*Journalism History* magazine

Endnotes to Chapter 2:

[1] Warren Bennis, "The 4 competencies of leadership," *Training & Development Journal* (August 1984): 16. A variation of this in the opposite order is in Warren Bennis and Burt Nanus, *Leaders: The Strategies for Taking Charge* (New York: Perennial Library, 1986), 21.

[2] John E. Flaherty, *Peter Drucker: Shaping the Managerial Mind* (San Francisco: Jossey-Bass, 1999), 119. Copyright © 1999, Jossey-Bass. Reprinted by permission of John Wiley & Sons, Inc.

[3] Thanks and a tip of the hat to Dr. Paul Christiansen, retired professor of biology at Cornell College in Mount Vernon, Iowa, who kindly straightened me out on this law, which I had totally mis-named in my first draft.

[4] Flaherty, *Peter Drucker: Shaping the Managerial Mind*, 281.

[5] Ibid.

[6] Frederick Herzberg, Bernard Mausner and Barbara Synderman, *The Motivation to Work* (New York: John Wiley & Sons, 1959), 132-134.

[7] "Salaries by employer type," Grady College of the University of Georgia, <www.grady.uga.edu/annualsurveys/grd00/grd2000sal.htm>, as accessed on April 11, 2003.

[8] Warren Bennis and Burt Nanus, *Leaders: The Strategies for Taking Charge* (New York: Perennial Library, 1986), 87.

[9] Shelby Coffey III, *Best Practices: The Art of Leadership in News Organizations* (Arlington, Va.: Freedom Forum, 2002), 59–61.

[10] Dan Herrera, assistant managing editor of the *Albuquerque Journal,* in remarks to a media management class at the University of New Mexico, April 4, 2002.

[11] Coffey, *Best Practices: The Art of Leadership in News Organizations,* 66.

[12] Ibid., 65.

[13] Ibid.

[14] "Most powerful black executives: Robert Johnson," at <www.fortune.com/fortune/blackpower/snapshot/0,15307,25,00.html>, accessed May 20, 2003.

[15] "Most powerful black executives: Cathy Hughes," at <www.fortune.com/fortune/

blackpower/snapshot/0,15307,34,00.html>, accessed May 20, 2003.

[16] "Women still missing from executive suites," *Mediaweek,* September 2, 2002, 21.

[17] Ibid.

[18] Coffey, *Best Practices: The Art of Leadership in News Organizations,* 103.

[19] Barclay Jameson, remarks to a media management class at the University of New Mexico, April 2, 2003.

[20] John D. Rockefeller, as quoted by Robert H. Giles in *Newsroom Management: A Guide to Theory and Practice* (Detroit, Mich.: Media Management Books, 8th ed., 1995), 10.

[21] Loren B. Belker, *The First-Time Manager: A Practical Guide to the Management of People* (New York: AMACOM, 1978), 1.

[22] David B. Martens, "The first-time manager's survival guide," *Presstime* (November 1997): 41.

[23] Ibid., 12–15.

[24] James Redmond and Robert Trager, *Balancing on the Wire: The Art of Managing Media* (Boulder, Colo.: Coursewise Publishing, 1998), 4.

[25] Ibid., 9.

[26] Nielsen Media Research, "The sweeps—local market management," at <www.nielsenmedia.com>, accessed January 13, 2003.

[27] Robert H. Giles, *Newsroom Management: A Guide to Theory and Practice* (Detroit, Mich.: Media Management Books, 8th ed., 1995), 10.

[28] Ibid., 12.

[29] Martens, "The first-time manager's survival guide," 42.

[30] Ibid.

[31] Roderick M. Kramer. Reprinted by permission of *Harvard Business Review.* From "When paranoia makes sense," (July 2002): 62–69. Copyright © 2002 by Harvard Business School Publishing Corporation, all right reserved.

[32] Andrew S. Grove, *Only the Paranoid Survive: How to Exploit the Crisis Points that Challenge Every Company* (New York: Doubleday & Co., 1999).

[33] Ibid.

[34] Susan Schwartz, "Into work it should creep: Moderate paranoia at the office is warranted, prof says," *The Gazette,* Montreal, Canada, August 26, 2002, formerly at <www.canada.com/montreal/montrealgazette/columnists/story.asp?id=11C8264F-7EF4-4F83-84F0-187ADEBDD5B2>, accessed September 6, 2002, but no longer available on the Web.

[35] Kramer, "When paranoia makes sense," 63.

[36] Peter F. Drucker, *The Effective Executive* (New York: Harper & Row, 1966–67), 51.

[37] Malcolm Forbes, as quoted by Steve Maller on Web site, "List of Quotation Authors," <www.maller.com/quotes/default.html?xauth=Malcolm%20Forbes>, accessed May 10, 2001.

[38] Flaherty, *Peter Drucker: Shaping the Managerial Mind,* 322.

[39] Drucker, *The Effective Executive,* 26.

[40] Joe Sulentic, remarks to a media management class at the University of Iowa in January 1999.

[41] Tom Gorman, *The Complete Idiot's Guide to MBA Basics* (New York: Alpha Books, 1998), 53.

[42] Brian Tracy, *Eat That Frog!* (San Francisco: Berrett-Koehler Publishers, 2001), 22.

[43] Ibid., 52.

[44] Ken Blum, "Worked to death: You need to break the job addiction to make your newspaper succeed," *Publishers' Auxiliary,* May 5, 1997, 15.

[45] D'Val Westphal, news editor of the *Albuquerque Journal,* remarks to a media management class at the University of New Mexico, February 12, 2002.

[46] Robert T. Kiyosaki, *Rich Dad, Poor Dad* (New York: Warner Books Inc., 1997), 173.

[47] Francis Dale, former publisher of *Los Angeles Herald Examiner,* as quoted by Doug Underwood in *When MBAs Rule the Newsroom* (New York: Columbia University Press, 1995), 14.

[48] Loren Ghiglione, "Two faces of Mickey Mouse," *Media Studies Journal* (Spring–Summer 1996).

[49] University of Illinois, "Joint master's degree in journalism and business administration," <www.comm.uiuc.edu/Journlsm/joint.html>, accessed May 27, 2001.

[50] Galaxy Quest, dir. Dean Parisot, 104 min., DreamWorks LLC., 1999, videocassette.

[51] Calvin Coolidge, as quoted at <www.ksu.edu/qsa/inspiration.htm>, accessed June 20, 2001.

[52] Gay Talese, *The Kingdom and the Power* (New York: The World Publishing Co., 1969), 319.

[53] Joe Strupp, "'Post' Modern Murdoch," *Editor & Publisher* (December 16, 2002): 15.

[54] Jim Romenesko's MediaNews, ©2001 The Poynter Institute, <www.poynter.org/medianews>, accessed May 18, 2001.

[55] Andrea Petersen, "Motorola goes into mea culpa mode to atone for its cellphone blunders," *The Wall Street Journal* Interactive Edition (May 18, 2001) e-book, 117.

[56] "S.F. Examiner publisher fired by his mother," ©2001 United Press International, as reported by *Wall Street City.*

CHAPTER 3
MOTIVATION AND THE WORK FORCE

PROFESSOR Bob Gassaway of the University of New Mexico recalls being interviewed for a job years ago with the publisher of a Missouri daily. Looking around the newsroom, Gassaway asked his boss-to-be how many people worked at the newspaper. "Well," drawled the old publisher, leaning across his desk, "as near as I can figure, about one in three."[1]

Motivating people to higher productivity than that always has been a major challenge for managers.

Luckily, a big part of managing the creative types who work at media companies comes from just appreciating their skills and turning them loose to do the job. "Perhaps nothing is more important to media employees—and thus, to their employer—than the employees' ability to create, react constructively, or see the meaning of their work," noted Ardyth Sohn and her co-authors in *Media Management: A Casebook Approach.*[2] Managers need also to work in a constructive manner with their talented and highly motivated staff and show their appreciation for each employee's skills. Much of this chapter deals with how to work with media employees to the best advantage of the employee, the manager and the company.

Part of any manager's success must start with hiring the best possible employees to begin with and then helping them become even better. How do you find such people, or know what you've found when you spot it? Businessman Harvey Mackay offered tips on how to recognize valuable employees (sometimes it's more difficult than you might think) and how to encourage them to become better employees.

Mackay noted that winners surround themselves with other winners. A winner knows he or she is a winner. Winners don't need go-alongs to massage their ego. Winners are confident and know they will go further with associates who not only can keep up but who also are capable of contributing good ideas themselves.

Mackay's advice is that if you are about to form a new business connection, whether it's a job or a joint venture, don't just look at your opposite number. Look at that person's subordinates, too. Does your opposite number trust them? Does he or she delegate to them? Do subordinates complement the leader's talents by being strong managers? Or are they just clones of their boss?[3]

Colin L. Powell has what he calls "Powell's rules for Picking People." One of America's best-known generals, he also has served five presidents in leadership roles, most recently as Secretary of State under President George W. Bush.

"What I looked for was intelligence and judgment, and most critically, a capacity to anticipate, to see around corners," Powell wrote in his autobiography. "I also valued loyalty, integrity, a high energy drive, a certain passion, a balanced ego and the drive to get things done."[4]

In response, Oren Harari, a professor and business consultant, makes the following points:

"How often do our recruitment and hiring processes tap into these attributes? More often than not, we ignore them in favor of length of résumé, degrees and prior titles . . . . You can train a bright, willing novice in the fundamentals of your business fairly readily, but it's a lot harder to train someone to have integrity, judgment, energy, balance, and the drive to get things done. Good leaders stack the deck in their favor right in the recruitment phase."[5]

Unionism in media companies

UNIONS. Now there's a fighting word in business. We might as well talk about it right up front. Extremely strong emotions are evoked in every workplace with owners and their managers on one side and the rest of the employees typically either on the other side or uncommitted. Most companies are willing to spend a fortune to stop a union from organizing—and that certainly includes newspapers, broadcast entities, magazines, and other media companies.

Without exception, if you become a manager you will be expected by your bosses to close ranks with them and to do everything possible legally to stop any union-organizing movement among the employees. Many of these employees might be long-time personal friends of yours. It's a difficult time for everyone, but especially for managers.

The view from the top is that unions interfere with the ability of owners to run their company as they want and that unions inevitably become costly because they force higher wages and benefits and affect the way the company can operate. Between the owner/manager and the rank-and-file employee, the typical management perception is that unions insert a third entity of "interference"—a union official, lawyer or negotiator.

Conrad Fink's book, *Strategic Newspaper Management*, forcefully states, "If you accept management responsibility, you implicitly agree to support management attitudes and efforts. That includes helping management avoid unions or, if they are unavoidable, helping fashion a relationship with them that will ensure management attitudes will prevail . . . . If you cannot accept that, a manager's career is not for you, because few areas of management require such deep commitment."[7]

Of course, the employees interested in organizing see the issue from a very different point of view. Good managers, no matter what they believe, will do their cause the most good if they understand the viewpoint of any opponent, inside or outside of the company, as well as they know their own viewpoint.

In general, employees do not feel a need for a union until they come to believe they are being treated unfairly or are about to be treated unfairly. Satisfied and secure employees do not seek company-wide confrontations with their bosses over their conditions

> "The boss don't listen when one guy squawks,
>
> But he's gotta listen when the union talks."[6]
>
> —*Old union song*

of employment. As the saying goes, companies that get unions usually deserve them.

Granting all of that, it was the writer Alexandre Dumas who noted, "All generalizations are dangerous—even this one."[8] Totally unexpected rebellions can occur in any workplace out of what seemed at the time to be innocent actions. However, it usually is long-standing grievances that coalesce into union solidarity. Put another way by John B. Jaske, senior vice president of labor relations at Gannett, "Nothing will turn an employee to a union faster than being taken for granted."[9] That's why Jaske has this advice for managers: "A commitment must be made at all levels of management to find out what employees are thinking, why they are thinking it, and how to make the best possible response."[10]

John M. Lavine and Daniel B. Wackman present a more tolerant and cooperative perspective than Fink toward unions in their book, *Managing Media Organizations*, noting:

"Some media managers are intent on driving unions out of their organizations. Others believe that unions serve a valuable function and they are able to work effectively with their union employees. These managers view unions as just one of many methods for employee-employer decision making; as having pluses and minuses, just as other arrangements do."[11] Probably most executives have strong emotions about unionism that are more in agreement with Fink's approach.

Both support and opposition to unions ordinarily is expressed in economic terms by both labor and management. However, the major (but usually unstated) reason business executives oppose labor unions is over control, not just economics. Unionization inserts the union between the supervisor and the supervised. Executives believe that kind of situation "threatens to circumscribe the customary prerogatives of management" by challenging the way business should be conducted.[12]

Several unions are present in media companies. They include some unusual unions—such as the United Auto Workers, which became the unusual choice to represent employees of the *Sault Ste. Marie (Mich.) Evening News* in a 25–14 vote in 1992.[13] The UAW is the largest union in Michigan, so that newspaper's staff turned to the UAW rather than one of the unions we ordinarily see representing newspaper employees.

Unions have had a long and influential history in the production and distribution departments of newspapers, but not in the newsrooms. Most newsrooms have never been unionized. Similarly, unions are established for many television, radio and magazine companies—but again, as a rule usually not in the newsroom.

Rules often are broken, of course. And it is a direct result of the take-over of media properties from families by national, publicly-traded and extremely wealthy conglomerates that unions are starting to have some success again in organizing reporters and others in the newsroom. Therefore, by the time you become a manager you might run a greater risk than your predecessors ever did of encountering a union drive in your newsroom.

The most prominent union representing newsroom and business department employees is The Newspaper Guild. In 1933, led by columnist Heywood Broun, traditionally self-reliant reporters unhappy with their pay established the Guild as an independent union. In 1936–37, the Guild affiliated with the AFL-CIO, and in 1995 it merged with the Communication Workers of America (CWA). The CWA's 630,000 members mostly come from other industries, but it had moved into newspaper organizing in 1987. That's when the International Typographical Union, in its death throes because of the end of the hot metal type composing room and the increase of mail room automation, merged its members into the CWA. In 1997, the Guild modified its merger with CWA by becoming a more independent "sector" of the CWA.[14]

In books of the 1980s and 1990s on the subject, you will read statements such as, "Guild membership is dropping precipitously."[15] Be aware that recent developments do not bear this out. In 1987, the Guild reported 34,828 members, and that indeed did decline to 26,202 by 1993.[16] By 2001, however, the Guild's membership had rebounded to

34,000 in the United States, Canada and Puerto Rico.[17] Guild president Linda Foley said membership was holding steady at that total in 2003.[18]

The Guild has expanded far beyond its original roster of newspaper reporters, which is why in 2001 it began talk of changing its name to The Media Guild to more accurately describe its membership. Today, with the muscle of the CWA and the AFL-CIO backing it up, the Guild represents online writers and designers, reporters, editorial assistants, photographers, editors, paginators, editorial artists, correspondents, typographers, advertising sales people, marketing, information systems specialists, commercial artists, technicians, accountants, business, customer service reps, drivers, maintenance, mail room, pressroom, telephone operators, circulation and distribution staff. The Guild also has branched out to include public relations staff, wire services, magazines, broadcast news, public service and dot-com companies.[19]

Early victories by the Guild include one of the first successful strikes by a group of white-collar workers in the United States when news staff employees struck the *Seattle Post-Intelligencer* in 1936 over arbitrary dismissals.[20] One of the Guild's more interesting victories came on March 20, 2001, when employees of *The Chinese Daily News*, a Chinese-language paper in Los Angeles, voted 78 to 63 for Guild representation.[21]

Still, the Guild represents only a small number of daily newspapers. Jaske thinks that is because of the famously independent streak in most news-side employees.

"Perhaps the Guild's greatest problem has been the fact that it attempts to organize the unorganizable," Jaske said. "Journalists are by disposition and training naturally skeptical of anyone who seeks to limit their freedom or group them together."[22]

The largest media union is the Graphic Communications International Union, representing 150,000 active and retired press operators and others. Also active in media companies are the International Association of Machinists and the International Brotherhood of Teamsters. The Teamsters probably represent the fewest media employees, but where they are present they are not to be trifled with. The Teamsters struck the *Pittsburgh Press* in 1992 and the paper was closed permanently.[23]

At broadcast stations, the major unions include the National Association of Broadcast Employees and Technicians (NABET), International Brotherhood of Electrical Workers (IBEW), the CWA and the Writers Guild of America.[24]

The strike is probably the most potent weapon of a unionized work force, but not the only one. Media employees can also confront management short of going on strike. In 2002 at *The Washington Post*, for example, bylines were withheld by print journalists. There also have been refusals to go on camera by broadcast journalists.

Strikes usually affect newspapers, and they are always very disruptive. A 1963 strike by several unions shut down New York City newspapers for 114 days, and a strike in the late 1990s against Detroit's dailies was still being fought in courts and before federal agencies years after the end of active picketing.

In every strike, managers are called on to keep the newspaper publishing and the TV or radio station broadcasting. Any non-union people hired to replace the striking workers are referred to as "scabs" by those on the picket line, and there are many law firms who specialize as "strike-breakers" to advise companies on how to win a strike.

Frequently, a union striking against a newspaper will publish a "strike paper" to compete for subscribers and advertisements against any attempts by the struck paper to continue publication without union workers. Most of these strike papers fade away when settlement is finally reached, with the notable exception of the *Green Bay* (Wis.) *News-Chronicle*. It was started as a strike paper in 1972 and afterward sold to publisher Frank Wood, who continues to publish it against the Gannett-owned daily there.

There also are some internal unions. They are formed with an owner's acquiescence because such unions tend to be more cooperative with management and less militant. The largest internal union probably is the Independent Association of Publishers' Employees (IAPE). For many years it represented staffers at *The Wall Street Journal*, with its officers having a reputation as being just mild-mannered reporters when it came to union business. Non-aggressive tactics began to harden when the IAPE eventually affiliated with the CWA. Finally, in 1999, the union publicly clashed with owner Dow Jones & Co., Inc., when the company announced it was unilaterally ending its profit-sharing retirement plan.[25] The IAPE won the right for staffers to convert instead to a money-purchase pension plan and a 401(k) retirement plan during its negotiation of a three-year contract that October.[26]

No matter how vehement the owner and other higher-ups to whom you answer become, an important fact for you to keep absolutely foremost as a manager facing a union organizing drive is this: Whether the boss likes it or not, employees do have a legal right to try and form a union.

The National Labor Relations Act (NLRA) of 1935, also known as the Wagner Act, states:

Section 7: "Employees shall have the right to self-organization, to form, join, or assist labor organizations, to bargain collectively through representation of their own choosing, and to engage in other concerted activities for the purpose of collective bargaining."

And furthermore:

Section 8(a): "It shall be an unfair labor practice for an employer to interfere with, restrain, or coerce employees in the exercise of the rights guaranteed in section 7."[27]

By ignoring this legal right and acting illegally yourself, you not only could cost your company a victory in the union organizing drive but probably also bring down ruinous lawsuits, incur disciplinary action against your company by the National Labor Relations Board, and get yourself fired. The Taft-Hartley Act of 1947 protects management's rights to campaign against unions, but only under strict guidelines that you must follow. Make sure you know them. They are enforced more strictly under some White House administrations than others.

Everyone (well, just about everyone) agrees that the best way to avoid a union is to treat employees fairly and keep their working conditions acceptable. In an effort to accomplish this, one alternative is in a company choosing paternalism, which usually ends up being counter-productive, at least in the long run. Many companies have been able to stave off unionism at least temporarily as they transitioned from blue-collar work forces to less militant "knowledge" workers in the computer age. But unions are redirecting their appeals to these new workers of the information age, who have their own complaints about treatment.

Business consultant Peter F. Drucker shares the same ambivalence that many inside and outside of business feel about unions. Despite his concern that unions often invest too much power in individual officers (he concedes that the same charge is true of boards of directors anointing their CEOs), Drucker also believes that unions can play an important role in American business.

"The trade union is beneficial and desirable today because it counterbalances some of the more obvious ills of our social body," he wrote in 1942. "It is an anti-organization, an antibody against social toxins. But it is not a constructive institution—nor designed as one."[28]

As years went by, Drucker became more disillusioned with much of the union movement, believing that its constitutional and social goals often became deeply compromised by its methods of operation. Union leaders often became too self-serving, putting union members into the position of simply trading one tyrant in the executive suite for another in the union hall. "Like corporate management, union leadership would disintegrate into an illegitimate, self-interested bureaucracy, more interested in its own power than in the needs and aspirations of its constituents," John E. Flaherty wrote of Drucker's concerns.[29]

If you are to succeed as a media manager, however, you certainly need to understand that Chicago columnist Finley Peter Dunne's oft-quoted mission of journalism, to "afflict the comfortable and comfort the afflicted,"[30] is rarely applied by media owners when it comes to dealing with any union's members. There are hundreds, perhaps even thousands, of business reporters in the nation's newspaper, magazine and broadcast outlets, but only a handful of reporters who cover organized labor's perspective. In the 2000 book *Rich Media, Poor Democracy,* author Robert McChesney observed, "If one read only the commercial media, it would be difficult to determine what on earth good was served by having labor unions at all."[31] A.J. Liebling observed earlier, "No newspaper anywhere in the nation, apparently, has had a kind word for the working man since about 1936."[32]

There are all kinds of actions media companies undertake to keep unions out of their companies. The most legitimate are steps taken to treat non-union employees so well that they do not feel any need for a union to protect them. As noted in the next section, for example, Advance Publications has long honored its pledge of no lay-offs for its non-represented employees, providing much-desired job security that would be lost if the employees joined a union and sought a contract through collective bargaining.

Union contracts spell out all of the terms of employment, not just salaries. Because they also set in stone issues that management reserves for itself in non-union workplaces—such as severance pay, hiring and firing procedures, workplace environment, overtime rules and promotion eligibility—management typically considers unions to be interference rather than cooperation in how a company is to be run.

In a statement that the senior management of nearly every media company would stand by, the Human Resources Committee of the American Newspaper Publishers Association went on record in the 1980s as being committed to "wherever applicable, a union-free environment."[33] That attitude still prevailed in 2003 when Charles Kamen, vice president of human resources at MediaNews Group, on his way to fight a Guild representation drive in Brattleboro, Vt., declared, "We don't believe it's in the best interests of our employees to be represented by a union."[34]

A model U.S. media contract is available on the National Newspaper Guild Web site at <www.newsguild.org/barg/display.php?StoryID=181>.

Unless unforeseen circumstances change the situation over the next few years, you are likely to some day face a union organizing attempt or be required to work with an already established union when you eventually become a manager. Numerous volumes have been written on unions and the subject of labor relations, many of which you undoubtedly will be required to read up on after becoming a manager for any media company that already has union representation or anticipates facing an organizing drive.

When you become a manager, or soon afterward, your employer will provide far more information through intensive training inside and outside the corporation than this book could give.

It is not this book's purpose to do any more than alert you to the situation, to identify the major players, acquaint you with some history, and introduce you to the challenge that could await you in a managerial role.

Layoffs in hard times

THE CHANCES OF meeting the local union organizer will rise dramatically during or soon after poor economic times, such as the recession of 2001, which was exacerbated by the terrorist attacks on America, followed by the wars in Afghanistan and Iraq, and further aggravated by accounting and personal scandals in some of America's largest corporations.

When sales go down, employees often go down with them. Call it downsizing, layoffs, corporate reorganization, work force restructuring, or anything else you want to, the result is that people lose their jobs—including longtime faithful employees who feel they have held up their end of the bargain. No greater test of a company's sense of fairness, foresight or patience exists than a depressed economy. That's when you find out what company vision the corporate owners and managers really have.

Matters certainly can deteriorate to where owners and managers have no choice but to pick the painful one of laying off employees. The test is when and how they decide to pull the plug.

Many bad times can be predicted, although no two economists ever seem to agree on the specific time lines. Most managers are not dummies, so they understand that every business has its ups and downs in prosperity.

Sometimes it is a predictable cycle common to the industry. For example, auto manufacturers know the times of year when cars and trucks are not selling and when they need to pause to retool for the coming year's models. For decades, temporary layoffs were a scheduled event in the auto companies—so structured that assembly line workers lacking sufficient seniority would arrange vacations, part-time jobs or a budget based on unemployment checks that were in turn based on easily predictable layoff periods.

Similarly, nearly all media companies face a severe decline in advertising sales during January and February, after the cash-register-ringing-days of the Christmas and Hanukkah seasons and the hangover doldrums of New Year's, when everyone starts thinking about saving up for their income taxes rather than spending money in the marketplace.

Knowing that, a publisher or station owner can build up a slush fund during the good times to spend on salaries in January and February, when not even the best salespersons are able to pay their way, thus keeping employees on the job out of a sense of mutual loyalty and teamwork. Many companies, especially smaller ones, do this.

Or, the publisher or station owner can put the money from the good times into a handy accounting basket called retained earnings, pocket the extra cash, and then declare hard times when sales drop in January and February. Such owners then can lay off staff while shedding crocodile tears all way to the bank, saying they had no choice but to let some staffers go because income was not meeting expenses—for those months anyway.

Thankfully, not all media companies opt for the latter tactic.

Small companies often have no choice but to lay off employees if hard times persist for several months, because they do not have an adequate cushion. However, large national corporations such as the ones running America's newspapers, magazines and broadcast outlets have much greater resources. The test of big companies' priorities over maintaining high profit margins versus employee jobs occurred in the recession of 2001. Economists said that recession started in March, and by the end of November more than 1.2 million Americans had lost their jobs, including a loss of 468,000 jobs in October—the biggest one-month loss in 21 years—plus 331,000 more lost jobs in November.[35]

While newspaper and broadcast owners, big and small, were announcing one round of layoffs after another throughout the recession of 2001, at least one company stepped forward to reassure its employees there would be no layoffs for them. Advance Publications, the fourth largest newspaper chain in the United States, is privately owned by the Newhouse brothers, Donald and Samuel I., Jr., (Si), instead of by stockholders. They only need to account to each other, not to investors. On July 2, 2001, the trade magazine *Editor & Publisher* reported on how Advance Publications was facing the same tough times as everyone else but that the company intended to just tighten its belt instead of laying off employees.

"The policy that every Newhouse publisher must live by, in good times and bad, is that no non-represented employees will lose their job because of economic conditions or technological change," explained

Raymond L. Gover, retired president of *The Patriot-News* in Harrisburg, Pa.[36]

"The thought behind it," said Stephen A. Rogers, publisher of Syracuse (N.Y.) Newspapers, "is that if your employees know they have job security, they focus on the job. It pays back in much higher morale." Larry McDermott, another Advance publisher in Springfield, Mass., added: "It is a struggle, but we continue to operate this way . . . . We look at other ways to cut expenses."[37]

It should be noted that Advance's "job guarantees" policy never has applied to its union employees. Exactly six months after *E&P* patted the corporation on the back, Advance notified the three unions at *The Jersey Journal* in Jersey City, N.J., that each needed to agree to layoffs for half of their members or Advance would cease publication of the 130-year-old daily.[38] All three unions finally consented, to save the remaining jobs.

Jersey City notwithstanding, the Newhouse brothers and their Advance Publications deserve credit for being a large group that nevertheless kept at least their non-union staffs fully employed during the recession crisis.

The McClatchy chain could be as ruthless as any conglomerate in its earliest days, but CEO Gary Pruitt's stand on layoffs since at least 2001 indicates that success has brought a greater sense of responsibility toward employees. Pruitt said it would take "an economic cataclysm" before McClatchy would resort to layoffs now, adding: "Job cuts just do not make good business sense."[39]

It is true that, during the days when many more media companies were privately owned, layoffs were rare during the inevitable down business cycles, especially in newsrooms. Family owners tended to ride out the storm, wanting the team intact when normal business conditions returned.

Not so with most of today's conglomerates. Unlike Advance Publications, which is privately owned, and unlike McClatchy, which has most of its stock controlled by the McClatchy family, many of today's media corporations sell stock, and thus their souls, to shareholders.

These public shareholders in turn are disproportionately represented by institutional investors representing pension funds, universities, banks and insurance companies. In the past 15 years or so, these institutional investors have become the main owners of publicly traded companies in all developed countries.[40]

Corporate governance power has shifted to these new institutional owners, who can hold such huge amounts of any one company's stock that they often can dictate to the executives what actions are to be taken.[41] What's more, institutional investors often have the power to force out any executives who dare to balk at their desires for more and more profits. Consequently, the executives who survive at publicly traded media companies tend to be the ones who most fiercely believe that their fiduciary responsibility to investors is more important than any social responsibility to others. Customers, employees, the local community where the company is located, and other stakeholders all can be sacrificed to the bottom line. Some CEOs are even willing to jeopardize the company's long-term viability for the sake of short-range returns.

It is economics Darwinism in the executive suite, in which only the profit-builders survive.

There is more about this in the discussion of the profit chase in Chapter 7 and values-based leadership in Chapter 8. Suffice it for now to say that the pressure on CEOs, especially CEOs of stockholder-owned corporations, to make ever-larger profits is why only those who answer the call become the heads of the giants.

The natural first choice for CEOs of stockholder-owned corporations with their relatively easy access to capital through cash or stock is to grow by acquiring other corporations.

But when an acquisition is not underway, you might wonder why these profit-maximization executives so often prefer to downsize a company by cutting costs rather than growing the company the old-fashioned way—by increasing sales. Both strategies are used, of course, but it is a fact that cost-cutting is a much faster fix than increasing sales. A dollar realized from a sale is worth only a few cents to the bottom line once the proportionate operating expenses have been deducted. But every penny of a dollar saved by cutting costs goes straight to the bottom line. So cost-cutting is often the first choice of a publicly traded corporation trying to increase profits before the next quarterly report, while increasing sales is a more likely tactic for a privately owned company interested in long-term growth and stability.

The Davey Committee in Canada identified this phenomenon in 1970, noting that newspapers are highly profitable but that many companies supply an inferior paper. "Their 'give-em-as-little-as-possible' syndrome is reflected, among other things, in the lack of journalistic resources and in a whole raft of decisions aimed at generating greater profits rather than a better newspaper," observed the Canadian Heritage program in its report on Concentration of Newspaper Ownership.[42]

Journalistic resources include employees, and employment is becoming more unstable in publicly traded companies because the CEOs, pressured by institutional and other stockholders to increase profits in both good times and bad, know that the quickest way to do that is to cut costs—and the easiest way to cut costs is by laying off employees. Consequently, despite all of their talk about how they cherish quality journalism, CEOs of publicly traded companies resort to that quick-fix strategy with regularity regardless of long-range consequences.

This harsher approach to layoffs by stockholder-owned companies led to a public confrontation in 2001, when Jay T. Harris resigned as publisher of San Jose's *Mercury News* rather than carry out budget-slashing and staff-layoff directives issued by the newspaper's owner, media giant Knight Ridder. "I resigned because I was concerned about the future of the whole of the paper, the business side and the news side," he later told other editors. "I resigned because I could no longer live with the widening gap between creed and deed."[43]

Harris' resignation caused such a stir that CEO Tony Ridder felt compelled to respond in a public letter, rare in corporate internecine warfare. Ridder said quality was not being sacrificed by the cuts and that, despite fears expressed by Harris, no newsroom layoffs were planned at the *Mercury News*. (About two weeks later, about 20 news staffers were laid off.)[44]

Rem Reider, editor of the *American Journalism Review*, later wrote that it was "clear (Harris) hopes his high profile exit will be a catalyst in reversing the direction in which the newspaper business seems to be careening."[45]

Many other non-management figures weighed in with comments and columns decrying the effects that such budget cuts and layoffs would have on what they see as the essential role in a democracy of reporting the news—both in newspapers, as epitomized by Harris, and in broad-cast, which was also seeing its news budgets and staffs reduced in 2001.

The Poynter Institute and the Committee of Concerned Journalists both created sections on their Web sites to receive feedback from editors and reporters on the effects of cutbacks on their newsrooms. *E&P* conducted a poll of publishers and editors across the nation and found widespread opposition to "margin management," with about 80 percent reporting that their newspapers had operating profit margins of at least 20 percent and up to almost 40 percent, which many felt were so high as to make any layoffs unjustified.[46]

High-profile media commentators such as Poynter President Jim Naughton, national columnist Geneva Overholser and *Columbia Journalism Review* writer David Laventhol were among those expressing concern that the layoffs were endangering the ability of the press to carry out the trust implicit in its Constitutional protection to inform the public.

None said it better than Harris himself, however, as he explained to the American Society of Newspaper Editors what prompted his resignation:

"What troubled me—something that had never happened before in all my years in the company—was that little or no attention was paid to the consequences of achieving 'the number.' There was virtually no discussion of the damage that would be done to the quality and aspirations of the *Mercury News* as a journalistic endeavor or to its ability to fulfill its responsibilities to the community. As important, scant attention was paid to the damage that would be done to our ability to compete and grow the business."[47]

His last sentence, implying that short-range decisions taken to build up the bottom line for a temporary fix can have long-range negative repercussions, seems borne out in a 1998 study done of the notoriously bottom-line Thomson Newspapers chain. Journalism educators Stephen Lacy and Hugh J. Martin of Michigan State University compared the economic performance of Thomson papers with other papers in comparable communities.

"The results," they reported, "indicate that short-run profit margins are associated with declining circulation and circulation revenue."[48] Not too surprising, perhaps, but Lacy and Martin for the first time quantified the losses in circulation and made an attempt to estimate what effect the lower circulation had on depressing advertising revenue as well.

They estimated that Thomson's high profit requirements between 1989 and 1990 (Thomson sold all of its papers in 2000–2001), cost the company $1.33 million in subscription revenue alone, supporting the warnings of many media analysts that "cutting costs to obtain high profits will have negative long-term effects on newspapers."[49]

Educator Edmund Lambeth concluded that the Thomson study showed that "if newspapers expect to compete successfully with emerging technologies, they must retain as many readers as possible. Trying to maintain above normal profits in the face of growing competition will only lead to reductions in newsroom expenditures and lower quality."[50]

Research led by educator Philip Meyer of the University of North Carolina showed how cutbacks in budget and news staff harms a newspaper's credibility, which in turn results in lost revenues in both circulation and advertising. That loss of readership seriously jeopardizes the newspaper's future economic health, Meyer said.[51]

The result of all these eloquent protests? Media layoffs rolled on across the country right through to the end of the year. The Newspaper Guild surveyed 178 dailies with circulations over 50,000 and found that both privately held and publicly held newspapers cut an average of 3 percent of their staffs in 2001. However, because Knight Ridder pared 10 percent of its staff, "it alone accounted for an astonishing 60 percent of net cuts in 2001 among publicly held newspapers."[52]

In most cases, reporters and editors had little protection because newsrooms of most media companies are not unionized.

The Newspaper Guild represents the newsrooms of only about 120 newspapers, almost all dailies, in the United States, Puerto Rico and Canada. Reporters, editors and photographers at the vast majority of newspapers, large and small, do not belong to a union. Even fewer people in the advertising, circulation and business departments are unionized.

Therefore, many reporters could only dream of any of the protective measures in place at, for example, the Eccentric group of community newspapers scattered through the suburbs of the Detroit metropolitan area. Layoffs were announced there in late 2001, too. Editors were handled in what one Detroit area journalist called an arbitrary way—one of the two editors sent packing was one of the chain's most experienced, longest-employed and highest-paid editors. Because reporters were represented by the Guild, the group's management announced that layoffs and reassignment of duties of reporters would adhere to terms of the Guild contract; that is, limited by seniority and other negotiated provisions.[53]

At most non-union papers, determining who will be laid off, and how, is entirely at the discretion of the owner, just as it was for non-unionized editors at the Eccentric papers.

If layoffs (managers now reserve the term "firing" for non-economic reasons) are not handled in a fair way—or perhaps even if they are—they might become seeds in fertile ground for union organizing. In the aftershocks of recessions, it is common for surviving employees to explore unionizing options at some companies to obtain at least some level of protection for the future.

From the management side, as media consultant Lisa Dixon pointed out, employees are considered by many successful companies to be one of the company's greatest assets. "They have the power to make, or break, a business," she said.[54] This is becoming especially true in today's corporation, where "knowledge" workers have to a large extent replaced the manual workers who had been a staple of employment for many years.

Managers who value their employees for knowledge and skills believe that ensuring employees have the tools they need is the most effective way to serve customers.

But no matter how enlightened the company and how considerate the management, sometimes circumstances coalesce darkly and employees must be let go for the welfare of the company as a whole. In nearly every business, including media companies, one of the largest single expense items is payroll, and sometimes it just needs to be cut.

When you must fire or lay off someone

U NFORTUNATELY, not all employees work out, regardless of whether it is their fault, your fault or nobody's fault. Sooner or later, as a manager you will need to terminate some employee's job, either through a "permanent layoff" or by firing. Layoffs can occur without warning. Layoffs are the term used when terminating an employee's job for economic reasons. Firing is the term when a job is terminated for non-economic reasons, such as insubordination, violations of company policy, and failure to perform a job satisfactorily.

"Firing for cause," as disciplinary termination sometimes is known, should never come as a surprise to an employee. Terminating an employee's job should not be done until after the employee has received a formal advance warning and a chance to correct the problem for which he or she is being fired. This is called "progressive discipline," and its steps must be documented and follow rules required by law in many states. Wrongful termination leads to lawsuits, so make sure you follow company policy and abide by state and federal laws.

When employees are laid off or fired, they should be asked to leave the premises immediately, and any trip they make to their office or work area should be under supervision. This may seem harsh, but being extra nice will result in some people stealing or sabotaging something on their way out the door. If they threaten to sue you, simply reply that they will need to proceed in whatever way seems appropriate for them, and leave it at that.

Severance pay is usually little more than an attempt to try to soften the blow of the firing and a bribe to reduce the likelihood of a lawsuit. When severance pay is offered, ideally the employee should sign a statement accepting the payment as a full settlement and promising no further action. Severance pay is voluntary for a company unless a contract requires it, and at some companies it is only offered if the employee agrees to sign a letter of resignation.

Most states have employment-at-will laws that allow an employer to fire an employee for any legal reason.

When it comes time for this extreme situation, which is usually stressful for both the manager and the employee, the following are tips frequently offered to managers.

• First of all, make sure you know your rights and the employee's rights under state and federal employment laws before you venture into this arena.

• Meet with the employee privately, but preferably with at least one witness present from the Human Relations office, if you are a large company, or the next highest ranking person in your organization if you are a small company.

• Give the person verbal notice of termination. If anyone insists on a dismissal in writing, you can bet there is already thought about retaining a lawyer, so keep such a letter as bland as possible with no specifics. You might even want your lawyer to draft it.

• Do not apologize. Do not debate the merits or reasons for the layoff or firing. This is the time to offer severance pay, perhaps only in return for a written letter of resignation from the employee. (With a resignation, a fired employee saves face and does not have a dismissal besmirching his or her record, but in most states a person also gives up rights to unemployment benefits with a resignation. It might be a desirable tradeoff and one that works for you, too.)

• The best strategy is to tell all terminated employees to leave the property immediately and to ship their belongings from their desk that same day. A poor alternative is for you (or a security guard if you have a large company) to accompany them back to their desk so they can remove their personal belongings. Whatever you do, fired employees who are stressed-out and upset should not be allowed to return to their desk alone. Unpleasant thoughts about retribution might be dancing in their heads, which could lead to all kinds of mischief, such as erasure of computer data, crying, a shouting match in front of employees, or worse.

Firing an employee is one of the most unpleasant tasks of a manager. If you become a manager, it assuredly will be required of you someday. If you dread doing it, remind yourself of the old business saying: "It isn't the people you fire who make your life miserable, it's the people you don't."[55]

Broadcast companies are especially notorious for firing employees. Gallows humor at television stations includes the oft-repeated belief that "everyone gets fired in television." The book *Management of the Electronic Media* resorts to classic understatement in its observation: "One type of turnover that occurs regularly in the electronic media is termination."[56]

Here's one last thing to keep in mind about firing and layoffs. The most important dimension in people's lives other than family is their livelihood—their jobs. As a manager, you're in charge of a critical physical and emotional need of other human beings. Your firing of them will leave most people at least temporarily devastated personally.

Wise hiring in the first place will eliminate many problems. But when an employee needs to be fired or laid off, you have an obligation to ensure that your hiring, retention and termination policies are sensible, responsible, respecful and ethical.

CHAPTER 3

Approaches to managing employees

MANAGERS constantly seek ways to motivate their employees. Keeping them happy is one way, but not the only way. There is no question that maintaining and improving productivity is one of the most important responsibilities any manager has to his or her higher-up, whether it be still another manager, the owner, or the Board of Directors. Every manager feels pressure to improve production. Since the end of slavery, at least, that inevitably has meant a manager must find ways to motivate the employees to improve the production for which the manager will take credit. Coercion will take a manager only so far.

The concepts of management in business have coalesced around two principal approaches: scientific and humanistic.

Managers mix aspects of both to varying degrees. A successful manager cannot rely on any one of these main approaches or their subcategories exclusively, because working with a wide variety of people requires judgment on what management approach will work the best at a given time, under certain circumstances, with a particular employee.

No one management style will work for everyone all of the time with every employee.

Scientific (or classical) management

Based on organizational structure, such as chain of command, and efficient division of labor, the scientific approach is the oldest management style. It ruled American workplaces throughout the first part of the 20th century. Its principles were put forth in a 1909 book by Frederick W. Taylor, who is considered the "Father of Scientific Management." Taylor's premise was, "The principal object of management should be to secure the maximum prosperity for the employer, *coupled with the maximum prosperity for the employee*"[57] (emphasis added).

This premise would seem to be self-evident, Taylor said, but it was not, because "a majority on either side do not believe it is possible so to arrange their mutual relations that their interest become identical."[58]

Taylor argued that the greatest mutual prosperity can be achieved only as a result of the greatest possible productivity of the employees and machines in a business. The most important object of both employees and managers was thus in the training and enabling of each employee to work at the fastest pace and with the greatest efficiency possible. This led directly to the establishment of a whole new profession—efficiency experts—and a constant effort by all businesses to improve their efficiency and therefore their productivity and their profits.

In Taylor's time, many industrial working people believed that working harder and more efficiently would result in many of them losing their jobs because products would be produced faster or more plentifully than they could be sold or consumed. This attitude of avoiding a productive day was even known by the phrases of "soldiering" in America and as "hanging it out" in England. Working slowly, in other words, was seen to be in a worker's best self-interest. "Under this fallacious idea, a large proportion of the workmen of both countries each day deliberately work slowly so as to curtail the output," Taylor noted.[59]

Taylor contended that such an attitude defied historical fact. History had shown, he argued, that each invention, each improvement, each rise in productivity had the effect of leading to lower prices, greater prosperity and more jobs.

Many of Taylor's ideas were not original. But he had the ability to quantify various concepts into measurable management practices, and he was a writer who was able to bring the ideas to corporate America's attention.

Since at least the 1880s, he had worked with industrial companies looking for ways to make their operations more efficient and productive, despite the very real prejudices and fears against such improvements from workers, unions and even many in management. Taylor's impact has been so great because he developed a concept of work design, work measurement, production control and other functions that completely changed the nature of industry. Before scientific management, such departments as work study, personnel, maintenance and quality control did not exist. Taylor was called before a congressional committee in 1911 and 1912 and criticized for some of his tactics, such as using stop-watches to time an employee's work. Taylor's system was controversial because it was frequently abused by unscrupulous managers who sought only the company's greater prosperity and ignored Taylor's dual call for employee prosperity as well.[60]

Accel-Team.com, an employee productivity consultancy, summarized the four objectives of scientific management:[61]

(1) The development of a science for each element of a person's work to replace the old rule-of-thumb methods

(2) The scientific selection, training and development of workers instead of allowing them to choose their own tasks and train themselves as best they could

(3) The development of a spirit of hearty cooperation between workers and management to ensure that work would be carried out in accordance with scientifically devised procedures

(4) The division of work between workers and the management in

almost equal shares, each group taking over the work for which it is best fitted.

Scientific management, Taylor believed, could be applied to all situations and implemented successfully with managers as well as with workers. Criticism of his scientific management approach, in addition to the ease with which it was abused, also included contentions that it treated workers like machines and considered them to be only motivated by money. In fact, Taylor considered wages to be the greatest motivator.

Peter F. Drucker expressed doubts about scientific management and its use of the worker as a "machine tool" as early as 1949, calling it "the lazy man's way out and an attempt to avoid coming to grips with the problem."[62]

Despite such misgivings, however, scientific management saw worldwide adoption. It is still in use today because—at least to a degree under many circumstances—it does improve productivity.

Humanistic (or behaviorist) management

Many people, concerned about callous treatment of workers under scientific management, began exploring the possibility that improved efficiency could come about by treating people more humanely.

That led to what is today known as humanistic management.

Probably the most famous breakthrough in the humanistic management approach toward motivating employees occurred in 1945. It led to the startling—and often still ignored—revelation that employees need to know they are regarded as important members of the company team and are not looked down on as mere automatons or cogs in the corporate wheel.

The breakthrough is known as the **Hawthorne Effect,** from the conclusions of a study done on the morale of workers at the Chicago Hawthorne plant of the Western Electric Company from 1927 to 1932.

Disturbed about poor morale among its workers, Western Electric called in a team of Harvard researchers including Elton Mayo to experiment by changing the plant's physical conditions to see what would improve morale. The researchers kept a control room unchanged, and then they would alter factors one at a time with a group of workers in an experimental room, working with variables such as lighting, noise, incentive pay and heating.[63] Sometimes the changes the researchers implemented were negative; sometimes positive. Regardless, productivity nearly always increased compared with the control room.

"The results were perplexing," Mayo said. Those running the experiment were exasperated because they were not able at first to understand why productivity rose regardless of whether the physical variables were positive or negative.[64]

Mayo came to realize that the only constant in the situation was that the researchers were paying a lot of attention to the workers. The workers appreciated the attention being paid to them, and that was the cause of the improved productivity—not the physical changes in environment. The workers concluded that the Hawthorne management cared about them. Why else would these researchers be conducting studies? Out of gratitude and a sense of fairness, the employees were motivated to work more productively.[65]

The mere act of showing people that you're concerned about them usually spurs them to better job performance. This is what is known as the Hawthorne Effect.

The Hawthorne Effect changed the way of thinking that productivity was controlled solely by working conditions and pay—the scientific approach to management. It introduced the idea that attention to the well-being of workers—a humanistic approach—can have major impact.

The Hawthorne Effect introduced the humanistic approach to personnel management. The humanistic approach states that it is through treatment of employees that results are achieved in productivity, morale and loyalty. This approach emphasizes treatment of workers as social beings who have their own needs but who also have a work ethic that wants the company to succeed if the company is fair to them. A company might have an efficient and effective formal organizational structure, but according to the humanistic approach, optimum goals will not be achieved unless it has a work force willing to cooperate with managers. The employees must be competent and well-trained, and they must share the same vision and goals as the management.

An appreciation of the overwhelmingly important value of teamwork also is one of the major findings to come out of the Hawthorne studies, though it is rarely mentioned in connection with the Hawthorne studies except by Mayo.

"Management, in any continuously successful plant, is not related to single workers but always to working groups," Mayo said in reflecting on the Hawthorne studies in *The Social Problems of an Industrial Civilization* in 1945. "In every department that continues to operate, the workers have—whether aware of it or not—formed themselves into a group with appropriate customs, duties, routines, even rituals; and the management succeeds (or fails) in proportion as it is accepted without reservation by the group as authority and leader . . . . The most important finding of all was unquestionably in the general area of teamwork and cooperation."[66]

Management and the Worker, the 600-page detailed review of the

Hawthorne studies, has to be the most famous and frequently reprinted work of flawed research in business. It was written originally in 1939, but I found the 8th edition that was printed in 1947. The research team was oblivious to the fact that the workers were responding to their presence. It was left to Mayo in his follow-up work of *The Social Problems of an Industrial Civilization* to finally point out that his fellow researchers themselves caused what has become known as the Hawthorne Effect.[67]

The researchers did pick up, however, on the power of teamwork demonstrated through their experiments. Women workers at Western Electric's Hawthorne plant were transferred from a team of 100 to teams of five (because the researchers realized there would be fewer variables, not out of a desire to test the small-group dynamics), and the result was a surprising increase in productivity. The researchers observed:

"No longer were the girls isolated individuals . . . . They had become participating members of a working group . . . . A growing amount of social activity developed among the test room girls outside of working hours and outside of the plant . . . . The girls began to help one another out of the common good of the group. They had become bound together by common sentiments and feelings of loyalty."[68]

Fitting in with the humanistic approach and the concept of teamwork is what is known as a "cooperative system" in business. It is based on the concept that a manager's authority depends on the subordinates' approval and willingness to cooperate.

The cooperative system was first articulated by a telephone company executive, Chester I. Barnard, in 1938.

Barnard was one of the first theorists to identify the importance of human motivation as a critical part of productivity. He postulated the still prevailing idea that a company (or a government) was a way for people to accomplish things cooperatively that they could not do individually, concluding: "Only as they (executives and employees) choose to work together can they achieve the fullness of personal development." [69] Barnard's findings, mostly based on empirical evidence gathered from years of being an observant and thoughtful manager, were an early recognition of the value of teamwork.

Theories of management

PERHAPS THE BEST KNOWN phrases in management theory are Theory X, Theory Y and Theory Z as applied to managers and employees. Douglas McGregor explained Theory X and Theory Y in 1960 in *The Human Side of Enterprise*. Theory Z was presented in 1981 by William G. Ouchi in a book titled *Theory Z: How American Business Can Meet the Japanese Challenge.*

An understanding of all three of these different takes on human nature is needed, because all three kinds of managers usually are present in any organization. Indeed, any manager can exhibit any one of these three natures at a given time depending on circumstances because each approach is effective in some circumstances and not in others.[70]

McGregor prefaced his discussion of Theory X and Theory Y with the observation: "Every managerial decision has behavioral consequences. Successful management depends—not alone, but significantly—upon the ability to predict and control human behavior."[71]

THEORY X: The manager following this theory of management believes the average human has an inherent dislike of work and will avoid it when possible. Therefore, this manager believes, rewards and appeals will not work; "only the threat of punishment will do the trick."[72] In fact, this manager is convinced the average human prefers to be directed, avoids responsibility, has little ambition and wants security without having to work for it. Theory X is seen as the management style practiced under the scientific approach.

Of course, there are occasional employees who only respond to a Theory X kick in the pants. Even the nicest manager, to be effective, has to know how to be tough when necessary. Robert H. Giles, who became editor of several daily newspapers, learned this lesson early from the crusty editor of the *Akron (Ohio) Beacon Journal.* In his first job as city editor, Giles was called into the editor's office and regularly reminded of his shortcoming as a nice guy. "Bob," the editor would tell him, "you've got to learn to be a son of a bitch."[73]

THEORY Y: Managers subscribing to this theory, on the other hand, see employees who enjoy work and derive satisfaction from their jobs, can be committed in the service of achieving goals, and can learn not only to accept responsibility but also to seek it. Theory Y managers believe employees can exercise imagination and creativity in the solution of their occupational problems, and that this type of human nature is widely distributed among people.[74] Theory Y "places the problems squarely in the lap of management," McGregor asserted. "If employees are lazy, indifferent, unwilling to take responsibility, intransigent, uncreative, uncooperative, Theory Y implies that the causes lie in management's methods of organization and control."[75]

In 1967, McGregor explained that he never meant to imply that Theory X and Theory Y were opposites, as they often are portrayed, nor that they were the only alternate theories to be found in management, nor that management might not exhibit characteristics of both.[76]

THEORY Z: Ouchi described this approach to management in 1981, saying that the Buick Division of General Motors exemplified Theory Z at its final assembly plant in Flint, Mich.

Buick officials adapted Japanese management tactics to turn the Flint plant into GM's top plant in quality and efficiency. Ouchi said those efforts became the basis of the Theory Z approach to management. "Quite simply," Ouchi said, "it suggests that involved workers are the key to increased productivity." [77]

Theory Z is oriented to the culture of an organization, managing people in ways so they can work together more effectively. Ouchie said, "Productivity . . . is a problem of social organization." [78] Productivity cannot be solved by simply working harder, he believed, because most employees already work as hard as they can.

As Ouchi's book title indicates, Theory Z came from the way Japanese industries were organized and reflected the rising success they had and the admiration (envy) of them by U.S. business executives. His book quickly became a best-seller. The book resulted in many American companies adopting Theory Z to emulate the Japanese firms, although with American twists required for a dramatically different culture.

American capitalism, for example, could not exactly copy Japanese firms in offering lifetime employment. But they could copy the Japanese in other ways, such as letting factory workers perform different tasks instead of only one repetitive task all day and developing qualities of Theory Z such as trusting employees and being more concerned with and aware of their problems and personalities.

In an attempt to achieve the kinds of success Japanese firms were experiencing, American firms began Theory Z efforts to improve their workers' Quality of Work Life (QWL). Efforts included improving work conditions and security, increasing worker responsibility, enhancing the worker's sense of self-worth and providing opportunities for social relationships to develop within the organization. [79]

Maslow's Hierarchy of Needs

ANY DISCUSSION OF motivation should include what has become known as Maslow's Hierarchy of Needs, developed in the mid-1900s. Students of business management always are introduced to the thoughts of Abraham H. Maslow on what motivates people to achieve, or even to simply persevere.

Maslow said people must go through a progression of needs. He pictured the needs as if arranged on a ladder to be climbed, though his concept usually is illustrated as a pyramid (this book compromises with an illustration that sort of resembles both).

Maslow placed the basic physical or physiological needs such as food, water, sleep and shelter at the bottom. These needs then led to safety needs that include religion, peace and health. Then came "belongingness and love needs," shown in the illustration[80] as love needs. The next level was for esteem and status needs such as self-respect and the respect of others, culminating at the top in self-actualization needs.[81]

"The clear emergence of these (the self-actualization needs at the top) usually rests upon prior satisfaction of the physiological, safety, love and esteem needs," Maslow wrote.[82]

In other words, Maslow said each stage must be satisfied before people can move fully to the next stage.[83]

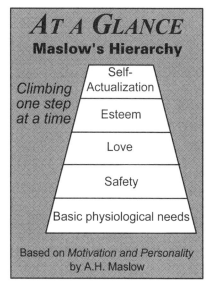

AT A GLANCE
Maslow's Hierarchy

Climbing one step at a time

Self-Actualization

Esteem

Love

Safety

Basic physiological needs

Based on *Motivation and Personality* by A.H. Maslow

Similarly, Kenneth A. Starck, a journalism professor at the University of Iowa, referred to this same perspective in his study on the ethics of journalists in the struggling Third World economy of Romania in the 1990s.

Yes, journalists there take bribes, shill for the government and do other sordid things that American journalists would consider highly unethical, Starck said. But he points out that it is difficult to concern yourself with fine ethical points when you are worried about how you are going to feed your family.[84] The basic, physical needs come first.

The self-actualization needs at the top of the hierarchy of human needs are defined as the striving to fulfill oneself, to become all that one is capable of becoming.

Maslow generalized that, among other characteristics, self-actualizing people tend to focus on problems outside of themselves, have a clear sense of what is true and what is phony, are spontaneous and creative, and are not bound too strictly by social conventions.[85]

Most thinking about human psychology up to that point had been on what made a person ill or abnormal. Maslow, on the other hand, was interested in what constituted positive mental health.[86]

Some consider Maslow's approach to be too all-encompassing, especially when trying to apply his Hierarchy of Needs to exceptional individuals. They point to numerous examples of people self-actualizing as artists, for example, while half-starving in hovels and receiving no recognition, as well as to writers like foreign correspondent Ernie Pyle, who finally achieved his fame in World War II when he was most beset by danger and deprivation.

Nevertheless, Maslow's thinking has been instrumental in getting many companies and their managers to start thinking of their employees as humans with needs and motivations, instead of as mere myrmidons.

Management by Objectives (MBO)—it's everywhere

MANAGEMENT BY OBJECTIVES is an organized way of (1) forming clear, concise and realistic goals; (2) developing action plans to achieve the goals; (3) evaluating employees' performance in working toward those objectives in regular appraisals by management, at least annually; and (4) amending the plans when necessary to achieve the goals.[87]

Some managers say there is still another MBO requirement put on managers, and that is allocating the resources of time and money so that the objectives can be achieved.

Geneva Overholser, a former Gannett editor, is among those who think many modern media giants have perverted the original intent of MBO in the way they apply it to top-level journalism management. She would approve of the approach by Advance Publications, which is one of the few conglomerates that pay publishers and editors a regular salary not tied to corporate performance.[88] Virtually all others pay publishers and editors bonuses and incentives to meet their MBO goals—the emphasis being put not on journalism goals but on financial ones, such as meeting profit targets.

It is difficult for editors to stand up for journalism values when they are golden-handcuffed to financial goals through the way their MBO is structured, Overholser observed.[89]

The concept of Management by Objectives, by the way, was another idea from Drucker, who first put the basics of the theory into writing in 1954. That one chapter in his book *The Practice of Management* has launched an entire industry of articles, books, seminars and university courses on MBO alone, explaining and expanding on what Drucker originally envisioned.

The basic premise of MBO is that goals must be established,

progress toward reaching them must be monitored, and failures to reach goals must be examined.

This emphasis on setting and reaching goals is confirmation of the importance of goals in a successful company. Without clear goals, as the Cheshire Cat implies in the quote box, a company is heading somewhere, but it is not really heading anywhere specific.

Drucker's book was concerned with encouraging managers to use MBO as a self-directed way toward goals and to control the manager's personal performance (self-control). It is later theorists who added the component of directly involving employees as well, through employee participation in goal-setting and employee evaluations.

> "(Alice) was a little startled by seeing the Cheshire Cat sitting on the bough of a tree a few yards off . . . . 'Cheshire Puss,' she began . . . . 'Would you tell me please, which way I ought to go from here?' 'That depends a good deal on where you want to go,' said the Cat. 'I don't much care where,' said Alice. 'Then it doesn't matter which way you go,' said the Cat."[90]
>
> —Lewis Carroll
> Through the Looking Glass

If you have ever been called in by your boss to discuss how good a job you're doing—or not doing—then you have experienced the modern version of MBO.

Companies large and small have embraced some variation of this management system, which grew out of the humanistic approach and now involves employees in the company's planning and implementation of goals, which Drucker seems to accept even though that was not part of his original concept.

Business needs to give individual strength and responsibility to the manager, Drucker said in introducing the MBO concept, "and at the same time give common direction of vision and effort, establish teamwork and harmonize the goals of the individual with the common weal. The only principle that can do this is management by objectives and self-control."[91]

The principle behind MBO is to make sure all managers and employees have a clear understanding of the organization's objectives, as well as an awareness of their own roles and responsibilities in achieving those objectives. Everyone's efforts, including the manager's and the employee's, is measured against the success or failure of achieving goals, and therefore management efforts are focused on goals.

"An effective management must direct the vision and efforts of all managers toward a common goal," Drucker noted. "It must ensure that the individual manager understands what results are demanded."[92]

The balance between management and employee empowerment has to be struck by managers. To turn their aims into successful action forces managers to master five basic MBO operations:[93]

(1) Setting objectives

(2) Organizing the group

(3) Motivating and communicating

(4) Measuring performance, and

(5) Developing people, including themselves.

The actual implementation of MBO, of course, will be subject to negotiations in a unionized workplace.

One of the most difficult aspects of MBO, which has been the subject of numerous reactions from cartoons to union complaints, is how the evaluation interview is handled between the manager and the employee. The point of the evaluation interview should be to determine how everyone, including the manager, can improve, and how this teamwork between manager and employee can achieve the goals that are set. The tendency of some managers, unfortunately, is to simply either praise or gloss over inadequacies, or, even worse, act as a hanging judge in condemning the employee.

All of us would rather be spoiled by praise than improved by criticism.

So, if we have the former, everyone leaves happy; if we receive nothing but the latter, many are going to be discouraged or angry. The manager needs to use a reinforcing approach, especially in criticizing an employee whose performance has not been satisfactory. Studies, and my experience, have shown that employees who are praised or worked with in a positive way tend to improve their performance, while those who are criticized regularly tend to grow resentful and even less productive.

As many employees can attest from personal experience, the basic problem with MBO is that some managers do not have the interpersonal skills and sensitivity to make the performance evaluation a constructive experience for the employee. To minimize problems, the manager and the employee should work together in determining both the employee's objectives and what performance will be required to achieve those objectives. In some companies, large and small, authoritarian managers mistakenly hand down the objectives as a directive to employees, rather than as a shared vision.

A real problem for media managers using MBO is that the creative types of people who typically work for media companies, compared with workers at many other kinds of jobs, are more independent, more confident in their abilities, and take more pride in doing their work. That's a roundabout way of saying that some of them do not take any criticism of their performance very well and may lack the very inter-personal skills they accuse their managers of not having.

It is often said that managing the creative reporters, editors, photographers, videographers and various artists in media companies is like herding cats. It takes a special kind of manager, probably with a thick skin and a firm will, tempered by an insider understanding of the difficulty of many media jobs, to be successful in media management.

The book *Newsroom Management* notes, "Editors going through the MBO process for the first time are often surprised by the amount of time it takes to do it right. Discussing ideas, documenting goals, coordinating the roles of the news staff or other departments, and laying out realistic timetables are complicated and demanding tasks."[94]

Employees need to feel they're being treated fairly

THIS IS A good time to bring up the social science theory of equity, defined and explained by J. Stacy Adams in a psychology journal in 1963. Adams summed up his 14-page theory in one sentence: "Whenever two individuals exchange something, there is the possibility that one or both of them will feel that the exchange was inequitable."[95]

Equity theory is a major consideration in both employee morale and motivation. A manager always should be aware of how equity theory might be working either positively or negatively with an employee. Whether in dealing with employees on strict labor issues or in handling them effectively in their MBO evaluation interview, equity theory can help explain why people act the way they do.

Equity theory states that people evaluate how fairly they are being treated by an organization in four steps.[96]

(1) People evaluate how they personally feel they are being treated;

(2) People evaluate how other people are being treated by whom they have picked, rightly or wrongly, as being comparable to them in responsibility and value;

(3) People then compare the treatment of themselves with the treatment of their comparable others;

(4) People make a judgment on whether they are being treated equitably, that is, fairly, based on how they see their comparable others being treated.

If they conclude they are being treated fairly, they will work to continue the status quo.

However, if they conclude they are being treated unfairly, they will take steps to try to correct the imbalance until they feel they have regained equity. This "corrective" action can take a number of either positive or negative forms. And it can be logical or illogical from a manager's point of view.

For instance, employees may seek additional schooling to improve their skills to be on a par with their comparable other. Or they might become far less conscientious in their work, showing up at the office late, leaving early, and making life unpleasant for others until they feel they have achieved some sort of psychological equity. Employees asking for a pay raise might be doing so because they know that others they consider comparable to them are making more money than they are, and they have inequity feelings. People who have been chastised too aggressively in an evaluation meeting might work less hard, not harder, to get even.

Equity theory is probably the simplest of several motivational concepts available to managers. Others include **expectancy theory,** which holds that people will work toward a goal if they believe they have a reasonable chance of achieving it; **reinforcement theory** (behavior modification), which implies that desired behaviors can be obtained by linking them with positive consequences; **goal setting theory,** which assumes people are motivated to set and work toward goals; **participative management,** which states that employees will be satisfied and inspired to higher performance if they have the opportunity to participate in decision making; and **attribution theory,** which holds some employees perceive their motivation to be internal; that is, they work because they enjoy doing the task. In this latter situation, which is common, the best incentives are intrinsic rewards such as recognition for people who seek a measure of self-worth. This is the opposite of the best incentive for those who perceive their motivation as external, for they are motivated more by pay and fringe benefits.[97]

A good way to measure whether employees are happy, fulfilled, and motivated is to measure the employee turnover rate. There always will be turnover, of course, but if the turnover rate is high, a company loses productivity and institutional memory, resulting in operational disruptions.

Turnover rates can be measured and compared within a company over periods of time and also across companies. The turnover index[98] is calculated as: TTR = (S/N) × 100

In this formula, TTR stands for Total Turnover Rate, S is the number of employees lost in a time period, and N is the average number of employees in that same time period. By substituting the S in the formula with letters such as R for retired, F for fired, Q for quit, and so forth, the manager also has a tool for measuring reasons for employee turnover.[99]

There is a rule of thumb for the number of full-time equivalents

(FTEs) that a newspaper should have in its newsroom, but there's little advice on circulation, advertising or other departments—other than that you need whatever number is necessary to get the work done. In newspaper newsrooms, the rule for years has been one FTE per 1,000 circulation, which was for the most part held up in a 2001 survey of 178 dailies with circulations over 50,000 conducted by the Poynter Institute and the Project for Excellence in Journalism. Their survey found that the prevailing ratio now is 1.2 to 1.3 FTEs per 1,000, with it higher for papers below 200,000 circulation and lower for the largest papers.[100] An Inland Industries survey ratio was 1.1 to 1.2 per 1,000 at dailies.

Television stations will carry a fraction of the number of news employees found at the same city's daily newspaper, usually about 30 to 40 for a mid-sized station. Most radio stations typically have no reporters. Thus, the advantages broadcast news programs have in being able to get news out faster are often offset by the depth that the more numerous print reporters can put into a story.

Owners and their managers are always looking for ways to minimize labor costs, which can represent half or more of any media company's budget. In addition to concerns about losing elements of control in a company's operation, owners and managers also oppose unions because they tend to be successful in driving up wages. This is true even for neighboring non-union companies that must be competitive with nearby union wages to attract the workers they need.

Union contracts usually stipulate a "top minimum" wage. The contracts are written with step increases over a given period, usually four or five years. After that period, an employee will make no less than the top minimum, expressed as a weekly wage. However, some companies such as the *Patriot-News* of Harrisburg, Pa., also have a merit factor. Thus, even with the top minimum there at $34,273 a year, there are valued reporters earning far more than that.[101]

Newsroom wages at U.S. and Canadian newspapers that have contracts negotiated by the Newspaper Guild are listed on page 98.

Reporter/photographer top minimums as of April 1, 2002 at North American dailies represented by Newspaper Guild[102]

Contract	Top Min.	After Yrs.	Contract	Top Min.	After Yrs.
Alameda, Calif.	720.00	6	Albany, N.Y.	836.21	4
Allentown, Pa.	876.62	4	Bakersfield, Calif.	570.65	5
Baltimore	1,069.00	5	Bellevue, Wash.	546.00	5
Boston Globe	1,260.16	5	Boston Herald	969.49	4
Bremerton, Wash.	767.77	6	Brockton, Mass.	803.25	4
Buffalo, N.Y.	1,042.47	5	Canton, Ohio	758.05	5
Chicago Sun-Times	1,182.01	5	Cincinnati (2)	962.50	5
Cleveland	1,130.61	4	Dayton, Ohio	660.50	5
Delaware County, Pa.	912.75	10	Denver Post	1,061.00	5
Denver Rocky Mt. News	1,068.00	5	Detroit Free Press	808.16	4
Detroit News	841.01	4	Dow Jones & Co., N.Y.	1,201.00	6
Duluth, Minn.	767.82	5	Erie, Pa.	933.07	5
Eugene, Ore.	882.73	6	Fall River, Mass.	754.68	4
Fresno, Calif.	775.00	6	Harrisburg, Pa.	659.10	4
Hazelton, Pa.	598.71	4	Hilo, Hawaii	842.90	5
Honolulu Advertiser	1,122.46	5	Honolulu Star-Bulletin	1,110.68	5
Indianapolis	874.17	6	Jersey City, N.J.	805.03	4
Joliet, Ill.	858.98	4	Kenosha, Wis.	883.26	5.5
Kingston, N.Y.	678.37	4	Knoxville, Tenn.	713.16	4
La Prensa (N.Y.) El Diario	758.74	4	Lexington, Ky.	575.00	4
Long Beach, Calif.	721.19	6	Los Angeles Daily News	735.57	6
Lowell, Mass.	751.14	5	Lynn, Mass.	658.56	6
Manchester, N.H.	897.93	3	Massillon, Ohio	504.85	4
Maui, Hawaii	993.78	5	Memphis, Tenn.	967.93	6
Milwaukee	886.00	5	Minneapolis, Minn.	1,147.75	5
Modesto, Calif.	700.00	6	Monessen, Pa.	610.00	5
Monterey, Calif.	835.00	6	Mt. Clemens, Mich. (2)	805.52	5
New York Times	1,445.17	2	Norristown, Pa.	496.89	5
Norwalk, Conn.	543.68	2	Noticias del Mundo, N.Y.	457.25	4
Pawtucket, R.I.	692.02	4	Peoria, Ill.	788.00	5
Philadelphia (2)	1,197.47	5	Pittsburgh, Pa.	1,105.00	6
Portland, Maine	879.54	4	Pottstown, Pa.	837.44	5
Providence, R.I.	968.91	4	Pueblo, Colo.	695.22	5
Quincy, Mass.	962.00	5	Rochester, N.Y.	419.00	4
Sacramento, Calif.	850.00	6	San Francisco Chronicle	1,070.22	6
San Jose, Calif.	1,090.42	6	San Juan El Vocero	700.00	5
San Juan Star, Puerto Rico	548.00	6	Santa Rosa, Calif.	943.31	6
Scranton, Pa.	828.66	3	Seattle Post-Intelligencer	898.88	6
Seattle Times	911.73	5	Sheboygan, Wis.	783.47	5
Sioux City, Iowa	678.53	4	St. Louis, Mo.	1,054.00	5
St. Paul, Minn.	1,112.63	5	Terre Haute, Ind.	589.82	5
Toledo, Ohio	1,041.07	5	Utica, N.Y.	387.50	5
Washington, D.C. Post	1,002.30	5	Waterville, Maine	571.16	5
Waukegan, Ill.	869.94	5	Wilkes-Barre, Pa.	538.00	4
Woonsocket, R.I.	621.40	4	Yakima, Wash.	777.60	4
York (Pa.) Dispatch	709.58	4	York (Pa.) Daily Record	730.00	4
Youngstown, Ohio	713.55	4			

CANADA

Contract	Top Min.	After Yrs.	Contract	Top Min.	After Yrs.
Cape Breton, Ontario	763.66	6	Fredericton, New Brunswick	802.96	5
Halifax, Nova Scotia	1,000.00	4	Kingston, Ontario	834.93	5
Lindsay, Ontario	550.29	5	Medicine Hat, Alberta	599.62	5
Moncton, New Brunswick	912.71	6	Montreal, Quebec	1,166.00	5
North Bay, Ontario	859.99	5	Ottawa, Ontario	1,142.42	5
Peterborough, Ontario	741.58	6	Sault Ste. Marie, Ontario	807.35	4

CASE STUDY   *Who Will Get the Pay Raises?*

by WILLIAM A. BABCOCK, Ph.D.
California State University, Long Beach

You are the city editor of a 45,000-circulation newspaper. The paper's managing editor has informed you that you will have a pool of $20,000 in raises for reporters in your department in the coming year, and she has asked you to let her know how you would like to distribute these monies among your four reporters.

Here are brief profiles of your reporters.

Jesus Gonzalez, 26, has been with your newspaper for one and one-half years. This is his first full-time journalism job. He has a green card and is from Puerto Rico. Jesus is extremely hard working and dependable. You have never given him an assignment that he has failed to complete, and he never complains about workload-related issues. He is married and has three children, ages 2, 3 and 6. He has a bachelor's degree in journalism from California State University, Chico. Jesus' writing has never been outstanding, and his work needs a great deal of editing. In fact, of all four of your reporters, he is the weakest writer. His mother, who has been diagnosed with a rare bone disease, lives with his family, and his health benefits are able to cover only a portion of her and his family's medical-related expenses.

Susan Clymer, 29, has worked four years at your newspaper—her first two years in the features department, and her last two years on the city side. She is the most talented writer on the newspaper and has won one regional and two state writing awards in the past three years. She is a superb wordsmith and storyteller. She also can be difficult to work with and temperamental, and she is the least dependable member of your staff of four when it comes to meeting deadlines. Susan is unmarried and has a bachelor's degree in English literature from the University of Minnesota and a master's degree in journalism from Columbia University. While this is her first journalism job, she interned at three newspapers prior to being hired at your paper. Her father is a U.S. Congressman from your state, and her ancestors came to the United States on the Mayflower.

Jackson Boyd, 34, joined your newspaper and your staff seven years ago. He has a bachelor's degree in journalism and black studies from Howard University and was your newspaper's first—and only—African

American hire in the past 15 years. Jackson's writing is clear and readable, though pretty bland for the most part. A long-time member of the Gay and Lesbian Journalists Association, he tends to focus much of his energies on covering minority issues and is reluctant to accept assignments that do not have a minority component to them. You and other editors have noticed that he tends to use more unnamed sources than do other reporters, and you have received occasional phone calls from persons complaining of being misquoted in his stories. Jackson's partner is the brother to your publisher.

Danny Giovanni, 62, is a fixture at your newspaper, where he has worked ever since graduating from high school. In his years at the paper he has covered everything from sports to county school boards to city politics to church dinners. You name it, he's done it. And he'll tell you about it again and again. Danny still uses his black manual Royal typewriter and then has a copy assistant scan his stories into the newspaper's computer. Danny and his wife Jane now have six grandchildren by their two grown children. Twenty years ago, when Danny worked on the editorial page, one of his editorials was a finalist in the Pulitzer Awards. He has been chapter president for the Society of Professional Journalists on three different occasions. He writes on the same topics in a predictable, uninspired manner. His sister owns a small Italian bistro in town.

So, who will get what raise? On what will you base your decision? From the standpoint of awarding raises, what information that you know about each person is relevant, and what is irrelevant? From what you know of each individual, what is your strategy or strategies in giving or withholding raises—reward, punishment, encouragement, etc.? And once you have determined what raises to assign, how will you notify each person, and what will you say to each individual?

AUTHOR:

William A. Babcock is professor and chair of the Department of Journalism at California State University at Long Beach. He was former senior international news editor for the Christian Science Monitor.

🖥 Suggested Web sites:

www.newsguild.org—The Newspaper Guild
www.fcc.gov/mb/policy/eeo—FCC and EEO rules and regulations
www.shrm.org/mhra—Media Human Relations Association
www.newsguild.org/barg/display.php?storyID=181—Model U.S. media labor contract
www.geocities.com/CollegePark/Quad/6460/AmLabHist—American labor union history

Endnotes to Chapter 3:

[1] Professor Bob Gassaway of the University of New Mexico, in remarks to author on December 12, 2001.

[2] Ardyth B. Sohn, with Jan LeBlanc Wicks, Stephen Lacy, and George Sylvie, *Media Management: A Casebook Approach* (Mahwah, N.J.: Lawrence Erlbaum Associates, 2nd ed., 1999), 69.

[3] Harvey Mackay, *Swim with the Sharks without Being Eaten Alive* (New York: William Morrow & Co., 1988), 155–156.

[4] Colin L. Powell, with Joseph E. Persico, *My American Journey* (New York: Random House, 1995), 355.

[5] Oren Harari, "Quotations from Chairman Powell: A Leadership Primer," *Management Review* (December 1996): 36.

[6] "Laborquotes: solidarity, at <www.ks.uiuc.edu/~braun/personal/den/laborquotes/solidarity.html>, accessed August 8, 2003.

[7] Conrad C. Fink, *Strategic Newspaper Management* (Boston: Allyn & Bacon, 1996), 174–176.

[8] Alexandre Dumas, as quoted by Ted Gup in "Media means so much, it means nothing," *Chronicle of Higher Education*, November 23, 2001, B12.

[9] John B. Jaske, "Labor relations in the newspaper industry," in *The Newspaper,* edited by D. Earl Newsom (Englewood Cliffs, N.J.: Prentice-Hall, 1981), 191.

[10] Ibid., 188.

[11] John M. Lavine and Donald B. Wackman, *Managing Media Organizations,* (New York: Longman, 1988), 214.

[12] Sidney Fine, *Sit-Down: The General Motors Strike of 1936–37* (Ann Arbor: The University of Michigan Press, 3rd ed., 1979), 29.

[13] Fink, *Strategic Newspaper Management,* 177.

[14] The Newspaper Guild, <www.newsguild.org/mission/history.php>, accessed May 29, 2001.

[15] Fink, *Strategic Newspaper Management,* 177.

[16] Ibid., 177.

[17] The Newspaper Guild, <www.newsguild.org/mission/today.php>, accessed May 29, 2001.

[18] Linda Foley, interview at the national convention of the Association for Education in Journalism and Mass Communication in Kansas City, Mo., July 31, 2003.

[19] The Newspaper Guild, <www.newsguild.org/mission/today.php>, accessed May 29, 2001.

[20] Historylink.org, "Seattle Post-Intelligencer news staff strikes on August 19, 1936," <www.historylink.org/output.cfm?file_ID=2519>, accessed June 3, 2001.

[21] Stephanie Moore, "TNG gains first Chinese-speaking unit," *The Guild Reporter,* April 20, 2001, 1.

[22] Jaske, "Labor relations in the newspaper industry," 189.

[23] Fink, *Strategic Newspaper Management,* 177.

[24] Alan B. Albarran, *Management of Electronic Media* (Belmont, Calif.: Wadsworth/Thomson Learning, 2nd ed., 2002), 140.

[25] Rifka Rowenstein, "Workers of the Journal unite," *Brill's* (May 1999).

[26] Dow Jones & Co. Inc., *Annual report, 1999.*

[27] The Newspaper Guild, <www.newsguild.org/org/index.php>, accessed May 29, 2001.

[28] Peter F. Drucker, *The Future of Industrial Man* (New York: John Day, 1942), 295.

[29] John E. Flaherty, *Peter Drucker: Shaping the Managerial Mind* (San Francisco: Jossey-Bass, 1999), 43. Copyright © 1999, Jossey-Bass. Reprinted by permission of John Wiley & Sons, Inc.

[30] Though attributed to many sources, the originator of this phrase appears to be Finley Peter Dunne, a 19th-century Chicago columnist, who wrote: "Th' newspaper does ivrything f'r us. It runs th' polis foorce an' th' banks, commands th' milishy, controls th' ligislachure, baptizes th' young, marries th' foolish, comforts th' afflicted, afflicts th' comfortable, buries th' dead an' roasts thim afterward," as quoted by Dr. Ink at <www.poynter.org/column.asp?id=1&aid=2852>, accessed August 7, 2003.

[31] Robert W. McChesney, *Rich Media, Poor Democracy: Communication Politics in Dubious Times* (New York: New Press, 2000).

[32] A.J. Liebling, *The Press* (New York: Ballantine Books, 1964), 121.

[33] George Garneau, "Labor union gets tough," *Editor & Publisher* (February 14, 1987): 39–40.

[34] Alex Beam, "Sticky state of the union in Vermont," *Boston Globe*, May 22, 2003, E1.

[35] Martin Crutsinger, The Associated Press, as printed in "Massive job losses continue," *Albuquerque Journal*, December 8, 2001, C1.

[36] Raymond L. Gover, retired president of *The Patriot-News* in Harrisburg, Pa., in letter to the author, December 16, 2002.

[37] Joe Strupp, "Newhouse won't give pink slips," *Editor & Publisher* (July 2, 2001): 6.

[38] Joe Strupp, "Stopping the clock in Jersey City: 'Journal' fate hangs in balance," *Editor & Publisher* (February 4, 2002): 8.

[39] Aaron J. Moore, "Job security," *Columbia Journalism Review* (September–October 2001): 41.

[40] Peter F. Drucker, *Management Challenges for the 21st Century* (New York: HarperCollins Publishers, Inc., 2001), Rocket e-book edition v. 1, 2002, 330.

[41] John Soloski and Robert G. Picard, "The new media lords: Why institutional investors call the shots," *Columbia Journalism Review*, September–October 1996, 11–12.

[42] "Concentration of Newspaper Ownership," Canadian Heritage at <www.pch.gc.ca/progs/ac-ca/progs/esm-ms/prob4_e.cfm>, accessed May 14, 2003.

[43] Mark Fitzgerald, Todd Shields, and Joe Strupp, "Creed vs. Greed: Harris reports from the front," *Editor & Publisher* (April 9, 2001): 7-8. (Harris was misquoted in the *E&P* article as having said creed and greed, but a tape recording revealed he actually said "creed and deed," resulting in an *E&P* retraction a week later. Harris' misquote has become more famous than what he actually said. The "creed and greed" misquote has been attributed to him many times subsequently, including in the Fall 2001 issue of *Media Ethics*.)

[44] "As layoff toll mounts, KR workers rally," *The Guild Reporter*, April 20, 2001, 1.

[45] Rem Rieder, "A sacred profession?" *American Journalism Review* (May 2001): 6.

[46] Edmund B. Lambeth, "Journalism educators and the journey to Pluto: Who will go and how?" *Media Ethics* (Fall 2001): 27.

[47] Jay T. Harris, full text of his remarks to ASNE on April 6, 2001, <www.asne.org/index.cfm?id=1525 >, accessed August 7, 2003.

[48] Stephen Lacy and Hugh J. Martin, "Profits up, circulation down for Thomson papers in the '80s," *Newspaper Research Journal*, 19, 3 (Summer 1998): 63.

[49] Lambeth, "Journalism educators and the journey to Pluto," 28.

[50] John Maxwell Hamilton, "The importance of being relevant," *Journalism & Mass Communication Educator* (Autumn 2001): 18.

[51] Philip Meyer and Yuan Zhang, "Anatomy of a death spiral: Newspapers and their credibility," paper presented in August 2002 at the annual convention of the Association for Education in Journalism and Mass Communication.

[52] *The Guild Reporter*, "Poynter: Private papers just as short-staffed," at <www.newsguild.org/gr/gr_display.php?storyID=1113>, accessed January 5, 2003.

[53] Journalist in the Detroit area, who asked for confidentiality, in an e-mail to the author on November 21, 2001.

[54] Lisa Dixon, "Employees: The competitive marketing advantage," as published in *Publishers' Auxiliary* and the Basic Business Builders newsletter issued by her company, AdWorks.

[55] Mackay, *Swim with the Sharks without Being Eaten Alive*, 167.

[56] Albarran, *Management of Electronic Media*, 133.

[57] Frederick W. Taylor, "The principles of scientific management," (1911), <www.socserve.mcmaster.ca/~econ/ugcm/3ll3/taylor/sciman>, accessed December 12, 2001.

[58] Ibid.

[59] Ibid.

[60] "Scientific Management: Frederick Winslow Taylor," <www.accel-team.com/scientific/scientific_02.html>, accessed December 12, 2001.

[61] Ibid.

[62] Peter F. Drucker, *The New Society* (New York: Harper & Row, 1949–50), 171.

[63] Elton Mayo, *The Social Problems of an Industrial Civilization* (Andover, Mass.: The Andover Press, 5th ed., 1945), 69.

[64] Ibid.

[65] "Motivation theory: Elton Mayo's Hawthorne experiments," <www.accel-team.com/motivation/hawthorne_01.html>, accessed December 12, 2001.

[66] Mayo, *The Social Problems of an Industrial Civilization*, 81–82.

[67] Ibid., 71–72.

[68] F.J. Roethlisberger and William J. Dickson, *Management and the Worker* (Cambridge, Mass.: Harvard University Press, 8th ed., 1947), 86.

[69] Chester I. Barnard, *The Functions of the Executive* (Cambridge, Mass.: Harvard University Press, 7th ed., 1948), 285.

[70] John J. Morse and Jay W. Lorsch, "Beyond Theory Y," *Harvard Business Review—On Management* (New York: Harper & Row, 1975), 378.

[71] Douglas McGregor, *The Human Side of Enterprise* (New York: McGraw-Hill, 1960), 4.

[72] Ibid., 33–43.

[73] Robert H. Giles, *Newsroom Management: A Guide to Theory and Practice* (Detroit, Mich.: Media Management Books, 8th ed., 1995), ix.

[74] McGregor, *The Human Side of Enterprise*.

[75] Ibid., 48.

[76] Douglas McGregor, *The Professional Manager* (New York: McGraw-Hill, 1967), 79–80.

[77] William G. Ouchi, *Theory Z: How American Business Can Meet the Japanese Challenge* (Reading, Mass.: Addison-Wesley, 3rd ed., 1981), 4.

[78] Ibid., 5.

[79] "Exploring psychology: work motivation," <www.dushkin.com/connectext/psy/ch09/workmot.mhtml>, accessed December 12, 2001.

[80] A Google search will provide more than 10,000 Web sites, almost all of them carrying an illustration identical or similar to this. Some depictions of Maslow's theory carry six or eight levels, but this illustration is based on Maslow's original concept.

[81] A.H. Maslow, *Motivation and Personality* (New York: Harper & Bros., 1954), 80–92.

[82] Ibid., 92.

[83] "A science odyssey: People and discoveries," <www.pbs.org/wgbh/aso/databank/entries /bhmasl.html>, accessed December 12, 2001.

[84] Kenneth Starck, "Groping toward ethics in transitioning press systems: The case of Romania," *Journal of Mass Media Ethics,* 14, 1 (1998): 28–41.

[85] Chris Jarvis, "Abraham Maslow and human motivation," formerly at <sol.brunel.ac.uk/ ~jarvis/bola/motivation/masmodel.html>, accessed December 12, 2001. Site is no longer on the Web.

[86] "A science odyssey: People and discoveries."

[87] Giles, *Newsroom Management,* 351.

[88] Gover, in an e-mail to the author, January 13, 2003.

[89] Geneva Overholser, "Editor Inc.," a chapter in the book, *Leaving Readers Behind: The Age of Corporate Newspapering,* Gene Roberts, editor in chief, and Thomas Kunkel and Charles Layton, general editors (Fayetteville, Ark.: University of Arkansas Press, 2001), 174.

[90] Lewis Carroll, *Alice's Adventures in Wonderland,* first published in London in 1865 (London, England: Puffin Books, 1962), 87.

[91] Peter F. Drucker, *The Practice of Management* (New York: Harper & Row, 1954), 136.

[92] Ibid., 126.

[93] "The art of management: Management by objectives," <www.1000ventures.com/ business_guide/mgmt_mbo_main.html>, accessed December 13, 2001.

[94] Giles, *Newsroom Management,* 360.

[95] J. Stacy Adams, "Toward an understanding of inequity," *Journal of Abnormal and Social Psychology* 67 (November 1963): 422–436.

[96] Ibid.

[97] Ricky W. Griffin and Gregory Moorhead, *Organizational Behavior* (Boston: Houghton Mifflin, 1986), 171.

[98] Robert G. Picard, *The Economics and Financing of Media Companies* (New York: Fordham University Press, 2002), 241–242.

[99] Ibid., 242.

[100] Rick Edmonds of The Poynter Institute, "Public companies no worse than private," at <www.poynter.org/content/content_view.asp?id=12122>, accessed January 6, 2003.

[101] Gover, in an e-mail to the author, January 13, 2003.

[102] The Newspaper Guild, "Salary info—2002," at <www.newsguild.org/salary/display .php?contract_id=26&year=2002&sortBy=contract_name&sortOrder=ASC>, accessed January 6, 2003.

CHAPTER 4
QUALITIES OF
LEADERSHIP AND MANAGEMENT

WHAT'S THE SECRET to building a great organization? Herb Kelleher, twice-retired CEO of Southwest Airlines, says the answer lies in just two words: "Be yourself."[1]

Whether you are an aggressive, hard-charging tyrant, or a soft-spoken, thoughtful team player, the experiences of countless CEOs prove you can succeed as long as you remain true to who you are.

> "Reason and judgment are the qualities of a leader."[2]
>
> — *Tacitus*

"There are many different paths, not one true path," Kelleher maintains. "That's true of leadership as well. People with different personalities, different approaches, different values succeed not because one set of values or practices is superior, but because their values and practices are genuine."[3]

So there is hope for all of us, after all.

There was a time when it was believed that certain traits made people into leaders—the "leaders are born" attitude. Modern research indicates that leaders tend to share some traits, but that leadership is more dependent on personality, knowledge, skills and drive than on physical characteristics such as height or distinguished gray hair.

The sources of power

LEADERSHIP derives its influence from power—power of some kind, whether freely given or subconsciously deferred to. Sociologist Rosabeth Moss Kanter says power is "America's last dirty word," explaining: "People who have it deny it; people who want it do not want to appear to hunger for it; and people who engage in its machinations do so secretly."[4]

The connotation of the word "power" seems to be one of evil or of exploitation of the weak, but power can be used in a very constructive way. Indeed, it is doubtful that much of anything in human society could be accomplished without someone's power causing things to change or advance.

Genghis Khan had power, but so did Mother Teresa when we see power for what it really is: the ability to get tasks done. If no one has power in an organization, there is chaos and nonproductivity. Someone has to be in charge. Their power might be in the background most of the time, but it only exists when others know that the leaders are able and willing to use the power if that is what it takes to get things done.

The importance of good leadership must not be underestimated in its impact on employees. "Quality of leadership is the single most important factor in the morale of journalists—followed by the ability to be creative and editors who listen to you," concluded a survey of journalists published in the *Columbia Journalism Review.*[5]

Research culminating in the 1947 book *The Theory of Social and Economic Organization* by Max Weber concluded that leadership rises from "three pure types of legitimate authority."[6]

(1) Rational grounds, based on the right of those elevated to positions of rank to exercise legal authority; (2) Traditional grounds, based on a belief in the sanctity of long-held traditions of who holds authority; and (3) Charismatic grounds, based on devotion by others, heroism or exemplary character that commands respect.[7]

Those never seemed adequate to me in describing all of the people I have known and thought of as leaders. Closer to the mark are the seven sources of power for leaders described in the 1982 book, *Management of Organizational Behavior*, which include Weber's three earlier cited sources,[8] and I have added an eighth category. The first two of these additional organizational sources of power borrow from Weber, and are:

• **Legitimate.** Distinction between Weber's definitions of "rational" and "traditional" sources of power never seemed very evident. The term of "legitimate" nicely combines them both. A person with legitimate power is one who exercises power simply by virtue of his or her position. We do what this person wants because, well, this person is the boss. We might barely physically recognize the absentee owner of a business, and make jokes about it, but if the owner actually shows up at the office and makes a request, we will hop to it.

• **Referent.** A person with this type of power has a great personality. Even when they have no "legitimate" authority, we tend to go along with referent-power people just because we like them and probably even admire them. Maybe we even envy them. This is the closest category to the "charismatic" leader from Weber's original three sources.

In addition, the 1982 book goes on to list the following sources of organizational power:

• **Coercive.** We've known or heard about people who use power in this way. They are not hesitant to force the rest of us to do as we're told. They are classic Theory X leaders/managers in forcing their agenda on everyone with threats of firing, demotion and downright bullying. Yet, they get things done—at least for a while, or until toppled in a rebellion.

• **Expert.** Expert-power people command respect and willing service because of their knowledge. When leaders like this give an opinion in their area of expertise, others defer to that opinion and are willing to do whatever is recommended that is based on that expertise. Unlike the category of "legitimate," this kind of leader might not even have organizational rank or be anyone's boss in the true sense of the word. But he or she definitely is a leader, complete with willing followers of both higher and lower rank.

• **Reward.** Some people are leaders just because they have the ability to do desirable things for us. They receive obeisance simply because they have power over salary, promotions, junkets, hiring, access to the boss, etc. Like the "expert," people who have "reward" power often possess more influence than their job or title suggests. They are people who we really need to talk with if we want a favor, regardless of rank in the company hierarchy.

• **Information.** Some people are leaders just because they have knowledge or access to knowledge that we consider important. They are not necessarily an "expert," but they know where to get the information. We need people who can track down necessary information, no matter where they fit in the organization's structure.

• **Connection.** Some universities require business students to take courses in golf or tennis so they can more easily make friends with outsiders who can assist them in achieving more profitable or social advancements. Some of our fellow co-workers have the ear of the boss or other powerful insiders. A person with these kinds of connections, outside or inside the organization, stands a good chance of becoming our boss someday, and we know it.

And finally, an eighth power source seems appropriate for this age:

• **Wealth and/or celebrity.** In today's age, when the mass media in general lionize the wealthy and perpetually promote the famous, these attributes constitute the newest source of power. People with wealth hold an economic power that often instills confidence and compels deference, while celebrities usually have wealth and the additional power of their celebrity, in which they are "famous for being famous."

The great leaders have a combination of most or all of these sources of power. Most of these sources are based on attributes that a person can decide to acquire or to ignore.

That leads to the perennial question. Are leaders born, or are they made? Or are they, as management expert Peter F. Drucker contends, neither born nor made, but self-made?[9]

His distinction is an interesting one, placing greatest importance on the desire of individuals to become leaders and to mold themselves into the kind of people whom others want to follow.

While it is true that "all men are created equal" in rights and responsibilities, they are not all equal in attitudes and aptitudes. Human determination can be an indomitable force, but nevertheless most leaders still are "born" to leadership—at least to the degree that you generally need better than average ambition, intelligence, confidence and common sense to become a leader respected by others. Attitude is often more important than skills. If determination can be matched with skills, all the better, but often it is a person's desire to achieve that counts most.

Even if we concede that most people have what it takes, management consultants Warren Bennis and Burt Nanus state another limiting factor. "Leadership seems to be the marshaling of skills possessed by a majority, but used by a minority," they wrote.[10]

Then, of course, there are those who are literally born to their positions, as in taking over mom's or dad's company when they grow up, which was discussed in the last chapter.

Drucker insists there is one essential trait for someone to possess or develop if he or she is to become an effective leader for the long run. Drucker's one indispensable trait is integrity

"(Integrity) might not lend itself to an easy definition," wrote John E. Flaherty in his book analyzing and explaining the master's thinking, *Peter Drucker: Shaping the Managerial Mind.* "But its absence should disqualify a person for a management position. In amplifying this point, he (Drucker) wrote: 'Trust is the conviction that the leader means what he says. It is a belief in something very old fashioned, called integrity . . . . Effective leadership—and again this is very old wisdom—is not based on being clever; it is based primarily on being consistent.'"[11]

History's most famous weekly newspaper publisher, Benjamin Franklin, would have agreed on the utmost importance of the virtue of integrity in a responsible media leader. Franklin observed in his classic autobiography, finished shortly before his death in 1790, "I grew convinced that truth, sincerity and integrity in dealings between man and man were of the utmost importance to the felicity of life; and I form'd written resolutions, which still remain in my journal book, to practice them ever while I lived." Later he returned to that theme, concluding that "no qualities were so likely to make a poor man's fortune as those of probity and integrity." [12]

It takes still another major step forward to become an effective leader. Having integrity and wanting to do the right thing will carry you only so far. In the inevitable times of crisis and indecision, when the right course of action is not at all clear, a leader must be willing to accept calculated risk. That risk will come in your willingness to challenge the status quo, which is where all change originates, and to have the courage once you are sure you're right to go ahead no matter what the nay-sayers believe. More on this in the chapter on decision-making

Drucker's main point stands. Leadership is not the exclusive claim of a few men and women who are wealthy, charismatic, talented, knowledgeable or just lucky. To a large degree, through the enabling force of the human spirit and will, many people can successfully learn to practice the traits of leaders—and therefore become leaders. It is mostly up to you whether you want to learn and develop them.

Now before you get the book version on leadership, read first the plain-spoken, unvarnished opinion of Gannett's Al Neuharth, one of the most famous U.S. media business leaders (notice I didn't say one of the most popular).

As CEO, Neuharth built Gannett from America's seventh largest newspaper company into its largest in a single decade, from 1970 to 1980. By press time for this book, Gannett owned 100 dailies in the United States and 15 in Great Britain.

Never afraid to express an opinion, Neuharth will tell you what he is sure the single most important quality is for a leader.

"Some CEOs call that strategic planning," Neuharth wrote in his autobiography, "and employ a squadron of MBAs to tell them why—or generally why not—to do it. I never did that. Instead, I relied on common sense. The CEO should have the smarts and the instincts to plan ahead, then employ experts to help him figure out 'how' to do 'what' his vision envisions." [13]

Leadership practices

IN THEIR BOOK, *The Leadership Challenge*, authors James M. Kouzes and Barry Z. Posner identified five fundamental leadership practices—accompanied by 10 corresponding behavioral commitments—that are common to many successful leaders and that enabled them to achieve extraordinary results. When at their personal best,

Kouzes and Posner said these leaders would:[14]

PRACTICE	COMMITMENT
Model the way	(1) find your voice by clarifying your personal values
	(2) set the example by aligning actions with shared values
Inspire a shared vision	(3) envision the future by imagining exciting and ennobling possibilities
	(4) enlist others in a common vision by appealing to shared aspirations
Challenge the process	(5) search for opportunities by seeking innovative ways to change, grow and improve
	(6) experiment and take risks by constantly generating small wins and learning from mistakes
Enable others to act	(7) foster collaboration by promoting cooperative goals and building trust
	(8) strengthen others by sharing power and discretion
Encourage the heart	(9) recognize contributions by showing appreciation for individual excellence
	(10) celebrate the values and victories by creating a spirit of community

These practices are available to anyone who wants to learn them. They can be the blueprint for someone to follow so they can rise to a leadership position and then be an effective leader.

Model the way

Employees take their cue from the top. If the leader of the business has a certain style and personality, you can bet it will be reflected, for better or for worse, throughout the company, from vice presidents right down to the receptionist.

Kouzes and Posner believe that "credibility is the foundation of leadership."[15] The most frequent response by employees when asked how they know if a leader has credibility is that credible leaders do what they say they will do. "A judgment of 'credible' is handed down when words and deeds are consonant," Kouzes and Posner write. "If people don't see consistency, they conclude that the leader is, at best, not really serious, or, at worst, an outright hypocrite."[16]

Leadership requires letting everyone in the company know your ideas on what is important for the company. The leader needs to set the example in both skills and values to properly motivate the employees looking to him or her for direction. If they don't, the people they are counting on will lose faith in them. A leader must set a good example.

Inspire a shared vision

Some believe the most important job of a leader is to create a vision, a dream, a goal—whatever word you put upon the forward-thinking force that invents a potentially new future. The importance of having a vision was stated succinctly by business author Harvey Mackay, who is still the king of business bromides, when he observed "If you don't have a destination, you'll never get there."[17] Sometimes reaching the goal requires a change in direction. As the Pogo comic strip once famously warned, if you don't make that required change, you're going to end up exactly at the unhappy conclusion that you are heading for. And we already saw the Cheshire Cat's opinion in the previous chapter about people who do not have a clear idea how to reach their goal.

Leaders live their lives in the future, creating goals and breathing life into them with intense personal commitment.

But vision alone is not sufficient. A person with no followers is not a leader, and people will not become followers until they accept the leader's vision as their own. You cannot forever just order obedience, except possibly in the military. Even in the military, however, and especially in business, the most effective leadership will come from inspiring commitment among the followers about the vision. Leaders work to turn their vision into a shared vision. They open up the exciting possibilities that their vision holds for the future. Leaders get others to join in their dream by showing how all will be served by a common purpose.

People must believe their leader understands their needs and has their interests at heart as well as the interests of the company. No one will work with any commitment, at least not for long, if they come to believe the only reward is for the leader alone.

Challenge the process

Leaders are willing to take calculated risks, to try ideas for the first time or even pick up failed ideas and use a new approach that might work this time. They are relentless in finding new ways to do things, in exploring new ideas, in challenging the status quo.

Everyone makes mistakes, and CEOs are no exception. But William Dean Singleton, CEO of MediaNews Group, said the risk of failure should never frighten a leader away from making a risk that is thought out and considered worth the chance of failure. The secret, Singleton said, is to "fail fast and fail cheap." [18]

Here is where we encounter one of the major differences often seen between entrepreneurs and managers. Entrepreneurs often are not always good managers, but many good managers are not always willing to accept the risks required to be entrepreneurs.

New ideas often come from entrepreneurs, who set the work processes in motion but sometimes lack the ability to manage them afterward. Improvements in marketing the ideas often are developed by managers. They sometimes lack the initiative of the entrepreneur, but their skills in work processes can take the company to new levels of success. Regardless, leaders are innovators or early adopters of new products, new ideas and new ways of doing things.

The ability to innovate, according to Robert Metcalfe, chairperson of 3COM, ". . . requires gambling and risk-taking," with an inevitability of mistakes. [19]

Similarly, Robert Townsend in *Up the Organization* admits, "My batting average on decisions (as CEO) at Avis was no better than .333. Two out of every three decisions I made were wrong. But my mistakes were discussed openly and most of them corrected with a little help from my friends." [20]

Harvard Business Review encourages a company culture that is led by "failure-tolerant leaders," as illustrated by the title of a 2003 book by well-known business authors Ralph Keyes and Richard Farson: *Whoever Makes the Most Mistakes Wins: The Paradox of Innovation.*

However, mistakes must be minimized because many companies are less tolerant of management mistakes than they sound. Robert Lloyd, former executive editor of New York's *Erie Times-News* and assistant managing editor of *The Post-Standard* in Syracuse, has this precaution: "From my experiences, making mistakes has hurt people. People are in power or stay in power because they make really good decisions." [21]

The mantra you hear repeatedly from management and leadership training seminars is that you must not avoid action out of a fear of making mistakes. At least, not in the ideal company. Not only that, you also must be willing to work past operational mistakes made by employees.

Of course, you must learn from your mistakes and move forward. Success in business is not simply stumbling around until you get lucky. However, you must keep your perspective. In *Leaders: The Strategies for Taking Charge*, Bennis and Nanus tell us that of the 90 successful leaders they studied, "almost every false step was regarded as a learning opportunity and not as the end of the world."[22] You will see this referenced again in this chapter as one of four competencies of leadership.

By the way, it is important to emphasize that this willingness to accommodate mistakes refers to management ranks, where experiments in different product ideas, marketing strategies and management procedures are being attempted.

In media companies, such latitude is not possible when talking about mistakes in the skills of journalism. A reporter who makes frequent factual mistakes, for example, cannot be tolerated for long in journalism, where credibility, truthfulness and reliability must be paramount. As only one example, if an *Albuquerque Journal* reporter misspells a source's name, the reporter must write a letter of apology to the source that is then approved and mailed by an editor. Assistant Managing Editor Dan Herrera said any reporter who has to write many of those letters is going to end up unemployed. Some newspapers, including the *Miami Herald*, have sent out letters to sources asking if they were quoted accurately and if a story's facts were correct.

Enable others to act

Leaders understand better than anyone else the value of teamwork. In bringing others on board to achieve their goals, they usually give careful thought about whom they invite to join them. As Southwest Airlines' Herb Kelleher puts it this way, "We've always believed that business can and should be fun . . . . we try not to hire people who are humorless, self-centered, or complacent, so when they come to work, we want them, not their corporate clones. They are what makes us different, and in most enterprises, different is better."[23]

Notice his use of the word, "we." The choice of that word rather than "I" helps immediately identify Kelleher as a team leader. The most effective leaders never think in terms of "I."

The best leaders build collaborative teams enabling others to act. Several management studies have indicated that team-building is possibly the most important of these five practices of a successful leader.

This sense of teamwork includes all of a company's stakeholders—its customers, suppliers, community, shareholders and its complementary businesses. All must support the vision in some way.

Rosabeth Moss Kanter, a Harvard business professor, confirms this in her research on successful innovations inside large corporations, reporting, "The few projects in my study that disintegrated, did so because the manager failed to build a coalition of supporters and collaborators."[24]

CHAPTER 4

A mantra in business is that information is power. Ineffective leaders hoard information while effective and credible leaders make sure information is shared. Kouzes and Posner point out that teamwork can not work unless information and resources are shared. Just as important as disseminating information is the skill of listening to others. True communication must be two-way. "If you want people to trust you," *The Leadership Challenge* says, "the listening-to-talk ratio has to be in favor of listening."[25]

Encourage the heart

This could have been in the chapter on motivation because that's what this section is all about. Leaders must encourage the heart of their followers to persevere against inevitable frustrations, setbacks and even tedium, because it can be so difficult to achieve goals. Showing staffers that their efforts are appreciated and that they are valuable to the company can be done many ways.

Many managers mistakenly think the best way to motivate employees is by giving them pay raises, but repeated research has shown that pay often is not the prime motivator, especially for the creative types of people who work for media companies. A book, *1001 Ways to Reward Employees*,[26] makes it clear that many other things are important to employees, too.

"Everyone needs to feel appreciated. Most businesses aren't very glamorous," Mackay points out. "If you want to (improve) morale a little bit among your middle managers, give them some unexpected recognition . . . . Bragging rights are just as important as money."[27]

In *Up the Organization*, Townsend writes that the simple elegance of saying thank you is "a really neglected form of compensation."[28]

Finding imaginative ways to extend recognition to people can motivate people without, as Mackay says, locking the owner into "a costly and ever-escalating (salary) program."[29]

Of course, you cannot buy people's commitment with gimmicks and pats on the back. That alone is not enough to get them to want to care, to stay late or come in early. The word "want" is the key. Any good manager can get people to do work, at least to a point. But a person who can develop attitudes in people that have them wanting to work is a step beyond a manager's goal of production efficiency—someone who can do that is a leader. Such a leader will enjoy the fruits of productivity and accomplishment, giving proof to Colin Powell's ideal definition of leadership, which he described as, ". . . .the art of accomplishing more than the science of management says is possible."[30]

For such a leader, and the team he or she has motivated into action in a spirit of community and shared goals, anything is possible.

Characteristics of leaders

VANCE PACKARD, in his 1962 book *The Pyramid Climbers*, offered one of the most basic, to-the-point definitions of leadership you will find anywhere. "In essence," he wrote, "leadership appears to be the art of getting others to want to do something you are convinced should be done."[31]

Notice that Packard's definition is also built on the phrase "to want" because it shows the power of persuasion coming from leadership as opposed to the power of force from mere management. As already mentioned, not all managers are leaders, and neither are all leaders good managers. But both managers and leaders need some degree of the other's principal ability if they are to succeed in business.

The difference between people doing work because they want to do it as opposed to being required to do it is the ultimate proof of leadership.

Creating this desire, within others, to take a stake in their employer's company and to achieve their manager's goals often relies on what Kouzes and Posner describe as a paradox of power—"We become most powerful when we give our power away,"[32] They illustrate it with the observation of a military general who said his leadership came not from the stars on his shoulder but from the men and women that he led.

Research continually shows that the more people believe they have influence and control in an organization, the more effective and satisfied they will be in their work. As Kouzes and Posner noted, "People who say 'Yes, I Can' and realize that 'I Make A Difference' in their organizations know that what they do matters."[33]

Effective leadership in this regard comes from assigning people to their strengths, giving them the opportunity to develop their weaknesses and providing them the resources and access to their managers that they need to perform their duties.

Of course, let it be noted that no amount of doing the right thing will work with a small minority of people who, for whatever reasons, busy themselves by putting up hurdles to a manager's success. Who really knows what drives some people?

When all else fails, a beleaguered manager can turn to baseball legend Casey Stengel's comic-relief advice on dealing with recalcitrant employees. "The secret to being a good manager," he said, "is keeping the people who hate me away from those who are undecided."[34]

There are many kinds of leaders. Despite the strong traits we already have seen that are commonly associated with leadership, it is interesting to note that researchers have found no single set of characteristics that worked for every leader in every situation.[35]

Indeed, Al Neuharth was demonstrative and arrogant, bombastic and charismatic, in transforming Gannett into one of the nation's earliest media companies traded on Wall Street in 1977 and in founding *USA TODAY* in 1982.

On the other hand, as executive editor of *The Philadelphia Inquirer*, a Knight Ridder paper, Gene Roberts was quiet and thoughtful, sensitive and nurturing with his staff in leading the paper to win more Pulitzer Prizes in 1986 than any other major newspaper group had ever won in a single year up to then.

Thus, despite their vast differences, both Neuharth and Roberts are legendary media leaders.

Dramatically different kinds of people have the ability to lead. But researchers have concluded, after years of debate and conflicting theories, that there are some core traits common to virtually all leaders despite differences in physical characteristics, temperament and style.

The researcher getting much of the credit for debunking the "leaders are born, not made" myth is Warren Bennis, who published his findings in 1984. For nearly five years, Bennis kept in touch with 90 leaders (60 corporate executives and 30 from the public sector), interviewing them and observing them in action. He stipulated that they be leaders, not just managers.

Bennis was convinced that American organizations were underled but overmanaged, so he wanted to see what worked for those executives who he felt were truly leaders.

Of the corporate CEOs, the median age was 56. Predictably, the vast majority were Caucasian males, but Bennis did include six African American men and six women in the group because that was probably typical of corporate leadership ratios in the 1970s and 1980s.

Bennis discovered four important similarities, which he called "competencies of leadership," that still stand as benchmarks.[36]

Management of Attention. One trait Bennis found most often among the executives was their ability to draw others to them because of an extraordinary focus of commitment. These leaders managed the attention of the organization and the people in it by a compelling drive to succeed. They had a vision of what the organization and the people in it could accomplish through a clear sense of goals and outcome.

The late Harvey Mackay recounted on how the best definition of a goal he ever heard came from a woman executive whom, regrettably, he did not name in his book. He gave her credit nevertheless for telling him, "A goal is a dream with a deadline."[37]

Management of Meaning. Effective leaders invariably are outstanding communicators, able to make others understand their goals and to enlist them in working together to achieve the goals. They manage, or direct, if you will, the meaning of their vision. "Effective leaders can communicate ideas through several organizational layers, across great distances, and even through the jamming signals of special interest groups and opponents," Bennis explained.

Kouzes and Posner devote an entire chapter in *The Leadership Challenge* to envisioning. They describe vision as "an image of the future," with its connotations of long-range planning, future potential, standard of excellence and quality of uniqueness.

"Leaders are possibility thinkers, not probability thinkers," the authors explain. "All new ventures begin with possibility thinking, not probability thinking. After all, the probability is that most new businesses will fail and most social reforms will never get off the ground. If entrepreneurs or activists took this view, however, they'd never start a new business or organize a community. Instead, they begin with the assumption that anything is possible . . . . It's this belief that sustains them through the difficult times."[38]

Management of Trust. Trust is essential to all organizations, Bennis maintained. A major part of this management of trust is to follow what you truly believe. People are willing to follow even a leader they disagree with if they feel the leader is being true to long-held convictions.

An important aspect of this is decisiveness. Few things are more frustrating to employees, clients and co-workers than people who continually change their minds. A manager who acts that way is violating the trust that employees want to have in a manager.

Indecisiveness is just another term for aversion to risk. It is seen as such a serious shortcoming when seen in managers—even as a fatal flaw—that one business owner insisted he will not change his mind on routine decisions, even if he has come to believe he made a wrong decision. He will stay faithful to such a decision until the most opportune time when it can be reoriented in such a way that it is not obvious he has changed his mind. "I'd rather be wrong than appear indecisive," he declared, regarding at least the decisions that are not critical.[39]

Another important quality of leadership is sound and trustworthy character that merits the respect of subordinates. General H. Norman Schwarzkopf described it in this way: "Leadership is a potent combination of strategy and character. But if you must be without one, be without the strategy."[40]

Management of Self. A good leader knows his or her own skills and how to effectively use them. Everyone knows their strengths, but the best leaders are perceptive enough to also know their weaknesses.

Both Drucker and Bennis considered management of self to be critical. After all, how can you manage others if you cannot manage yourself?

The executives in the group "seemed unacquainted with the concept of failure," Bennis noted.[41] He said they used many euphemisms and descriptive words for mistakes, but never used the word failure. They saw mistakes as a learning process, not a disaster.

A big part of managing yourself is being able to handle the inevitability of errors on your part, let alone all of those by others. Earlier we learned that successful leaders accept the fact that they'll make mistakes, and that such mistakes are "not the end of the world." An Iowa attorney, Frank J. Nidey, pointed that out to me during a discussion of one of my business mistakes that cost me an additional $140 just to talk with him about it. He asked me if I had learned anything from the mistake. I replied that I certainly had, that I had analyzed what went wrong, and vowed I would never be so foolish again. That mistake cost me thousands of dollars.

Then he quoted to me the line first used by Barry LePatner: "Good judgment comes from experience, and experience comes from bad judgment."

We learn from our mistakes, and grow wiser in the process.

There are many reasons why you should not get unjustifiably angry at employees. Not the least of the reasons is the fact that when an employee makes a mistake, as often as not it is you—as that person's manager—who is at least partly to blame. Perhaps it is something as basic as not having provided the required training, supervision or resources. Look for ways to correct what caused the mistakes. You cannot be so forgiving of mistakes that there is no effort by an employee to avoid making another, but you do need to keep your perspective when a mistake is made.

Developing strong leadership ability requires self-analysis, the management of self. As a leader, you should be able to list your strengths, but you should also know your weaknesses and acknowledge them.[42]

While vice president of personnel at the national media company Knight Ridder, Doug Harris said his company had identified 14 values commonly shared by successful leaders:[43]

(1) Communication ability, both oral and written

(2) Creativity in coming up with imaginative solutions

(3) Decisiveness

(4) Delegation and control over management processes

(5) High energy

(6) Impact in making a good first impression and then commanding attention and respect

(7) Flexibility in modifying self-behavior

(8) Leadership by employing the appropriate management style

(9) Personal motivation

(10) Planning and organizing effectively for self and others

(11) Common sense

(12) Sensitivity in reacting to others and listening

(13) Stress tolerance under pressure and opposition

(14) Tenacity in following through to a solution

The immeasurable value of optimism

YOU COULD add a 15th tenet of leadership, based on my observations of those who are leaders and those who are not. That 15th tenet is optimism. Or, think of it as positive thinking. Pessimists simply do not achieve much success—except as lawyers, who are trained in law school to be pessimists and who take considerable pride in always identifying the downside and foretelling the doom to come if their advice is not followed. With that exception for the barristers, however, it is the optimists (the positive people, if you will) who usually end up as leaders. By that, I do not mean to imply naivete or Pollyannaism. I am referring to people who tackle problems with confidence and positive attitudes, who enjoy the challenge of jumping the hurdles placed in their path.

They are optimists, like John Madigan, who as president and CEO of the Tribune Co., said, "There's never been a more exciting time to be involved in an organization like this. There are so many challenges. There is so much competition. There are so many things to do." [44] Now there's a leader unfazed by difficulties—a leader who relishes facing challenge and will get things done. As Max De Pree noted in *Leadership is an Art,* "It is natural for a leader to be a person who is primarily future-oriented." [45] You can see that trait in Madigan's comment.

We want our leaders to have enthusiasm, energy and a can-do attitude. We draw strength for ourselves from our leaders when our leaders are confident and optimistic. Witnessing that attitude among our leaders inspires us to believe we are part of a successful enterprise with the odds in our favor because of the abilities of ourselves and of our leaders together.

Keep in mind that it isn't just the spiritual weaklings who can be adversely affected by the pessimism of others. Even Benjamin Franklin, an exuberant publisher who believed utterly in himself, testified to the power of pessimism over others when he recalled in his autobiography:

"There are croakers in every country, always boding its ruin. Such a one then lived in Philadelphia; a person of note, an elderly man, with a wise look and a very grave manner of speaking; his name was Samuel Mickle. This gentleman, a stranger to me, stopt by one day at my door, and asked me if I was the young man who had lately opened a new printing-house. Being answered in the affirmative, he said he was sorry for me, because it was an expensive undertaking, and the expense would be lost; for Philadelphia was a sinking place, the people already half-bankrupts, or near being so; all appearances to the contrary . . . . And he gave me such a detail of misfortunes now existing, or that were soon to exist, that he left me half melancholy. Had I known him before I engaged in business, probably I never should have done it." [46]

The expectations we hold about ourselves or other people often become self-fulfilling prophecies. You probably have noticed that other people act in ways in line with your expectations, whether high or low.[47]

"If we expect others to fail, they probably will. If we expect them to succeed, they probably will," Kouzes and Posner observed.[48]

Our expectations shape others' behavior as well as our own. Optimists are healthier, more successful, and score higher on aptitude tests.[49] Pessimists have a negative attitude toward health and aging, and a recent study showed that people with a negative self-perception die 7.5 years before the positive-thinkers.[50]

You really can help yourself succeed and be happy by looking at the sunny side of the street. A primary tactic in getting others to cooperate with you is showing confidence and enthusiasm. That assures others that your joint efforts will be successful.[51]

While a commercial real estate agent, I remember an incident when I began enthusiastically telling my manager how I intended to complete a certain deal, describing how I would overcome the obstacles and successfully make the sale. Then, just for a moment, I worried that I might be considered over-confident. But my manager, Al Weaver, gave me a nod of approval and dismissed my sudden self-doubt, declaring, "If we weren't optimists, we'd never get anything done."

As educator and former editor Robert Lloyd noted, "Believe in yourself, even when nobody else does."[52]

Such optimism percolates all through a company, no matter what its product. And if I'm going to add the 15th tenet of optimism, I should note its close cousin, humor.

Some owners and managers think business is no laughing matter, but the most successful ones have a culture from the top down that keeps everything in perspective. At my newspaper, I always thought work should be fun as well as challenging and fulfilling. After all, we're spending half our waking hours there, a significant part of our limited life span, so let's make it a pleasant place. Everyone there was serious about getting work done right, and making a profit, but the office always had laughter and friendly banter floating around. Customers coming in would find themselves joking and laughing, too.

On many a staff there is not always laughter and friendly banter. I remember one reporter at a paper who won writing awards but could not get along with her fellow staffers. Everyone tries to weed such people out in the interview process, but somehow she slipped under the editor's radar. As the months went by, it became disturbingly obvious that she did not know the difference between mischief and meanness, between teasing and taunting, between disagreeing and being disagreeable. Her people skills were lousy, offending the other employees. Her reporting and writing skills were excellent, however, and readers loved her.

The editor fired her.

Having good-natured and happy people in the office who could get along with each other was more important than mere skills that could be acquired elsewhere in a more pleasant person.

Business columnist Dale Dauten, who bills himself as the "corporate curmudgeon," describes laughter in a company as an antidote to organizational fear, which he defines as corporate bureaucracy.

"If you create a place known for laughter and playfulness, guess what?" Dauten wrote. "Cheerful people want to work there. Laughter is an employee benefit and a consumer benefit. In bad companies, upper management makes jokes at the expense of employees; in mediocre companies, employees joke about upper management; in a few great companies, employees and upper management joke with each other and with customers about everything."[53]

Mary Edrington, assistant dean of the College of Business Administration at Drake University, said that business can and should be fun. "Employees should not be humorless, self-centered or complacent," she said.[54]

Ad agency president David Ogilvy urged his managers: "Try to make working at Ogilvy & Mather fun. When people aren't having any fun, they seldom produce good advertising. Kill grimness with laughter. Maintain an atmosphere of informality. Encourage exuberance. Get rid of sad dogs that spread gloom."[55]

You should enjoy going to work. If you don't, then go find a company where you will enjoy your work. There are companies where you can work hard and, ironically, still be relaxed. Luckily for us (perhaps because of the irreverent sorts that are attracted by creative jobs), such companies often are media companies.

Pointers on being an effective leader

LET'S TURN to a military analogy, to the positive role model of General Colin L. Powell. He served President Jimmy Carter on the Department of Defense staff in the Pentagon and later was National Security Advisor to President Reagan. He served President George Bush and briefly President Bill Clinton as chairman of the Joint Chiefs of Staff from 1989 to 1993, and he was appointed in 2001 by President George W. Bush as Secretary of State, becoming an even more visible statesman.

A little known fact is that Powell also earned a master's degree in business administration after two tours in the Vietnam War.

Familiar now to all business students are the 18 leadership lessons gleaned from Powell's autobiography, *My American Journey*. Actually, it's more accurate to say that they are leadership lessons from Powell as explained by Oren Harari, who selected them and then added his own commentary for an article in *Management Review* in 1996. Since then they have been copied and printed hundreds of times around the world in company publications, motivational speeches, articles and college professors' handouts—often without attribution. Several examples of Powell's rules and Harari's perceptive commentary can be found in an Internet search of "Powell's Leadership Primer," or words to that effect.

Because of the popularity of the original article, Harari wrote a book in 2002 further expounding on leadership quotes and opinions from Powell, titled *The Colin Powell Leadership Primer.*"[56]

A couple of Powell's leadership quotes are in this book to illustrate points. One of the most apt ones is based on a quote Powell paraphrased from book publisher and editor Michael Korda, saying, "Great leaders are almost always great simplifiers, who cut through argument, debate and doubt, to offer a solution everybody can understand."[57]

Harari's commentary: "Effective leaders understand the KISS principle, or Keep It Simple, Stupid . . . . Their visions and priorities are lean and compelling, not cluttered and buzzword-laden. Their decisions are crisp and clear, not tentative and ambiguous. They convey an unwavering firmness and consistency in their actions . . . . The result? Clarity of purpose, credibility of leadership, and integrity in organization."[58]

Regardless of the power they seem to wield, even top-ranking managers need to answer to someone else. Sometimes it is another manager above, but even at the supposed top the CEO owes an accounting for his or her job to a board of directors and, if the company is publicly traded, ultimately to stockholders.

The Poynter Institute for Media Studies gained insights into the mindset of professional managers when Harvard faculty member Marty Linsky conducted extensive interviews with 14 CEOs of major media companies, publishing the results in a report titled *The View From the Top*. Linsky, who is director of the Poynter Institute's research project on Media Ownership and Leadership, found all 14 CEOs to be fearless in tackling the media industry challenges and optimistic about the future. That was in stark contrast, Linsky noted, to "the gloomy mood of the working stiffs . . . . reporters are pessimists, dissatisfied with the present, with little expectation that things will get better in the future."[59]

One wonders: Are reporters pessimists or are they only disappointed optimists,[60] beaten down by a profit maximization culture among executives more interested in selling advertising than in filling empty newsroom slots, paying good wages and aggressively pursuing news?

Reporters seem to understand better than many media executives that the unique First Amendment protection afforded to the press confers special privilege, which should require special responsibility in return.

It's common for reporters to become discouraged by a management system in many media companies that cares less about the journalism end of the business than they do.

Taken too far, however, this pessimism (or disappointed optimism) solves nothing. This is a good place to reinforce an earlier point: If you aspire to a management position some day, then you must be a positive person, a person who believes in solving problems rather than just carping about them. It can be difficult to rise above the camaraderie that comes from newsroom grumbling and self-righteous judging of others. But if you are an optimist and doer rather than a pessimist and complainer, you are much more likely to rise to a position where you can actually do something about fixing the problems.

Back to Linsky. His 14 CEOs are a confident bunch who see the challenges they face as part of what makes their jobs so exciting. "It is as much a question of attitude as it is an objective assessment of where the industry is headed," Linsky observes. "They recognize that their readers, viewers and listeners are changing, that technology is changing, that the sources and presentation of information is undergoing a transformation and that they want their organizations to be on the boat as it leaves the dock. Being left on the shore is their worst-case scenario."[61]

A couple of pages later, Linsky makes a point about his 14 print and broadcast moguls that is important for all of us to understand about this new generation of media managers. He concludes, "One of the clearest ways to gauge the differences in vision between the newsroom and the corporate suite is the extent to which the bosses see themselves as corporate managers rather than journalist managers, the extent to which they identify with CEOs of widget companies more than Pulitzer Prize-winning reporters. How do the people who are sitting at the top of these large media organizations think about their role and responsibilities as corporate leaders? . . . . Do they see themselves as corporate leaders or as journalism leaders?"[62]

The context of his questions tells you that Linsky believes these top-level media managers are much more in tune with the principles of business rather than the principles of journalism—at least the principles of journalism held dear by most editors, reporters, students and professors. Journalist Doug Underwood reached the same conclusions in his 1993 book condemning the takeover of the nation's newsrooms by people holding MBA degrees instead of journalism degrees, concluding that the MBAs were concerned only about the business side of journalism and not at all in touch with the editorial side.

The MBAs arrive in media companies

THERE HAVE been several books and magazine articles on venture capital journalism, including "Small Links, Big Chain" in the *Columbia Journalism Review*. In that article, I was quoted as worrying that a purely bottom-line investment approach by media owners and managers might erode the public's perception of the information responsibility role of newspapers in society,[63] perhaps ultimately even threatening the privileged position afforded to the press by the First Amendment.

The bottom-line approach is not limited to just venture capital firms. It is endemic also to many of the publicly traded chains. Deborah Howell, a former editor of Knight Ridder's *St. Paul Pioneer Press*, says that, "editors are often looked on as sellouts" because they are profit-oriented rather than journalism-oriented.[64] "A lot of editors feel they are slowly taking the paper down," Howell added.[65]

Bottom-line management by business-oriented publishers and

editors is well documented in Doug Underwood's indictment of the new newspaper industry, *When MBAs Rule the Newsroom.*

"It's probably no surprise that in an era of mass media conglomerates, big chain expansion, and multi-million-dollar buyouts, the editors of daily newspapers have begun to behave more and more like the managers of any other corporate entity," Underwood writes. "The executives of today's daily newspapers have decided to treat their readership as a market and the news as a product to appeal to that market."[66]

Even Underwood concedes that directing of newspapers and other media companies by professional business managers is no new phenomenon. He quotes Gerald Baldesty, press historian at the University of Washington, who had noted that, "by the late 19th century, the formula of the newspaper-as-business-first-and-foremost was firmly established."[67]

Underwood gives example after example where he feels management decisions were made by heretics with no regard for sacred tenets of journalism.

A similar hatchet job on all managers, but in a much more humorous way, is carried out by Scott Adams in his Dilbert cartoons ridiculing modern business, in which all managers are buffoons and all workers are, well, much brighter.

Adams' cartoons have led to what is actually being considered a plausible business theory in some quarters, known as "The Dilbert Principle" after Adams' leading cartoon character and one of his many books of humorous business cartoons.

Adams' book, and the theory it expostulates, is the latest in what John Flaherty and Peter Drucker call a guerrilla approach to improved productivity that is more an attitude than a frontal attack. Flaherty writes, "It (the guerrilla approach) was a satirical indictment of the pomposity of academic theorists, the hubris of executive skepticism, the insouciance of bureaucratic administrators, the pretentiousness of charismatic leaders, and the myopia of businessmen."[68]

Flaherty says the chief representatives are Shepherd Mead, *How to Succeed in Business Without Really Trying;* C. Northcote Parkinson, *Parkinson's Law;* Lawrence Peter, *The Peter Principle;* and Scott Adams, *The Dilbert Principle.*[69] All are well known books and often even required reading for business students.

Flaherty explains: "Drucker considered the guerrilla writers to be intellectual terrorists (a description that no doubt would please them), who worked assiduously to undermine the questionable assumptions of conventional wisdom in the field of management. He found them amusing but not helpful in promoting executive effectiveness. Moreover, he thought that a focus on constantly telling others what is wrong results in an essentially barren and sterile exercise that does not address the issue of executive results."[70]

The Peter Principle states that capable workers get promoted until they reach a level where they finally surpass their competence, and thus become incompetent. At that position, they then stay, neither promoted nor demoted from that day forth.

In his mocking and ironic way, Adams maintains that the Peter Principle now is giving way in modern companies to the Dilbert Principle. Adams first put forth the Dilbert Principle in a *Wall Street Journal* article, following that up with his book by the same name in 1996. "The basic concept of the Dilbert Principle," Adams writes, "is that most ineffective workers are systematically moved to the place where they can do the least damage: management."[71]

To Adams, the Peter Principle days were "Golden Years when you had a boss who was once good at something . . . . Now, apparently, the incompetent workers are promoted directly to management without ever passing through the temporary competence stage."[72]

Both Underwood and Adams, in their very different ways, would have us believe that all employees and, I presume, all businesses as well, can manage themselves, thank you—in defiance of Drucker's opinion that all businesses tend toward destruction when left to non-management.

While we can grant that incompetent managers can speed the process of destruction, nevertheless a good manager can inspire a staff and an entire company to greatness. And we certainly can concede that good managers and bad managers alike exist in abundance.

Not that even a good manager or entrepreneur always will be likeable, or without faults—sometimes massive ones built on ego. But time can heal wounds, or at least compromise memory.

Thus, the legendary status of past broadcasters, publishers and editors often burns brighter while their faults dim over the years.

Being an effective manager of others

WHEN IT COMES TO managing others, there are certain tasks and standards that will mark a person as a professional manager who is getting results. You need management skills to implement sound management effectively, of course, and these skills are timeless and cross all kinds of business (and even social) organizations.

Here are the five most important ones you should develop if you want to be a successful manager.

(1) A skilled manager controls the use of his or her time. When he or she can't, the reason usually lies in Parkinson's Law. Managers need to beware of the unchallenged validity of this law, as its effects are seen in nearly every company and organization to a larger or lesser degree. By minimizing the effects of Parkinson's Law, you will be doing a big favor to the future profitability and efficiency of your firm.

The book also titled *Parkinson's Law* was published in 1957 by C. Northcote Parkinson. It is a slim volume satirizing the British Civil Service bureaucracy and drawing many conclusions about bureaucratic structure as a result. It was Parkinson who had correctly predicted two decades earlier that the British Navy would eventually end up with more admirals than ships.[73] One of the effects of Parkinson's Law with application in business is that the number of managers continues to increase even if there is not enough work for all of them.

The actual law is known by just about everyone, but nevertheless ignored by far too many, so it bears repeating here:

"Work expands so as to fill the time available for its completion."[74]

Its truth is seen in every disorganized, unfocused manager and employee in the company. Anyone attempting to undertake an effort to manage his or her time better will soon recognize that much, if not most, of the problem exists because of the repercussions of Parkinson's Law. Either too much time is spent on tasks, or time is spent on the wrong tasks. Delegation is an important part of managing one's own time.

(2) A skilled manager is adept at planning and its related counterpart, goal-setting. Here you can remember the 5-P Rule: "Proper Planning Prevents Poor Performance." A plan is the actual starting point in management, and it must be in writing. It points the direction unerringly toward the goal identified by the manager and for which everyone is working.

(3) A skilled manager is a confident but careful decision maker who is willing to assume calculated risks and even willing to move before all of the facts are in. Decision-making is at the heart of effective management. Or it should be. We all know of managers incapable of making a timely or firm decision, and we have no respect for them.

(4) A skilled manager works well with others. Some executives claim that this is the most important ability they look at when deciding whether to promote someone. If you want others to want to work for you, and therefore accomplish the goals you have set, then you must have respect for them and treat them as you like to be treated. Also, you must

create an atmosphere where people do not have excessive fear of making a mistake. Not all ideas will work, and people need to be encouraged to keep trying new ideas.

(5) A skilled manager is customer-oriented. Every decision is influenced by a desire to attract and satisfy customers while keeping professional goals and ethical standards in mind. Or, as Drucker sees it, a product has no value until it has a customer, and a customer is the only reason for the existence of a business.

Jerks and vampires don't see themselves in the mirror

DALE DAUTEN'S syndicated business column recently made the imaginative observation paraphrased in the headline above. Dauten was explaining why so many incompetent bosses never seem to change.

"I used to assume that if you made fun of one premier jerk, then secondary and tertiary jerks would be forced to confront their Inner Jerks and change," Dauten wrote in confessing his early naiveté about the mysteries of corporate management. "But that's not how it works," he explained. "Years ago I was forced to realize that jerks are like vampires—you hold up a mirror, and they don't see a thing."[75]

Dauten said this conclusion has been borne out in the seminars he gives around the country. "You might think that mediocre bosses would come, eager to learn from the greats," he wrote. "Not so. It's the best bosses who tend to show up, eager to learn. Meanwhile, mediocre bosses seek out some comfortable rehashing of old theories, programs that ought to be called 'What Used to Work,' ones that sell the reassurance that you've again heard just what you expected to hear."[76]

Perhaps you have even noticed that in everyday life, among some of your friends or among acquaintances with whom you'd never want to be friends. The important lesson for employees is that if your boss is a jerk, it's unlikely the jerkdom will ever end unless change is forced by someone higher up. It might be time for you to move on because, as I say elsewhere in this book and have repeatedly told myself, life's too short to work for jerks.

This is also a warning to you. Be honest with yourself, and see yourself in the mirror as you really are, not as you think you are.

CASE STUDY   *Using Leadership*
to Improve Staff Morale

by HUGH S. FULLERTON, Ph.D.
Sam Houston State University

(Second in a series of five related case studies)

When Jerry takes over as owner of the weekly newspaper, *The Call*, he finds he has a staff that is in the doldrums. The employees seem like nice people, but they are not very effective. They spend too much time chatting on the phone and drinking coffee, records are kept rather haphazardly, and there is a bit of office infighting going on.

Advertising revenue is stagnant, in part because the competition includes a local shopping guide, which is aggressively pursuing business, as well as a small radio station. At least one employee—one of the best ones—is looking for a better job. The employees are pretty poorly paid, even by small-town standards.

Jerry, however, does not have a lot of extra cash. The down payment took most of the capital he had been able to commit, and he knows he has to have some cash available for expenses for the first few weeks, as well as his own family living expenses. Simply put, he cannot afford to give raises now.

Suddenly, leadership, not money, becomes an issue. Jerry has never been in a supervisory position except when he was acting as copy chief at *The Record*, so he has no real managerial experience. He knows that he must keep his best employees happy and quell the minor quarrels that divert employees' attention from their jobs. The office manager sometimes acts as she were a queen, and the employees do not give the perception that they really want to provide the best service.

How is Jerry going to improve morale and performance, convince the somewhat skeptical employees that *The Call* is going to be a good place to work, and do it without throwing money around or spending all his time on employee issues?

AUTHOR:

Hugh S. Fullerton was a reporter at daily newspapers and also was publisher of weekly newspapers in Michigan for several years. He teaches journalism at Sam Houston State University in Huntsville, Texas.

CASE STUDY   *Recruiting and Retaining*
Volunteer Staff

by LOUISA HA, Ph.D.
Bowling Green State University

Your university's Radio News Organization (RNO) comprises the news departments of WBGU-FM and WFAL-AM, which are the two university radio stations. It provides news updates five times a day, five days a week on each of the two stations. In addition, it airs *Front and Center*, a weekly talk show focusing on campus and community issues on WBGU.

The entire organization of RNO is run by student volunteers. Any student can join the organization. The station provides all of the training.

Students can choose from a variety of positions, both on-air and behind the scenes, ranging from anchoring to production and reporting. Apart from radio production jobs, students can choose other management and administrative positions such as sales, promotion, public relations, writing and working on its Web site.

Listeners of the RNO's radio programs range from university students to long-time community residents. The audience is diverse with a wide range of musical interests.

The benefits of joining the RNO are not limited to the practical hands-on experience in running a news department and producing news shows on radio. Unlike a structured course, the students have complete freedom to choose the news and create new programs. For key officer positions such as the news director, the assistant news director and promotions director, students can request for independent study credits in the department.

The station is suffering problems in recruiting and retaining staff members. As with other student organizations, all staff members at RNO are volunteers. In addition, the station has many competitors on campus, especially the university's student-run TV newscast.

Even when the organization was able to recruit some students at the beginning of the semester, retention was poor. During the last fall recruitment, only two of 10 volunteers stayed until spring. Although there is a broadcast journalism major at your university, almost no journalism students have participated in RNO in recent years.

Maggie Monty, a senior who is graduating this spring, is the current news director. Jenny Johnson, another student, is the assistant news director. All training duties fell on the shoulders of these two students. Positions such as promotion director have not been filled.

Due to the lack of volunteers, not all newscasts could be filled and the weekly talk show was also not aired. No original news reporting or gathering has been done because of the lack of staff. The news service and the RNO are both close to collapse if no one is able to succeed Maggie and Jenny.

Several options are under consideration. (1) Leave the organization as a student organization and totally independent of course work. (2) Incorporate station duties as part of the requirement in the university's radio production courses, such as radio production or radio workshop. (3) Create a hybrid of a student organization and course work, where majors who take radio classes hold executive officer positions. Their performances at the stations will be part of the grade in those classes.

You may also suggest another option outside these three, but be sure to provide justifications and feasibilities of any option.

As a media management leadership team, your group should identify the strengths and weaknesses of the organization as a hands-on practical experience and as an extracurricular activity for students. Discuss and compare the pros and cons of each option with specific reference to the recruitment and retention of quality personnel. Recommend which option the organization should use and justify your choice.

AUTHOR:

Louisa Ha is associate professor in the Department of Tele-communications at Bowling Green State University, in Bowling Green, Ohio. She has published over 30 articles in refereed scholarly journals.

CHAPTER 4

💻 Suggested Web sites:

www.poynter.org/geneva—Geneva Overholser's Weblog on media management issues
www.newsroomleadership.com—Edward Miller's reflections on leadership
www.asne.org/kiosk/editor/tae.htm—*The American Editor* magazine
www.poynter.org/subject.asp?id=14—Poynter site on leadership
www.poynter.org/subject.asp?id=47—Poynter on journalism and business values
www.freedomforum.org/templates/document.asp?documentID=16166—Art of Leadership
www.poynter.org/content/content_view.asp?id=1211—Media leadership links
www.roguecity.com/reference/MediaEthics.html—Comprehensive list of journalism links

---

Endnotes to Chapter 4:

[1] Herb Kelleher, "A culture of commitment," *Leader to Leader*, 4 (Spring 1997). Also available at <www.pfdf.org/leaderbooks/L2L/spring97/kelleher.html>, accessed August 13, 2003.

[2] Lewis C. Henry, ed., *Best Quotations for All Occasions* (Greenwich, Conn.: Fawcett Publications, 1962), 129.

[3] Kelleher, "A culture of commitment," *Leader to Leader*.

[4] Rosabeth Moss Kanter, "Power failure in management circuits," in *Executive Success: Making It in Management,* Eliza G.C. Collins, ed. (New York: John Wiley & Sons, 1983), 249.

[5] "Low and getting lower," *Columbia Journalism Review* (September-October 2001): 37.

[6] Max Weber, *The Theory of Social and Economic Organization,* A.M. Henderson and T. Parsons, trans. (New York: Oxford University Press, 1947), 328.

[7] Ibid., 238.

[8] Paul Hersey and Kenneth Blanchard, *Management of Organizational Behavior* (Englewood Cliffs, N.J.: Prentice-Hall, 4th ed., 1982), 178–79.

[9] Peter F. Drucker, *Managing the Non-Profit Organization: Principles and Practices* (New York: HarperBusiness, 1992), 21.

[10] Warren Bennis and Burt Nanus, *Leaders: The Strategies for Taking Charge* (New York: Perennial Library, 1986), 27.

[11] John E. Flaherty, *Peter Drucker: Shaping the Managerial Mind* (San Francisco: Jossey-Bass, 1999), 277. Copyright © 1999, Jossey-Bass. Reprinted by permission of John Wiley & Sons, Inc.

[12] Benjamin Franklin, *The Autobiography of Benjamin Franklin*, RocketEdition 1999 (Berkeley, Calif.: Treeless Press ePublishing, 1999), 119, 185.

[13] Al Neuharth, *Confessions of an S.O.B.* (New York: Doubleday, 1989), 108.

[14] James M. Kouzes and Barry Z. Posner, *The Leadership Challenge* (San Francisco: Jossey-Bass, 3rd ed., first paperback edition, 2003), 13–22. Copyright © 2002, John Wiley & Sons, Inc. This material is used by permission of John Wiley & Sons, Inc.

[15] Ibid., 32.

[16] Ibid., 37.

[17] Harvey Mackay, *Swim with the Sharks without Being Eaten Alive* (New York: William Morrow & Company, 1988), 76.

[18] William Dean Singleton, in keynote address at the state convention of the New Mexico Press Association, November 2, 2002.

[19] Ralph Metcalfe, "Innovation in industry," a 1981 presentation quoted in, *Leader to Leader*, Frances Hesselbein and Paul M. Cohen, eds. (New York: Free Press, 1999), 8.

[20] Robert Townsend, *Up the Organization: How to Stop the Organization from Stifling People*

and Strangling Profits (New York: Alfred A. Knopf, 2nd ed., 1970), 115.

[21] Robert E. Lloyd, in interview with Ben Berger at the Newhouse School of Communication in Syracuse, N.Y., March 17, 2003.

[22] Bennis and Nanus, *Leaders: The Strategies for Taking Charge*, 72.

[23] Kelleher, "A culture of commitment," *Leader to Leader*.

[24] Rosabeth Moss Kanter. Reprinted by permission of *Harvard Business Review*. From "The middle manager as innovator," (April 1982): 102. Copyright 1982 by Harvard Business School Publishing Corporation, all rights reserved.

[25] Kouzes and Posner, *The Leadership Challenge*, 269.

[26] Bob Nelson, *1001 Ways to Reward Employees* (New York: Workman, 1994).

[27] Mackay, *Swim with the Sharks without Being Eaten Alive*, 172–173.

[28] Townsend, *Up the Organization*, 184.

[29] Mackay, *Swim with the Sharks without Being Eaten Alive*, 173.

[30] Colin L. Powell, with Joseph E. Persico, *My American Journey* (New York: Random House, 1995), 264.

[31] Vance Packard, *The Pyramid Climbers* (New York: McGraw Hill, 1962), 170.

[32] Kouzes and Posner, *The Leadership Challenge*, 284.

[33] Kouzes and Posner, *The Leadership Challenge*, 287.

[34] BrainyQuote, <www.brainyquote.com/quotes/quotes/c/q130921.html >, accessed August 7, 2003.

[35] John M. Lavine and Daniel B. Wackman, *Managing Media Organizations: Effective Leadership of the Media* (White Plains, N.Y.: Longman Inc., 1988), 218.

[36] Warren Bennis, "The 4 competencies of leadership," *Training & Development Journal* (August 1984): 14–19.

[37] Mackay, *Swim with the Sharks without Being Eaten Alive*, 78.

[38] Kouzes and Posner, *The Leadership Challenge*, 124.

[39] Michael S. Herrick, owner of Matter*form* Media, interview with author, June 15, 2001.

[40] H. Norman Schwarzkopf, quoted at <www.vfmac.edu/acad_leadership.shtml> (he was a 1952 graduate of Valley Forge Military Academy and College), accessed August 3, 2002.

[41] Bennis and Nanus, *Leaders: The Strategies for Taking Charge*, 69.

[42] Ardyth Sohn with Christine Ogan and John Polich, *Newspaper Leadership* (Englewood Cliffs, N.J.: Prentice-Hall, 1986), 16–17.

[43] Ibid., 20.

[44] Marty Linsky, *The View From the Top* in The Poynter Papers: No. 10 (St. Petersburg, Fla.: The Poynter Institute for Media Studies, 1997).

[45] Peter F. Drucker, *Managing the Non-Profit Organization: Principles and Practices* (New York: HarperBusiness, 1992), 40.

[46] Franklin, *The Autobiography of Benjamin Franklin*, 119.

[47] E.C. Jones, "Interpreting interpersonal behavior: The effects of expectancies," *Science* (1986): 41–46.

[48] Kouzes and Posner, *The Leadership Challenge*, 322

[49] D. Coleman, "Optimism leads to health, wealth, research shows," *San Jose Mercury News*, February 5, 1987, 1F–2F.

[50] Aparna Surendran of Knight Ridder Newspapers, as published in "Outlook on aging tied to length of life," *Albuquerque Journal*, July 29, 2002, C3.

[51] Kouzes and Posner, *The Leadership Challenge*, 322.

[52] Lloyd, March 17, 2003.

[53] Dale Dauten, King Features Syndicate, as published in "Why Southwest is hiring," *Albuquerque Journal*, November 22, 2001, in Business Outlook section, 10.

[54] Mary Edrington of Drake University in a telephone interview with Ben Berger, March 20, 2003.

[55] Thomas J. Peters and Robert H. Waterman Jr., *In Search of Excellence: Lessons from America's Best-Run Companies* (New York: Harper & Row, 1982), 291.

[56] Oren Harari, *The Colin Powell Leadership Primer* (New York: McGraw-Hill, 2002).

[57] Colin L. Powell, with Joseph E. Persico, *My American Journey* (New York: Random House, 1995), 395.

[58] Oren Harari, "Quotations from Chairman Powell: A Leadership Primer," *Management Review* (December 1996): 36.

[59] Linsky, *The View From The Top*, 5.

[60] The "disappointed optimists" point of view was provided by Thomas L. Beell, a journalism professor at Iowa State University, in an e-mail to the author, December 27, 2002.

[61] Linsky, *The View From The Top*, 5.

[62] Ibid., 7.

[63] Aaron Moore, "Small links, big chain: Community Newspaper Holdings and the power of the cluster," *Columbia Journalism Review* (July–August, 1999): 14.

[64] Geneva Overholser, "Editor Inc.," a chapter written for *Leaving Readers Behind: The Age of Corporate Newspapering,* Gene Roberts, editor in chief, and Thomas Kunkel and Charles Layton, general editors, (Fayetteville, AR: University of Arkansas Press, 2001), 176.

[65] Ibid, 179.

[66] Underwood, *When MBAs Rule the Newsroom*, 15.

[67] Underwood, *When MBAs Rule the Newsroom*, 42–43.

[68] Flaherty, *Peter Drucker: Shaping the Managerial Mind*, 249.

[69] Ibid.

[70] Ibid.

[71] Scott Adams, *The Dilbert Principle* (New York: HarperCollins Publishers, 1996), 14.

[72] Ibid., 12.

[73] "Parkinson's Law," on <www.wikipedia.org/wiki/C._Northcote _Parkinson>, accessed September 16, 2002.

[74] C. Northcote Parkinson, *Parkinson's Law, or the Pursuit of Progress* (London: John Murray, 1957), 2.

[75] Dale Dauten, King Features Syndicate, as published in "Jerks, like vampires, see nothing in a mirror," *Albuquerque Journal,* May 23, 2002, Business Outlook section, 10.

[76] Ibid.

CHAPTER 5
DECISION-MAKING

NOTHING IS MORE fundamental to leadership and effective management than the ability to make the right decisions, make them in a timely way, and implement them correctly. A close second is, on those times that you make the wrong decision, to be insightful and courageous enough to admit you made a mistake and come up with a better alternative decision.

Ironically, the most effective decision-makers spend little time, relatively speaking, in actually making decisions. They spend more of their time obtaining information and processing it, they delegate authority so others closer to the problem can respond to it with them providing only oversight and ultimate responsibility, and they organize their systems so that many decisions are on automatic pilot.

On the last point, it is not necessary, for example, to continually reassess and therefore re-decide many issues that repeatedly come before a business in the course of a day. In other words, reserve decision-making for the important decisions that arise only at your level in the organization. Until others prove to be unreliable, trust those below you with their decision-making duties and do not ambush those above you. Concentrate on the decisions expected of you, and even then first ensure they are worthy of your attention before spending time and energy on them.

Resist the very real temptation to tackle easy questions—don't waste your talents on trivia or routine decisions, neither of which have any meaningful consequences. Those should be delegated or at least designated as a low priority. Robert Lloyd, a former editor and a visiting professor at the Newhouse School of Communication at Syracuse University, believes that, "A key concept of time management is to get the hardest or most difficult task done first."[1]

The first test of a decision-worthy issue is whether there is both risk and opportunity involved.

Frame the problem as an opportunity versus risk situation, if you want, but consider the opportunity first and then look at the risks. Many people mistakenly look at the risks first and become preoccupied with all of the things that can go wrong. The natural consequence of such an approach is "analysis paralysis." Usually nothing gets done by such a person—and we all have met managers who fall into this trap. If you want to lose the respect of your staff, peers and bosses, just become the type of manager who either cannot make a decision or is constantly changing decisions, which are two manifestations of the same problem.

What is decision-making?

FOR STARTERS, we should define what we mean by decision-making. It sounds at first as if making decisions comes naturally to leaders, but most will tell you that making decisions—wise ones, anyway—is the most challenging aspect of their work and one that requires insightful analysis to at least minimize the doubts. And there always are doubts for the big ones.

Peter F. Drucker points out that most business books advise decision-makers to start their process by considering the facts. But he notes that what makes business management so difficult (and so interesting) is that there usually are far more opinions to start with than facts.

"A decision is a judgment," he tells us. "It is a choice between alternatives. It is rarely a choice between right and wrong. It is at best a choice between 'almost right' and 'probably wrong'—but much more often a choice between two courses of action, neither of which is probably more nearly right than the other."[2]

Not only that, he says, it is a "risk-taking judgment," and it is irresponsible for an executive to approach a problem while thinking there is only one answer because that is the classic definition of a closed mind.

One alternative always is to do nothing. Many problems do indeed work themselves out without need for intervention, and others really should be delayed. The danger comes when managers mistakenly think they have found one of those kinds of problems, when in fact a decision actually is needed. You must make a decision, for example, if the condition will degenerate through inaction, and you must make a decision if an opportunity is about to be lost.[3]

Decisions usually are made under conditions of uncertainty, in which not all the information is available on the situation, the possible alternatives, or the consequences of different actions.[4] Economist Herbert A. Simon explored this aspect of decision-making in detail, and subsequently he received the Nobel Prize in economics for his study.

It is frustrating, perhaps even maddening at times, but virtually no significant decision is 100 percent certain in its outcome. This is as true in business as it is in gambling or the big and little decisions we all have in our personal lives. Uncertainty sometimes can be reduced by analyzing the alternatives and their outcomes.

Colin L. Powell even has a mathematical formula of sorts to demonstrate the need for a manager to make a decision **before** all the facts are in. "I have a timing formula, P=40 to 70, in which P stands for the probability of success and the numbers indicate the percentage of information acquired . . . . I don't wait until I have enough facts to be 100 percent sure of being right, because by then it is almost always too late. I go with my gut feeling when I have acquired information somewhere in the range of 40 to 70 percent."[5]

Commenting on that, educator and consultant Oren Harari states, "Powell's advice is don't take action if you have only enough information to give you less than a 40 percent chance of being right, but don't wait until you have enough facts to be 100 percent sure, because by then it is almost always too late. His instinct is right: Today, excessive delays in the name of information-gathering breeds 'analysis paralysis.' Procrastination in the name of reducing risk actually increases risk."[6]

Stay mentally in charge in your decision-making. As former editor Robert H. Giles emphasizes, "A decision born of strong anger or disappointment often is an unwise decision."[7]

In making their decisions, the managers' only tools for implementing the decision are the company's resources.

As for resources, the study of macroeconomics tells us there really are only two: (1) **Time,** and (2) **Money.** They are the universals, or common denominators, of macroeconomics theory.[8]

To a degree, time and money are interchangeable. For example, if you have enough money, but need time, you can hire more people to get the job done. If you have time, but not enough money, you can work longer and cheaper. Obviously, there are other forms of resources, but all of them can be traced back to time and money.

Decisions can be made by one person or by two or more people working together as a group. It takes less time, and is certainly less troublesome, for one person to make a decision. However, the more important and complex the decision, the more likely it is that the best decision might be reached by the "two (or more) heads are better than one" dynamic of the group decision-making process. Groups make some decisions better than individuals do, and there's more on these dynamics later.

Every decision made in business is intended in some way to advance toward the organization's goals, or in some other way support the organization's goals. One might think that the maximum effect of every decision would be the objective, but Simon noted that is impossible because no one can know everything they need to know about a complex problem. Therefore, he coined the term "bounded rationality" to describe how managers try to achieve a satisfactory result—not necessarily the maximum result—in moving the organization forward toward its goals.

The steps to making decisions

SEVERAL MODELS for the steps of decision-making have been developed for quality decisions. Despite their differences, they all include in their first step the task of addressing Drucker's main concern, which is to define what the problem is. Besides Drucker, there are several different decision-making sequences from other theorists such as G.P. Huber, Ricky W. Griffin, and Ardyth B. Sohn. They share much common ground; all call for defining the problem, generating alternative solutions, implementing a solution, and then evaluating whether the solution worked.

The different lists of steps in the process of making decisions are all merely variations on Drucker's first list in *The Practice of Management,* published in 1954. There he listed five steps:[9]

(1) Define the problem. You must distinguish between the problem and its symptoms. As Drucker explains: "What appear at first sight to be the elements of the problem rarely are the really important or relevant things. They are at best symptoms. And often the most visible symptoms are the least revealing ones . . . . The first job in decision-making is therefore to find the real problem."[10]

This first step is the most important and deserves a lot of time, despite all of the books purporting to tell you how to make a fast decision. As an example, suppose a survey reveals that readership of a magazine is declining. That poses a need for an aggressive solution, but to define the problem, management needs to consider all possible causes and then determine the most likely culprit. In this example, the problem might eventually be identified as lackluster photography and writing compared with rivals—revealing that the declining readership is the symptom, not the problem.

(2) Analyze the problem, or put another way, classify it by determining who must make the decision (individual or group), who must be consulted in making it, and who must be informed. The manager will never be able to get all of the facts he or she would like to have, but there must be an understanding of what facts are and are not obtainable so a determination of risk can be made on when the decision will be reached.

(3) Develop alternative solutions. By this, Drucker specifically states he does not mean an "either-or" situation. Those are only two out of many alternatives available for every problem.

In the magazine example, possible solutions might be to reorganize the copy desk over the next month so it is more efficient in catching errors; to hire a hotshot writer within three months; to hire a page designer in the next month; to re-train the current photography staff by sending each person to seminars over the next six months; to determine what digital photography equipment is needed and acquire it in two months; to investigate and change printers for better quality in two months; to promote the new look of the magazine in a series of print and broadcast ads developed by the magazine's public relations and advertising staff as soon as the first issue with new personnel is on the racks, no later than the fourth month; and to print color on more inside pages.

These are just some of the many possible solutions, all of which, like the goals, have specific time frames for completion.

Depending on resource limitations, perhaps the company can afford to risk only enough time or money to implement one solution, possibly involving the merger of a couple of proposed solutions. It is unlikely that any company can afford to risk enough resources to implement all of the solutions, no matter how helpful they might be in the overall plan.

(4) Decide upon the best solution. In weighing the different alternatives, the manager must use four criteria to pick the best solution out of the possibilities: (1) the risk versus the gains of each alternative; (2) what will give the best returns for the least effort; (3) the timing, depending on whether the solution needed is an urgent one or if it is one that can be long-range; and (4) the limitation of resources. The manager must gradually weed out the alternatives until the most promising ones remain.[11]

Management, probably through a group or teams, selects the solution that will have the greatest impact for the least risk of time and money, and that decision is made after thoroughly collecting and analyzing pertinent facts for each solution. No matter what solution is ultimately picked as the one promising the most return for the least risk, the alternatives are kept as a backup. If the first solution does not work, then one of the others might be revived and tried.

Keep in mind the advice of business executive Chester I. Barnard: "The decision may be not to decide. This is a most frequent decision, and from some points of view probably the most important."[12] Some problems really do solve themselves if just left alone. *New York Times* publisher Arthur O. Sulzberger Jr. said it a different way when he advised that no problem should be solved before its time.

(5) Making the decision effective. Implementing a decision requires that people understand what changes are needed. "A manager's decision is always a decision concerning what other people should do," Drucker points out.[13] So implementing a decision requires the manager to make sure people not only understand what changes and actions are needed, but that they also share the manager's goal for the action to be taken.

There really has been no decision made until someone is assigned to implement it. And no decision is final until it has been put into place, and then re-evaluated for effectiveness and possible change. Murphy's Law, and our own personal experiences, alert us to the fact that rarely, if ever, will every detail go according to plan satisfactorily. Every action plan coming out of a decision needs to be changed, or at least adjusted. You should assume that as a given and not be concerned when you find you need to fine-tune a decision down the road—or even change course completely.

Therefore, once you have made a decision, you must commit to putting it into action. Otherwise, you have only a good intention—and we all know what the road to hell is paved with. Remember, there are only two resources available to a business to implement a decision: time and money. Every decision must be accompanied with a detailed plan of action on the exact commitment of these resources in any of the myriad forms either can take.

Everyone including Drucker seems to agree that a sixth step also is crucial to the decision-making process. After the decision is implemented, it needs to be monitored so that adjustments—or perhaps an entirely different solution—can be made in a timely and effective way.

Monitoring the solution is an important, and often neglected, part of the decision-making process. Too often, a solution is implemented with grandiose assumptions. If the solution is not working, then selection of a new alternative is required.

All of these steps can apply to either individual or team decision-making, both of which will be discussed in more detail later.

Risk-taking in the decision process

YOU CAN'T GET something for nothing. You can't win without taking some risks. Facing and handling risk is what gets the adrenaline going for the best managers and entrepreneurs, though that is exactly what unnerves lesser people.

"Most of the significant decision-making in contemporary organizations is done under a state of uncertainty," management professor Ricky W. Griffin warns. "Intuition, judgment and experience always play major roles in the decision-making process under conditions of uncertainty."[14]

No decision can be made without some chance of losing resources of time and money committed to accomplishing the goal. The risk determines the importance of a decision. No organization would allocate a large percentage of its resources to an unimportant decision or project. Similarly, if the stakes are high, such as the survival of the organization, significant resources might be allocated in an all-or-nothing attempt to succeed. The greater the risk for the company, the more important is the decision. (Risk is a relative term, of course. Allocating $10 million and the time of 100 employees would be an overwhelming proportion of resources for even a large daily newspaper or television station, but it would be almost dismissively small and routine for the likes of the Walt Disney Company and Gannett.)

Decisions have different levels of risk, as we noted earlier, based on the resources needed to solve them. The first of what Drucker says are three kinds of risks is the trivial or **routine decision,** which he defines as, "The risk we can afford to take. If it goes wrong, it is easily reversible with minor damage."[15]

The real test of a manager's ability comes in the next two categories of decisions described by Drucker: the **irreversible decision,** when failure may do serious harm, and the **reactive or proactive decision** where the risk is great but one cannot afford not to take it.[16] In the latter decision, both the uncertainty and risk are so great that they are major decisions. As a result, they often will be delegated to a group or teams, which will be called on to recommend a final decision to the manager or at least provide the research and discussion the manager needs to make the final decision.

The presence of dissent is a positive and provocative asset in deciding important issues. There are many who say an important decision cannot be decided, or at least should not be decided, unless there is dissent, because disagreement forces everyone to consider more options and in turn leads to a much more effective understanding of both the opportunities and the risks at stake. Effective decision-makers often will, in fact, postpone an important decision if there is no one in disagreement. Unanimity on a critical solution you offer is not an affirmation of your genius, as you would like to think it is. Instead, it is a warning sign that you either have surrounded yourself with yes-people or that others have not come to comprehend the complexity and seriousness of the decision before them.[17]

While chairman of General Motors, Alfred P. Sloan Jr. reportedly said at a meeting of GM executives, "Gentlemen, I take it we are all in complete agreement on the decision here." When everyone nodded assent, Sloan added: "Then I propose we postpone further discussion of this matter until our next meeting to give ourselves time to develop disagreement and perhaps gain some understanding of what the decision is all about."[18]

You need the benefit of someone willing to challenge your solution, to force you to investigate it further. As Drucker puts it, "You want a critic—and one the organization respects."[19]

Drucker goes on to observe, "If you can bring dissent and disagreement to a common understanding of what the discussion is all about, you create unity and commitment. There is a very old saying—it goes back all the way to Aristotle and later on became an axiom of the early Christian church: 'In essentials, unity; in action, freedom; and in all things, trust.' And trust requires that dissent come out into the open, and that it be seen as honest disagreement."[20]

Neither Drucker's indispensable critic, nor an open discussion that includes dissent to reach a collaborative understanding, is possible in the approaches taken by some hard-charging and aggressive managers who have reputations as "strong leaders."

What are such people really like? Too often, bullying, rank-pulling and authoritarianism is mistakenly called strong leadership by those who are intimidated by such managers. CEOs or other ranking managers who insist on having their own way, and who railroad others with their narrow opinions, destroy all motivation for a team effort on anything.

Drucker says that such managers are guilty of using advocacy instead of inquiry in their decision-making process. In the long run, their strong-arm tactics do harm at many levels.

A manager pushing his or her ideas across through advocacy creates winners and losers among the members of what can only be considered a dysfunctional team, if it is a team at all. Whatever decision is reached is the sole property of the manager, for there is no sense of collective ownership involving anyone else.

By embracing inquiry instead of simple advocacy, a leader will encourage an open exchange of ideas by several people in an interplay of dissension and agreement that will lead to much more effective decisions.

Instead of handing down edicts, modern managers are turning to team-building, bringing several key persons into the analysis and alternative-forming stages. These steps lead up to "the buck stops here" decision that the managers ultimately will need to implement.

Two team-building models gaining favor with many corporations in recent years were explained in a recent issue of the *Harvard Business*

Review. They involve appointing two sub-groups instead of just turning a decision over to a single committee for consideration, as has been the traditional approach to both team-building and group decision-making in the past. These two models are called "Point and Counterpoint" and "Intellectual Watchdog." [21]

The first half of the process is the same for both models, wherein Sub-group A develops a proposal or solution, depending on the mandate. Its members then present their proposal with the arguments supporting it to the members of Sub-group B.

The second half of the process differs.

In Point and Counterpoint, Sub-group B meets separately and comes up with one or more alternatives, making a counter-proposal to Sub-Group A. Then the two sides sit down together and work out their differences to reach a consensus.

In Intellectual Watchdog, however, Sub-group B responds with critical analysis of what's both right and wrong with Sub-group A's proposal, engaging immediately in discussion. This leads to revisions by Sub-group A members in their proposal, which they re-present to Sub-group B until both groups reach a consensus.

As a leader, you cannot permit disagreement to escalate into conflict. It is the responsibility of a leader to ensure that disagreement is maintained as a positive provocateur for new thinking and creation of alternative actions, not as an agitator for personal and acrimonious conflict between those trying to arrive at a mutual understanding.

Generally speaking, the more difficult the decision, the more likely it is that the best decision will be reached through a team effort rather than through a unilateral decision by one authoritarian figure.

There certainly are grand examples of leaders making lonely but brilliant decisions, like Thomas Jefferson writing the Declaration of Independence mostly by himself. But teamwork is the way to the best solution in most complicated cases.

Categorizing decisions

ECONOMIST HERBERT A. SIMON noted that decisions are either **programmed** or **non-programmed.**[22] The first is really a non-decision of sorts because it is made automatically, according to a non-programmed decision that had to have been made in the past. Programmed decisions are repetitive with a routine procedure set up to deal with them. For example, writing a salary check each pay period is a programmed decision, with the amount and time of payment set up in advance. No manager sits around thinking about it. The decision is made automatically.

If a decision has low uncertainty and low risk, it often can be programmed effectively, instead of treating it as a question demanding additional time and effort. In a way, converting a problem into a programmed decision is a way of managerial delegating, although technically it is consigned to the organization's system rather than delegated to other people.

Unlike their counterpart, non-programmed decisions are novel, unstructured, and consequential. They have not arisen before, or are so important they require special attention. They require additional information and need to be considered by a manager or a delegated group. They require decision-making, full of uncertainty and risk.

Programmed and non-programmed decisions can exist in the same overall action. For example, accepted news values of proximity and impact make covering an accident that kills several people a programmed decision. Of course we will cover it. On the other hand, how we cover it might involve non-programmed decision-making at both the managerial and reporter levels.

For example, determining whether to use photographs of the corpses of local citizens could be a programmed positive decision with a supermarket tabloid, but it would be a controversial non-programmed negative decision for the local newspaper or television station.

Now we can see how the three levels of risk, discussed earlier by Drucker, fit in with Simon's two basic types of decision-making. In outline form they are:

    I. Programmed decision

        A. Routine

    II. Non-programmed decision

        A. Proactive

        B. Reactive

Analytical decision-making tools

ANALYTICAL TOOLS have been developed that enable the manager to work out on paper the right solution from several alternatives. Some of the most commonly encountered analytical tools developed for managers in resolving non-programmed challenges are Program Evaluation and Review Technique (PERT), Critical Path Method (CPM), the Decision Tree, various economic value of information formulas, and the "basic decision tool," which we'll discuss first.

The basic tool

This is the most basic decision-making tool of all. Some decisions are not nearly so difficult, and can be solved rather adequately with this simple tool. All that's required is a sheet of paper with a line drawn down the middle. Many of us learned this simple decision-making aid intuitively as an adolescent.

Simply write down all the reasons why you should do a particular action on one side of a page, and write down all of the reasons why you shouldn't do that same action on the other side. Go with whichever side has the most reasons. Of course, you need to be honest about listing all of the reasons on both sides for this to have any value.

Critical Path Method (CPM) and
Performance and Evaluation Technique (PERT)

Far more sophisticated are CPM, PERT and other analytical tools. Developed at about the same time, CPM (1957) was created by J.E. Kelly of Remington Rand and M.R. Walker of DuPont as a tool for scheduling maintenance in chemical plants,[23] while PERT (1958) was developed by the U.S. Navy to evaluate its Polaris Missile submarine fleet.[24] Both are used today as effective tools to estimate project completion times and thus determine and control project costs.

Originally, there were minor differences between the two methods. For example, PERT dealt more with probabilities while CPM was based on certainties in time and cost. Today, however, they are often thought of as one technique and are referred to together as PERT/CPM.[25]

Readers should be forewarned that what follows is an extremely simplified explanation of PERT/CPM, the Decision Tree, and analytical tools to determine the economic value of information, such as the Pay-Off Matrix.

Business books go into considerably more detail, with layers of diagrams, algorithms, algebra, and other details in construction of the tools. If you want that level of expertise, you need to either obtain an MBA degree or hire an accountant or some other consultant trained in such analysis.

The explanation here, though reduced to the basics, still should be helpful to anyone trying to solve problems that are not too complex.

Through the use of technology, the PERT/CPM visual tool for decision-making now can be quickly worked out on a computer loaded with the proper linear programming software. But this explanation sets forth how relatively uncomplicated problems can be set up and solved the old-fashioned way, on paper.

The first three steps in both PERT and CPM always were the same: (1) determine the tasks necessary to complete a project and how long each will take, (2) determine the sequence in which the different tasks need to be performed, and (3) construct a diagram showing the time sequences of the various activities.[26]

Think of PERT/CPM as a visual tool that can be used to diagram a complex problem in such a way as to find how to do two or more tasks simultaneously, thereby completing the work in the most efficient time.

A task list comprises the first two steps, listing all of the tasks and the time it will take to complete each as well as to determine what tasks must be preceded by others before they can be done.

An example follows for startup of a weekly newspaper or shopper. With slight changes, it also could be modified to apply to the basic steps of starting a radio station or some other media company. First there is the tasks list [27] that includes the first two steps of PERT/CPM. Arrange tasks in the order they must be done, then organize them into tracks that can be done simultaneously, along with an "implementation track" where all tracks come together to be implemented.

Tasks List

Task	Task Description	Predecessors	Time (e.g., wks.)
FACILITIES TRACK			
A	Find office location	None	6
B	Negotiate lease	A	2
C	Do renovations	A, B	8
D	Purchase computers, equipment	with C	2
PERSONNEL TRACK			
E	Hire editor	None	6
F	Planning of operations	with E	2
G	Hire and train staff	E, F	8
IMPLEMENTATION TRACK			
H	Do mockup and sales calls	A–G	4
I	Publish first issue for distribution	All	1
TOTAL			39 wks.

In this example, the tasks have been divided into a "facilities track" and a "personnel track" because it is felt the tasks in each could be accomplished concurrently.

With the chart as a guide, you then diagram it (the third step mentioned) in such a way as to determine what is the most efficient path—the critical path—through the diagram to determine how long it will take to accomplish all tasks.

Each task is assigned a code under the "task code" column. The "predecessors" column uses these codes to describe which tasks need to be completed before the particular task on that line can be completed. The estimated time for each individual task is noted in the final column. Obviously, the Herculean effort of starting up a weekly newspaper has been greatly over-simplified here for purposes of illustration.

Each task has been assigned, after careful study, a "most likely" time for its completion. At a glance, it would appear that the completion of the startup would take 39 weeks of total effort.

Can it be done faster?

Certainly, because the facilities and personnel tracks can be underway at the same time, and even some tasks, indicated by multiple "task codes" under the "predecessors" column, can be done concurrently.

The next step in PERT/CPM analysis is to diagram the tasks visually, using the task codes and putting in the times required for each in parenthesis, so the relationships can be seen among them. For example, Task A will take six weeks to complete and it is placed in the first box of the following diagram as A(6).

Facilities Track

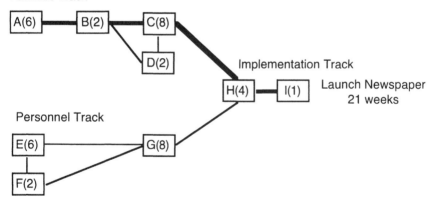

In working up the diagram, this exercise provides for three tracks of action: facilities (getting the physical location of the office ready), personnel (hiring the staff and getting ready to operate), and product creation through implementation (doing the mockup and actual issue).

The diagram lines up the facilities track on the top line and the personnel track on the lower line because these tasks will be completed concurrently. In the facilities track, we can drop Task E into a concurrent subtrack because the equipment can be purchased and installed while the remodeling is going on. Similarly, in the personnel track, we also can drop Task F into a separate subtrack because the editor can help do planning and newsstands once on board.

As you plot out the critical path, each square represents a task from the chart. The weeks in parenthesis will be added as they occur along the critical path to attain the expected time for completion. Some tasks are done concurrently. The "critical path" is the path taking the comprehensive start to completion time through the project, depicted here as the dark bold line going through the top line and dropping to the middle line leading to the newspaper's launch—a total of 21 weeks instead of the 39 indicated in the tasks chart.

Remember Murphy's Law at all times in your planning. If you need to answer to someone else for the successful completion of the project, it probably would be reckless to guarantee the 21-week completion time. But at least you know you can get it done much more quickly than the 39 weeks that would be required if each task was done one at a time.

The advantage and major addition that PERT originally provided over CPM was in PERT's break-down of the time required for each activity into optimistic, most likely, and pessimistic estimates.[28]

The original PERT users calculated a weighted average for the time of an activity by assigning a value of "1" to the pessimistic and optimistic guesses, and a value of "4" to the most likely estimate. The values are used in the following PERT formula:[29]

$$\text{EST. TIME} = \frac{(\text{optimistic} \times 1) + (\text{most likely} \times 4) + (\text{pessimistic} \times 1)}{\text{divided by 6}}$$

The exact equation as used in business texts, is:

$t_o + 4(t_m) + t_p \ / \ 6 = \text{estimated time of project.}$

You divide by six because one plus four plus one equals six, and you are calculating a weighted average of the time estimates, giving more weight to the most likely estimate than to the optimistic and pessimistic estimates. Again, PERT can involve complex statistical techniques and even include scheduling of "slack" times. This is a simplified version.

Re-consider the previous CPM flow diagram, and let's assume you used your "most likely" estimate for each step in the original Tasks Chart, which would mean that the answer of 21 weeks reached in your CPM diagram is your best guess. However, if everything went right, you can envision an optimistic completion estimate of 19 weeks, even while your most likely guess remains at 21 weeks. You also can see where things could go wrong, leaving you with a pessimistic worst-case estimate of 35 weeks. Using the PERT formula on these three completion alternatives would give you an estimated weighted average time of 23 weeks—which would be a more reliable estimate than the 21 weeks reached in the original critical path diagram.

For greatest accuracy, those weighted average times also could be calculated for each step in the process. The PERT estimate for each task then would be plugged into the diagram you've drawn, making it more reliable in coming up with a final reckoning of completion time. For example, on the first task:

Tasks list modified with PERT formula's calculation

Task Description	Optimistic time	Most Likely time	Pessimistic time	PERT calculation
FACILITIES TRACK				
Find office location	5	6	10	6.5

In this example, the first block on your diagrammed CPM chart would read "A(6.5)," thus containing the PERT calculation of 6.5 weeks instead of the original chart's most-likely estimate of 6 weeks. Each task would be recalculated for a PERT value.

It takes judgment and experience to come up with time estimates for PERT/CPM. Business author Tom Gorman suggests giving pessimistic estimates for tasks over which you have no direct control, as when you must depend on someone else to accomplish the task. When reporting to senior management using PERT/CPM, he suggests playing it even safer by giving only your pessimistic guess as if it's your best guess.[30] That might not fly in some organizations, but it is indicative of how these projections are, after all, only "guesses," even after research.

The Decision Tree

Another visual decision-making tool that also considers probability factors, like PERT, is the Decision Tree. PERT/CPM is used on a single project, while a Decision Tree usually is used when comparing alternative projects against each other.[31]

Let's use as our example a newspaper owner considering the possibility of starting a shopper in Albuquerque or Santa Fe. The owner has the resources of time and money only to do one or the other, but which one should it be? After hours of research, she finally believes she has some optimistic, most likely, and pessimistic estimates for the profits she could make at each city. Following are the owner's estimates for profits over the next five years:

Expected Profits Chart

Estimate	Albuquerque	Santa Fe
Optimistic	$600,000	$500,000
Most Likely	300,000	400,000
Pessimistic	200,000	200,000

The owner becomes an odds-maker now. Her market research leads her to believe the following percentages of possibility that the most likely guess will occur or that either the optimistic or pessimistic estimates will occur for each alternative. She draws up the following Decision Tree, showing the probability percentage of each possible outcome.[32]

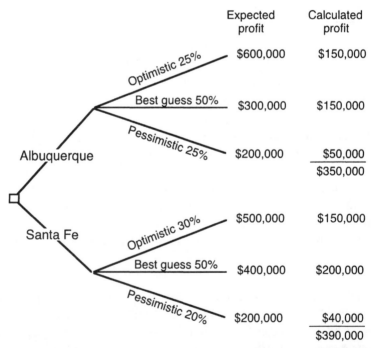

In this simplified Decision Tree, she multiplies the "expected profit" for each alternative by the probability percentage that research has assigned to each scenario to obtain the more accurate "calculated profit."

Of course, you can always decide to do nothing. That will avoid the risk of any loss, but it also will avoid the possibility of making any gain whatsoever. If nothing else, this exercise demonstrates the importance of doing something if you want to make a gain.

One other interesting development comes out of this particular Decision Tree. The figures in the Expected Profits Chart would seem at a glance to make Albuquerque the best choice. But multiplying each alternative's expected profit by the probability that could be expected, using the Decision Tree, shows that starting the shopper in Santa Fe would actually have a substantially higher overall calculated profit of $390,000, contrasted to Albuquerque's $350,000.

In actual practice, of course, this would be just one more helpful tool in making the final decision.

Decision Trees can become complex structures. In this example, perhaps there is a need to include an event (usually depicted with a circle) or another decision (usually depicted with a square)[33] occurring before the "calculated profit." These events might have their own probabilities branching off before a final estimate of profit can be obtained. There are several software programs to draw Decision Trees.

Decision Trees can be modified in many ways to determine almost any goal, not just financial ones as in this example.

The pay-off matrix

Innumerable formulas and mathematical computations have been developed to measure the economic value of information. Our Pay-Off Matrix solution requires the manager to come up with an estimate of the probability of success.

An example adapted from economist Robert H. Hayes involves a new product with an initial investment of $1,000,000.[34]

You calculated that if the product is successful there will be cash flows from that new product totaling $1,500,000. That would result in a 50 percent return, which sure sounds good to you and your accountant.

However, if the product performs poorly in the market, market research warns of a worst-case scenario of new cash flow totaling only $800,000—definitely a failure with a $200,000 loss from your original million-dollar investment.

Your job as the manager is to determine whether to take the risk that the product will be unsuccessful. You need an estimate of the probability of success or failure. Your research concludes that the probability of success is 70 percent, while the probability of failure is 30 percent. Instead of just crossing your fingers and picking whether to go with the product launch, you can more rationally base your decision on a weighted average of these two alternatives with the following "expected value" formula, which gives a weighted average for profit:[35]

Weighted Average Formula

Pct. × pos. estimate + pct. × neg. estimate – investment

In other words, for the stated example:

0.7(1,500,000) + 0.3(800,000) – 000,000 = weighted avg. profit

So: 1,050,000 + 240,000 – 1,000,000 = weighted avg. profit

And finally: 1,290,000 – 1,000,000 = $290,000 (your expected value)

You also could have a "most likely" probability in the equation.

Because the weighted average profit is a figure significantly larger than zero (which would be the profit you'd get if you sat on your hands), you as a manager can be more confident in taking the plunge and introducing the product. This is literally a calculated risk, with a number you can cite to justify your decision.

Your return in this example, as calculated by using weighted average, is not 50 percent, as projected in your most optimistic projection, but it is still a 29 percent return even when the pessimistic projection is played against it.

If your company needs a minimum 15 percent return on all its investments, you are justified in taking a chance on this project, and have a stronger argument for taking the chance when presenting it to your superiors in the company.

If the same calculation had resulted in zero or a minus number, because of different percentages of probability for success and failure, then you probably would not take the chance on introducing the product. The temptation of high profits from a successful product launch would be tempered by the realization that the product would be a big gamble.

By the way, actually you would be concerned with the "discounted present value" of this example's cash flows, but we won't be discussing that term until Chapter 8, so that bit of complexity was not included.

The best use of this formula is for those problems that deal with expected value or profit. This formula can assist you in deciding on a price for a product.

The computer spreadsheet

As mentioned earlier, linear programming software now is available to solve some of these decision-making problems. All of these tools depend to some degree on the ability to forecast the future, and nothing is more helpful and efficient in this regard than the computerized spreadsheet, using programs such as Excel and Lotus, to name just two.

A computer spreadsheet answers faster and better than anything else the question, "What if?"[36] Simply plug in different cost alternatives, and the spreadsheet program immediately recalculates everything else based on the new numbers. Because so many numbers are related throughout the budget, with later ones derived from the earlier ones put in, any changes in any stage of calculations will ripple mathematically through the rest of the spreadsheet.

The efficiency of the spreadsheet ensures that a manager can quickly try out every alternative that seems worth exploring, with little more time than what is required to simply type in the changes.

Hidden traps of decision-making

BLOCKING THE ability to reach prudent and perceptive decisions is the fact that we, as humans, are our own worst enemy in the decision-making process. We have a tendency to overestimate our abilities, to under-estimate many of the variables, and to make leaps of faith that often end up being much regretted in the glaring insight that comes with that damning retrospective observation of "if I had known then what I know now."

Because bad decisions can ruin a business or career, while good decisions can advance the cause of both, it is essential for managers to understand as much about decision-making as possible.

There are any number of strategies to follow, as mentioned earlier, to ensure that decisions are made rationally after thorough and insightful analysis. So why do some of the richest and smartest corporations still make huge mistakes? It is at least partly because the best research can be compromised by the hidden traps of decision-making, starting with heuristics.

Heuristics. Ordinarily heuristics help us in decisions, even if we don't know the meaning of the word. But it also can subconsciously fool us into making poor judgments. Our minds use "unconscious routines" to comprehend complex situations. These routines are called heuristics, and they serve us well—most of the time.[37]

For example, we don't spend a lot of our brain power on the minute-by-minute efforts to judge distance. Instead, our minds frequently rely on a heuristic (call it a mental short-cut) that equates size and clarity with proximity. The clearer or nearer to its actual size that an object appears, the closer we consider it to be. Similarly, if the object appears indistinct and smaller than it should be proportionately, then the farther away we assume it to be. This heuristic manifests itself in our depth perception.

However, most heuristics are not 100 percent reliable. While driving in foggy weather, for example, our eyes will trick our minds into thinking objects are farther away then they actually are, because they appear indistinct. The result can be disastrous for drivers. Researchers have found people tend to drive faster and closer together on fog-shrouded highways, their heuristic on distance judgment mistakenly leading them to believe they have more distance to the next vehicle than they really do. The results are frequent news reports such as the following (all in the spring of 2000): Sixty cars and trucks slammed into each other in thick fog near Windsor, Ontario, in Canada, killing 7 and injuring 45; a 63-vehicle chain-reaction pileup injured 15 people on a foggy highway near San Bernardino, Calif.; and 22 cars and trucks crashed into each other on a smoke-obscured highway near Wellborn, Fla., killing 3 and injuring 21 others.[38]

The devastating possibility of this heuristic failing even the most experienced operators is why pilots are required to rely on their cockpit instruments in addition to their eyes when landing in nighttime, fog or inclement weather.

Researchers have discovered a number of ways in which our minds, our biases and our at least occasional irrationality trick us into making poor judgments. The most dangerous aspect is that they are, as mentioned earlier, subconscious decisions, so that we fail to recognize them as mistakes even as we commit them. The best defense is awareness and knowledge about the most common traps.[39]

According to three authors of a *Harvard Business Review* article by the same title as this section, the primary decision-making traps are:[40]

The anchoring trap: Our minds give disproportionate influence to the first information we receive, making that initial information an anchor to subsequent judgments and decisions. This is true even if the first information is as innocuous as something you read in the paper or overheard in a conversation.

The most pernicious aspect of this trap is that others can purposely anchor you to their self-serving figures and impressions simply by mentioning them to you. And of course, you can use the same tactic against them.

The anchoring trap is used by adversaries all the time in negotiations, such as when they give you a proposed price that they know is too high. You also realize it is too high, so you counter it, but you unwittingly have nevertheless anchored your thinking to the originally suggested price and thus might very well make a counteroffer that is still higher than it should be.

Not only must you be aware that a savvy opponent might be trying to anchor you to their way of thinking, you must avoid anchoring your own staff to your preconceived notions when attempting to obtain honest feedback from them. Staff always will be influenced by a manager's opinion. Once they realize what answer the manager wants, they tend to give it.

Sometimes we don't need any outside influence. We are very capable of self-anchoring. For example, anchoring traps include stereotypes we carry about people, locations and situations. In business we frequently self-anchor to past events or a trend.

The anchoring trap probably is the most commonly encountered of the hidden traps, and you should be especially vigilant about it.

The status quo trap: All of us have a strong subconscious bias toward alternatives that perpetuate the status quo. Even the rebels among us don't want to change their own present state of being—only the status quo of others. We can see this tendency whenever a radically new product is introduced. The first automobiles, called "horseless carriages," looked very much like the horse-drawn buggies they replaced. The first news sites on the Internet looked like newspaper pages. Breaking from the status quo often takes a lot of self-confidence because it exposes the pioneer to criticism and ostracism.

The adoption of new technology is at least partly slowed by this status quo trap. I was an "early adopter" when Apple Computer began marketing its laser printers in 1985, buying one that year to set type for my newspapers. It replaced the unreliable, high-maintenance, chemical-loaded photo-typesetters used in nearly all weekly newspapers at the time, as well as at quite a few dailies, public relations and advertising firms, and magazines.

When I attended the Iowa Newspaper Association convention the following spring, my use of laser printers was greeted by other publishers with skepticism and even ridicule. Virtually all other publishers had numerous reasons why they should continue with the status quo of using their photo-typesetters. It was at least the devil they knew.

However, within five years, nearly all weekly newspapers in the state had converted to laser printers. Many publishers were forced to dump their photo-typesetters in the landfill or in an out-of-the-way storeroom because there no longer was a resale market for them.

An interesting thing to keep in mind when defending the status quo is that as more people adopt the change, at some point the status quo becomes seen as being old-fashioned and the new idea, though once scorned, becomes the new status quo.

"The more choices you have, the more likely you will want to stick with the status quo," the *Harvard Business Review* authors note. "In business, where sins of commission (doing something) tend to be punished more severely than sins of omission (doing nothing), the status quo holds a particularly strong attraction."[41]

The sunk cost trap: To protect our egos, we have a strong likelihood of making choices that justify past choices we have made, even when it seems obvious that the past choice was a poor one. The well-known aphorism that describes this trap is "throwing good money after bad."

Our past decisions become what economists call "sunk costs"—old investments of time or money that are now irrecoverable. Some corporate cultures, which do not look kindly on mistakes, make it difficult for managers, or anyone else for that matter, to come forward and admit that a previous decision was a poor one and that a new direction is required. Instead, people fearful of drawing repercussions on themselves will allow a failed project to flounder along, hoping some miracle will save them and bail them out of their predicament.

The best thing you can do once you realize a mistake has been made is to correct the mistake, or at least cut your losses by ceasing any actions set in motion by the original decision. It was Will Rogers who was first credited with the comment, "If you find yourself in a hole, the first thing to do is stop digging."

The confirming evidence trap: Common in all fields, we like to have people agree with us, and so we tend to seek affirming statements about our ideas from people we know will agree with us. The confirming evidence bias not only affects where we go to collect evidence but also how we interpret the evidence we receive.

"There are two fundamental psychological forces at work here," the *Harvard Business Review* authors state. "The first is our tendency to subconsciously decide what we want to do before we figure out why we want to do it. The second is our inclination to be more engaged by things we like rather than things we dislike."[42]

The framing trap: This goes to Drucker's point that the first step in making a decision is to frame the question (define the problem). Everything else goes wrong if the problem is defined incorrectly in the beginning. It can be like buttoning a shirt but starting with the wrong button. Everything seems to be going fine as you work with one button after another, and it is not until the very end that you discover that the whole process was ruined by the very first mis-step.[43]

The framing trap is closely related to other traps. A frame can establish the status quo or introduce an anchor early on in the decision-making process. It can dwell on sunk costs, or lead people to confirming evidence.

Estimating and forecasting traps: Many of us think we are competent, perhaps even brilliant, at making estimates of variables such as time, distance, weight and volume. Such estimates are the very stuff of heuristics again. Our biggest danger is when we assume that our abilities with such variables carry over into making estimates or forecasts about uncertain events.

This particular trap usually manifests itself in one or more of the following uncertainty traps, listed here as three subcategories of estimating and forecasting traps.[44]

(1) Overconfidence—we tend to be overconfident in our accuracy, which can lead to errors in judgment when, for instance, we're determining optimistic, most likely and pessimistic projections in PERT/CPM or decision tree analysis;

(2) Prudence—when faced with risky decisions, we tend to "play it safe" by being overly prudent, or overly cautious. But this can skew results, especially if a decision is going through several departments and every one of them puts a worst-case spin on the outcome, resulting in a totally unrealistic probability model in the end. Too much prudence can sometimes be as counter-productive as too little;

(3) Recallability—A dramatic or traumatic event in your own life can distort your thinking, leading you to believe that the likelihood of it happening again is far greater than it really is. For example, my car was once rear-ended while I was trying to make a left turn, and I now find myself with a far greater dread about this happening again than is statistically reasonable.

The worst news about these hidden traps is that not only can they be encountered in isolation, each can also be piled on top of another so they work in concert, really exacerbating the situation. Your best defense is to know these hidden traps exist and understand how they work.

Who are the decision-makers?

DECISIONS can be made either by individuals or groups. In some cases where quick and authoritative decisions are required, strong leaders will not hesitate to make the decisions themselves. Other times, when issues are complex, require intensive research or there is no need for quick action, the best decision-making might come from groups.

All leaders need to be aware of when decisions are best made quickly by an individual and when the organization is better served through consideration by a committee, board or other group. Both forms of decision-making have their strengths and weaknesses.

The main advantage of the individual making a decision is speed. Major advantages of a group making a decision are that the decisions often are based on more complete research and analysis of alternatives, and also that people involved in a group decision are much more inclined to go along with a decision than if it is handed down by one individual.[45]

Individual decision-making styles

One great intangible advantage in individual decision-making by the best leaders is that their judgment and experience can result in an intuitive decision of a quality that no one else in the organization can match. This intuitive ability enables them to make creative break-throughs in making decisions that are seen as ingenious. Others are left wondering, "How did he figure that out?" and, "How did she know that would work?" When a person of such intuitive abilities is leading the organization, none of the usual rules apply on whether a decision is better handled by a group or by the individual.

On the other hand, not all organizations are led by the brilliant— though they usually are led by competent people who genuinely want to accomplish the best job possible. To such people, timing and action can be an effective tactic.

In business, sometimes doing something only half-right immediately is better than waiting for a committee to come up with a more perfect solution days, weeks or months later. Similarly, even making a wrong decision is sometimes less harmful than failing to make a decision.

The Dynamic Decision Maker makes a point that managers are either "satisficers" or "maximizers" in their decision-making styles. It defines the first as a fast-action, worry-about-it-later type, and the latter as analytical and wanting to know all the information available before acting.[46]

The authors also identify two styles that you don't want to be. They talk about "searchers" who can never reach a decision, and "lurchers" who seemingly make a decision without giving any thought to it at all.[47]

They describe five styles used by individuals, though they note that no one style is best. Each style has its own strengths and weaknesses, and the one used by an individual will depend on the personality of the decision-maker and the situation.[48] The five individual styles are:[49]

Decisive Style: This is favored by satisficers who are uni-focused in the sense that once they make a decision they rarely alter the course afterward. These folks prize action, speed, efficiency and consistency, and once a decision is made they move on to the next problem. Sometimes decisions are made too fast.

Flexible Style: Like the decisive style, the flexible style decision-makers also are satisficers who move fast, but they are more adaptable in being willing to change direction if the first decision does not seem to be working. These leaders never fall in love with an earlier decision and can quickly drop one tactic in favor of another as the situation changes.

Hierarchic Style: These leaders are uni-focused, like the decisive style, but are maximizers. They use all of the information they can get to make detailed and specific solutions. They are looking for the one best solution, not necessarily the most expedient or quickest decision. They often will have layers to the solution, with various back-up strategies in place in case their first decision fails them.

Integrative Style: Multi-focused, like the flexible style, these leaders also are maximizers. Like the hierarchic decision-makers, the integrative folks use a lot of information in researching their decision. However, rather than trying to settle in on one decision, these leaders come up with a variety of alternatives and often pursue two or more courses of action simultaneously.

Systemic Style: Some maximizers make frequent use of both the hierarchic and integrative styles, proceeding in a two-stage decision process. First, they approach a problem as an integrative would, using information from different perspectives and laying out alternatives. Then the systemic style of decision-maker shifts into a hierarchic mode, judging the alternatives from one or more values they hold. It is multi-focused like the integrative style in the beginning but more like the hierarchic in the later stages.

Often managers will exhibit a combination of these styles and are not so easily categorized as the researchers might indicate. From this list, can you pick out the individual decision-making style that you seem to prefer?

Group decision-making styles

Group decision-making obviously is more time-consuming than individual decision-making, but sometimes that can be an advantage. Both governmental and corporate bureaucracies are criticized for having lengthy, complicated procedures for making decisions that involve legions of people before anything is finalized. But the lengthy process might actually be advantageous because it gives sufficient time to determine and fully explore all of the alternatives.

Committees can use this additional time to over-analyze problems, leading to the observation that a labyrinth is a hallway put together by a committee.

The most serious danger of group decision-making, however, is the very human phenomenon known disparagingly as "groupthink." First explained by Irving I. Janis in 1982, it occurs when group members identify so closely with other members of their group that they go along with each other and achieve unanimity without adequately analyzing the alternatives.[50]

Janis pointed out that groupthink can destroy any advantage of group decision-making if people "become more concerned with retaining the approval of the fellow members of their work group than with coming up with good solutions to the tasks at hand."[51]

When delegating problems to a group, managers must be ever vigilant of the possibility of groupthink emerging instead of a sound decision. Janis said the groups most vulnerable to groupthink are those that have an exaggerated opinion of power or infallibility, are closed-minded, or impose pressures on members for conformity.[52]

Generally speaking, however, if over-thinking and groupthink can be avoided, groups usually have the "two heads are better than one" advantage in making decisions. The quality of a group's final decision usually is superior to any one individual's ability.

Just like individuals, groups also exhibit different decision-making styles. There are at least 10 ways that groups reach decisions. The first seven were described in the 1975 book *Joining Together*, which was in its eighth edition by 2000. They are:[53]

Decision by authority without group discussion: The boss appoints a committee, and then the boss or a designated sub-boss heads the committee and tells everyone what the decision is going to be. This is a group decision in name only. Ill feelings among group members usually lead them to not support the decision, and perhaps even sabotage it.

Decision by expert: Sometimes there is one person in the group whose expertise on the issue at hand is so superior to anyone else's that other members simply defer to the expert. While other members might concede that the expert is right, there are no group dynamics to ensure that the members will work to support the decision. There might even be resentment by members not happy about being on a group where their opinions were not valued.

Decision by averaging individuals' opinions: This is often used when it is difficult to get everyone together for meetings, when a decision is so urgent that there isn't time for group discussion, and when there are not enough skills and information among the members to make the decision any other way. There is little commitment from the members to work for the goal decided on, and there is little to no group discussion.

Decision by authority after group consideration: There's some benefit of group discussion, but in the end everyone has to do what the authority running the group wants, and they know that and sometimes resent it. This tends to lead to meetings where everyone nods their heads in agreement as the boss tells them what to think. Sometimes a brave soul will speak up and be able to alter the authority's direction.

Decision by majority vote: If the issue before the group is hotly contended, this can leave an alienated minority after the decision is shoved down their throats by a majority vote. Majority vote can be used best when complete member commitment is not necessary to put a plan of action into effect, or when a decision is not very important. Most people do not like serving on such groups because they believe the situation gets too politicized.

Decision by minority: This is useful for routine decisions, or when the group's work must be delegated to a subcommittee because all members cannot meet together or the members are under excessive time pressure. Any member not serving on the subcommittee is effectually shut out of the process, which can lead to resentment or lack of commitment.

Decision by consensus: This is the most time-consuming, energy-intensive route in group decision-making, but almost invariably it also is the most successful in coming up with high-quality, well-thought-out decisions. When serious or complex problems are to be solved and commitment from everyone is needed to ensure the decision's success, this uses the talents of all of the members. This method is difficult to use in an emergency situation very effectively.

The final three types of group decision-making were added to the original seven in the 1997 book, *Leading Your Team to Excellence*. Its author made a point of noting that a group is not necessarily a team. All members need to share the same mission and the same commitment to realizing the goals of that mission and be able to trust each other, if a group is to coalesce into a team.[54] The remaining three types of group decision-making profiles are:[55]

Decision by default: Sometimes a decision is arrived at by reaching no decision. Remember, no decision always should be one of the alternatives at least considered in the decision-making process. Sometimes the best action is to do nothing—at least for the time being. Doing nothing might be the right response, though it can leave people elsewhere in the organization somewhat confused if there is no communication on the outcome.

Self-authorized decisions: There are times when one or more strong-willed individuals may assume they have the authority to make the decision for the group, whether they do or not. Other members might even be taken by surprise by the authority wrested from the group by these self-authorized individuals. This can lead to the most contentious aftermath of any of the scenarios.

Decision by clique: One of the hallmarks of human interaction in any situation is that people tend to join forces into little groups, or cliques, and try to impose their will on everyone else who is not a member of the clique. This can even happen in committees appointed to study a corporate problem. When it does, the usual result is the formation of an opposing clique—and nothing gets done.

Whether non-programmed decisions are being made by individuals or groups, they can be placed into three categories on the basis of time.

• "Immediate" decisions must be made quickly, within hours, minutes or even seconds. Deadlines often force decisions to be made immediately in media companies, and they virtually always are individual decisions by reporters and editors.

• "Short-term" decisions don't need to be made immediately, and are often done by small groups in a formal or informal basis. A short-term decision can even be two people talking together about what course of action to take, or an individual making a unilateral decision.

• "Long-term" decisions are complex and look to the future, and therefore they almost always are delegated to a group decision-making process. Thus, they take longer to finalize. Many immediate and short-term decisions typically are implemented in the process of making the final long-term decision.

When making decisions or engaging in any kind of planning a leader should first conduct a "S.W.O.T. analysis," which means that every step of decision-making and planning must take into consideration the strengths and weaknesses of the company and the opportunities and threats of the situation. Not only is a S.W.O.T. analysis conducted of your own company, but it also is conducted of any and all competitors.

As with most human activity, decision-making can be made more effective and productive with study and experience. There are innumerable books in libraries and Web sites on decision-making dynamics.

CASE STUDY   *Ok, Folks, You Can*
                    Stop Meeting Now

by LESLIE-JEAN THORNTON
State University of New York, New Paltz

What do you do when a team of journalists in your newsroom simply won't disband?

This was the case for a group of education writers who worked for a large newspaper in the country's heartland. The paper, which had gone through troubled times that included top management crises and significantly declining circulation, created the team when a new editor arrived full of vision and change.

Although there was much grumbling and dissension at first about the move from a traditionally hierarchical newsroom to one built around teams, this group found the new structure worked well, allowing the reporters greater breadth in their coverage and a system in which they felt they had "backup."

In short, they bonded—helped, perhaps, by their location in a suburban bureau rather than in the main newsroom downtown.

When that editor left the paper a few years later, the education team had established routines, goals and interpersonal ties. But the editor had left under duress and that was to have an effect on the team. The newsroom had complained about him in strong terms, and the changes he had made at the paper in both structure and tone were still not to everyone's liking. When a new editor was hired, it was announced that many of the changes that had been made would be changed back—including a move away from teams.

The education team decided to take a stand: No. We like things the way they are, and we don't want to go back to working independently of each other. We like sharing story ideas and brainstorming. We like working together. We even like being away from the newsroom.

The new editor, intent on imposing discipline and order, didn't buy it. Although some of the education writers were told they would continue covering education issues but would answer to an assignment editor with responsibilities beyond education, others in the team were reassigned to new beats. Everybody was ordered back to newsroom desks. Within weeks, two of the reassigned writers left for jobs on other papers.

The members of the former team, however, didn't let go of each other

—even those who had changed jobs and papers. They set up an Internet "ring" so that they were in contact with each other on a daily, if not more frequently, basis. They continued to run story ideas by each other and share information. More than a year after the transition, they were going strong. Several of them were bitter, though. If pressed, they'd tell you they felt underappreciated and, frankly, betrayed. The best that could be said about the ex-team's general reaction to the new administration was "we'll wait and see."

ASSIGNMENT:

• Drawing on what you know of management theories, explain what's going on in this newsroom.

• How might both of the new editors have created a more amicable and workable newsroom?

• There are advantages and disadvantages to creating strong teams. What are they and what consequences do they have for non-team colleagues in the newsroom? For management? For team members? Explain the dynamics involved.

• What do you make of the e-mail connections that continued to link former team members? As a manager, is this something you would nurture or discourage—assuming you even knew about it? Are there positive aspects that are good for the profession or does the practice simply undermine authority?

ACKNOWLEDGEMENT:

The scenario is hypothetical but loosely based on true events at more than one newspaper.

AUTHOR:

Leslie-Jean Thornton teaches news media management and journalism at the State University of New York at New Paltz. She was editor of several newspapers in Connecticut and New York. Before beginning work on her doctorate as a Freedom Forum Fellow, she was an editor at The Virginian-Pilot.

 *Suggested Web sites:*

www.auburn.edu/~garriro/tam.htm — Roger W. Garrison on time and money macroeconomics
www.poynter.org/subject.asp?id=47 — Poynter on journalism and business values
www.Accel-Team.com — Management productivity tips

Endnotes to Chapter 5:

[1] Robert Lloyd in an interview with Ben Berger at the Newhouse School of Communication at Syracuse University, March 17, 2003.

[2] Peter F. Drucker, *The Effective Executive* (New York: Harper & Row, 1966–67), 143.

[3] Ibid., 155.

[4] Ricky W. Griffin, *Management* (Boston: Houghton Mifflin, 1984), 203.

[5] Colin L. Powell, with Joseph Persico, *My American Journey* (New York: Random House, 1995), 393.

[6] Oren Harari, "Quotations from Chairman Powell: A Leadership Primer," *Management Review* (December 1996): 36.

[7] Robert H. Giles, *Newsroom Management* (Detroit, Mich.: Media Management Books, 8th ed., 1995), 169.

[8] Roger W. Garrison, "Time and money: The universals of macroeconomic theory," on <www.auburn.edu/~garriso/b6time.htm>, accessed August 1, 2002.

[9] Peter F. Drucker, *The Practice of Management* (New York: Harper & Brothers, 1954), 350–369.

[10] Ibid., 353.

[11] Ibid., 362–363.

[12] Chester I. Barnard, *The Functions of the Executive* (Cambridge, Mass.: Harvard University Press, 7th ed., 1948), 193.

[13] Ibid., 364.

[14] Griffin, *Management*, 201.

[15] Peter F. Drucker, *Managing the Non-Profit Organization: Principles and Practices* (New York: HarperBusiness, 1992), 123.

[16] Ibid.

[17] David A. Garvin and Michael A. Roberts. Reprinted by permission from *Harvard Business Review*. "What you don't know about making decisions," (September 2001): 110. Copyright 2001 by Harvard Business School Publishing Corporation, all rights reserved.

[18] Drucker, *The Practice of Management*, 470.

[19] Drucker, *Managing the Non-Profit Organization,* 125.

[20] Ibid.

[21] Garvin and Roberts, 110.

[22] Herbert A. Simon, *New Science of Management Decisions* (New York: Harper & Row, 1960), 5.

[23] Israel Brosh, *Quantitative Techniques for Managerial Decision Making* (Reston, Va: Reston Publishing, 1985), 292.

[24] Ibid., 276.

[25] Jack Byrd Jr. and L. Ted Moore, *Decision Models for Management* (New York: McGraw-Hill Book Company, 1982), 110.

[26] Brosh, *Quantitative Techniques for Managerial Decision Making,* 292.

[27] Adapted from Gilbert Gordon and Israel Pressman, *Quantitative Decision-Making for Business* (Englewood Cliffs, N.J.: Prentice–Hall, Inc., 1978), 486; Tom Gorman, *The Complete Idiot's Guide to MBA Basics* (New York: Alpha Books, 1998), 102; and John M. Ivancevich, Peter Lorenzi, Steven Skinner with Philip B. Crosby, *Management: Quality and Competitiveness* (Burr Ridge, Ill.: Irwin, 1994), 481.

[28] Byrd and Moore, *Decision Models for Management,* 112.

[29] Brosh, *Quantitative Techniques for Managerial Decision Making,* 277; and Griffin, *Management,* 239.

[30] Gorman, *The Complete Idiot's Guide to MBA Basics,* 104.

[31] Alexander H. Cornell, *The Decision-Maker's Handbook* (Englewood Cliffs, N.J.: Prentice-Hall, 1980), 184.

[32] Diagram is adapted from Saul I. Gass, *Decision Making: Modes and Algorithms* (New York: John Wiley & Sons, 1985), 349; Tom Gorman, *The Complete Idiot's Guide to MBA Basics*, 105; and Mind Tools, "Decision theory and decision trees, at <www. psywww.com/mtsite/dectree.html>, accessed August 12, 2003.

[33] Gordon and Pressman, *Quantitative Decision-Making for Business,* 102.

[34] Robert H. Hayes, "Qualitative Insights from Quantitative Methods," *Harvard Business Review—On Management* (New York: Harper & Row, 1975), 80–81.

[35] Ibid.

[36] Michael R. Czinkota, Masaaki Kotabe, and David Mercer, *Marketing Management: Text and Cases* (Cambridge, Mass.: Blackwell Business, 1997), 191.

[37] John S. Hammond with Ralph L. Keeney and Howard Raiffa. Reprinted by permission of *Harvard Business Review*. From "The hidden traps in decision-making," (September–October 1998): 47. Copyright 1998 by Harvard Business School Publishing Corporation, all rights reserved.

[38] Associated Press articles from March of 2000 printed in the Cedar Rapids, Iowa, *Gazette* under the headlines, respectively, of "Pileups leave 7 dead on Canadian highway," "63-vehicle pileup hurts 15 in California," and "Pileup kills 3, injures 21 in Florida."

[39] Hammond, Keeney and Raiffa, "The hidden traps in decision-making," 47.

[40] Ibid., 48–58.

[41] Ibid., 48.

[42] Ibid., 52.

[43] U.S. Rep. Dale E. Kildee of Michigan demonstrated this example effectively to me as he was discussing the perils of the wrong first step in decision-making back in the 1970s; it has stuck with me ever since.

[44] Hammond, et al., "The hidden traps in decision-making," 52.

[45] Rensis Likert, *New Patterns of Management* (New York: McGraw-Hill, 1961).

[46] Michael J. Driver with Kenneth R. Brousseau and Phillip L. Hunsaker, *The Dynamic Decision Maker: Five Decision Styles for Executive and Business Success* (San Francisco: Jossey-Bass, 1993), 4.

[47] Ibid., 5–6.

[48] Ibid., 15.

[49] Ibid., 11–14.

[50] Janis, Irving I., *Groupthink: Psychological Studies of Policy Decisions and Fiascoes* (Boston, Mass.: Houghton Mifflin, 2nd ed., 1983).

[51] Ibid., vii.

[52] Ibid., 174–175.

[53] David W. Johnson and Frank P. Johnson, *Joining Together: Group Theory and Group Skills* (Englewood Cliffs, N.J.: Prentice-Hall, 1975), 76–81.

[54] Elaine K. McEwan, *Leading Your Team to Excellence: How to Make Quality Decisions* (Thousand Oaks, Calif.: Corwin Press, 1997), 35.

[55] Ibid., 2.

Chapter 6
Media Ethics, Regulation and Laws

HOLDERS OF THE Master's in Business Administration degree are recruited fiercely by companies, large and small alike, to lead them into the competitive future. And that's becoming true in journalism and communications fields, as evidenced by Doug Underwood's book, *When MBAs Rule The Newsroom*, and in other reports throughout media companies.

The arrival of the "suits," as some journalists disparagingly refer to their business-trained managers and owners, has created an unprecedented confrontation between the newsroom and other departments in many news-oriented organizations. Journalists see themselves in the role of chasing the money-changers out of the temple— their newsroom—but with no real savior in sight to actually pull it off.

Herein lies the most troubling aspect of what is often a true clash of philosophies. News organizations such as newspapers, television networks and stations, and magazines (radio long ago mostly abandoned the battlefield) are dual citizens of both the society they function in and the world of commerce.

As a part of society, with First Amendment protections and the responsibility that those protections imply, American newspeople strongly believe their over-riding duty is to report information citizens need for them to function in a democratic society.

Their highest-level bosses, however, often feel that their first duty is to make a profit and become more dominant in the marketplace. Many of them look on the news as simply a commodity that should be marketed like anything else the company produces.

The book *The Business of Media* described these two basic approaches as being a conflict between the "public sphere model" and the "market model" of news-oriented media companies.[1]

As Marty Linsky of the Poynter Institute concluded after he compared responses of newspeople (representing the public sphere model) to his interviews with 14 media CEOs (market model), it is as if the newspeople and the executives live on two different and mutually hostile planets. Neither side listens to the other, Linsky concluded, so there never can be a reconciliation of two such conflicting standards.[2]

CHAPTER 6

Do the right thing

L INSKY'S VIEW seems reinforced by a troubling research conclusion reported by *Business Week* magazine. Many of those who are critical of the media's growing reliance on business-trained managers might not be too surprised to read the results.

A pair of professors from Ball State University and Miami University of Ohio surveyed a group of MBAs and then posed some identical questions to 300 prisoners at three minimum security prisons. The study's conclusions gave the felons the edge in at least several areas of business ethics. The convicts showed higher loyalty and obedience in some ethically charged situations, according to the study. And while MBAs put shareholders' interests first, the convicts—as a matter of ethics—put customers first.[3]

Educated to think along the shareholders-first market model for at least a generation or more, MBAs are now firmly in charge of at least the largest publicly traded media companies. Their profit-driven influence is becoming steeped throughout the industry, especially since the emergence 40 years ago of the first publicly traded media conglomerates.

The result, as journalism educator Ted Gup observes, is that, "The media are depicted as an octopus-like creature whose tentacles indiscriminately package news, entertainment, commercials, music, and movies, all driven by crass motives. Media scholars like to speak of concentration of ownership and of hegemony. One such scholar, James Lull of San Jose State University, defines it 'as the process of perpetual social domination by the relatively powerful over the relatively powerless.' We've come a long way from the days when the press was said to afflict the comfortable and comfort the afflicted."[4]

Columnist Jill Porter noted how many citizens might have been less than surprised that the press was singled out along with members of Congress for anthrax attacks in late 2001. "Oh, sure, we in the media see ourselves as missionaries of truth, indispensable to the foundations of freedom upon which this country was founded," she wrote. "The public, however, has a slightly dimmer view. They tend to think we're spreaders of spin, hustlers of hysteria, broadcasters of bias, celebrity cultists, and divas of distortion."[5]

Surveys show that a growing number of U.S. citizens mistrust and even actively dislike the press and have come to believe that newspaper and TV reporters are sensationalistic, unethical and, in general, not nice people.

Many of the ethical violations by reporters and photographers that plagued newspapers across the country just in 2003, from *The New York*

Times to the *Los Angeles Times*, could be blamed in large part on failures of managers to spot problems early and act on them before unethical behavior created a credibility crisis. Most unethical employees leave clues to their behavior in a series of poor judgments long before the one that finally brings notoriety and shame down on everyone.

But, of course, the blame also lies with the reporters, photographers, editors, videographers, and producers who need to take individual responsibility for their behavior. As ethicist John C. Merrill of the University of Missouri noted, "A journalist needs a will to be ethical. This is the starting point, this desire to be ethical, and without it journalists and their journalism will not improve."[6]

Nearly all university and college journalism programs require their students to enroll in ethics and media law courses. But many news side employees in print, broadcast, magazines and the Internet were not journalism majors and never were exposed to ethical and legal media perspectives. Others were, but nevertheless practice a modern-day workplace version of Machiavellian ethics (non-ethics?) in which the ends—their success—justifies any means, no matter how inappropriate. This Machiavellian approach results in such common situations as photographers Photoshop-ing pictures to distort reality, so that their cameras lie, and reporters faking news sources and quotes or committing plagiarism.

Decisions about ethics are made every day by almost every editor and reporter, though many are small decisions without major repercussions if a mistake is made. Because of the constant struggle over ethical decision-making, many news organizations have put strict guidelines into place through written policies.

One of the most complete policies is *The New York Times'* 52-page manual titled "Ethical Journalism: Code of Conduct for the News and Editorial Departments" covering the company's newspaper, television and Internet enterprises.

There are 155 situations detailed in the manual covering ethical questions that can arise in pursuing the news; protecting the newspaper's neutrality; the staff's civic and journalistic activities outside *The Times;* dealing with advertisers, marketing and production; conflicts of interests in personal and professional activities; dealing with contributions and gifts; and even specifying separate rules as needed for specialized departments at the newspaper.[7]

The January 2003 edition recognizes financial conflicts in that it prohibits any reporter or editor from owning any stock or having any other financial interest, outside of mutual funds and similar investments outside their control, in any company or industry for which he or she writes, edits, packages or supervises news coverage. Their spouses also are prohibited from holding such investments. For some on the news staff, this tightening of financial restrictions means they can own very few individual stocks outside the New York Times Co.

A PDF file of the entire ethics handbook is available on the Web at <www.nytco.com/company-properties-times-coe.html>.

"In addition to this code," the manual states, "we observe the Newsroom Integrity Statement, promulgated in 1999, which deals with such rudimentary professional practices as the importance of checking facts, the exactness of quotations, the integrity of photographs, and our distaste for anonymous sourcing."[8]

The manual also states flatly, "Staff members must obey the law in the pursuit of news."[9]

Many beginning reporters and editors, perhaps influenced by the unethical and overly aggressive reporting practices often portrayed by Hollywood in movies from "The Front Page" on, enter the news business thinking that laws against trespassing do not apply to them. Some feel they can engage in deception and thievery in the pursuit of an important story. Some important stories have indeed been published using these tactics over the years, but today's media managers are expected to stop such Machiavellian attitudes among their news staffers.

"They (reporters) may not break into buildings, homes, apartments or offices," the manual states in detail. "They may not purloin data, documents or other property, including such electronic property as databases and e-mail or voice mail messages. They may not tap telephones, invade computer files or otherwise eavesdrop electronically on news sources. In short, they may not commit illegal acts of any sort."[10]

So long, Hollywood.

Welcome to an adult world of responsible journalism.

Times publisher Arthur O. Sulzberger Jr. also read from a separate and additional code of conduct for his company's managers in a Freedom Forum video titled "The Art of Leadership in News Organizations."

Referring to them as "the rules of the road" for *Times* managers, Sulzberger said, "Success at The New York Times Company means more than just achieving our financial and journalistic goals. All of us should conduct ourselves in a manner consistent with the following tenets of behavior."[11]

These rules for managers at *The Times*, and appropriate for anyone hoping to be an ethical manager at any media company, are:[12]

• Treat each other with honesty, respect and civility.

- Strive for excellence. Don't settle for less.
- Contribute your individual excellence to team effort.
- Embrace diversity.
- Take risks and innovate, recognizing that failure occasionally occurs.
- Information is power—share it.
- Give and accept constructive feedback.
- Accept responsibility; delegate authority.
- Maintain perspective and a sense of humor
- Our journalistic work is sacrosanct.
- Strategy is a joint responsibility of both the news and business departments.
- Demand the tools you need to get the job done.

The *Times* rules of the road have a final point, that managers need to be willing to change their budgets if circumstances change. Stating that final point even more strongly is Eugene Meyer's statement of principles for *The Washington Post*. Meyer published his seven principles on the front page in 1935. They embody what he felt makes a newspaper truly great, and include the principle, "In the pursuit of truth, the newspaper shall be prepared to make sacrifices of its material fortunes, if such a course be necessary for the public good."[13]

Such a policy of self-sacrifice would seem far too idealistic to executives and boards of directors of most public corporations. But many media companies, especially privately owned newspapers, have a similar stated or informal code of honor, and it is a telling point about what a different kind of business the news media are in. It goes to the heart of the debate as to what degree that kind of mission is being compromised by today's prevailing economic pressures at even the most responsible newspaper and broadcast companies. A complete text of the principles is at <www.washpost.com/gen_info/principles>.

Needed are a combination of the many excellent ethical codes of conduct for news staffers, management practices as detailed in the *Times* rules of the road and the *Post* principles, and continuing emphasis in colleges and universities on ethical journalism practices. Infractions will always be committed by rogue journalists, and managers must always be alert for any sign of a lack of professionalism among news staffers. Constant vigilance is required if the negative ratings reported by the public toward the media are ever going to reverse their downward trend.

Another reason for less-than-ethical or professional journalism often is attributed to conglomerates cutting their way to prosperity by slashing newsroom budgets and salaries, leaving too few people to do too much work and for too little money. Overworked and harried employees make mistakes in ethical judgments, just as do those who put profits first before the mission of informing the public.

Conglomerates look at newspapers, TV broadcasters and magazines as just "profit centers," columnist Molly Ivins said, as she questioned whether some have any regard for the constitutionally protected role of the press in disseminating information citizens need in a democracy.[14]

Government and the press

GOVERNMENT plays a huge role in the growth and profitability of media business, as Ivins' comment about the Constitution indicates. This is why media companies pay so much attention to what goes on in Washington, D.C., and the state capitals and are major lobbyist forces. There is a continuing massive impact from the Newspaper Preservation Act of 1970 and the Telecommunications Act of 1996 on the newspaper and broadcast industries in recent years.

From the earliest days of the United States, starting with the First Amendment to the Constitution in 1791, government actions have directly affected the media in many ways, both good and bad, through legislation, policies and the courts.

As the book *The Business of Media* puts it, "The media's role in facilitating democracy and encouraging citizenship has always been in tension with its status as a profit making industry. Mediating between these two has been the government, whose regulations (or lack thereof) have fundamentally shaped the environment within which the media operate."[15]

With the administration of George W. Bush taking office in January 2001, with its boldly pro-business slant dominating both agenda and policies, it was not long before there were major reversals of previous policies and the advancement of new initiatives. Indeed, as early as April of 2001 the trade magazine *Advertising Age* observed that after only three months it was obvious that under the new Bush Administration "the political tide has turned to media owners."[16] All of the Bush Administration policies and actions favor even more consolidation and giganticism within the media industries.

As just one example of the importance of government policies for media companies, *Advertising Age* summarized how major developments on the FCC's proposal to ease media ownership rules got off to a fast start in the first few months of 2001.

It reported on how conglomerates were able to get around existing ownership limits, starting with a temporary order that April from the U.S. Court of Appeals for the District of Columbia stopping the FCC from enforcing its cap on broadcasters from owning stations that reached more than 35 percent of the nation's households. Viacom had bought some UPN stations that would have put it over the FCC limit, but with the court decision it was able to avoid selling stations to get back under 35 percent.

Very quickly, other networks began looking at the possibility of buying more stations. Only weeks later, News Corp purchased Chris-Craft's TV stations and the UPN network, which also jumped it over the existing 35 percent cap. That purchase also put News Corp. in violation of an FCC ban against owning two networks, as well as giving it a second TV station in the New York City market, where News Corp. already owned the *New York Post*. The U.S. Justice Department approved the purchase.

Those developments were followed by new FCC Chairman Michael Powell announcing soon afterward that, "he had abandoned, at least for the moment, any attempt to look at market competition or diversity issues in radio station sales."[17] Powell's rationale was that action by Congress in 1996 to raise the number of licenses that any one company could own in the largest markets to eight left the FCC's only duty as defining the market and certifying compliance.

"Finally, Mr. Powell has acknowledged the current FCC newspaper cross-ownership rules are on shaky ground and need review," *Advertising Age* reported. "The rules bar newspapers in a city from buying a local broadcaster, and vice versa, and could face a challenge in the News Corp. case."[18] In a matter of only a few weeks, the forces of deregulation suddenly were in charge of a new era.

Six weeks later, The Associated Press reported what it called a mostly behind-the-scenes effort by the Bush Administration and its supporters to make it easier for big media companies to consolidate and expand.

The battle to end the cross-ownership ban was on in earnest, and it resulted in a rare lobbying alliance by the National Association of Broadcasters (NAB), often called the most powerful lobby in America, and the Newspaper Association of America (NAA), whose members are publishers of the nation's dailies and perhaps second in influence only to the NAB. Politicians speak mostly through the media, and few are courageous enough to defy the wishes of the nation's broadcasters and newspaper publishers.

AP's story focused on the possibility of ending the cross-ownership ban against newspapers owning TV stations in the same town, which was seen as the last stand of those who favor some regulation of the media conglomerates. The possibility that the cross-ownership ban would be eliminated quickly alarmed Jeff Chester of the Center for Media Education. "This is radically going to change the nature of our media institutions," Chester warned. "These properties are going to be held by fewer and fewer companies."[19]

Newspaper and broadcast executives expressed a different perspective, of course. With 84 percent of Americans subscribing to cable or satellite television, plus the growing reliance on the Internet, they said it is necessary for media companies to be able to combine newspapers and broadcast properties just to stay competitive. In addition, they pointed out that more than 40 cities already had newspaper-broadcast combinations under the same owner because such arrangements existed before the cross-ownership ban went into effect in 1975 and thus were grandfathered in or were granted waivers by the FCC afterward.[20]

Plans and intentions never can be certain in politics, and that became glaringly evident in the unexpected power shift in the U.S. Senate shortly after the *Advertising Age* and The Associated Press reports. The emphasis changed from the near-certitude of results in the first article to speculation by the second article about whether any of it would happen. In that short time, the Republicans and the Bush Administration lost control of the U.S. Senate to the Democrats, therefore relinquishing all of the GOP committee chairmanships. On June 5, 2001, Senator Ernest Hollings, D-S.C., replaced Senator John McCain, R-Ariz., as chairman of the Senate committee overseeing the FCC and its rules. Hollings always had been more skeptical than McCain about allowing increased consolidation in the media industry.[21] And just before he took over the committee, he confirmed on May 25 that he would fight to keep the cross-ownership ban intact. On that same day, Powell observed that the changing of the Senate guard would cause his FCC to rethink its leniency toward News Corp. picking up the two New York TV stations.[22]

But again, matters changed abruptly. With the 2002 election, McCain was back in the chairmanship. Michael Powell and Republican leaders announced that media deregulation was back on track.

Even under Hollings' chairmanship, however, Powell resumed his drive to loosen or eliminate the cross-ownership ban. Powell's position was summarized by the trade journal *Editor & Publisher:* "Show the prohibition (against cross-ownership) is justified, or kiss it goodbye."[23]

In a joint filing on Dec. 3, 2001, the Consumer Federation of America and other public interest groups advocated continued regulation. *E&P* reported, "Yes, they said, there are more TV outlets today, but the number of local TV news operations has dropped about 10 percent. Yes, the Internet exists, but it mainly channels established media's news products. Yes, there are new TV networks, but there are one-third fewer broadcast owners today than 25 years ago. As for newspapers, they said, the number of daily newspapers is down nearly 20 percent, while the number of owners is down almost two-thirds, to 290 from 860."[24]

The nonprofits tried to make the point that even multiple outlets, if they all had the same owner, still were only one voice.

E&P reported that Gannett Co., Cox Enterprises, Belo, Tribune Co., and others considered the 1975 cross-ownership ban to be an outdated relic from a pre-Internet world of "information scarcity," and that the corporations contended there was "no factual basis for assuming that common ownership necessarily reduces . . . media to a single, monolithic viewpoint."[25]

A hands-off attitude on media ownership controls by the Bush Administration certainly was in keeping with its other business policies favoring a loose rein on the race horses of commerce.

Finally, on June 2, 2003, the FCC voted 3 to 2 to ease the cross-ownership ban and TV national broadcast ownership limit. As of press time for this book, some members of Congress were threatening to overturn the FCC action with new laws reinstating some limits.

According to the Newspaper Association of America, one corporation (in most cases a predominately newspaper chain) could end up owning in one of the nation's 70 largest markets the daily newspaper, up to two TV stations, the cable system and channels, and up to four radio stations —plus weekly newspapers, niche publications and shoppers.[26]

Newspapers are likely to buy TV stations rather than vice versa, because TV stations are much more profitable than newspapers.

Unless overturned by Congress, the new FCC regulation (or perhaps more accurately, deregulation) of the media is expected to reshape the media industry over the next five to ten years, with more cities becoming dominated by one media corporation for all news and views.

Tara Connell, Gannett's vice president of corporate communications, undoubtedly was expressing the attitude of most conglomerates after the FCC vote when she noted, "We're always in the market for properties."[27]

Assessing the FCC action, a media analyst for a New York investment firm concluded, "The big guys will get bigger and the little guys will have to decide whether they want to exist anymore."[28]

If there is any company that appreciates the difference a political environment can make, that company has to be Microsoft Corp. Subjected to horrendously expensive litigation and threatened with breakup as a monopoly by President Bill Clinton's administration, Microsoft was able to quickly reach a settlement with the federal government shortly after the new Bush administration assumed its stewardship of governmental agencies in 2001. Some states continued appealing that settlement, and a Massachusetts antitrust suit still was alive against Microsoft in 2003.

Legal issues in media businesses

L EGAL ISSUES abound across all aspects of media business, some of them common with all other businesses in the myriad of local, state and federal laws that affect commerce, and some of them unique to different parts of the media industry. Some of the legal issues especially relevant to media companies are in the areas of libel, slander, privacy, obscenity, advertising, copyright, lotteries, antitrust, wage and hour, child labor, fraud, contempt of court, search of newsrooms, and access to public records and public meetings.

It is not the intent nor the competence of this book to provide legal advice. Anyone needing legal advice should consult a lawyer and not rely on this book or any other book written by a non-lawyer for legal advice. That being established, what follows is only the most general of information on some of the legal issues confronting media companies.

The specific torts of libel, slander, copyright infringement and invasion of privacy are among those that are extensively covered in other books and classrooms dealing with journalism and communications. Though critical to media companies, those torts will not be covered again here. Instead, this book will discuss some legal principles dealing specifically with the business side of media companies.

Unionism was discussed earlier, and it should be reiterated here that very specific federal and state laws spell out what a company can and cannot do in dealing with unions or with union organizing drives.

One thing to remember in labor relations is that people must not be singled out for disciplinary action. In addition, people cannot be discriminated against in hiring, firing or lay-offs on the basis of any "protected category" listed under five different federal laws—including race, color, gender, national origin, religion, disability or age (40 years or older). Details on each of these protected categories is available at <www.eeoc.gov/facts/qanda.html>. In some states, people also cannot be discriminated against on the basis of sexual preference.

In other words, even if you have a good work-related reason to fire somebody, if they can prove your main motivation in terminating their employment was on the basis of any protected category, they can successfully sue both you and your company in federal court.

This is true even in **employment-at-will** states, which give legal sanction to the principle that an employee works only at the will of the employer and can be dismissed at any time for "any" reason. What such state legislation really is saying is that the employee can be fired for any reason—except those specifically protected by federal legislation,[29] or other "public policy" exceptions.

The doctrine of employment at will, like almost everything else in business, is neither clear-cut nor absolute. The New Mexico Court of Appeals rejected an employer's employment-at-will defense in late 2001 in upholding an employee's lawsuit for unlawful dismissal. A 32-year employee who had risen to president was summarily fired by the CEO/owner. The fired employee had no written contract, but the court ruled that the company's staff manual had procedures for dismissal that constituted a contract for everyone, and they were not followed.[30]

The moral of the story is to make sure your staff manual is followed for everyone, and don't fire anyone illegally.

This employment-at-will concept must not be confused with legislation known as **right to work** in some states, most of which are in the South and the West. In most states, people being hired at a company whose employees are represented by a union must join that union and be represented by the union in collective bargaining with the company about the terms of their employment. In 22 states as of mid-2003, however, state legislation gives employees the "right to work" at a company without being required to join the union at the company or to pay union dues,[31] even though the union still must represent them in negotiations and grievances. The executives of large corporations (who are the ones most likely to have unions) are strong supporters and lobbyists for right-to-work legislation because they believe no one should be forced to join a union in order to work at the company—and they also see this as another strategy to weaken unions at their companies. Unions, as you might already have guessed, consider such laws as akin to government-sanctioned union-busting.

Many employees of media companies, especially in television, will find that they will not even be offered a job unless they agree to sign an employment contract that includes a **non-compete covenant.** This provision of their contract will forbid them from working for any competitor—usually, but not always, another television station—in a certain geographic area for a certain period of time, like two to five years. These covenants exist to protect the employer, not the employee, so anyone asked to sign one should consult an attorney or an agent.

Hey, this is a free country, some folks new to the work force might be inclined to declare. I can quit anytime I want and go to work for anyone else that I like.

Not if you sign a legally-binding contract with a non-compete covenant, you can't. One humorously instructive scenario is illustrated in a Dilbert cartoon.[32]

DILBERT reprinted by permission of United Feature Syndicate, Inc.

Courts definitely will enforce provisions of any contract, including the non-compete covenant, as long as the terms are reasonable in geography and time. So, what is reasonableness in geography or time? That depends. Ask your lawyer. Generally speaking, however, the courts will protect your employer from you being able to take knowledge, skills and celebrity to a competitor if doing so would constitute breach of a written contract. But courts will not enforce a non-compete that they feel simply prevents you from making a living.[33]

For example, I was once forced to sign a non-compete as a requirement for employment that stated I could not work for any similar company anywhere in the world for 10 years. When I decided to go to work for another similar company in a different state, I showed the non-compete to my lawyer, Richard Hileman. He actually laughed aloud at the over-reaching language of the non-compete. Then he dashed off a simple letter to my soon-to-be-jettisoned boss about the utter unenforceability of such a covenant. I was on my way. Non-competes must be reasonable in time and geography to be enforceable.

As a business manager, you should never try to hire someone who is barred from working for you under a non-compete clause or other provision of their employment contract. That person's current employer could sue your business for knowing interference with a contract.[34]

A concept frequently battled over throughout the media industry is the distinction between the legal term of an "employee" and an **independent contractor.** There are major advantages for any company to consider a worker as an independent contractor, because such a worker is not entitled to a fixed wage, training, equipment, facilities, overtime, fringe benefits or reimbursed expenses. Another advantage for companies is an exemption from payroll taxes, which brings the much-dreaded U.S. Internal Revenue Service (IRS) into the discussion. The IRS has rules spelling out what constitutes an independent contractor. These rules are designed so employers cannot label someone who really is an employee as an independent contractor instead just to save on taxes and other costs.

Very briefly, independent contractors are considered to be operators of their own independent businesses who choose to work in tandem with your company, but not "for" the company.

Don't hire someone and call them an independent contractor and then try to dictate work hours, training, supplies or a desk. If such a situation is brought to the attention of the IRS (by one of these people after you have fired them, for instance), the IRS probably will rule that such a person is an employee, not an independent contractor. If so, the company will be held liable for back taxes, interest and penalties. In such a ruling, the company is retroactively responsible for tax withholding, Social Security and all benefits given to its employees. This is one of the most commonly abused areas of employment law—and the IRS sometimes checks on it.

Child labor can become an issue, especially for newspaper companies using youngsters as carriers, a tradition started by New York City newspapers in 1833.[35] The newspaper industry has a 1949 exemption to the federal Fair Labor Standards Act allowing them to use children as young as 12 as carriers. Some states regulate minors employed as newspaper carriers more strictly than federal law does.[36] This is becoming controversial lately after a researcher reported that teenagers make up almost half of the nation's 450,000 newspaper carriers and that between 1992 and 1995 there were 10 minors under the age of 18 killed while delivering newspapers.[37] A story on that report was carried the following year in *Editor & Publisher* magazine.[38]

And the issue won't go away. *The Wall Street Journal* published a Page One article in 2002 noting an updated figure of 16 youths killed between 1992 and 2000 and pointing out that only five states require newspapers to provide any kind of insurance for the children. It gave credit to one daily, the family-owned *Columbus* (Ohio) *Dispatch*, for voluntarily providing workers' compensation insurance and life insurance to its young carriers.[39]

Costly lawsuits over **sexual harassment** have been filed and won against managers, fellow workers and entire companies. Callous and insensitive behavior with a sexual connotation in the workplace by men toward women, or by women toward men (or even same-sex scenarios), can be actionable. Unwelcome sexual advances and other verbal or physical actions of a sexual nature can be the basis for a sexual harassment lawsuit. It is considered harassment when submission to or rejection of the conduct explicitly or implicitly affects the terms of an individual's employment, interferes with an individual's job performance, or creates an intimidating, hostile or offensive work environment.

A new area of trouble is the forwarding of sexual jokes and innuendo between employees over a company's e-mail system. *The New York Times,* for example, fired several employees in 2000 because of some suggestive e-mails sent around an office. Other companies have fired employees for posting suggestive photos or drawings in or around their desk, locker, or work station.

Tax payments are another major problem area. All companies are required to make the appropriate payments according to strict deadlines to local, state and national governments for such payroll expenses as Social Security withholdings, unemployment compensation levies, workmen's compensation insurance, pension deductions, state sales taxes, and both state and federal income taxes.

Though this is seldom a problem with large companies, it is notoriously common for small businesses of all kinds to yield to the temptation of using some of these funds for their own purposes, such as to tide them over during a slow sales period. The cash being withheld from employees' wages for taxes, for example, might end up paying for some pressing overdue bill of the company's. The owner or manager usually intends to make it up later before the tax payment is due to the government. Such robbing of Peter to pay Paul often ends badly when a tax payment eventually is missed because of one too many other pressing overdue obligations. Once that happens, IRS agents come calling, and another entrepreneur is drawn into either expensive entanglements with the IRS or even forced out of business—frequently both.

Keep in mind that business owners who delay or fail to make deposits of employees' pension or 401(k) account funds, under the assumption that no one will find out, are in violation of federal law.

There are many legal tactics available to owners of privately held businesses to minimize their taxes while still maximizing their income, including but not limited to bestowing perks on themselves. But one point must be emphasized: While it certainly is legal to minimize taxes as much as the tax code allows, **it is illegal to avoid paying taxes by hiding or not declaring all of a company's income.**

All businesses must be aware of federal laws prohibiting acts that are anti-competitive in nature and constitute **restraint of trade.** Basically, any attempt by two or more businesses to set prices, assign customers, or otherwise make business policies coincide could be considered in violation of laws dealing with restraint of trade. You might decide on your own to charge the same prices as your competitor, but to actually discuss the possibility with the competitor is de facto restraint of trade and is prosecutable.

If you are ever in a convention session, as one example, and one of your competitors stands up and announces that he or she charges a particular advertising rate and urges others to do the same, you should run—don't walk—to the nearest exit, protesting loudly all the way that you want nothing to do with this discussion. Then, if a restraint of trade legal action is later brought against every single person in the room, you *might* have a chance of escaping prosecution. That's how serious such matters can get, and how unexpectedly the incidents can arise.

Finally, keep in mind that a **contract** is enforceable by a court if it is done under circumstances that make it legally binding. This is true whether it is a contract in writing or not. It was Samuel Goldwyn's aphorism that "a verbal contract isn't worth the paper it's written on,"[40] but in fact an oral contract can be as legally binding as a written one.[41] The major difference is that an oral contract might be harder to prove and almost certainly will result in a longer and more expensive civil suit to get it enforced. (Under the Statute of Frauds, however, written contracts are required to transfer certain kinds of property, including real estate, so Goldwyn was right about that field.)

Simply as a practical matter, it is important for both employees and managers to acquire an understanding of key basic points of contract law, including non-compete covenants, penalty clauses, employment at will, sexual harassment, etc. You need to understand what your rights and your responsibilities are in the inevitable contracts you will encounter in the workplace. To be legally enforceable, an oral or written contract must include an **offer**, an **acceptance**, and what is legally termed **consideration,** which may or may not be represented in cash.[42]

Heaven forfend that you should ever need to deal with **bankruptcy** in your own company, but you probably will encounter it eventually in business dealings with your suppliers or customers. There are two kinds of business bankruptcy. A Chapter 11 is a court-supervised reorganization in which a company tries to stay in business and work out payments on its debts. The most extreme form of bankruptcy is a Chapter 7, which is a liquidation of all of the company's assets.

Those are the two types of business bankruptcy—different chapters can apply to individuals. If a company or individual going through bankruptcy procedures owes you money, you are very limited by law in how to go about collecting on that debt, and you must do it through the bankruptcy court. Woe to you if it's discovered you are trying to collect a debt on your own from some company or person under the bankruptcy court's protection.

A quick recommendation about **corrections** for news organizations: Studies have shown that you will increase your credibility if you admit to your mistakes, and you also might avoid a lawsuit for libel, slander, or invasion of privacy.

Your viewers and readers know you're not perfect (even if you're in denial about it), and they will respect you more if you clear up mistakes as soon as possible in a clear and visible way. And at least one study has shown that the leading cause of these lawsuits is by aggrieved readers or listeners who could not get the newspaper or TV station to admit that a mistake was made that damaged the plaintiff's reputation or business. When they cannot get a correction, they sue to set the facts straight.

As so well put by Barclay Jameson, former president of the Associated Press Managing Editors Association: "People will protect their reputation more fiercely than almost anything else."[43] If a media company corrects a mistake, and in the most serious cases apologizes for it as well, that is often all that the aggrieved party is really interested in.

Managers need to be knowledgeable about both the laws and regulations that affect their companies. Though listed by their federal names, the following governmental agencies also have state counterparts, and any one of them can give a manager ulcers in their oversight of activities common to media companies:

- Equal Employment Opportunity Commission
  (enforces discrimination laws)
- Securities and Exchange Commission
  (prosecutes cases of securities fraud)
- Environmental Protection Agency
  (prosecutes environmental violations)
- U.S. Department of Justice
  (enforces anti-trust laws)
- Occupational Safety and Health Administration
  (concerned with workplace safety)

Be proactive instead of reactive to their requirements and standards.

CASE STUDY   *Jayson Blair*
                 and the New York Times

by LESLIE-JEAN THORNTON
State University of New York, New Paltz

Macarena Hernandez, a reporter for the *San Antonio Express-News*, knew plagiarism when she saw it—after all, it was her work that had been stolen. There, in *The New York Times* under Jayson Blair's byline, were almost the precise words Hernandez had written after interviewing the woman whose son was then the last missing U.S. soldier in Iraq. Problem was, Blair had twisted some of the facts. Because of that, try as she might, Hernandez had trouble believing Blair had ever visited the woman.

Two days after the *Times* story, she was waiting with other reporters outside the same woman's home. News had broken that the body of the son, Edward Anguiano, had been found. Hernandez mentioned her doubts about Blair to a *Washington Post* reporter. Soon after, she was contacted by *Post* media columnist Howard Kurtz, who wanted to know more. The *Express-News* quickly notified the *Times* by e-mail of Blair's transgression.

Thus began a tumultuous and embarrassing investigation into a situation that damaged the credibility of one of the country's most respected newspapers and exposed serious flaws in the 1.5 million–circulation daily's management process. Here's how it unfolded:

• April 28—The *Times* learned from the San Antonio paper of Blair's plagiarism and the possibility Blair had never visited the Texas woman he purportedly interviewed.

• May 2—The *Times* printed a correction to Blair's April 26 story; in a separate story, it reported Blair's resignation and noted that five reporters and three editors were to investigate Blair's work during his four years as a *Times* reporter.

• May 11—In a front-page article that jumped to four full inside pages, the *Times* reported problems in at least 36 of the 73 articles Blair had written since being assigned national stories. Plagiarism was cited, as were instances of made-up comments and scenes. Blair had pretended to report from places he had not visited. The *Times* set up an e-mail address for readers to report suspicions.

The article noted that Blair had been reprimanded for unprofessional behavior and multiple errors in the past. In April 2002, the metropolitan editor had written a memo that said, "We have to stop Jayson from writing for the *Times*. Right now." Blair had been told his job was in jeopardy unless he changed, but by late October the paper's top editors, Howell Raines and Gerald Boyd, were assigning him to important national stories. Several of Blair's reports on a Maryland-area sniper brought objections and queries from law officials.

• May 12—Executive Editor Raines sent an e-mail message to the staff detailing steps he would take to stop a recurrence of journalistic fraud. He said a committee would be led by the assistant managing editor and would answer to the publisher.

• May 14—Publisher Arthur Ochs Sulzberger Jr., Raines and Managing Editor Boyd held a "town hall" meeting for the newsroom to talk about the Blair case. Raines said he accepted blame for a "failure of vigilance," but would not resign. Much of the two-hour meeting was given to angry comments from staff members, some of whom said they had "lost faith"; they protested Raines' authoritarian management. Some said he had pushed young "star" reporters too hard, too fast. Others questioned whether race was a factor since Blair, an African American and 27, had begun at the *Times* as a minority intern. Raines said he could not entirely rule that out.

A storm of comment ensued. Blair fueled discussion by giving an "exclusive" interview to *Newsweek*, which promoted the story on its cover. He was portrayed as having many personal problems. A few days later, in the *New York Observer*, he mocked the "idiot editors" he had bamboozled at the *Times*.

• May 21—A 22-person committee was named "to conduct a comprehensive review" of newsroom policies. The *Times* called the scandal "a low point in the 152-year history of the newspaper."

• May 23—The *Times* suspended Pulitzer Prize–winning reporter Rick Bragg for using the work of a willing but uncredited intern in a story carrying Bragg's byline. Bragg said it was common practice to use the work of interns or stringers—freelance reporters—in bylined stories. Outraged *Times* writers countered that Bragg's behavior was another manifestation of Raines' "star" system. Comments flew fast and heavy to Romenesko, a popular media news Weblog, fanning continued discussion as to how newsroom management might have contributed to Blair's plagiarism.

• May 28—Bragg resigned, saying he didn't want even one more day of animosity.

• June 5—Executive Editor Raines and Managing Editor Boyd both resign. Former Executive Editor Joseph Lelyveld is brought back as interim executive editor.

• June 12—The *Times* reports that ten additional articles by Jayson Blair contain passages that appear to have been fabricated or stolen.

DISCUSSION:

The *Times*' May 11, 2003, exposé deserves a closer look. Call up a copy through Lexis-Nexis and read it carefully. Where would you have taken disciplinary action and against whom? Are there ways in which editors made it easier for Blair to do what he did? Are there problems in the way editors interacted—or failed to interact—with each other? What are they, and what might have been the consequences of those behaviors?

Some praised Sulzberger and Raines for quick action. Others said they overreacted in arrogance. How do you feel? What alternative actions could they have taken and how might the consequences have been different?

Chief among staff complaints was that the paper was managed hierarchically or "top-down," and that top editors played favorites, thereby creating double standards. What are the advantages and disadvantages of such management ploys and how did they play into Blair's career there?

Did the Bragg scenario lessen or increase the importance of examining management practices at the *Times*? Why? Did it make what Blair did seem less important?

Should Raines and Boyd have quit? Discuss advantages and disadvantages of their leaving.

This case was still developing as this book went to press. Check <www.mediatextbook.com> for more information.

AUTHOR:

Leslie-Jean Thornton teaches news media management and journalism at the State University of New York at New Paltz. She was editor of several newspapers in Connecticut and New York. Before beginning work on her doctorate, she was an editor at The Virginian-Pilot.

CHAPTER 6

CASE STUDY   *An Ethical Dilemma*

by HUGH S. FULLERTON, Ph.D.
Sam Houston State University

(Third in a series of five related case studies)

The Call is successful under Jerry's ownership in large part because he has pleased his advertisers. Circulation has increased steadily, and people in the community are talking about what they read in *The Call*. Jerry has been able to train his ad sales people, as well as the layout staff, to provide good customer service and create attractive, effective ads. Ad revenues are growing faster than circulation.

One day Jerry is faced with a problem with an advertiser, John Small. It seems that Small's son, Arthur, got a ticket when he caused a minor boating accident on Woods Lake near Jamestown. The kid was operating the boat too fast. No one was hurt, and the damage to the boats was only a few hundred dollars, but the boy is going to have a minor police record. As a news item, the accident is trivial, and would probably be put near the end of the Sheriff's Department roundup story.

Small is in the insurance business, and his reputation is important to him. He is not a big advertiser, but he is in the paper week after week—one of a group of advertisers who have been very supportive.

Small calls Jerry and politely asks him to withhold the story. Small says his wife is very upset, and he is afraid she will have some kind of breakdown. The kid, he says, deserves the ticket but not the publicity. It could also hurt his business. Finally, he threatens to pull his advertising if Jerry does not see the matter his way.

Jerry knows something that Small may not. Small's wife has been running around with another local businessman. It's not the kind of thing that gets into small town papers, for a lot of reasons.

Should Jerry tell his reporter to spike the story? What factors should he consider before making the decision?

AUTHOR:

Hugh S. Fullerton was a reporter at daily newspapers and also was publisher of a group of weekly newspapers in Michigan for several years. He is an associate professor of journalism at Sam Houston State University in Huntsville, Texas.

🖥 *Suggested Web sites:*

www.business-ethics.com — *Business Ethics* magazine

www.journalism.sfsu.edu/www/ethics.html — Media ethics

http://commfaculty.fullerton.edu/lester/ethics/media.html — Ethics on the Web

www.poynter.org/subject.asp?id=32 — Poynter site on newsroom ethics

www.journalism.sfsu.edu/www/ethics.html — Journalism ethics

www.asne.org/index.cfm?id=387 — Links to numerous media ethics codes

www.freedomforum.org/first — Information on the First Amendment

http://bailiwick.lib.uiowa.edu/journalism/mediaLaw/index.html — Media law and technology links

www.dol.gov/dol/topic/youthlabor/Newspaper.htm — U.S. Department of Labor on carriers

www.fcc.gov/ownership — Media ownership policy re-examination

www.roguecity.com/reference/MediaEthics.html — Media ethics and journalism resources

Endnotes to Chapter 6:

[1] David Croteau and William Hoynes, *The Business of Media* (Thousand Oaks, Calif.: Pine Forge Press, 2001), 13.

[2] Marty Linsky, *The View From the Top* (St. Petersburg, Fla.: The Poynter Institute for Media Studies, 1997), 38.

[3] Business Wire, January 29, 1999.

[4] Ted Gup, "'Media' means so much, it means nothing," *Chronicle of Higher Education,* November 23, 2001, B12.

[5] Jill Porter, "Anthrax no surprise to vilified media members," as printed in *The Daily Lobo,* University of New Mexico, November 1, 2001, 4.

[6] John C. Merrill, *Journalism Ethics: Philosophical Foundations for News Media* (New York: St. Martin's Press, 1997), 27.

[7] *Ethical Journalism: Code of Conduct for the News and Editorial Departments, The New York Times* (January 2003), 1–52.

[8] Ibid., 5.

[9] Ibid., 9.

[10] Ibid.

[11] "The Art of Leadership in News Organizations," 55 min., The Freedom Forum, 2002. Videocassette.

[12] Ibid., for a partial list with the remainder provided by The New York Times Co.

[13] "Eugene Meyer's Principles for The Washington Post," on *The Washington Post* Web site at <www.washpost.com/gen_info/principles>, accessed May 31, 2003.

[14] Molly Ivins, "And how much blame for the Fourth Estate?" (November 1, 2001) <http://web.star-telegram.com/content/fortworth/columnist/molly_ivins.htm>, accessed November 26, 2001.

[15] Croteau and Hoynes, *The Business of Media*, 38.

[16] Ira Teinowitz, "Broadcast consolidation bulldozer speeds up," *Advertising Age*, April 16, 2001, 38.

[17] Ibid.

[18] Ibid.

[19] Kalpana Srinivasan, "Media facing more competition," The Associated Press, June 2, 2001.

CHAPTER 6

[20] Ibid.

[21] Ibid.

[22] Todd Shields, "Hollings: Keep FCC ownership ban," *Editor & Publisher* (June 4, 2001): 9.

[23] Todd Shields, "Funhouse-mirror images: 'The Ban,'" *Editor & Publisher* (December 17, 2001): 8.

[24] Ibid.

[25] Ibid.

[26] Mark Fitzgerald and Todd Shields, "FCC ruling sparks buzz and bites," *Editor & Publisher* (June 9, 2003): 7.

[27] Alec Klein and David A. Vise, "Media giants hint that they might be expanding," *The Washington Post,* June 3, 2003, A6.

[28] Ibid.

[29] Richard G. Hileman, attorney and specialist in corporate law, in remarks to media management classes at the University of Iowa and in interviews with the author in 1999 and 2000.

[30] Martin Paskind, retired attorney, "Don't bet on employment-at-will doctrine," *Albuquerque Journal,* December 31, 2001, Business Outlook, 7.

[31] National Right to Work Legal Defense Foundation Web site at <www.nrtw.org /rtws.htm>, accessed December 22, 2001.

[32] Scott Adams, "Dilbert" cartoon strip reprinted with permission, © United Feature Syndicate Inc., May 26, 2002.

[33] Hileman.

[34] Martin Esquivel, attorney and specialist in media employment law, in remarks to media management class at the University of New Mexico on February 26, 2002.

[35] History Buff Library, at <www.historybuff.com/library/refnewspeters.html>, accessed December 23, 2001.

[36] U.S. Department of Labor from the Web site <www.dol.gov/dol/topic/youthlabor/ Newspaper.htm>, accessed December 22, 2001.

[37] Marc Linder, "What's black and white and read all over? The blood tax on publishers — or, how publishers exclude newscarriers from workers' compensation," *Loyola Poverty Law Journal* 3 Spring 1997), 76.

[38] Robert Neuwirth, "Quiet tragedy: Violence against carriers," *Editor & Publisher* (September 12, 1998): 8–10.

[39] Patricia Callahan, "Children injured on paper routes often go uninsured," *The Wall Street Journal,* July 19, 2002, A1.

[40] Aphorisms Galore! from the Web site <www.ag.wastholm.net/aphorism/A-1515>, accessed December 22, 2001.

[41] Hileman.

[42] Esquivel.

[43] Barclay Jameson, in remarks to media management class at the University of New Mexico on March 19, 2002.

CHAPTER 7
OPERATIONS AND STRUCTURE
OF NEWS MEDIA COMPANIES

T OM ROSENSTIEL is director of the Project for Excellence in Journalism, and he summed up the present state of the operations and structure of media companies: "The era of the individual, patriarchal local (daily newspaper) owner is gone—long gone," Rosenstiel has concluded. "There are a handful left, but they are the exception. This is the era of corporate media."[1]

In this new era, the business pressures media companies are facing are different, according to Cole C. Campbell, a Poynter Institute Fellow. Campbell explained, "The world of journalism is marked by great tension between boardrooms and newsrooms, between those who count the beans and those who spill them . . . . We work in a time of economic transformation—and disruption—that is as vast as the global economy and as near at hand as the particular newspaper, broadcast station, cable channel or online venture we serve. Amid this turbulence, we ponder how we can continue to reward both those who do quality journalism and those who invest in it."[2]

His conclusion, written in an essay for the Poynter Institute's special Journalism and Business Values project, is that the newsrooms cannot ignore the requirements and values of either good journalism or good business.

Newsroom staffers are caught in the middle between two sometimes conflicting missions in that they must be accountable to both the public and to their employers.[3]

In another essay for the same project, Reid Ashe, publisher of *The Tampa Tribune*, wrote, "Who hasn't cursed the demands of the business side? . . . Though we're often tempted to wish otherwise, most of us work for commercial enterprises. They can be infuriating and distracting . . . . Until somebody figures out how a newsroom can generate its own revenue, we'll have to live within the larger enterprise . . . . The market can be fickle, but at least it makes our mission clear. It's to serve readers (and viewers) and to gain more of them. That's about as constant a mission as you can find, and it's our best assurance of long-term independence."[4]

Gadfly columnist Molly Ivins does not believe that quality translates into more resources. In discussing how serious journalism such as foreign correspondence has been losing the race to more profitable—but far less enlightening—pursuits such as celebrity journalism and infotainment, Ivins said, "Thirty years ago, the publisher of a good-sized city daily expected a return of 7 to 8 percent (refer to William Allen White's 1925 commentary on Frank Munsey near the end of Chapter 1). Today, there is virtually no competition, and getting less than 20 percent is considered a failure . . . . That the media have a public responsibility so important that it is protected by the Constitution gets lost in the profit chase."[5]

Ivins is mixing up the financials a little. The 8 percent return expected in a less sophisticated accounting past was more likely net profit, while today's 20 percent that she is referring to is operating profit. (Net profit should not be confused with operating profit. Operating profit is before taxes and some other expenses, such as interest. Net profit, on the other hand, is what remains after all expenses (the amount actually left for the company to use for acquisitions, retained earnings, etc.). Most business stories report a company's operating profit, not its net profit.

Still, some media companies today are much more lucrative, and even an 8 percent net profit for today's much larger companies brings in a far greater cash flow.

A benefit of stockholder ownership of media companies is that now there is financial information available on newspaper and broadcast companies. Such details always were carefully guarded before. The following chart shows the net profit margins for several media companies interspersed with the net profit margins for several non-media companies for perspective.

Operating profits are not shown on this chart. For one example, Gannett's operating profit for 2002, called EBITDA (Earnings Before Interest, Taxes, Depreciation and Amortization) was 33.5 percent. After taxes and all other expenses, Gannett's bottom-line net profit was 18.1 percent. Tribune Company had an operating profit margin of 23.19 percent and a net profit margin of 8.2 percent.

The list starts with Microsoft, which *The Wall Street Journal* reports as being among the "most profitable (companies) in the world."[6]

It can be misleading to report a specific year's income, as success can vary annually. All examples are in dollars unless otherwise specified and are for the fiscal year 2002, as compiled by researcher Ben Berger.[7]

2002 Net profit margins
of leading corporations in several industries

Company	Net Profit (in millions)	Gross Sales (in millions)	Profit %
Microsoft Corp. *	7,829	28,365	27.6
Oracle	2,225	9,673	23.0
GlaxoSmithKline (£)	3,920	21,200	18.5
Gannett	1,160	6,422	18.1
Lee Enterprises	82	460	17.8
Coca Cola	3,050	19,564	15.6
Hearst-Argyle	108	721	15.0
Anheuser Busch	1,934	13,566	14.3
AOL Time Warner**	5,663	40,961	13.8
Dow Jones & Co.	202	1,559	13.0
McClatchy Company	131	1,081	12.1
Journal Register Co.	48	407	11.8
E.W. Scripps	188	1,609	11.7
Intel	3,117	26,764	11.7
American Express	2,671	23,807	11.2
General Electric	14,118	131,698	10.7
Pulitzer	35	325	10.7
Knight Ridder	282	2,842	9.9
New York Times Co. ***	300	3,079	9.7
Belo	131	1,428	9.2
Meredith Corp.	91	988	9.2
Clear Channel Communications	725	8,400	8.6
Campbell Soups	525	6,133	8.6
Tribune Company	443	5,384	8.2
Nike	663	9,893	6.7
General Mills	458	7,949	5.8
Lowe's	1,472	26,491	5.6
Reebok	137	3,128	4.4
Royal Dutch/Shell	9,420	235,600	4.0
Reed Elsevier (£)	181	5,020	3.6
Wal-Mart Stores	8,040	244,520	3.3
Volkswagen AG (euro)	2,580	86,950	3.0
Viacom	726	24,606	3.0
Best Buy	570	19,597	2.9
Fuji Photo Film Co. (yen)	65,000	2,560,000	2.5
Honda (yen)	65,000,000	2,560,000,000	2.5
John Deere	319	13,947	2.3
Korean Air Lines (won)	111,900	6,250,000	1.8
Barnes & Noble	64	4,870	1.3
Apple Computer	65	5,742	1.1
General Motors	1,736	186,763	0.9
Sony	115	57,117	0.2

* - The previous year, the Microsoft net profit margin was 29%
** - Not counting massive write-down of paper losses in company value
*** - New York Times net profit margin the previous year was 14.8%

Many media critics are fond of saying that media companies are the most profitable businesses in America. They are far more profitable than retailing and industrial companies, but it is not true to say that they are the most profitable. Successful biotech pharmaceutical companies and computer software companies lead all others for the highest returns. That might be expected for firms at the front edge of the new technological age. In the next category are the banking and financial services companies along with the best of the media companies. Many media conglomerates enjoy double-digit net profit returns. The S&P 500 is dominated by retailing and manufacturing corporations that are satisfied with low single-digit margins, however, and it is to them that media companies often are compared.

The ethics of the media profit chase

ALSO LOOKING at the new corporate culture, Jonathan Kwitny, formerly of *The Wall Street Journal* and PBS, has questioned whether any premium is really placed on ethics any more in journalism. His question is an extension of the ethics discussion raised in the previous chapter, but in a different light in that he is talking about the business ethics rather than the journalism ethics.

Host of the PBS series "The Kwitny Report," and author of books and articles about the media, Kwitny said changing ownership patterns in the press have led to a disturbing neglect of serious national and international news gathering.

Media consolidation is certainly not new. It has been going on since 1741 when the *Boston Gazette* merged with the *New England Weekly Journal*.[8] But there has been a dramatic consolidation of ownership since media companies started going public in the 1960s. In a paper on "The Ethics of Ownership," presented at the Poynter Institute of Media Studies, Kwitny said America's new giant media owners are changing the attitude of the press toward its own function, and thus its performance.[9]

Some of Kwitny's indictments included: Pandering for audiences and advertisers has put entertainment and profits ahead of public service; public news ethic has been supplanted by an elitist business ethic; news of substance has been supplanted by fluff, photo ops, and soft news; diversity among competing local new media has been supplanted by blandness born of monopolistic control; authoritarian management has eliminated the spirit of participatory leadership; and lip service is paid to recruiting the best while low wages are being paid to graduates.[10]

Journalists should not get too sanctimonious, however. Many managers making exactly the type of decisions that Kwitny and others complain about are people who came up through the ranks in the newsroom. They are journalists who cherish the First Amendment and who embrace the mission of the press outlined by the 1947 Hutchins Commission on the importance of serving the public interest. So the question naturally arises—how can people as dedicated as journalists become a willing party to market-driven management tactics, which many feel compromises the news gathering and news reporting roles?

The answer at least partly can be found in what economist John Kenneth Galbraith calls "the approved contradiction."[11]

The increasing consolidation of previously independently owned newspapers, broadcast stations, magazines and now Internet companies through purchases by large national and international conglomerates has brought about a managerial revolution throughout the media. Owners no longer run the day-to-day decision-making at most media companies because the corporations are so large that such a role must be delegated at each outlet to professional managers. And yet, it would seem that human nature would dictate that managers—at least the ones who come from reporting and editing careers—would not share the same profit maximization goals as an owner.

One researcher wonders, "How can organizations managed and controlled on a daily basis by professional managers rather than the owners be expected to maximize rewards for others (owners) but not themselves?"[12] It would seem on the surface that human nature would direct the managers to pursue their own interests rather than the bottom-line interests of the owners and those they represent—whether they are the shareholders in a publicly traded company such as Gannett or a family in a closely held company such as Advance Publications.

Nevertheless, Galbraith's "contradiction" indicates that, at least in most cases, middle and lower level managers do set aside selfish personal interests to pursue the corporate interests of the owners. He refers to managers as the "technostructure" of an organization. These managers are not nearly as well paid as the owners nor the very top echelon of managers, but labor on their behalf anyway in fulfilling their role in corporate culture, seeking to maximize profits for owners rather than maximizing wealth for themselves.[13] "It is now agreed," Galbraith wrote, "that the modern corporation is quite typically controlled by the management."[14]

James Burnham's 1941 book *The Managerial Revolution* reported how managers were replacing the old-style capitalists of American business. David Demers of Washington State University said the managerial revolution resulted in managers with operational knowledge effectively replacing the capitalist owners in control of corporations.

"Research on this question strongly suggests that the role of owners in the day-to-day operations decreases as the organizations grow," Demers reports, "that the proportion of manager-controlled firms has increased, and that most large companies today are manager- rather than owner-controlled."[15]

But unlike Galbraith, who contends that these managers are overwhelmingly market-oriented, Demers believes that this control by managers results in a more socially conscientious corporation. Demers says his research shows that chains (he calls them corporate newspapers) place less emphasis on profits and more emphasis on other goals such as product quality precisely because "they are controlled by professional managers and technocrats, not the owners."[16]

On the other hand, Max Weber, a pioneer in management research, refused to concede that the managerial revolution was giving managers the upper hand over owners. Taking over managerial functions from owners, he argued, only removed ownership's managerial headaches, not ownership's control.[17]

Many incidents indicate that owners usually are still in very firm control—regardless of whether those owners are stockholders led by large institutional investors, individual owners such as the Newhouse brothers of Advance Publications and Rupert Murdoch of News Corp., or publicly traded companies led by strong CEOs like Tony Ridder of Knight Ridder or Douglas McCorkindale of Gannett.

To cite only one example of many that exist, this book discussed earlier how Jay T. Harris found that his views as a top manager of a Knight Ridder newspaper were no match against a determined CEO and board of directors who had a different view.

Galbraith maintains that most managers toe the line on corporate objectives because of corporate culture and because the result would be "a chaos of competitive avarice"[18] if managers used insider knowledge to pursue their personal interests. "These are not the sorts of things that a good company man does," Galbraith explains. "A generally effective code bans such behavior."[19]

Misfeasance and malfeasance require some privacy, he notes, but the structure of companies with team decision-making does leave room for managers to run wild without someone finding out.

Therefore, Galbraith says, "Management does not go out ruthlessly to reward itself—a sound management is expected to exercise restraint. Already at this stage, in the accepted view of the corporation, profit maximization involves a substantial contradiction. Those in charge forgo personal reward to enhance it for others . . . . They must be willing to do for others, specifically the stockholders, what they are forbidden to do for themselves."[20]

Well, in a perfect world, perhaps. However, the late 1990s and afterward brought to light rogue CEOs and other self-enriching managers of companies such as Enron, Global Crossing, Adelphia, ImClone, Tyco, etc., which called such a selfless attitude into serious question, as did the inherent conflicts of interest publicized at Wall Street brokerages and accounting firms in those financial piracy years.

Business columnist William Pfaff believes managers have become so brazenly corrupt in recent years that Galbraith's depiction of a selfless manager operating under the "approved contradiction" no longer applies to today's managerial class—at least not in many of the largest corporations.

"The corporate scandals revealed (in 2001–2002) all have one thing in common," Pfaff observed. "In all of these cases, the corporation was being run to profit its managers, in complicity if not conspiracy with accountants and the managers of other corporations . . . . These managers often proved indifferent to the long-term interests of their companies."[21]

Another viewpoint was expressed by Roger C. Nagel, a CPA, in commenting about business scandals in a story in the *Albuquerque Journal*. Nagel said, "Shareholders and analysts have driven management for years (to grow earnings) in an unceasing fashion that is contrary to common sense. We as shareholders and analysts don't create an environment that affords honesty . . . . I think it's that kind of pressure that oftentimes causes controllers and chief financial officers to skew the truth in the most optimistic fashion possible."[22]

The decline of local news coverage

THE RELENTLESS quest for ever-higher profits has resulted in a noticeable decline in the quality and quantity of local news coverage by newspapers, TV and radio.

CEOs of publicly traded media corporations admit they are under tremendous pressure to keep making ever-larger profits to satisfy their investors on Wall Street. Gannett takes considerable pride in boasting in its annual reports that for as far back as it could possibly matter it has always made an increased profit in every succeeding quarter.

In the journal *Media Ethics*, journalism educator Edmund Lambeth quotes the following exchange:

Q: Terence Smith, NewsHour correspondent: "What (operating) profit margin does Wall Street expect (from publicly held media companies)? If they average in the 20s, is that enough?"

A: Lauren Fine, media analyst for Merrill Lynch: "Well, it's never enough, of course. This is Wall Street we're talking about."[23]

The financial success investors crave often is a short-term gratification at the cost of long-term strength. Boards and CEOs, and through them their managers down the line, do everything they can think of to keep the profits growing.

Privately owned companies must keep pace with their publicly traded competitors, but are not under the same investor mandate. The Hearst Corp. is the oldest media company still under private ownership. Its president and CEO, Victor F. Ganzi, expressed the feelings of many private owners when he wrote in Hearst's employee magazine, "We at Hearst are in an enviable position. As a private company, we have the luxury of managing with a view to the long-term."[24]

The fear of many reporters, editors and producers is that the quest for short-term profits at the expense of long-term stability is inflicting irrevocable damage on print and broadcast newsrooms. Journalism researchers like Philip Meyer of the University of North Carolina and Stephen Lacy of Michigan State University are struggling to come up with empirical proof that diminishing news quality will hurt profitability over time. "I know in my heart (news) credibility has economic value," Meyer said. "What I need is to find evidence that will convince people."[25]

Newspaper economist Robert G. Picard told *Editor & Publisher*, "The other problem with linking quality and content is that advertisers provide about 85 percent of the income to the U.S. newspaper industry and they don't worry much about the quality of the content . . . . Acceptable quality is OK for them, not excellent quality."[26]

Newspaper editors complain about smaller news holes at many papers. A walk through almost any newspaper newsroom will turn up empty desks of bygone reporters and copy editors no longer considered necessary for getting that smaller news hole filled. Not everywhere, of course, but in most places.

The situation is even worse in broadcast, where Av Westin, former executive producer of ABC Evening News and World News Tonight, insists that broadcast news is in a "death spiral."

Westin explained to the *St. Paul* (Minn.) *Pioneer Press*, "Everywhere you look, the bottom line has trumped (quality TV journalism). The profit expectations of conglomerate news is such that if you're running a local newsroom, the only way you're going to meet your (financial) objectives is by going down market and cutting staff. You look around, and you see men and women today running (TV) newsrooms who got all their training in the past 10 years. They don't know any other environment."[27]

At a media ownership forum in Phoenix in 2003, Hugh Downs, the veteran ABC newscaster and former anchor of *20/20,* said that Walter Cronkite was right when he expressed fears that broadcast journalism itself is at risk. Downs said the current "media merger mania" is resulting in "dumbing down the news, where the bottom line is the only line."[28]

As Westin and Downs lament the current state of broadcast journalism, the local version is disappearing altogether in St. Paul and other cities, where television stations are not just downsizing, they are eliminating their local broadcast newsrooms altogether. An increasing number of TV stations are shutting down their local news programs in many markets, while others buy local news programming from other stations in town.

Can local television news disappear?

Just a couple of decades ago, local radio news was a vibrant industry and an attractive career option for young reporters. Today, local news has mostly disappeared from radio. Conglomerates can own up to eight radio stations in a market, and they often combine all of the studios along the hallway of a central building. As you walk down those hallways or into the offices of even most smaller groups' radio stations, you will see an occasional D.J. but no news reporters. In many radio operations, there are no personnel at all, as computers hum along, coordinating all of the programming from satellite feeds. If an emergency happens in your town and you turn to your local radio station for information, all you might ever hear are commercials, music and talk-radio programs recorded somewhere else.

Meyer bemoaned the loss of local radio news in a recent article. Consolidation theoretically could improve news and all other pro-gramming by allowing everything to be delivered more efficiently, he said, but that is not happening. Instead, the conglomerates are providing media designed only as a cheap way of delivering advertising that is priced as high as the market will bear. While the number of independent radio owners has declined by 34 percent since the Telecommunications Act of 1996, the new conglomerate owners of radio have jacked up advertising rates by up to 90 percent.[29]

Meyer commented, somewhat bitterly, "A corporation has some of the legal characteristics of a person but with a huge moral difference. As George Washington University professor Lawrence E. Mitchell observed (quoting an English jurist), the corporation has 'no soul to be damned and no body to be kicked.' It's just a moneymaking machine."[30]

197

At least one example, however, exists of profits driving additional news coverage in TV—though the solution comes with problems involving deception and sets a worrisome precedent if it is picked up by other broadcast chains. Sinclair Broadcasting had been shutting down news programs on some of its 62 TV stations, such as in Greensboro, N.C., St. Louis and Tallahassee, because they were not profitable. In October 2002, however, Sinclair turned to "centralcasting" as a way to create news programs on some of its stations, including some of its affiliates with Fox, UPN and WB networks that never had news programs before.[31]

In centralcasting, TV and radio chains send tapes from a central location featuring corporate news anchors and D.J.s, respectively, to their local stations. Often, a serious effort is made to trick local viewers and listeners into thinking they are hearing local people. Clear Channel has been criticized for doing this at some of its radio stations—passing off satellite feeds as local programming—and viewers have noticed that the same reporters show up on both Viacom stations in Los Angeles.[32]

Sinclair has turned to this strategy more than anyone else, setting up a 40-person centralcasting operation near Baltimore. The national news studio set is identical to one at each local station. Commentators, meteorologists and sports reporters—often bantering back and forth with the local news staffers hundreds of miles away as if they were in the same room—then present "local" stories to be aired at the other station. Most of the program is provided by the centralcasting figures, allowing the local station to put on a news program with a much smaller news staff than usual.

People "ought to be applauding us," said Mark Hyman, a Sinclair vice president. He pointed out that at least now there is a local program.[33]

Others worry, of course, that centralcasting is just another portent of local TV news programming's death spiral, as convergence operations pioneered by some newspaper chains are heading in the same direction of centralizing operations with smaller news operations.

Jack Fuller, president of the *Chicago Tribune,* takes issue with the contention that corporate journalism is a profiteering new development that is contrary to the past, when media companies were in the hands of individual owners. He says the ideal of a past in which owners were said to have been selfless and cared only for their community is nostalgic nonsense.

"The basic argument critical journalists make against the corporate form is that corporations have taken money out of newspapers at a rate far higher than private owners did," Fuller wrote in his 1996 book, *News Values.* "I do not have the historical data from other papers, but in the 1920s during the *Tribune's* heyday under the proprietorship of Colonel

Robert R. McCormick . . . . the operating margin reached almost 29.8 percent in 1929, compared with 24.6 percent at its highest afterwards."[34]

Throughout all of this discussion, the word "corporation" is distorted in its use. As will be noted later in this chapter, a corporation does not need to be a monolithic, international powerhouse. A single person can establish a corporation. In fact, virtually every media business of any size—whether good, bad or indifferent—is a corporation. When critics of media companies condemn the corporation, they specifically are thinking of the publicly traded corporations owned by stockholders. The dynamics of these stockholder-owned corporations are to be discussed next.

Influence of stockholder interests

THROUGH HER magazine, *Business Ethics*, and in her 2001 book, *The Divine Right of Capital*, Marjorie Kelly is trying to start a dialog about what she sees as a core problem of the current embodiment of capitalism.

"The symptoms range from bloated CEO pay, sweatshops, and speculative excess to stagnant wages, corporate welfare, and environmental indifference," Kelly writes. "All spring from a single source: the mandate to maximize returns to shareholders. In major public corporations . . . this mandate amounts to property bias, which is akin to racial or gender bias. It arises from the unconscious belief that property owners, or wealth holders, matter more than others."[35]

While each stockholder owns a piece of the company, Kelly maintains the company owes far less fiduciary obligation to those who acquired their stock from previous investors rather than directly from the company through Initial Public Offerings (IPOs) and new stock issues. This argument is similar to the one by accounting professor Ralph W. Estes, who in *Tyranny of the Bottom Line* compared the stock market to the used car market. The money for a used car, or a re-sold share of stock, goes not to the home corporation but to the previous purchaser, with no direct effect on the corporation.[36]

Furthermore, Estes dismantles a favorite myth of corporate America when he observes, "Corporate management tells us repeatedly that the stockholders control the corporation and have full power over it and them. Some executives may believe this, but for many it is little more than a smoke screen to obscure the fact that *no one* has direct, significant control over top management . . . . Stockholder uprisings that realize any degree of success are exceedingly rare in large corporations. The CEO or a few top executives exercise autocratic control in the great majority of these colossal enterprises."[37]

Kelly looks at another angle of the idea of working for the shareholders, writing: "Corporations are believed to exist for one purpose alone: to maximize returns to shareholders. This principle is reinforced by CEOs, *The Wall Street Journal*, business schools, and the courts. It is the law of the land—much as the divine right of kings was once the law of the land. Indeed, 'maximizing returns to shareholders' is universally accepted as a kind of divine, unchallengeable mandate,"[38]

Kelly said this business philosophy is not at all controversial, but she contends that it should be. Because about 99 percent of the stock traded any given day is "used stock," according to figures from the Federal Reserve and the Securities and Exchange Commission, she considers stock investors as little more than gamblers. They bet their money in a purely speculative market where none of the cash actually reaches the corporations, but instead circulates only among the other investors.[39]

"The truth is, the commotion on Wall Street is not about funding corporations. It's about extracting from them," Kelly maintains.[40]

The only time corporations receive cash is when they sell the stock for the first time. That is the only time productive corporate wealth is created.

Kelly concludes, "Those who buy stock at sixth or seventh hand, or 1,000th hand, also take a risk—but it is a risk speculators take among themselves, trying to outwit one another like gamblers. It has little to do with corporations."[41]

Kelly's perspective clearly is not conventional. Some in business even might classify her as holding radical views. But even national economist John Kenneth Galbraith wonders why stockholders receive so much attention from companies. Galbraith and Kelly's way of thinking about corporate mission appeals to some who believe that what they perceive as the greed and short-term gratification of the past few decades is not the way for managers to continue operating their companies.

Like Kelly, Galbraith also thought the typical stockholder was really owed little by the business managers, although they received much obeisance anyway.

"The managerial revolution—the assumption of power by top management (from owners)—is conceded," Galbraith wrote. "So long as earnings are above a certain minimum, it would also be agreed that such management has little to fear from the stockholders. Yet it is for these stockholders, remote, powerless and unknown, that management seeks to maximize profits."[42]

The other point of view is that both Kelly and Galbraith are being unrealistic in the face of a very real business consequence. Ignoring owners of "used stock" could easily lead to a stockholder rebellion that could destroy the value of the company, as stockholders dumped rapidly devaluing shares to buy elsewhere. Thus, publicly traded companies are in fact held hostage by these later investors, who are not as remote, powerless and unknown as they might seem. Chastised company officials from many corporations occasionally discover this fact at their annual stockholder meetings.

A stockholder rebellion led by a New York institutional investor with more than 13 million shares of "used stock" forced Conrad Black to reduce his own compensation at Hollinger Inc.'s 2003 shareholders meeting, and also institute other operational changes.[43]

The Poynter Institute with its emphasis on social responsibility for newsrooms, as well as journalism and communication educators striving to inculcate ethics compatible with the Poynter mission in a future generation of media leaders, are urging that media companies embrace a corporate role as exemplified by Alvah H. Chapman Jr. While chairman of Knight Ridder, Chapman wrote in 1985, "We believe good journalism is good business. As an information company, our success depends on the excellence, reputation and usefulness of that information which is our product. We want our readers and viewers to have the highest possible confidence in what we produce. This is essential to maintaining our credibility and consequently the loyalty and following of our readers and viewers."[44]

However, while declaring good journalism to be the professional priority of his newspapers and broadcast properties, Chapman knew that even he must never slight his fiduciary responsibility as a business leader.

For that reason, when Chapman made a point of announcing to stockholders that Knight Ridder had won seven Pulitzer Prizes in 1986, he also made sure the stockholders were informed that corporate profits were up at the same time.[45]

Media ethicist Clifford G. Christians is a leading proponent of moving media companies to a social responsibility emphasis, referred to by some as communitarianism.

"Nothing is more difficult in the mass media enterprise than promoting the public good," Christians wrote in his book, *Media Ethics*. "In actual practice, it becomes extraordinarily difficult to separate the media's financial interests from the public's legitimate news interests. The Constitution protects the media from government constraint, but the news is under perpetual risk of corporate control . . . . Ever since mass communications took on the character of big business at the turn of the

20th century, there have been built-in commercial pressures . . . . As the ominous trend continues toward concentrated ownership of media properties, cost-conscious publishers threaten to overwhelm the press's noble mission."[46]

This rising influence of Wall Street was analyzed by three University of Iowa professors in a review of annual reports filed by the nation's 17 largest stockholder-controlled media companies in 2000. They presented their findings in the book, *Taking Stock: Journalism and the Publicly Traded Newspaper Company*.

In making the point cited in Chapter 1 about the Faustian bargain newspapers made to gain capital in return for stockholder control, the *Taking Stock* authors concluded, "The dominating and unrelenting expectation of the national investment markets are now being felt directly by newspapers. In the late 20th century the financial markets expanded rapidly, making capital easily available to larger and successful enterprises . . . . Newspapers were engines of untapped potential advertising revenue, unkempt and sloppily-run operations ripe for the cost-cutter's picking, enterprises whose product, hard news, could be stripped and made efficient because the product in its traditional form bore no relation to the news imperatives of focused audiences and premium advertising rates."[47]

Unlike other companies traded on Wall Street, however, the media companies—especially newspapers, magazines and broadcast—are more than just pure businesses. Media companies have an added responsibility granted under the First Amendment to also keep citizens informed adequately to meet the needs of a participative democracy. However, the *Taking Stock* authors concluded that the media companies' product—news—ends up being treated simply by Wall Street the same way they treat the manufacture of any goods.

"Newspapers were encouraged," they concluded, "to see news simply as the engine for, or instrument of, delivering eyeballs for advertising, because the advertisers paid most of the bill anyway. News could be stripped, made efficient, reshaped without concern about content or quality or public purpose, as long as the new product could attract the desirable advertising market or audience."[48]

Taking Stock makes the point that when newspaper companies and other media companies decided to exploit the financial and other advantages available through selling stocks to the public, they in effect also were agreeing to be treated just like any other business, their First Amendment status notwithstanding, noting that, "In consequence, they became subject to external and internal forces that oblige them to behave as do other businesses, but with special consequences for journalism."[49]

The wide range of these consequences provokes the rancorous debate found throughout journalism today and in media management classes on campuses across the country.

However, the controversies over how much profit is enough, and the corporate governance issue of stockholder power, also are being raised for non-media corporations. Peter F. Drucker believes a lot of conventional business wisdom, including some of his own in the past, must be and will be changed for corporations in the coming years. In his 2001 book, *Management Challenges for the 21st Century,* Drucker points out that the "emerging American theorem that business should be run exclusively for the short-term interest of the shareholders is also not tenable and will certainly have to be revised."[50]

With longer life expectancies and a growing elderly population in the United States and nearly all other nations, Drucker said, all corporations are going to feel more pressure to start operating for long-term prosperity and survival so as to protect pensions and other investment-based retirement incomes.

What are the current consequences of stockholder ownership of news media companies? They include the following—all of which are discussed in this book—directly affecting both the companies that are traded on Wall Street and also influencing to various degrees the privately owned companies competing against them.

The main points and the subpoints are:

• Consolidation, directly resulting in fewer independently owned media outlets and ever-larger sizes of the conglomerates that result.

• International expansion, as media conglomerates become large enough to become involved in business opportunities not only across the United States but also overseas.

• Less emphasis on the value of news and information by mega-corporations in which the revenue from journalism components are an increasingly insignificant part of their overall operations.

• More control over how news is covered and disseminated by corporate executives whose backgrounds are in business, not journalism.

• An increasing fragmentation of audience, resulting from rapidly developing technology opening up new opportunities for dissemination of news and information, and large media corporations finally able to exploit those opportunities.

• Profit maximization to satisfy investors and attract even more capital, all of which results in the following consequences:

—Market-driven journalism intended to attract more readers or viewers—and thus more advertisers—with its constant companions of less news and more sensationalism, trivialization and infotainment.

—Convergence, to cut costs and obtain maximum efficiency from employees even if it means increasing stress and workload of reporters and editors.

—A "death spiral" of local TV and radio news, manifested by the near elimination of local news on radio and an increasing number of TV stations dropping their news programs or turning to centralcasting.

—Operational sharing arrangements between competing companies, such as master-control mergers among broadcasters, the California Newspapers Partnership established in 1999 by three chains, and Joint Operating Agreements between newspapers.

—The elimination of the cross-ownership ban that prohibits one company from owning both newspaper and TV properties in the same market and elimination or loosening of the caps on the number of radio or TV stations that one company can own in a market.

—A talent drain, as some of the most able reporters and editors are lost to journalism because they become disenchanted with "bottom-line" mentality and then seek more fulfilling careers elsewhere.

—Possible challenges to First Amendment protections to media companies as the public sees news being treated only as another commercial commodity.

Uncommon types of ownership

NOT ALL NEWSPAPERS and TV stations are owned by corporations and families, wealthy or not. Other arrangements also have been tried with varying success and are still in effect today, albeit at only a few media outlets across the country.

Some media companies have been or are owned by private foundations. In the 1980s, Houston Endowment, Inc., owned the *Houston Chronicle* (since sold to the Hearst Corp.), and the Public Welfare Foundation, Inc., owned the *Spartanburg* (S.C.) *Herald-Journal, Tuscaloosa* (Ala.) *News,* and *Gadsden* (Ala.) *Times.*[51]

Surprisingly, one chain—Independent Newspapers, Inc., headquartered in Dover, Del.—is a for-profit tax-paying company owned by a nonprofit holding company. CEO Joe Smythe established the nonprofit holding company in 1991, "dedicated to preserving the company's independence and assuring that its newspapers would be published in a spirit of public trust."[52] In establishing the holding company, Smythe had to give up ownership of the chain. The holding company's trustees reinvest the chain's profits back into its more than 60 daily, weekly and monthly newspapers, niche publications and printing plants in Delaware, Maryland, Florida and Arizona.

A few individual dailies today are still owned by trusts.

Since the death in 1939 of its last private owner, Theodore Bodenwein, *The New London* (Conn.) *Day* has been owned by The Day Trust. Its board of directors is unable to sell the newspaper unless it suffers two consecutive unprofitable years. The board invests part of the profit from *The Day* back into the newspaper, and the rest is given to the Bodenwein Public Benevolent Foundation, which annually hands over about $300,000 to local charities.[53]

Similarly, *The Union Leader* of Manchester, N.H., became owned by a trust when publisher William Loeb died in 1981, and it remained that way until his widow died in 2000. The daily's ownership now is split, with about 75 percent owned by the Nackey S. Loeb School of Communications and 25 percent owned by the William Loeb Union Leader Trust. Dividends from the trust's ownership portion are divvied out annually to employees, while dividends from the school's portion fund its operating costs.[54]

Another daily published by a nonprofit organization is the *Northeast Mississippi Daily Journal* in Tupelo. As the state's third largest newspaper, it is owned by Create, Inc., a tax-exempt charitable corporation begun by the *Daily Journal's* late publisher, George A. McLean. Create distributes the newspaper's profits to a variety of educational, cultural and health programs in and around Tupelo.[55]

Two more dailies were turned over to nonprofit foundations in 2002 and 2003 in a possible intensification of the effort to keep locally owned dailies out of the grasp of the chains. Upon her death in December 2002, Marajen Stevick Chinigo bequeathed the *News-Gazette* of Champaign, Ill., to a nonprofit foundation that will support local charities. And H. Brandt Ayers, whose family owns two Alabama dailies—the *Anniston Star* and the Talladega *Daily Home*—announced his plan to eventually turn the papers over to a foundation that will offer a graduate degree in community journalism through the University of Alabama.[56]

In the best-known unorthodox arrangement, the Poynter Institute has owned the *St. Petersburg* (Fla.) *Times* since 1978, and the institute also reaches a national audience through its <www.poynter.org> Web site. Today, the nonprofit Poynter Institute is a leader in working to improve professionalism in journalism. Numerous seminars are conducted every year in Florida for working journalists in print and broadcast and for journalism students and educators. The institute produces films and books, and offers other educational resources, exploring new ideas in journalism and in training print and broadcast reporters and editors. Poynter owns the Times Publishing Co., which splits its after-tax profit equally between the Poynter Institute and reinvestment in the newspaper.

Along with nonprofit ownership, some newspapers also are experimenting with various Employee Stock Ownership Plan (ESOP) arrangements to fend off take-overs by conglomerates.

Newspapers with majority ownership by their employees include the *Omaha World-Herald; The Daily News-Miner* in Fairbanks, Alaska; *The Evening News* in Monroe, Mich.; and America's oldest employee-owned arrangement, the *Milwaukee Journal Sentinel.*

However, the board of Journal Communications, Inc., which owns the Milwaukee paper, proposed in May 2003 to dissolve the employee-owned trust that has owned the paper for 66 years. It would be replaced with a publicly traded structure with closely held super-voting stock plus the common stock that would be sold to the public.[57]

Employees own a significant percentage but less than a majority stake in many other dailies, including the *Daily News* in Longview, Wash., and the *Gazette* in Cedar Rapids, Iowa.

Ownership by employees or by trusts must be carefully structured, however, because these unusual ownership structures can have their vulnerabilities. Financier Robert Bass nearly took over the *St. Petersburg Times* in the 1980s when he managed to acquire large blocs of stock owned by two of the late Nelson Poynter's nieces. The takeover was thwarted, but only after a bitter and expensive legal battle.[58]

Employee-ownership attempts have failed at several dailies since the 1970s, leading to recent moves by owners to turn more to organizing trusts and nonprofit foundations instead.

There have been a few instances over recent years when weekly newspapers in financial difficulty have been taken over and published by a community organization, such as an economic development group, so they could survive as local papers.[59] This might very well happen with small radio stations as well, though I know of no instances.

There also was at least one long-term effort to run newspapers under co-op ownership arrangements. The most successful, the Iowa Co-Operative Publishing Co., was formed in 1936 to publish a labor newspaper, the *Dubuque Leader*. Shares of stock were owned by more than 300 working class people in and around Dubuque and labor supporters who also signed on as investors. The arrangement endured for nearly 30 years.[60]

General circulation labor newspapers were not uncommon in the 1920s and 1930s, when labor unions like the United Auto Workers were successfully winning their first collective bargaining agreements against corporations as large as General Motors in a nationwide reaction against exploitation of workers.[61] The 1925 *American Labor Press Directory* lists more than 200 newspapers of that time aimed at a working class audience, with 21 of them published under co-operative ownership arrangements.[62] These labor papers existed because union members nearly always found an unsympathetic chronicler of their problems and affairs in the daily newspapers—which were, after all, published by wealthy businessmen and businesswomen.

Though American journalism generally prides itself on secular independence, churches nevertheless own some broadcasting and publishing outlets across the continent. Two of the best known and most influential are daily newspapers—*The Washington Times*, published in the nation's capital by the Rev. Sun Myung Moon, head of the Unification Church, and the *Deseret Morning News*, published by the Church of Jesus Christ of Latter-day Saints in Salt Lake City, Utah.

There are, of course, several magazines and newspapers published by trade associations and educational institutions. Many of them have considerable influence in the industry, with two of the most influential ones dealing with the news side of the media industry being *American Journalism Review* and *Columbia Journalism Review*, published through the journalism schools at the University of Maryland and Columbia University, respectively.

In the broadcast industry, individual entrepreneurs and small family-owned corporations own many radio and television stations in small-town America. In the mid-sized to major markets, however, most broadcast outlets are owned by large corporations with many—often hundreds—of holdings.

One notable exception in a market that is at least large geographically is KTNN-AM in Window Rock, Ariz. As one of only six 50,000-watt AM stations in the United States,[63] KTNN was founded in 1986 and is owned by the Navajo Nation. It can be heard throughout the West, from Canada to Mexico. Unlike virtually all other radio stations today, KTNN is information-driven rather than entertainment-driven. The station maintains an active news staff that ranges over a four-state area to cover news of interest to the Navajo Nation—for example, its reporters were sent to Utah in 2002 to cover the Olympics in Salt Lake City.[64] The Navajo Nation also owns a 100,000-watt FM station, KWRK, and the weekly *The Navajo Times* in keeping residents of the sprawling Navajo reservation informed of issues that other media ignore.

Other tribes own several radio stations and weekly newspapers across the continent and, like KTNN, they often are bilingual in English and the tribe's own language. Native American newspapers trace their lineage back to the *Cherokee Phoenix,* established in 1828 by Sequoyah after he invented the Cherokee alphabet.[65] The largest newspaper today covering Native Americans is the weekly *Indian Country Today,* founded in 1981 and owned by the Oneida Nation since 1998.[66]

In addition to Rupert Murdoch's Australian-based News Corp. and Conrad Black's Canadian-based Hollinger chain, other foreign corporations also own media properties in the United States.

For example, a San Francisco Chinese-language daily, the *World Journal,* claims a nationwide circulation of 350,000.[67] That would put it among the 25 largest U.S. dailies, though few Americans are even aware it exists. It is owned by United Daily News Group of Taiwan. Claiming 181,000 circulation is the *Sing Tao Daily,* owned by a Hong Kong company. It publishes daily editions in San Francisco, New York, Los Angeles, Boston, Chicago and Philadelphia.[68]

Both of those Chinese-language dailies are part of a thriving U.S. ethnic press serving the millions who make up the Asian, Hispanic and African American audiences. Today's ethnic press includes many other daily newspapers, including *The Korean Times* in Los Angeles, competing Spanish-language dailies *El Nuevo Herald* and *Diario Las Americanas* in Miami, and *The Chicago Defender* for African Americans, to name a few.

Many ethnic publications have large circulations. For example, *La Opinión* in Los Angeles is the largest Spanish-language daily, with a circulation of more than 125,800.[69]

Foreign-language newspapers have been a part of the American immigrant press since at least 1794, and they reached a peak in 1914 when there were 140 dailies published in dozens of languages.[70]

In broadcasting, National Public Radio has more than 600 member stations across the country, and the Public Broadcasting System is owned and operated by about 350 television stations. Both entities cover most major markets. Both NPR and PBS are private, nonprofit media organizations, with NPR started in 1970 and PBS founded in 1969. Many NPR radio stations can be heard in multi-state regions, and both NPR and PBS pride themselves on independent and educational programming that cannot be found on commercial stations.[71]

However, the model for public broadcasting in radio and television has changed dramatically since an intense Congressional battle in 1995–96, when then–House Speaker Newt Gingrich led an effort to "zero out" federal funding for public broadcasting. The compromise resulted in reduced federal funding levels. That has resulted in commercialism pressures, and public stations have increasingly turned to corporate "sponsors" (avoiding the term "advertisers") for more income.[72]

According to *American College Media Directory*, there also are at least 1,300 newspapers (about 75 of them dailies), 1,000 radio stations and 700 television stations on campuses that reach 13 million college and university students across the nation.[73]

Three main kinds of ownership

NOT WITHSTANDING the more unusual forms of media ownership just cited, there are only three basic kinds of commercial ownership structure for any kind of business—sole proprietorship, partnership and corporate—with some variations on each. The differences in corporate structure, for example, are so major that choosing which kind of corporation you want your new business to be can be a major tax and operating decision. A new owner buying or starting up a business should consult with attorneys and accountants to decide which of the three forms of ownership is the best fit for the situation.

Sole proprietorship

About 70 percent of all U.S. businesses are sole proprietorships. It is the simplest type of business to start and is the organizational structure of choice for most one-person operations—especially among those who know very little about business. That last point should be your first clue that a sole proprietorship might not be the most advantageous type of organizational structure for a business. A sole proprietorship can have employees, though many don't.

Depending on where you live, starting a sole proprietorship can be as simple as just opening your doors for business. Most cities require an assumed-name filing if the business name is anything other than the owner's own name, and most also require a home occupation permit if the business is run out of the home. On the other hand, these requirements are often ignored and difficult to enforce. There are more proprietorships than any other kind of structure, and many large corporations started out as a sole proprietorship in a garage. (Think of Bill Gates.)

The owner of a sole proprietorship keeps all the profits, so all business income is taxed as personal income. However, the owner also has unlimited liability for business debts, which means that creditors can come after the business owner's personal assets as well as business assets. Another disadvantage is that the owner's ability to raise capital is limited to the owner's personal wealth or credit-worthiness. This limitation often means that the business cannot exploit new opportunities because of the inability to raise sufficient capital. Ownership of a proprietorship also can be difficult to transfer because it requires the sale of the entire business to a new owner,[74] and the business itself often is identified too closely with a specific individual.

Partnership

This form can be very similar to a sole proprietorship, except there are two or more owners and the profits or losses from the business are divided according to a partnership agreement drawn between the owners. There are two kinds of partnerships:

A general partnership can be organized with an oral or written partnership agreement. The smaller the business, the less formal this type of partnership tends to be. This is the most risky type of business arrangement, because both partners are equally responsible for all business debts and each partner has the right to obligate the other partner to debts of the partnership. Lack of written agreements in a partnership of any size is courting misunderstanding and potential economic disaster. A general partnership ends when one partner dies or when one partner wants to leave.[75]

A limited partnership requires a written agreement, if for no other reason than that it must withstand closer scrutiny from the IRS. In this type of partnership, a "general partner" actually runs the business and one or more "limited partners" have no say in the company operation but also have their risk limited by the amount of their investment. If a limited partner attempts to become involved in business decisions, the IRS and courts might very well reclassify him or her as a general partner despite any claims to the contrary. A limited partner's interest can be sold without dissolving the partnership, but finding a buyer might be problematic.

Corporation

This is the most complicated, but usually the most advantageous, business structure for a business of any size. A corporation is a legal entity, a "person" if you will, separate and distinct from its owners, and it has many of the rights, privileges and obligations of an actual person. Corporations can own property and borrow money, can sue and be sued, and can enter into contracts. A corporation can even be a general partner or a limited partner in a partnership, and a corporation can own stock in another corporation.

Because a corporation is a legal entity, distinct from the owners who are its officers, the owners are effectively shielded from claims against their personal property to satisfy debts of the corporation. A second major advantage of a corporation is the tax advantage corporations enjoy in being able to deduct expenses from income before paying taxes.[76]

For these two reasons alone, many business owners choose to incorporate even small companies—many times even one-person companies that appear on the surface to be sole proprietorships. The 1990s wealth-building book, *Rich Dad, Poor Dad,* emphasizes the tax advantages to being incorporated for any business, as follows.[77]

People who establish corporations for even one-person businesses:

(1) earn,

(2) spend,

(3) then pay taxes on income after expenses.

On the other hand, people who work for corporations:

(1) earn,

(2) pay taxes,

(3) then can only spend the smaller portion that is left.

The difference in the order of those sequences can result in a big reduction in taxes for an incorporated person over a wage-earner. The whole point of the book is to show people how to make money work for them, rather than having them do as most people and work for money.

To form a corporation requires preparing articles of incorporation and a set of bylaws, registering with the state in which the business is incorporated, and issuing stock, which can be closely held by a few individuals or, if so organized, publicly traded. Every corporation has stock, but there are four ways in which the stock is handled.

(1) Single-owner corporation. A small, privately owned corporation will possess just one certificate with all of the shares in the proprietor's name. Most small media companies, from weekly newspapers to advertising and public relations firms, are incorporated this way.

(2) Closely held private corporation. Some larger corporations are set up this way. All of the stock might be in one individual's name, as in the first example, but very often there are different amounts of shares, usually held by members of the owner's family.

This is the first of two arrangements used to maintain local ownership and deter an unfriendly takeover. Sometimes a minority interest in stock is issued to the public, with family members keeping the majority. In that way, the corporation cannot be sold unless the members of the family want to sell it. As stock gets diluted with each succeeding generation, however, with more family members not sharing the founder's interest in the company, eventually there often are enough like-minded family members to force the sale. Thus, the Chandler family finally sold the *Los Angeles Times,* and the Cowles family sold the *Des Moines Register.* The 80 family stockholders of Freedom Communications voted in 2003 to put their company up for bidding by the chains. Several media companies are closely held corporations, including Advance Publications and the McClatchy Co.

(3) Restrictive stock ownership corporation. Some corporations have put a twist on their stock plans to more effectively guard against the company being sold or lost in an unfriendly take-over by establishing "dual-class" stock structures, such as issuing voting and non-voting classes of stock. For example, the New York Times Co. and the Washington Post Co. issue voting stock that is held by family members, while non-voting stock is sold on Wall Street. Others arrange to have controlling blocs of stock owned by an Employee Stock Ownership Plan (ESOP). Nothing seems foolproof, however, when it comes to money. Even these plans can fall victim to a desire by stockholders to cash in lucrative holdings. The *Journal Star* of Peoria, Ill., was put into an ESOP as a strategy to keep it from going to the chains. But after 12 years, many of the employees (who owned 91 percent of the company) began opting for the money they could get by selling their stock. The resulting financial threat to the paper forced the directors to sell the *Journal Star* to the Copley chain in 1995.[78] Another grand experiment gone awry.

(4) Publicly held corporation. This is a corporation that has all of its stock sold on Wall Street and in brokerage houses across the nation. When most people think of a stockholder-owned company, they are referring to this kind of arrangement. Smaller companies might be listed on the NASDAQ exchange, while larger companies are listed on the New York Stock Exchange. Anyone can buy any amount of these corporations' shares, with the result that institutional investors such as pension funds and insurance companies can end up with influential blocs of stock. Members of the board of directors usually own only a small minority interest, and so they are prone to pressures from larger holders. Publicly held media corporations include the Walt Disney Company, Gannett, Knight Ridder, Dow Jones & Co., E.W. Scripps Co., and Cox Enterprises.

In a large corporation, the stockholders and managers are usually separate groups, but in a small corporation they may be the same individuals. The stockholders elect a board of directors, whose members are responsible for working with management in directing or at least overseeing the company.

As a result of separation of ownership and management (except in single-owner corporations), the corporate form has several advantages over a partnership or a sole proprietorship.

Ownership, represented by shares of stock, can be easily transferred, so the life of the corporation is theoretically perpetual. In fact, ownership can be changing continuously without affecting the continuity of the business. Corporations can and often do outlive the founders, and some have lasted for centuries. The corporation borrows money in its own name, so the stockholders have limited liability for corporate debts and cannot lose more than they have invested. With the help of a lot of paperwork and lawyers, the corporation also can issue and sell more stock to raise needed capital.[79]

The main reasons people form corporations are to give them legal and financial protections and to improve their ability to raise capital.

The main form of structure for the largest corporations is what is known as a **C corporation.** Smaller companies today usually are a different kind of corporation, although smaller companies that have been inherited often still retain their original C form of incorporation because the heirs neglect to change the structure.

Because it is a legal "person," any corporation can be sued, but the owner's personal assets are not nearly so much at risk. This is because the owner is just an employee of the corporation—just like the other people working for the corporation are employees.

In a partnership or sole proprietorship, the owner is liable both personally and as a business. To reiterate, stockholders of a corporation have limited liability for debts, but the owner of a sole proprietorship or a partnership has unlimited liability for business debts.

The one big disadvantage of a corporation is that because it is a legal "person," it therefore must pay taxes. In addition, money paid out to stockholders (the owners) in the form of dividends is taxed again as income to the stockholders. This is referred to as "double taxation" because corporate profits are in effect taxed twice—when they are earned, and when a portion is paid out as dividends. Both the owners and the corporation must pay taxes.

Even this problem can be avoided, however, by newer corporate structures—limited liability corporations and professional corporations.

Primarily to avoid the much-hated double taxation, but also for more nimble organizational reasons, most small and mid-sized businesses today are incorporated as an **LLC corporation.**

A similar and older limited liability corporation is the **S corporation,** named after a section of the tax code. The S corporation is being phased out for many reasons in favor of the LLC corporation. In both cases, profit passes through the corporation as personal income to the owners, and thus is only taxed once. Because of this tax advantage over the C Corporation, IRS approval is required for establishing either an S or an LLC corporation. Though it doesn't apply to media companies, incorporation as a professional firm also is available for lawyers, doctors, CPAs, etc.

Anyone starting a corporation should consult an attorney for the differences, advantages and disadvantages of each corporate structure. This book does not give legal advice.

The functional parts of any business

NO MATTER WHAT the organizational structure, and no matter what size it is, certain internal activities take part in any business to enable it to create, sell and make a profit from its products or services. In a major corporation, these activities are carried out in a several departments, though they might not be exactly as named in this book. In small companies, the owner might do them all, though they still will be separated as duties, even if subconsciously.

The eight functional parts of a business are: Administrative, finance, accounting, operations, marketing, sales, information systems, and support functions.

Don't take the title personally, but the following titles of the eight functional parts of a business are partly adapted from the book *The Complete Idiot's Guide to MBA Basics*.[80]

Administrative

This is the home of the chief executive officer (CEO) and the highest echelon of the company's officers. Sometimes known as the headquarters or executive office, the top officers of all of the other departments might also be located physically in this office in the largest companies. Most corporations reserve space here for a conference room where planning and operational meetings can take place, including meetings of the board of directors.

The smaller the company, the more likely that some or all of this and the following departments might be merged. In sole proprietorships, one owner will do everything. But even there, the owner tends to think of his or her duties broken down in the following ways.

Finance controls the money

This might come as a surprise, but companies always are seeking good investment opportunities for their cash reserves, often keeping cash in money market funds or investments that still provide easy and quick availability. The finance department makes sure the company has the money it needs to operate, including funds to buy or lease property and equipment, purchase raw materials, and pay for all operations.

Finance works with senior management, and sometimes its leaders are involved in setting the company's sales and profits. A person with the title of chief financial officer (CFO) often is found in this department. In large companies, this department is staffed with financial analysts and investment specialists.

Accounting counts the money

The accounting department works closely with finance, but it has a different role in that it tracks the flow of money within the company. In the accounting department, for example, are the accounts receivable (money the company is owed and paid) and the accounts payable (money the company owes and must pay). There also is payroll, which is the only part of the department that most employees encounter. This department includes the credit department, which decides how much credit to extend to suppliers and customers, and the tax department, which manages the company's federal, state and local tax payments. In large companies, this department is staffed with accountants. Small and mid-sized companies might turn all of these duties over to an outside accounting firm.

Operations makes what the company sells

This department goes by many names, depending on the company and its products or services. The operations department is also called the production function. In a service organization, operations includes the employees who serve the customers and the places where they work—such as the newsroom and advertising departments in media companies. The purchasing department, which buys the company's supplies, is included in this function, as are other back-office functions outside the public's view necessary to keep the company operating smoothly.

Newspapers and magazines also have a factory-like component, so operations also would include departments such as shipping and receiving, press rooms and sometimes even trucking terminals.

In media companies, operations is where you find the newsroom staffs. Many companies would refer to the top person in this department as the chief operating officer (COO), but there often are different titles at media companies, such as, for example, the editor at a newspaper and the general manager at a television station.

Marketing sells to groups

The marketing department works to publicize and promote the

company's products and services to customers and potential customers. Marketing does this through public relations, advertising campaigns, special promotions, direct mail, and other awareness-creating strategies. Staffs for telemarketing and direct mail can be included in this department. This function also can include market research. In large companies, people in marketing are specialists in one of these areas.

Marketing can make or break a company. A firm can have a product superior to any competitor, but unless marketing makes the public want to buy the product, the company will not generate sufficient sales to grow or possibly even to survive.

Sales brings in the money

This department includes the men and women who actually sell the company's products or services one-on-one to customers. A customer service department also is part of this function. In every media company, this department includes an advertising section, where the salespeople for local and national accounts are located. Print companies also have a circulation section staffed with salespeople. As with marketing, the success of individual salespeople is critical to a business. The dark humor about failed companies is that they did everything right, but they just didn't make enough sales.

Management info keeps the computers running

This department, which used to be known as data processing, is the one that runs the company's computer systems. It might go by the name of "management information systems" (MIS) or by the name of "information technology" (IT). In large companies, MIS people keep the systems running, and IT people are more apt to be considered computer repair and upgrading specialists. Whatever you call it, this department has experienced phenomonal growth in importance since the 1980s, when computers first became both ubiquitous and essential to virtually every company.

This department deals with the purchase, maintenance, programming and security of the company's computers. Its employees ensure that the company uses its high-tech sources in a competitively advantageous way and that computerized record-keeping needs are met in every other department.

Support functions do the rest

All of a company's other operations are categorized as support functions. They include human resources (formerly known as personnel), the legal department, investor relations, and facilities management. Any of the first three might be found in the administrative department.

However, they are placed in different departments in different companies. For example, facilities management might be a part of operations, just as investor relations might be a part of the marketing department.

Facilities management deals with real estate matters as well as the maintenance of the company's building(s), and it is responsible for upkeep of the grounds and of the heating, cooling, telecommunications and security systems.

Structure of media companies

ALL OF THESE functional departments come together to make up the organization. Small, independent newspapers, television stations, magazines, radio stations, public relations firms and advertising agencies all have the same similar structure, in which the owner of the company usually is the president, the CEO, COO, CFO and the relatively new position of chief information officer (CIO), all rolled into one.

The blended TV-print-Internet newsrooms under convergence are putting all job roles into a state of confusion at the middle and lower levels of organizational structure, but not at the top.

In the most general of terms, the leading executive of a newspaper is a publisher and the leading executive of a broadcast station is the general manager. In large conglomerates, however, these people still are not at the top of the heap, because they must report to senior management in regional or national offices of the company, and those senior managers must in turn report to corporate CEOs, COOs, and CFOs depending on the organization.

It doesn't stop there in publicly traded companies, where the president and/or the CEO must report to a board of directors, headed by a chairman of the board, which usually meets at least monthly.

In America's capitalistic system, the heart of the profit chase in publicly traded media companies lives in the corporate body known as the board of directors. Board members are elected by the stockholders. Their duties include hiring the CEO, establishing corporate policy, monitoring corporate operations, mission and strategy, and approving all major decisions before implementation. The board's heart beats for the stockholders.

In fact, board members owe a legal obligation known as **fiduciary responsibility** to stockholders. Even if board members want to pull back from the profit chase, they cannot. To do so would be to risk their own seats on the board at best and to be personally sued by disgruntled stockholders at worst. Thus, the profit chase is assured, regardless of philosophical struggles over whether it is diminishing a media corporation's journalism mission.

In some corporations, the chairperson of the board of directors is more influential in running the business than the CEO. A good example is CBS board chairman William S. Paley, who traditionally played the strongest role in charting the network's direction and mission.[81]

In a corporation, the CEO is the executive who directly presides over the layers on layers of senior, middle and line managers. To be sure, corporate bureaucracy can be as formidable and as difficult to navigate as anything dreamed up by the federal or state governments.

There are four bureaucratic principles of structure that apply to every large company—principles of authority, span of control, work specialization and departmentalization.

Principles of authority: How authority is distributed and exercised is a major building block of an organization. One of the first principles is "unity of command," which holds that there should be only one supervisor to whom a subordinate should owe responsibility and obedience. This is great in theory, but in actual practice it is a rare subordinate in any media company who doesn't need to keep more than one supervisor happy. There is just too much interaction between departments in a media company for unity of command to be observed strictly. Other authority principles are "decentralization" at the organizational level, where authority and responsibility are delegated system-wide to middle and lower-level managers, and "delegation," where power is distributed at the individual level as managers assign work for others to do.[82] Just as there is decentralization, of course, there also is centralization, and in periods of reorganization many companies that are decentralized become more centralized, and vice versa.

Span of control: This also is known as "span of attention" or "span of management." Companies have different ideas of how many subordinates a manager can handle. Representations of span of control often are pictured as a pyramid, with the top executive at the pinnacle. In a span of three, three managers would report to that CEO, and they in turn would have three sub-managers each reporting to them, and so on. Typically, the span of control for top executives ranges between three and nine, but the farther down the pyramid, the more people an operational manager is expected to be able to direct, up to 20 or 30.[83] For that reason, rarely is the span of control kept mathematically precise through all levels of management. Ideally, the wider the span, the more efficient an organization should be. Span of control is one of the first organizational principles looked at in company-wide reorganization efforts. Mid-level managers especially are vulnerable to layoffs when a company decides to increase the span of control at their levels.

> An early example of span of control is in the Old Testament where Moses is advised to designate "rulers of thousands, and rulers of hundreds, rulers of fifties, and rulers of tens."[84]
>
> —*Exodus 18:21*

Work specialization: This is also known as division of labor, generally attributed to economist Adam Smith, author of *Wealth of Nations*,[85] originally published in 1776. Under work specialization, certain jobs are the responsibility of a specific individual. For example, newspaper copy editors have the final say over wording and punctuation in a story, at least theoretically. Different individuals have different labors. It is effective in media organizations and many other kinds of companies where highly skilled people are needed to perform certain tasks. This is the area of bureaucratic structure with which efficiency experts often are concerned, checking on the efficiency of employees who have specific tasks to perform repeatedly day after day. For less skilled employees, there is a move on to eliminate work specialization so that each worker gets to do more than one kind of job, thereby relieving the boredom of a repetitive task.

Departmentalization: As individuals are separated by the kinds of jobs they do, the next step is to gather the ones doing similar work and place them in a department together, under the eye of a manager who is knowledgeable in the kind of work being done. Departments are created based on several factors, including the nature of the work, different kinds of customers being served (such as national and local), geographic locations of branch offices, and specialized employees (a foreign desk as a nearly autonomous department within the newsroom that is supervising widespread foreign correspondents, as an example).

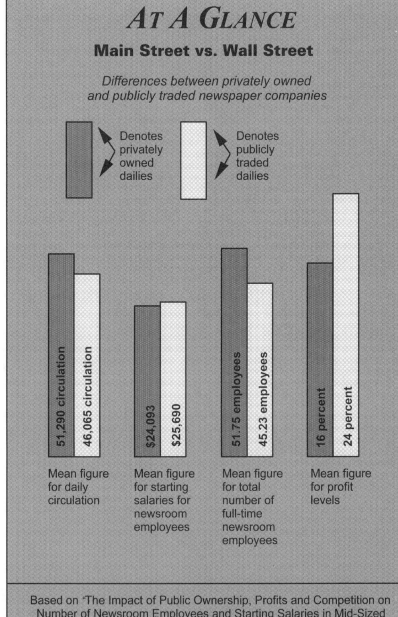

AT A GLANCE

Main Street vs. Wall Street

*Differences between privately owned
and publicly traded newspaper companies*

Denotes privately owned dailies

Denotes publicly traded dailies

51,290 circulation

46,065 circulation

$24,093

$25,690

51.75 employees

45.23 employees

16 percent

24 percent

Mean figure for daily circulation

Mean figure for starting salaries for newsroom employees

Mean figure for total number of full-time newsroom employees

Mean figure for profit levels

Based on "The Impact of Public Ownership, Profits and Competition on Number of Newsroom Employees and Starting Salaries in Mid-Sized Daily Newspapers," a research paper presented in August 2002 at the national convention of the Association for Education in Journalism and Mass Communication

CASE STUDY   *Serving Two Masters:*
                  The Boss and the News

by LINDA KAY
Concordia University

Bill Stanford is the sports editor of the largest daily newspaper in the state. A few days ago, the editor-in-chief dropped a bombshell on him. He told Stanford that the paper, which owns a handful of other newspapers around the country and several large broadcast outlets in the Midwest, intended to purchase the National Basketball Association franchise in his state within the week. Stanford was advised to keep mum about the purchase and not leak a word of it to his staff.

But already one of the staffers has gotten wind of the purchase. He's the senior sports columnist on the paper and has sources that reach far and wide. As Stanford peers out his office window into the sports department, he sees the columnist on the telephone trying to track down comment on the impending purchase.

The columnist's protégé, a young female sportswriter, has already come into Stanford's office to say she has tried to get some comment on the purchase from the publisher, but to no avail. She tells Stanford that the newspaper's top executives have all left town for a fishing retreat in Canada.

Stanford knows the purchase is a fait accompli, but still feels bound by his vow of silence. Now the reporters are looking to him for direction on the story.

It's a huge story that will surely make waves. He can just see the competing newspaper in town raising the specter of conflict of interest in its coverage—a question that screams loudly when a newspaper buys the team it covers. Stanford himself has mulled the question a thousand times since the editor-in-chief dropped the bomb.

Now the columnist and his protégé are knocking on Stanford's office door. They want to write the story. The sports editor hesitates and tells them he'll get back to them in a moment. He phones the editor-in-chief and requests advice. The editor-in-chief says the purchase of the team is a business story, not a sports story. He suggests Stanford hand it over to the business department. He says he'll be coming to Stanford's office in a few minutes with the editor of the business section.

Meanwhile, Stanford doesn't feel the business writers will have the same insight into the story as his sports staff. But if he must hand over the story to the business section, he thinks the senior sports columnist should be permitted to write critically about the purchase. And shouldn't the sports section, he ponders, if not the paper as a whole, be assuring its readers, in some kind of printed statement, that coverage of the NBA team will continue to be fair and impartial?

Stanford intends to raise these points with the editor-in-chief and business editor. He sees them walking across the newsroom to his office. Now that the cat is out of the bag, Stanford also ushers into his office the sports columnist, his protégé and the basketball writer.

Assignment:

1. In groups, take the part of the sports editor, editor-in-chief, business editor, sports columnist, his protégé and the basketball writer. Have each represent a position congruent with his/her role.

2. Examine the fundamental question of cross ownership. Let each participant in the discussion air his/her views on the merits and the pitfalls. Then examine the question of how the story should be handled in this case. Should it be handled by the sports or business section? Should critical pieces be written about the purchase? Let each participant comment on the ramifications of the paper's coverage.

3. Should the paper issue a statement to its readers about the purchase? If so, what should the statement say?

ACKNOWLEDGEMENTS/EXPLANATIONS:

Names and places have been altered in this scenario, but the underlying facts are true.

AUTHOR:

Linda Kay is an assistant professor in the journalism department at Concordia University in Montreal, Quebec, and director of the graduate program there. She was a daily newspaper reporter for 17 years, including a 10-year stint as a sportswriter for a large metropolitan daily in the United States.

⌨ *Suggested Web sites:*

www.newslink.org/menu.html—List of media properties
www.ajr.org/News_Wire_Services.asp?MediaType=10—Media companies
www.cjr.org/owners—"Who Owns What?" plus selected articles on ownership
www.naa.org/presstime/index.html—*Presstime* magazine of daily publishers
www.broadcastingcable.com—*Broadcasting & Cable* magazine
www.poynter.org/subject.asp?id=47—Poynter's Journalism and Business Values site
www.veronissuhler.com—Newspaper facts from Veronis, Suhler & Associates

---

Endnotes to Chapter 7:

[1] Jay Lindsay, *Herald to Buy Community Newspapers*, Associated Press, September 28, 2000.

[2] Cole C. Campbell, "Cash cow journalism and the changes in our business," at <www.poynterextra.org/centerpiece/jbv/campbell.htm>, accessed August 9, 2003.

[3] Ibid.

[4] Reid Ashe, "The only way to get more resources: Serve readers better," at<www.poynterextra.org/centerpiece/jbv/ashe.htm>, accessed August 9, 2003.

[5] Molly Ivins, "And how much blame for the Fourth Estate?" (November 1, 2001), formerly at <web.star-telegram.com/content/fortworth/columnist/molly_ivins.htm>, accessed November 26, 2001. Site is no longer available on the Web.

[6] David P. Hamilton, "As others sink, 2 biotech players have hit it big: Amgen, Genentech combine luck and skill to emerge enormously profitable," *The Wall Street Journal* (November 18, 2002): A1.

[7] Ben Berger, an M.A. student in accounting at the University of New Mexico, researched and compiled most of the information on the profitability of corporations by studying the 2002 financial reports of the corporations in early 2003.

[8] Michael Emery and Edwin Emery, *The Press and America: An Interpretive History of the Mass Media* (Englewood Cliffs, N.J.: Prentice-Hall, 5th ed., 1984), 39.

[9] Jay Black and Ralph Barney, "Journalism ethics since Janet Cooke," *Newspaper Research Journal* (Fall 1992–Winter 1993): 13–14.

[10] Ibid., 14.

[11] John Kenneth Galbraith, *The New Industrial State* (New York: Houghton Mifflin Co., 4th ed. 1985), 116–135.

[12] David Demers, "Corporate newspaper bashing: Is it justified?" *Newspaper Research Journal* (Winter 1999): 89.

[13] Galbraith, *The New Industrial State,* 122.

[14] Ibid.

[15] David Demers and Debra Merskin, "Corporate news structure and the managerial revolution," 13, *Journal of Media Economics* (2000): 111.

[16] Ibid., 114.

[17] Max Weber, *The Theory of Social and Economic Organization,* A.M. Henderson and Talcott Parsons, trans. (New York: Free Press, 1947), 248–249.

[18] Galbraith, *The New Industrial State,* 124.

[19] Ibid.

[20] Ibid., 125.

[21] William Pfaff, Los Angeles Times Syndicate International, as published in "U.S. capitalism has gone corrupt," *Albuquerque Journal*, September 7, 2002, A8.

[22] Winthrop Quigley, "Corporate scandals blamed on character," *Albuquerque Journal*, July 5, 2002, A2.

[23] Edmund B. Lambeth, "Journalism educators and the journey to Pluto: Who will go and how?" *Media Ethics* (Fall 2001): 26–27.

[24] Victor F. Ganzi, "From the desk of Victor F. Ganzi," *@Hearst* (Fall 2002): 1.

[25] Lucia Moses, "Profiting from experience," *Editor & Publisher* (February 3, 2003): 12, 21.

[26] Ibid., 21.

[27] Brian Lambert, "Network vet sees news in 'death spiral,'" *St. Paul Pioneer Press,* at <www.twincities.com/mld/twincities/entertainment/columnists/brian_lambert/536970.htm>, accessed March 12, 2003.

[28] Hugh Downs, in comments made as a member of a panel discussion on media ownership sponsored by FCC Commissioner Michael J. Copps at Arizona State University in Phoenix, April 25, 2003.

[29] "Radio," *Editor & Publisher* (March 17, 2003): 21.

[30] Philip Meyer, "Should limits on broadcast ownership change? No," *USA Today*, January 22, 2003, 11A.

[31] Paul Farhi, "TV's news central: One source fits all," *The Washington Post,* May 31, 2003, A1.

[32] Jim Rutenberg with Micheline Maynard, "TV news that looks local, even if it's not," *The New York Times,* June 2, 2003, with full text at <www.nytimes.com/2003/06/02/business/media/02TUBE.html>, accessed June 2, 2003.

[33] Ibid.

[34] Jack Fuller, *News Values* (Chicago: University of Chicago Press, 1996), 197-198.

[35] Marjorie Kelly, "Is maximizing returns for shareholders a legitimate mandate?" <www.business-ethics.com/TDROC-PBACK.htm>, accessed August 9, 2003.

[36] Ralph W. Estes, *Tyranny of the Bottom Line: Why Corporations Make Good People Do Bad Things* (San Francisco, Calif.: Berrett-Koehler, 1996), 50.

[37] Ibid., 48.

[38] Kelly, "Is maximizing returns for shareholders a legitimate mandate?"

[39] Ibid.

[40] Ibid.

[41] Ibid.

[42] Galbraith, *The New Industrial State,* 122.

[43] "Hollinger, Black vow to make changes," NewsInc. Web subscription newsletter, 15, May 26, 2003.

[44] Conrad C. Fink, quoting from a letter written to him by Alvah H. Chapman Jr., *Media Ethics: In the Newsroom and Beyond* (New York: McGraw-Hill Book Co., 1988), 105.

[45] Ibid., 139.

[46] Clifford G. Christians, *Media Ethics: Cases and Moral Reasoning* (New York: Longman, 6th ed., 2001), 35–36.

[47] Gilbert Cranberg with Randall Bezanson and John Soloski, *Taking Stock: Journalism and the Publicly Traded Newspaper Company* (Ames: Iowa State Press, 2001), 109–110.

[48] Ibid.

[49] Ibid., 41.

[50] Peter F. Drucker, *Management Challenges for the 21st Century* (New York: HarperCollins Publishers Inc., 2001), Rocket e-book edition v. 1, 2002, 134.

[51] "Newspaper interests ask for changes in tax laws," *Editor & Publisher* (August 6, 1983): 27.

[52] Independent Newspapers Inc., "Our company," <www.newszap.com/inprofile>, accessed April 11, 2003.

[53] Joe Strupp, "Owner's will was the way to ensure quality and profitability in perpetuity," *Editor & Publisher* (January 28, 2002): 21.

[54] Joe Strupp, "Primary colors paper's past, but school points the way to an independent future," *Editor & Publisher* (January 28, 2002): 12.

[55] John Cummins, "The Nonprofit Newspaper," *Editor & Publisher* (February 25, 2002): 24.

[56] John Morton, "Noble sentiments: Local owners devise ways to keep their newspapers away from the chains," *American Journalism Review* (March 2003): 60.

[57] Rick Romell and Kathleen Gallagher, "Journal Sentinel faces potential, peril as parent goes public," *Milwaukee Journal Sentinel,* May 25, 2003, complete text on <www.jsonline.com /bym/News/may03/143078.asp>, accessed June 2, 2003.

[58] Joe Strupp, "Using Poynter to make a difference—and growing circ along the way," *Editor & Publisher* (January 28, 2002): 12.

[59] One example is the *Springville* (Iowa) *Newsletter,* published for several years by volunteers and a local economic development group.

[60] James F. Tracy, "The voice of the common people: The founding and development of the Iowa Co-Operative Publishing Company," from a dissertation titled *Rekindling Class Consciousness: The Dubuque Leader, 1935–1940,* © 2001, James F. Tracy, 1. A revised version of the dissertation was published as, "From blueprint to reality: The Dubuque Leader's transformation under cooperative ownership," *American Journalism: A Journal of Media History,* 9, 4 (Fall 2002): 95–119.

[61] Sidney Fine, *Sit-Down: The General Motors Strike of 1936-37* (Ann Arbor: The University of Michigan Press, 3rd ed., 1979).

[62] Tracy, "The voice of the common people," 3.

[63] Chester Francis, general manager of KTNN-AM, in remarks made to media management class at the University of New Mexico, February 14, 2002.

[64] Jay Allen, program manager of KTNN-AM, in remarks made to media management class at the University of New Mexico, February 14, 2002.

[65] Emery and Emery, 115.

[66] Information from the newspaper's Web site at <www.indian country.com>, accessed March 1, 2002.

[67] Pui-Wing Tam, "New voices: Ms. Li's journalistic crusade is epitome of thriving ethnic press in U.S.," *Wall Street Journal* Interaction Edition, Rocket e-book, July 31, 2001, 97.

[68] Sing Tao Daily <www.asianmediaguide.com/chinese/pub/singtao.html>, on Web site of Kang and Lee Advertising Inc., accessed September 8, 2002.

[69] Michael J. McCarthy, "Texas dailies battle for Hispanic readers," *The Wall Street Journal,* August 4, 2003, B-1.

[70] Emery and Emery, 684.

[71] Information from the two organizations' Web sites at <www.npr.org> and <www.pbs.org>, both accessed March 1, 2002.

[72] Glenda Balas, *Recovering a Public Vision for Public Broadcasting* (Lanham, Md.: Rowman & Littlefield Publishers, 2003), 10.

[73] American College Media Directory, <www.webcom.com/shambhu/cmd/home.html>, accessed October 25, 2001.

[74] Stephen A. Ross with Randolph W. Westerfield and Bradford D. Jordan, *Fundamentals of Corporate Finance* (New York: Richard D. Irwin, 3rd ed., 1995), 5–6.

[75] Ibid., 6.

[76] Ibid., 6.

[77] Robert T. Kiyosaki, *Rich Dad, Poor Dad* (New York: Warner Books, 1998), 104–105.

[78] Morton, "Noble sentiments: Local owners devise ways to keep their newspapers away from the chains."

[79] Ross, et al., *Fundamentals of Corporate Finance,* 6–7.

[80] Tom Gorman, *The Complete Idiot's Guide to MBA Basics* (New York: Alpha Books, 1998), 26.

[81] Ricky W. Griffin, *Management* (Boston, Mass.: Houghton Mifflin, 1984), 181–182.

[82] Ibid., 272.

[83] Ralph Currier Davis, *The Fundamentals of Top Management* (New York: Harper & Brothers, 1951), 275.

[84] Thanks to Ricky W. Griffin for his mention of this Biblical passage on pages 273–274 in his book, *Management*.

[85] Griffin, *Management*, 261.

CHAPTER 8

BUDGETING AND

FINANCIAL MANAGEMENT

T WO PEOPLE with irreconcilable approaches in the philosophy of financial management of media companies are Bill Kovach, director of the Committee of Concerned Journalists, and William P. Hamilton, a former editor of *The Wall Street Journal.*

Kovach is a true believer in the idea that a media company receiving the benefits and protection of the First Amendment owes a debt of responsibility to the public in return. Kovach states firmly, "(News media companies) have a personal and direct obligation to the citizen first and the stockholder second. We need an ownership that understands that."[1]

Hamilton, however, saw a newspaper as simply a business, nothing more. Editor of *The Wall Street Journal* until 1929, Hamilton declared, "A newspaper is private enterprise owing nothing whatever to the public, which grants it no franchise. It is emphatically the property of the owner, who is selling a manufactured product at his own risk."[3]

William H. Vanderbilt, a 19th century railroad magnate who was characterized by the press of his day as a "robber baron," was

> "The public be damned! I'm working for my stockholders."[2]
>
> —*William H. Vanderbilt*
> *Oct. 2, 1882*

even more outspoken, as seen in the quote box. Vanderbilt was not a journalist, of course, but there is no reason to think he would have changed his approach even if he had been one.

It is likely that today's media companies are driven by executives somewhere between Kovach and Vanderbilt in philosophy. Some undoubtedly subscribe to Hamilton's approach, which implies the profit-maximization credo driving much of corporate America today.

Profit-maximization is sometimes credited to or blamed on (depending on your point of view) the 20th century's apostle of supply-side economics and free-wheeling capitalism, Milton Friedman.

A 1976 Nobel laureate in economics, Friedman set the tone for the 1970s through at least the 1990s, and perhaps beyond, when he wrote,

"There is one and only one social responsibility to business—to use its resources and engage in activities designed to increase its profits."[4]

A typical attitude of a profit-maximization executive is the phrase, "Money is how I've always kept score." In its many variations, this is a popular credo of many executives, including Tom Murphy when he was CEO of Cap Cities/ABC.

This capitalistic view of the press by Hamilton, Murphy and many other media executives, with not even a curtsey to social responsibility, was decried by the Hutchins Commission of 1947, which concluded that the newspaper publishers of the day and their scoop-driven cynics in the newsroom were too irresponsible in coverage of important news. The Hutchins Commission marked a turning point from the emphasis of unfettered freedom of the press to a new focus, supported in large part by several U.S. Supreme Court rulings since then, that the press needs to be a responsible citizen within the society of which it is such a critical part.[5]

Friedman's assertion, while it is certainly reminiscent of Hamilton's, is more problematic.

The profitability dilemma of media managers

IN THE FINAL analysis, all news media companies are indeed for-profit businesses—but with a difference, for they also fulfill vital roles as the providers of information, opinion and entertainment in America.

Seeing their companies as profit-making enterprises, concerned with tasks such as finding and pleasing customers, strikes many journalists as vulgar and compromising. But most of today's news media CEOs and managers see things far differently. They feel they have no choice but to embrace market-driven journalism if they are to survive in what they see as a highly competitive marketplace. Their reaction to the cries of those who believe the media's news role is being harmed is simply this: Diminished journalism is better than no journalism.

James Batten, while CEO of Knight Ridder Newspapers, said in his 1989 Press-Enterprise Lecture that newspapers need to develop a "new and fierce commitment to publishing newspapers that strain to please and satisfy our customers every day. The days when we could do newspapering *our* way, and tell the world to go to hell if it didn't like the results, are gone forever."[6]

Many working journalists would agree with Batten to a point.

But they also contend that many media companies are really more interested in maximizing profits than they are in informing the customers. The newspaper chains today routinely report pretax profit margins of 20 percent to 30 percent (Warren Buffet's *Buffalo News* boasts an operating margin of more than 35 percent[7]). Even more striking is that local TV stations often boast of operating margins ranging around 50 percent,[8] while at the same time refusing to pay interns any wage at all and offering low average starting salaries to broadcast grads.

As university student Wendy Apkarian, taking courses in both journalism and business, observed, "Free speech and the priority of the public interest has always been at the heart of journalism but certainly not at the heart of profit."[9]

Such profitability is the envy of most major national industries, many of which are deemed prosperous with single-digit to 15 percent margins. It is common for media companies to sell properties that are profitable—but not profitable enough—and to move quickly when doing so. For example, MediaNews Group Inc., purchased the small *Valley News Today* daily in Shenandoah, Iowa, as well as other publications nearby for $5.1 million plus working capital and noncompete covenant provisions on May 1, 1998.[10] Only a year and a half later, MediaNews Group announced it was putting those papers on the market because they were not as profitable as expected,[11] selling them in late 2000 to Omaha World-Herald Company.

Without realizing it, in opposing profit maximization, working journalists really are advocates of what Peter F. Drucker called "profit optimization," a principle that he defined as the most compatible ratio between risks and opportunity. Drucker considered the traditional definition that profit is a reward for taking risk to be crass. Rather, he considered profit to be the costs of covering today's unintended operating crises and tomorrow's uncertain innovative decisions; that is, a critical source of revenue to cover costs and risks. Drucker opposed the concept of profit maximization because it did not measure critical factors such as whether the company was adequately identifying and implementing new opportunities, developing human assets, and recognizing and responding to external factors threatening the company.[12] (More on Drucker's attitudes about profits in Chapter 10.)

Similarly, economist Herbert A. Simon concluded that managers knew that profit maximization was not possible. Therefore, perhaps even unconsciously, they would try to "satisfice" rather than "maximize" their need for profits.[13]

Ensuring profitability is life or death to the career of a manager. But profitability actually is only one of Drucker's eight required survival objectives required for any business as a whole.

"Drucker identified as key activities those that required at least minimum performance to ensure continued corporate vitality," John E. Flaherty reported. "He chose eight critical areas in which objectives were mandatory: (1) market standing, (2) productivity, (3) physical and financial resources, (4) innovation, (5) profitability, (6) worker contribution, (7) managerial performance, and (8) public responsibility."[14]

The area of public responsibility is where many journalists and academics believe the most serious disparity exists in the operation of today's media companies. If there is a remedy that would calm critics of today's management practices of media companies, it would be to take some of those massive profits and plow them back into the publications in the form of increased news hole, much improved wages and benefits, and public service projects.

That's really what Geneva Overholser is campaigning for with her "News Trust" proposal described in Chapter 1, it is what Neil Hickey discusses in his 1998 article titled "Money Lust" in the *Columbia Journalism Review*, and it is what many working journalists are thinking of when they accuse owners of greed and bottom-line journalism.

For perspective, a newspaper management textbook published in 1988 declared that, "the newspaper business is a lucrative and rewarding investment" because of a net profit margin for all U.S. newspaper groups averaging 9.6 percent.[15]

How much more lucrative it must be today with those same net profit margins approaching 20 percent for the most successful!

One of the few newspapers that can be purely idealistic about the profitability dilemma is the *St. Petersburg* (Fla.) *Times*, which is owned by the nonprofit foundation that also owns the Poynter Institute.

The editors at the *St. Petersburg Times* follow what they call "permissible moderation in the pursuit of profits," with an executive saying that they would be concerned if operating profits were below 10 percent, but they also would be concerned if operating profits were over 20 percent.[16]

Perhaps needless to say, other newspaper companies are not nearly so modest in their profit expectations. Even while daily newspaper circulation has declined overall by about 15 percent, Overholser reports that profit margins at the same newspapers rose by about 50 percent.[17]

From 1991 to 2000, newspaper analyst John Morton reports, Knight Ridder's operating margin increased from 13.6 percent to 20.8 percent, Gannett's operating margin increased from 19.7 percent to 28 percent, and E.W. Scripps Co.'s operating margin increased from 14.1 percent to 21.5 percent.[18] These margins are for the chains' newspaper operations only.

Even during the recession of 2001, the comparable figure for Gannett's newspaper margin in 2001 was almost 24.7 percent (equal to $1.4 billion), with a 5 percent increase in newspaper revenues.[19] Like Gannett, all of the chains weathered the recession well by imposing "employee reductions" and other cost-saving measures.

Knight Ridder's conflict with editor Jay T. Harris arose because corporation executives were not happy with operating margins that had ranged between 22 percent and 29 percent over recent years while many of their other dailies routinely reported profits in the 30 percentile range. Industry analyst John Morton reported that in 2001 (with advertising declines for newspapers and other media) that the newspaper industry's average operating profit was still 18.5 percent[20] (down from the 22.7 percent reported for the 12 largest newspaper companies in Chapter 1). Morton notes that at the worst of the 1991 recession, the newspaper industry still had a 12 percent profit margin, which he describes as "a level other industries would hope for in boom times."[21]

Gathering reliable and understandable data involving profits from the companies is difficult because there is no one definition of profit used by everyone.

Some companies find it to their advantage to report their profit as a pretax figure, others after-tax, others simply as gross revenues over expenses, others as retained earnings, others before or after one-time expensing, etc.—while some play such elaborate word games with the concept of profit that even accounting firms cannot clearly explain what is going on. This is not just a problem with media companies. In 2001, an energy trading company known as Enron Corp. saw its stock price plummet in a matter of weeks from $85 a share to eventual bankruptcy. It was revealed that Enron's profit figures were purposely mired in such convoluted accounting chicanery that even sophisticated institutional investors were blindsided.

As it stands now, it is difficult to know if a company is talking about apples or oranges, let alone the quality of the fruit.

This confusion over what exactly is profit might be cleared up in the future because of the Enron debacle. The nation's Big Five accounting firms of PricewaterhouseCoopers, Deloitte & Touche, KPMG, Ernst & Young and the now defunct Arthur Andersen—Enron's auditor—were working together in late 2001 and into 2002 to come up with improved financial reporting standards to be submitted to the Securities and Exchange Commission (SEC).[22] For now, however, all the SEC can do is keep re-issuing its standard warning that corporate financials be treated with "appropriate and healthy skepticism."[23]

Whatever the definition of profit, the clash of philosophies over what constitutes an acceptable or desirable profit margin is at the heart of the debate over the conduct of media companies today. This is especially true of the news/information sector such as newspapers, magazines, books and broadcasting. It is less controversial, though still open to debate nevertheless, in the entertainment sector of movies, most television programming, music and radio.

Sociologists David Croteau and William Hoynes, in their book, *The Business of Media*, note in their discussion of profit that "All of these quandaries are really variations on one recurring theme: the tension between profits and the public interest . . . . The media that the authors of the First Amendment knew were radically different creatures from the ones we have today. Not only have new types of media been introduced, but the nature of media owners and producers, and the scale of their operations has changed dramatically as well. The media conglomerates of today are unprecedented in human history. How these companies operate has been rapidly changing with the rise of Internet technology, conglomeration, integration, and globalization." [24]

There are indications that some corporate news executives in 2002 and 2003 were starting to sense that the time might be right to start using some of those heady profits from the past for reinvesting and rebuilding. MediaNews Group CEO William Dean Singleton, retired Gannett CEOs John Curley and Al Neuharth, and E.W. Scripps CEO Ken Lowe all made public statements along the lines of how profit maximization has gone far enough, and perhaps too far, and that news must be recognized as the key asset of journalism companies. [25]

Media executives often speak this way, however, even while their actions go in the opposite direction of their words. It remains to be seen if these comments really are a signal of a new emphasis on news responsibility or just empty rhetoric.

Many newspaper and broadcast owners argue persuasively that good journalism is made possible only because of their profits. It seems that part of the owner's rhetoric is invariably to argue for greater profits because the money can be used for better journalism.

James D. Squires, who has been on both sides as both a reporter and an editor of the *Chicago Tribune*, gave his perspective of the conflict between profits and journalism in his autobiographical account of compromise and betrayal in Wall Street newspapering, *Read All About It! The Corporate Takeover of America's Newspapers.*

"Editors complain to peers and friends that the demand for consistently higher profits keeps their newsroom in a perpetual state of contingency planning and crisis management," Squires wrote. "The real reasons are the corporate compulsion for higher earnings to support stock prices and their parent companies' need for money to invest in local cable systems, entertainment media expansion, or acquisition of new businesses."[26]

Many journalists, like Kirk Anderson, former editorial cartoonist for the *St. Paul (Minn.) Pioneer Press*, believe that good journalism often is not what necessarily results from media companies' business success. In the accompanying cartoon, Anderson pictures how an over-emphasis on profits often acts as a restraint on journalism's ability to protect the public interest.[27]

Reprinted by permission of Kirk Anderson

NEWSPAPER CHAIN

(Anderson said he asked an editor at Knight Ridder's *Pioneer Press* to publish the cartoon, but "he just laughed at me.")[28]

It seems a debate destined to persist forever and to remain as a great philosophical divide between those who report the news and those who pay for the operation that allows the news to be reported

Profit maximization and responsibility

WILLIAM Pfaff is a nationally syndicated business columnist who frequently takes issue with Friedman's credo, which has become the dominant view of U.S. business economics.

"For the past 30-some years, business ideology has declared that stockholder return is the be-all and end-all of economic activity," Pfaff wrote. "Not manufacturing goods for real people, promoting the wealth of society and of the nation, ensuring prosperity and security for all. Just return on investment."[29]

Pfaff said this ideology of what he calls "the new economy" has insisted that if you just maximize the return to stockholders that all of the rest will follow, and everyone will benefit.

"This belief, of course, will eventually pass into the history bin of discarded ideologies," Pfaff insists.

"In the past, corporate citizenship, stakeholder work forces, and community responsibility were the accepted values," he said. "One day they will be restored by the business community itself—or be imposed by the political will of the citizenry."[30]

Pfaff's commentary echoes a philosophy long espoused by Drucker, who nevertheless concedes that the profit maximization ideology has resulted in some remarkable short-term gains.

"One may argue (as I have) that the present concentration on 'creating shareholder value' as the sole mission of the publicly owned business enterprise is too narrow and in fact may be self-defeating," Drucker states, even while conceding, "But it has resulted in an improvement in these enterprises' financial performance beyond anything an earlier generation would have thought possible—and way beyond what the same enterprises produced when they tried to satisfy multiple objectives, that is, when they were being run in the 'best balanced interests' of all the stakeholders—that is, shareholders, employees, customers, plant communities, and so on."[31]

Pfaff argues that such spectacular gains are only a short-term benefit at best. The capitalism of the late 20th century now spilling over into the early 21st century is based on deregulation and removal of other government oversight over corporate behavior, Pfaff said, resulting in a retreat from responsible capitalism.[32]

"The new American capitalism," Pfaff wrote in reaction to the bankruptcy collapses of major corporations in 2001–02 such as Enron and Global Crossing, "has failed to produce the economic justice it promised. Its natural tendency has been to produce oligopolies striving to become monopolies. This has happened in airlines, media, communications, banking, aerospace and defense industries and most other major American industrial sectors . . . . It has subordinated both short- and long-term corporate interest to quarterly profit return and the logically absurd stock market demand for constant profit growth, an expectation resembling a belief in fairies."[33]

The observations of Pfaff and Drucker sound remarkably like the complaint of editorial and newsroom employees about today's print and broadcast media. Many reporters and editors express concern that short-term goals of maximum profitability are weakening and even endangering the long-term strengths of the media's responsibility to inform the public.

That viewpoint extends to some in the top management ranks as well, according to a 2001 national survey of top managers of chain-owned newspapers. "While these publishers and editors carried out the orders (to maintain a certain profit margin even during a temporary recession), most of them believe the cuts will have a negative impact, both in the short term and long term," the trade magazine *Editor & Publisher* reported. "And, by about a 4-to-3 margin, they feel that margin management is 'bad for the newspaper industry.'"[34]

More business people, including the analyst Pfaff and the philosopher/consultant Drucker—and maybe even *E&P*—all are alluding to a values-based concept of business ethics that is starting to see some emergence in large corporations.

In a Nov. 4, 2000, speech at the University of Iowa, Leonard A. "Len" Hadley, who had recently been re-named CEO of the Maytag Corp., noted a decline in the confidence level of Americans concerning corporate America and its leaders. In a report of his speech by a University of Iowa student, Kari Althoff, Hadley announced that a study found that 55 percent of Americans had confidence in corporate America in 1966, but this level of approval had withered to only 19 percent in a more recent poll.[35]

Disturbingly for us interested in communications and journalism companies, Hadley pointed out that only a few specific industries —including the media—have earned less confidence than corporate America in general.[36]

Marjorie Kelly, publisher of *Business Ethics* magazine, is among those attempting to introduce values-based leadership of the kind espoused by Hadley to other corporate leaders.[37]

In Chapter 7, the concept of "fiduciary responsibility" was discussed. Retired corporate securities attorney Robert Hinkley explained in a *Business Ethics* article why it is taken so seriously by executives and members of corporate boards of directors.[38] Current state laws governing corporations actually inhibit a values-based corporate governance that would require social responsibility to employees and other stakeholders, he pointed out. In most states, there are virtually identical legislative clauses declaring that the purpose of a corporation under law is to make money for its stockholders. For example, Section 716 of the corporations act in Maine reads, "The directors and officers of a corporation shall exercise their powers and discharge their duties with a view to the interests of the corporation and its shareholders."[39]

Many executives read that as meaning that their obligation to increasing profits for shareholders trumps the more general co-mandate that their acts also should be in the interests of the corporation.

This mindset has rarely been so dramatically illustrated than in the last 30 years or so that are lamented by Pfaff. Old business norms and values fell aside to be replaced by situational ethics that were driven by business leaders piling on profits to feed the insatiable hunger of stockholders. The stockholders in turn wanted ever greater returns on their investments all through the 1990s in history's largest sustained bull market—until stock prices peaked in March 2000, followed by the dot-com bust and a recession.

As stock prices lower, reflecting a more realistic view of company values and profit margins, some corporations are starting to return to emphasizing product quality and corporate responsibility to all stakeholders rather than to just stockholders. They also are embracing the philosophy of building for the company's future rather than just exploiting the present, 2001–2002 business scandals notwithstanding.

This turn to values-based leadership is not without controversy nor resistance, but it is very similar to what is the norm in another of the world's industrial powerhouses—Germany. Like Japan, Germany was hailed not so long ago as a model for the U.S. to follow. Its Rhineland model—marked by business–labor cooperation and a generous Vader Staat, or "nanny state"—took it from devastation to prosperity. Although unemployment was still above 8 percent in 2000, many unemployed Germans live better than many employed, low-wage Americans.[40]

Postwar Germans value a very different strain of capitalism from America's version. Big government isn't a bogeyman in Germany. By law, every company's supervisory board must have an equal number of worker and shareholder representatives. The German Constitution states, "Ownership entails obligations. Its use should also serve the public interest."[41] Most German business leaders seem to believe that Germany has benefited from stakeholder capitalism, which puts the needs of workers, unions, banks and communities alongside those of shareholders.[42]

However, the prevailing voice of American business, *The Wall Street Journal,* still trumpets the siren call of short-term shareholder returns.

In its edition of Dec. 13, 2000, the *Journal* published dueling front page articles on General Motors and Volkswagen. In the GM article, the newspaper reported that the giant U.S. automaker was restructuring operations, laying off 15,000 workers, and dropping its Oldsmobile line in an effort to boost its stock values up from its current 5 percent return on investment. Meanwhile, Japanese and European automakers continue to export the high-quality cars that have had all the U.S. automakers reeling for at least the past 15 years. One of those overseas operators is Volkswagen, which an accompanying article in the *Journal* berates for failing to produce the return that American investors have come to expect from global firms. "Shareholder Value Still Hard to Prove at Volkswagen," declares the *Journal* headline. The article notes that for years Volkswagen has "worried much more" about its 100,000 German workers "than about its stockholders," and has been making costly investments and accepting thin profit margins to manufacture "really good cars" and thus remain the most successful auto maker in Europe, increasing its market share from 16.7 percent to 19 percent in a year.[43]

Nowhere is there a clue that *The Wall Street Journal* sees any connection between long years of profit-maximization hurting GM nor today's values-based quality manufacturing benefiting VW.

The values-based concept has roots in the business principles of fidelity, social responsibility, honesty and stewardship. Several books have been published in recent years exploring how a company can be successful by acting responsibly toward employees and customers as well as to shareholders.

But corporations, especially tight-fisted companies owned by stockholders, live and operate by the budgets their managers write, so it is vital that anyone wanting to be a manager understand the budgeting process and its close relationship to operational planning.

Budgeting and planning

BUDGETING by its very essence involves planning for the future. What is not so clear in the policies and operations of many companies is whether that planning should be short-term, intermediate or long-range. Even when our mission is to think long-range, an American company thinking in terms of several years is defining "long-term" differently than, say, a Japanese company, which might have long-range plans on paper covering several decades in the future.

It is not that the Japanese are better planners. And it's not that they are infallible, as recent difficulties among Japanese companies and their national economy have demonstrated. But their basic planning tends to look much further into the future than the planning that typically takes place in a U.S. company—and certainly much further than the range viewed by a typical American media company. Drucker could have been commenting on the short-term profit obsession of U.S. media companies when he observed, "They (Japanese companies) start out by saying, where should we be 10 years hence? And we start by saying, what should be the bottom line for the quarter—which, contrary to what most people in the United States believe, is higher in Japan than it is in American business, precisely because they start with the long-range and feedback. As did all of the companies in this country that have succeeded in staying viable, producing results for the long term."[44]

Budgeting is a form of planning—financial planning—and nearly every business decision a manager makes has to be done with a consideration of what the decision does to the budget. A manager needs to understand the budgeting process, as well as all of its components such as time value of money, financial statements, cost control, cash flow, allocation of resources, etc. Accounting and budgeting do not take great mathematical skills. The ability to add, subtract, multiply and divide are all that are really necessary—and you can even dispense largely with them if you know how to run a calculator. In today's computerized business world, you also need to learn a spreadsheet program, such as Excel.[45]

There are two kinds of operating budgets: **sales budgets** and **expense budgets.** Every department in a company will have its own separate budget, and each department's manager usually submits a budget at least once annually to corporate headquarters. Because nothing ever works out exactly as planned, managers always need to deal with one or another "variance" from the budget, often being required to make a variance report in each instance to the higher-ups, sometimes immediately after their budget has been changed. Many managers use cash flow reports, which show the actual beginning total of assets for the present year versus the beginning totals for the previous year.

Planning a budget is difficult, and the further out the budget goes the more it becomes an art form rather than a science. Malcolm Forbes noted, "Anyone who says businessmen deal in facts, not fiction, has never read old five-year projections."[46]

Frankly, a sales budget is mostly just a motivational tool in most companies. Management always wants to increase sales, of course, but there are many reasons why that might be difficult or impossible to achieve. The recession of 2001 is the most recent example of an insurmountable hurdle to the sales budgets of nearly every company.

Budget-cutting, known also by its euphemism of cost control, is the manager's dreaded duty when sales budgets fall short of their goals, expense budgets go over their projected totals, or economic downturns cause both consequences. Budget-cutting never wins the hearts and minds of the staff, but the manager needs to be both timely and firm in applying any cuts needed to restore the department's budget.

The individual press barons of old, for all their faults, almost always could be counted on to use some of the profits from good times to carry their newspapers through the bad times with minimum disruption. Not so the chains, however, which strive mightily to keep the same profit margins or even increase them year after year, through good times and bad times alike. When something like the recession of 2001 strikes, profit pressures on managers remain as intense as ever—with the predictable result of cutbacks in news coverage, layoffs and hiring freezes.

The first place managers typically look when their paring knives are out are the "discretionary" expenses such as staff travel, entertainment, conventions, office parties, new office furniture, various staff perquisites, publications, memberships, and other such budget fat enjoyed when times are good. After the fat is gone, managers often also need to carve away at the budget's meat, taking a close look at whether new equipment purchases thought so necessary at the beginning of the year can be put off until a later time, as one example.

Newspapers look for ways to trim printing costs (shrinking the news hole, for example); broadcast stations look for cheaper programming and lower transmission costs; advertising and public relations companies look at overhead costs, perhaps even to the point of moving to cheaper office space; magazines try to lower production costs, from printing bills and postage to freelancers' pay. And everyone checks out the possibilities of doing more work in-house instead of farming it out, becoming more aggressive in managing credit extended to customers, and refinancing debts at lower interest rates.

James D. Squires is one of only about half a dozen daily newspaper editors to publicly describe the budgeting tug of war between editors and owners. While editor of the *Chicago Tribune* during the 1980s, he said, repeated efforts to add news staff and improve coverage always ended up giving way to just increasing profits.

Journalistic improvement of the paper "was talked about, planned for and then either watered down or postponed altogether while newspapers and their corporate owners became the earnings stars of Wall Street investors," Squires wrote in his book. "This decade of corporate development changed the *Tribune* and other newspapers across the country as dramatically as if they had been converted to fried chicken franchises. The pressure to profit became a straitjacket for the free press. And for the most part the people lacing it up did not understand or give much thought to what they were doing."[47]

Some editors would be satisfied if they could just keep the staff they have. However, they often need to resort to radical surgery—cutting the staff. This is where the fun of being a manager stops, because now people's jobs, careers and livelihoods suddenly are riding on the individual manager's decisions. Empty desks in newspaper and television newsrooms across the country are silent testimony to the cutbacks during 2001 and the hiring freezes that continued into 2003.

Budgeting and financial management are only two different dimensions of the same task. Budgeting is the roadmap for managing the finances, which are tracked and recorded through accounting reports. The main accounting reports are (1) the balance sheet and (2) the income statement (also known as profit and loss statement). Financial management is control over operations using the budget and also project planning tools such as Gantt and milestone charts.

Gantt and milestone charts

THE PROCESS OF budgeting is inseparable from the concept of planning because the availability and expenditure of money must be timed with the cash flow needed for expenditures. Much of a company's income and expenditure is dependent on the progress of the company's projects through the whole range of activities, from product creation, to production and launch, to marketing, to sustainability.

The progress of a project's activities can be mapped through creation of a Gantt Chart. An example of a Gantt Chart produced by Excel follows, with the numbers across the top designating the date corresponding to each vertical line in the chart:

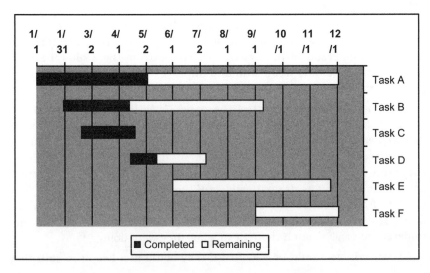

The chart represents a project that is to start Jan. 1 and be completed on Dec. 1. By looking at the line marking May 2, you can quickly see that Task A is running right on schedule, Task B is behind schedule, Task C is completed, Task D is running ahead of schedule, and the remaining tasks have not begun yet.

Developed by Henry L. Gantt (1861–1919), who was a disciple of Frederick Taylor's scientific management approach, Gantt Charts are also known as time line charts. Basically, a Gantt Chart is a bar graph that lists information such as tasks on the one side of the chart and the duration for each activity as horizontal bars.

Gantt Charts can be arranged to track various projects running concurrently, or to track concurrent tasks in a single project. They allow managers to see at a glance the status on a certain date of several projects or tasks. Gantt charts often are used by managers involved in planning a complex and long-running project.

Special software is available to produce Gantt Charts. If a manager does not have access to such software, however, he or she still can create an acceptable Gantt Chart using Microsoft Excel, found in nearly every office. Directions on converting an Excel document into a Gantt Chart can be found through a Google search for "how-to articles Excel Gantt."

The term "milestone" is sometimes given to the events plotted on a Gantt Chart because they are key events in a project.

A milestone chart can be done separately, just as a way to mark significant events in the life of an ongoing project. They usually are events that must be completed on time to avoid delay in the project. By closely monitoring milestone activities, a manager is able to keep up on the priority actions needed to achieve the deadlines. A milestone chart can be as simple as marking the deadline dates for key events on a calendar.

Once a milestone event is identified, a manager can break it down into a to-do list of all of the activities that must be completed to accomplish the milestone event on time.

Managers must keep their planning and financial management activities coordinated with balance sheets and income statements.

The balance sheet

THE BALANCE SHEET usually is described as a "snapshot" of the company's assets (what is owned) and liabilities (what is owed) on a given date. One is always prepared at the end of a fiscal year or just before a major financial event such as a loan application. Some companies issue balance sheets more frequently.

Following is an actual balance sheet for a weekly newspaper:[48]

BALANCE SHEET

Sterling Publications, Inc.

As of Dec. 31 — After Adjusting Entries

ASSETS		CURRENT LIABILITIES	
Regular checking acct.	258	Accounts payable	2,431
Corp. money market	21,512	Sales tax payable	31
Corp. payroll acct	2,284	Fed. inc. tax withheld	1,436
Petty cash	100	FICA withheld/accrued	1,763
Accts. receivable	21,407	State tax withheld	412
Goodwill	5,000	FUTA payable	24
Prepaid expenses	4,750	State unemployment	5
Rounding off adjust	0	401(k) payable	1,003
		Rounding off adjust	(1)
Furniture & equip.	226,638	LONG TERM LIABILITIES	
Accum. depr. F&E	(216,217)	Note payable-L.I.	23,014
Lease Improvements	49,096	Note payable-ind. loan	4,733
Accum. depr. L.I.	(10,163)	TOTAL LIABILITIES	34,851
		OWNERS EQUITY	
		Retained earnings	19,814
		Common stock	50,000
		TOTAL EQUITY	69,814
TOTAL		**TOTAL**	
ASSETS	**104,665**	**LIAB./EQUITY**	**104,665**

Note that the totals on each side of the balance sheet are equal. That clearly demonstrates how the formula for a balance sheet is:

Assets = Liabilities + Owners Equity

The balance sheet shows whether the company is in good financial health overall. Owners invest money in the company. This is represented on corporate statements as issuing of stock to the public if a publicly traded company or to the individual owner(s) who founded the corporation if privately owned. The company extends credit to customers and owns cash and physical properties (all assets) while suppliers and others extend credit to the company and loans are obtained (all liabilities). The difference (assets minus liabilities) creates owners or stockholders equity.

Another way to explain the same thing: Management uses the assets on the left side of the balance sheet to generate cash to pay liabilities on the right side, and whatever is left over is income to the owner as profit and/or retained earnings. The assets are listed on the left side of the page, and the liabilities and owners equity are on the right side. The totals for assets and for liabilities-plus-owners-equity must equal each other, the left side balancing with the right side (hence the name).

Because the balance sheet is only a snapshot of one moment or date in the company's financial health, it does not really reveal much about the company's operating dynamics or long-term health. If looking only at balance sheets, you need at least two periods to have any perspective. Looking at only one balance sheet is not very helpful.

Some other things to remember about a balance sheet are that assets are usually listed in order of their liquidity (the ability to convert them into cash), and the liabilities and owners equity are listed in the order in which they are scheduled to be paid. Parenthesis indicate a negative number. Current liabilities are payable within one year, as contrasted to long-term liabilities.

A careful reading of this balance sheet should reveal the key point that owners of small private corporations have great financial freedom.

For example, when I owned my weekly newspaper, I also owned the building it was in and thus paid rent (deductible as a business expense) to myself. My wife and both of my sons worked at various times at the newspaper, and I'll never forget the day my wife told me at lunch one day that she thought she deserved better pay (she got the raise, of course).

Unlike chains, which are trying to impress Wall Street every quarter, individual owners can put the long-term health of their business ahead of the short-term cycles.

For example, they can and often do avoid laying off employees except as a very last resort by having money set aside to carry them over relatively short periods of low business income.

They also can provide themselves with nice perks—notice the owner of the newspaper in the balance sheet carried an "individual" loan of $4,733. He didn't need the money (notice the money market balance), but he borrowed $5,000 from his father to give his father a safe high-interest investment.

Loans of such small sums within a closely held private company between the owner's family raise no concern with the IRS. However, the revelation in 2002 that many corporate CEOs were using their stockholder-owned businesses as their own personal banks for millions of dollars in loans to themselves led to major scandals and Congressional investigations.

The calculation of depreciation on equipment and buildings is a non-cash expense and thus can be legally pocketed by the owner or set aside in a fund for equipment repair and replacement. One publisher couple used their family-owned corporation's profits to buy a time-share condominium on the grounds that they would award stays there to visiting advertisers and to winners of subscriber contests—and to themselves most of the time, of course.

Such "assets" are legitimate business expenses, but a "Return on Assets" (ROA) analysis is badly skewed when such assets include time-share condominiums and country club memberships.[49]

"The truth is," two business professors wrote in *Harvard Business Review*, "standard financial statements tell only half the story in private companies. After all, when wealth flows freely between the owner and the business, personal finances are really part of the organization . . . . Return on equity, return on assets, return on investment, and debt-equity ratios are great for measuring the performance of large public corporations. But for small private companies, these measures are unreliable. And textbook methods for judging investment opportunities, like hurdle rates, payback periods and discounted cash flow aren't always useful in organizations that are privately owned."[50]

This is why banks don't distinguish between personal wealth and business wealth for owners. Anyone who wants to know how things are running in a privately owned company needs to count the money in both pockets.

As a newspaper broker, in analyzing newspapers for prospective buyers I always must do my best to prepare a "reconstructed cash flow" by trying to separate personal finances from the truly business finances of family-owned newspapers. I also need to reassure less sophisticated buyers that the profit reported in company financial statements is purposely manipulated to a low figure to minimize taxes. Buyers must be convinced that the small profit figure they might be looking at is often not a true measure of the cash actually flowing to the owners.

One last term to explain from the balance sheet is the difference between profit and retained earnings. Profit is the difference realized that year in income over expenses. Retained earnings, on the other hand, is a cumulative total kept on the company's books as potential re-investment capital to finance more operations instead of being paid out in dividends to the stockholders. In private companies, retained earnings often end up being converted into new equipment—or treated as additional profit that is paid to the owners.

A case study using Excel to enter different transactions into a balance sheet available over the Web is at the end of this chapter.

The income statement

ALSO KNOWN AS the profit and loss (P&L) statement, the income statement is as important as the balance sheet in understanding the financial operations and health of a company. The income statement is drawn up at least annually, and with most companies it is done on a quarterly basis.

This report shows the company's income and expenses for that period, and so some people refer to it as an income statement. It also shows the profit or loss for the period, which accounts for its second most common name.

Unlike the balance sheet, the figures on an income statement represent activity for its period alone. As with a balance sheet, you need at least two years of income statements to reach any meaningful understanding of how a company is doing. In business sales, buyers want to see three to five years of income statements.

There are numerous forms used by accountants and CPAs in drawing up income statements, depending on the size and complexity of the company. Some statements, for example, include a category called "cost of goods sold" that is a specific accounting term for production expenses. Other statements are simpler and do not include such a breakdown, especially in small privately owned companies.

Similarly, some income statements break revenue down into "gross income or gross profit"—sales before the selling, general and administrative expenses—and "net income or net profit" for the total after such expenses. In turn, some statements distinguish between pre-tax and after-tax profits, and some talk of operating profit. Unsophisticated reporters are apt to quote any one of these figures as "profit," which results in misleading confusion.

Following is an income (profit and loss) statement for the same year of the same weekly newspaper whose balance sheet ran earlier:[51]

INCOME STATEMENT

Sterling Publications, Inc.

Jan. 1 to Dec. 31

INCOME:
Subscription sales................................. 37,777
Display advertising.............................155,714
Classified advertising 53,539
Legals advertising 20,770
Newsstand sales 9,151
Circulars advertising............................. 9,187
Job printing (taxable) 13,738

Job printing (non-taxable) 15,797
Finance charges......................................497
Interest income..394
Miscellaneous income................................379

TOTAL INCOME $316,943

EXPENSES:
Newspaper printing............................... 19,938
Newspaper postage............................... 10,399
Shopper printing................................... 20,387
Shopper postage 16,583
Shopper carriers 3,462
Printing special issues...............................378
Utilities 2,737
Telephone.. 2,777
Equipment repair..949
Office supplies 5,378
Office postage 1,765
Mileage.. 1,550
Gasoline.. 1,150
Film and processing 457
Rent.. 9,600
Job printing expense............................. 11,776
Sales and promotion 1,769
Meals 296
Conventions and seminars 2,097
Insurance..414
Professional fees 2,194
Dues and publications 1,796
Donations.. 1,008
Miscellaneous expense 403
Interest expense.................................... 2,526
Correspondents 2,663
Sales discounts...................................... 4,512
Salary expense...................................... 56,579
Officers salaries 71,210
Employees.. 1,032
Payroll taxes.. 10,283
401(k) employers contribution 5,687
Depreciation expense (F&E)...................... 3,255
Depreciation expense (L.I.)...................... 1,558
Rounding off adjustment ....(2)

TOTAL EXPENSES $278,566

NET PROFIT $38,377

That last line is "the bottom line" that you're always hearing about. If expenses exceed revenue, then the company is "in the red" and the total would be reported as a loss instead of a profit, with the figure placed inside parenthesis to signify a negative number.

A cash flow statement, which many companies also use, especially larger ones, is done on at least an annual basis. The larger the company, the more likely it will use this accounting tool. A cash flow statement reports the cash received for the period (with its sources), the cash spent on expenses, the net cash flow, and the difference in the cash assets held by the company at the beginning of the period compared with what it held at the end of the period.

Financial analysis ratios

MATHEMATICAL RATIOS are used by bankers, investors and other business analysts to determine a company's financial health, using numbers taken from the balance sheet or income statement (or both), depending on the ratio being calculated. As a business owner, or buyer, these ratios are a quick way of determining a firm's business accomplishment when measured against published or otherwise known standards in that industry—if the figures reported in the balance sheet and income statement are sound.

At a minimum, there are four types of financial ratios: (1) liquidity, (2) leverage, (3) operating, and (4) performance.[52] The following explanations of the most common ratios are an amalgam of definitions from several sources, including business author Tom Gorman, syndicated business columnist Scott Clark, and a weighty tome titled *Fundamentals of Corporate Finance.*

The latter book adds a caveat to be repeated here: "Different sources frequently don't compute these ratios in exactly the same way, and this leads to much confusion. The specific definitions we use here may or may not be the same as ones you have seen or will see elsewhere."[53]

Liquidity ratios: These measure the company's capability to meet its short-term obligations and to convert receivables and other assets into cash without undue stress. They include:

The Current Ratio, also known as the working capital ratio, measures the firm's solvency by indicating its ability to pay current debts from assets. Banks usually like to see a ratio of at least 2.0. Its ratio is current assets/current liabilities, i.e., current assets from the balance sheet divided by current liabilities from the balance sheet.

The Quick Ratio, also called the quick asset ratio or the acid test ratio, measures how liquid assets can be used to meet current debts. Lenders and investors generally want this number to be above 1.0. It is current assets – inventory/current liabilities.

Leverage Ratios (also known as solvency ratios): These measure how much of the company's financing is supplied by the owners and how much by creditors.

>The Debt Ratio measures the percentage of company assets financed by its creditors. The higher the ratio, the greater the risk of default, where 1.0 would mean 100 percent of the assets are financed by debt. One of several formulas is total liabilities/total assets.

>The Debt-to-Equity Ratio, also known as the debt-equity ratio and the debt-to-net-worth ratio, compares what the business owes to what it owns. If it is below 1.0, the firm owns more than it owes. The formula is total liabilities/owners equity (net worth).

Operating Ratios: These are included by some analysts under liquidity ratios, and described by others as asset utilization ratios. They measure the company's earning power and management's effectiveness in using resources to run the company's operations.

>The Accounts Receivable Ratio measures the collectability of the money owed the company from customers buying on credit, which in the media business constitutes virtually all advertising sales. Keep in mind that an uncollectable account receivable is worthless, so lenders and bankers use this ratio frequently. This ratio divides the credit sales by the average accounts receivable.

>The Collection Period Ratio determines the average length of time taken for those accounts that do get paid. You are providing interest-free loans to customers who buy on credit, so the lower this number, the better. The ratio is accounts receivable × 365 days/annual credit sales or, if you did the above calculation first, then it is 365/accounts receivable turnover.

Performance Ratios: Also known as profitability ratios, these equations indicate how successfully the business is conducting business and making money.

>The Return on Assets Ratio, or ROA, is probably the single most widely used measure of business success. It measures management's ability to generate a profit. The formula is net income (net profit)/average total assets.

>The Return on Equity Ratio, or ROE, also called the return on equity, or ROI, measures the return earned on the owners' investment. This number is critical because managers must earn a good return for their owners. The formula is net profit (usually after taxes)/owners equity.

These are only some of the most commonly used ratios. There are many others, including inventory turnover, operating margin, gross margin, cash coverage, etc. Average ratios for industries are in the *RMA Annual Statement Studies*, available at many banks and libraries.[54]

More informally, but perhaps closer to the mark, a sense of the averages can be inferred from conversations with others you know in the same business with you.

Cash flow and cost-control

ONCE MANAGERS look over their financial reports, especially formal or informal cash flow statements, a natural conclusion often is reached that costs need to be reduced somewhere, somehow. As a matter of fact, an outstanding manager is always alert for ways to cut costs by trimming fat off the company's meat, or ending product lines whose lives have matured and ended. The problem is that a manager's definition of fat might be what the employees consider muscle and bone.

Cost-control (which is not necessarily the same as cost-cutting) is essential to a well-managed business even though it can, like anything else, be counterproductive if it is carried out without consideration of long-range consequences.

A company that holds back (cost control) or reduces (cost-cutting) its advertising budget is often taking the first step toward its eventual destruction unless it truly does not need to spend more on advertising or it truly was spending more on marketing than was merited.

Cost-cutting can be an obvious step. But always keep in mind that a perceived need for cost-cutting might really be a signal for the need of the mirror image of such action—increasing revenues.

For example, whenever a newspaper or magazine manager notices a large number of copies being sent to the recycling pile after a press run, that is a clear and obvious signal for both cost-cutting and revenue-raising. Such a situation means that too many copies are being printed because newsstand sales and/or subscriptions were down from the last time the press run was calculated. A manager should temporarily reduce the press run, thereby saving expense, while at the same time putting renewed vigor and emphasis on selling newsstand copies and annual subscriptions to increase revenue and, consequently, raise the press run back to its previous level or higher.

Too often, managers think only in terms of cutting expenses instead of also increasing revenue.

Similarly, you also can make the mistake of reducing your costs by cutting back or reducing a part of your business that is needed to generate revenue. Studies cited earlier in this text reported on how Thomson Newspapers often implemented reductions in staff and resources in the newsroom to save money and increase short-term profits, but that only resulted in reducing circulation, which ended up costing the corporation more in the long run than it saved initially.

Cost-cutting tactics can have the most immediate impact on the bottom line. If your company has a 25 percent profit margin, increasing sales by $1 gives you only 25 cents more for the bottom line. However, if you reduce your costs by $1, that adds a full dollar to the bottom line—or four times more than a dollar of additional sales.

This impact explains the appeal of cost-cutting over revenue-growing during difficult economic times. And because labor is the largest single cost for newspapers and television, as well as many other media companies, it explains also why the cost-cutting ax frequently falls so heavily on employees.

Cash flow is an engine that determines financial health for a company—even more so than profits. Business history is filled with accounts of firms that were profitable on paper but that could not survive because their cash flow was not adequate or timely to ensure that bills could be paid, payrolls met, product produced, marketing ensured, and growth continued.

In fact, studies indicate that insufficient cash flow—not ultimate profitability—is the main reason for business failure.[55]

Because most media companies depend on income from selling advertising on credit terms, they are especially prone to being whipsawed between the advertisers (who are their main source of income and who are trying to delay payment) and their own obligations to pay bills immediately due, such as printing, postage or payroll expenses. However, all companies suffer some degree of gap between income coming in and expenses being paid.

This fact of commercial life demands, at risk of total business failure, competent and eternal monitoring of cash flow with control over its constant companions—costs and revenue growth.

Some reasons for inadequate cash flow affecting a company's ability to pay its expenses are waste, over-investment, over-financing, excessive debtors, excessive creditors, over-financing through loans or credit cards, excessive extension of credit, and poor collection of credit accounts.[56]

There are specific forms for monitoring cash flow, but the quickest and most dramatic telling of the need for cash flow control is the first time a manager realizes that he or she cannot pay that day's bills. By then, of course, the hour already is late, so it is prudent for managers to begin monitoring the gap between debts and credits far before that situation arises through creation of a cash flow forecast in the beginning and maintenance of a cash flow budget thereafter on a monthly, weekly or even daily basis.[57] This is necessary to ensure that the business can pay its current obligations in a timely manner.

Identifying and monitoring cash flows can be difficult because the inflows and outflows of cash vary from period to period. At a minimum, cash flows from operations must equal cash flows to the firm's creditors and to its equity investors in each chosen period.[58] Cash flows from operations reflect earnings before interest but after taxes and after depreciation. Taxes take cash, of course, but depreciation is considered a noncash expense.[59]

As individuals, we think in terms of cash basis accounting, where income is recorded when cash is received and expenses are recorded when cash is spent. However, nearly all but the smallest businesses build their business records instead on what is known as **accrual basis accounting.**

The concepts of depreciation and amortization are manifestations of accrual basis accounting. Accrual basis of accounting is more accurate for businesses because revenues are recorded at the time of sale for services and merchandise, but expenses usually are not recorded until their benefits are realized. For example, under cash basis, a large piece of equipment would be recorded as an expenditure at the time of purchase. However, that would greatly distort the company's financial health for that period because that large expenditure would diminish the period's profit to the point where operations could actually show a loss—which would not be a true measure of the company's performance. Under accrual basis accounting, the cost of a large piece of equipment would be divided and assigned as an expense over the accounting periods that are receiving the benefit of the equipment.[60]

Time value of money

ALL FINANCIAL decision-making starts with the fundamental concept known as "the time value of money." This concept recognizes that a dollar in your hand today has a different value than one promised to you for sometime in the future.

Put another way, if given a choice between being given $1 today, compared with receiving the same $1 a year from now, prudent individuals and firms will elect to receive the money today when it can be invested at an interest rate and grow to an amount greater than $1 a year from now.

For example, if you can receive a 10 percent return on your investment, today's $1 is really worth $1.10 to you if you are willing to wait a year. Why? Because $1 multiplied by the 10 percent return that you could make equals $1.10.

Entire books of tables exist to show you the present and future values of money, so the ones in this book are barely representative. But both of the tables that follow illustrate the relationship between the future value and present value of money.

All of these tables are based on the one basic "time value of money" formula. It is Future Value equals Present Value multiplied by one plus the rate of return, squared by the number of time periods. The formula can be stated as **FV = PV $(1+r)^n$** for the future value of today's money. An example of a Future Value table, based on annually compounded rates, is as follows:[61]

FUTURE VALUE OF $1 at various compound interest rates:

Years	5%	6%	7%	8%	9%	10%
1	1.05	1.06	1.07	1.08	1.09	1.10
2	1.10	1.12	1.15	1.17	1.19	1.21
3	1.16	1.19	1.23	1.26	1.30	1.33
4	1.22	1.26	1.31	1.36	1.41	1.46
5	1.28	1.34	1.40	1.47	1.54	1.61
10	1.63	1.79	1.97	2.16	2.37	2.59

In other words, if you have the ability to gain a 10 percent return on your money, being given or making $1 today has the same value as being given or making $1.10 a year from now. Want to double your money in a decade? You can verify by the above table that if you invested $1 today for a return of a little over 7 percent (7.177 percent, to be exact), you will approximately double your money to $1.97 in 10 years.[62]

You also can calculate the value of money backward in time by taking into consideration a discount rate, based on an algebraic turn-around of our previous formula to determine the present value of a future amount.

In the below example, today's $1 is the present value of 90.9 cents after the dollar is discounted at a rate of 10 percent. The mathematical formula is **PV = FV / $(1+r)^n$** in which the future value of $1 is divided by 1 plus the interest rate and factored by the number of years the discount rate applies.

The following table illustrates the present value of $1 at various discount rates for various years:[63]

PRESENT VALUE OF $1 at various discount rates:

Years	5%	6%	7%	8%	9%	10%
1	.952	.943	.936	.926	.917	.909
2	.907	.890	.873	.857	.842	.826
3	.864	.840	.816	.794	.772	.751
4	.823	.792	.763	.735	.708	.683
5	.784	.747	.713	.681	.650	.621
10	.614	.558	.508	.463	.422	.386

If you can get a 10 percent return on your money, this chart tells you that $1 today is equal to 38.6 cents received 10 years from now, or conversely, 38.6 cents invested today will grow to $1 in 10 years.

Now you can see why state lotteries offer to pay you big winnings over a period of years or a smaller amount immediately. Depending on the rate of investment return available to you, a smaller amount of money might or might not be worth a lot more to you today in one sum than a greater amount (to a degree) is worth to you if it is parceled out over several years.

In every investment decision, you must ask yourself if the investment is worth it. By discounting future cash flows to their present value, it often becomes immediately obvious whether the investment is worth the risk and initial cash outlay.

There are scores of mathematical equations relating to the time value of money, but they all are derived from these two basic formulas on the future value and present value.

Small amounts can add up over long periods of time—most dramatically through what some have called civilization's greatest invention: compounded interest.

When we compound interest, we add the money received from interest at the end of each year. At 10 percent, we'd have $1.10 at the end of the first year. Then interest is recalculated for the second year not just on the $1 principle but on the $1.10 (principle plus interest). And so on for each following year, paying interest on both the principle and the accumulated interest.

The result can be staggering over long periods of time.

A true-to-life example comes from the will of our favorite publisher, Benjamin Franklin. At his death in 1790, Franklin bequeathed the equivalent of about $1,000 to Massachusetts and the city of Boston. He gave the same amount to Pennsylvania and the city of Philadelphia. The money was to be invested and paid out 100 years after his death. Due to a century of legal wrangling, the money was not paid out until 1990, which was 200 years later. By then, the Pennsylvania money had grown at a compounded average rate of 3.87 percent annually, resulting in the original $1,000 increasing to a worth of $2 million. But the Massachusetts money grew at a rate just a little bit better, 4.3 percent, and was worth about $4.5 million.[64]

Corporations do, and individuals should, fully consider the time value of money and the power of compounded interest in deciding upon their investments, whether it be for new equipment for the corporation or a retirement fund for individuals.

It is not unusual for corporations to place some of their cash balance in money markets, certificates of deposit or simply savings accounts so cash is easily available for anticipated expenses, such as an acquisition when money would be needed quickly.

Investment criteria

THE GOAL OF financial management is to create value for the stockholders. An investment is only worth taking if it creates greater value, and it is financial management skills that analyze these investments.

In a large corporation, financial management falls to the Chief Financial Officer (CFO), who is likely to be a certified public accountant. In smaller firms, financial management might be another one of the duties that befall a senior or even mid-level manager. Of course, in the smallest firms, financial management is the responsibility of the owner, along with just about everything else.

Three common analytical tools used by managers to assess the true value to a company of a particular investment are, (1) net present value, (2) internal rate of return, and (3) payback period.

The first two consider the time value of money, but payback period does not.

Net present value

The difference between an investment's market value and its cost is called the net present value, abbreviated as NPV. In other words, NPV is a measure of how much value is created or added by undertaking a certain investment. Determining NPV requires the computation of a discount rate to a series of future cash flows.[65]

Business author Tom Gorman explains it along these lines.[66]

Suppose you need to make a decision on whether to build a new facility that requires an investment of $2,200,000. You have a five-year horizon because you plan to sell the business then. But you're not sure if you will sell or not, so you need to have the facility work as a five-year investment regardless. Will it?

Over the next five years, you estimate the additional income realized from the new facility will be:

Year 1—$200,000
Year 2—$500,000
Year 3—$700,000
Year 4—$800,000
Year 5—$1,000,000
TOTAL—$3,200,000

Your next step is to determine what rate of return you need. That becomes your "discount rate" on these future cash flows.

For this example, let's say you need at least a 10 percent return on the investment. To discount the future cash flows, you do the following calculations using the present value table presented earlier in this chapter, taking each of the cash flows just calculated above and plugging them into the following chart:

Year	Cash Inflows ($)	Present Value of $1	Present Value of Cash Inflow
1	200,000	× 0.909	$181,800
2	500,000	× 0.826	413,000
3	700,000	× 0.751	525,700
4	800,000	× 0.683	546,400
5	1,000,000	× 0.621	621,000
Present Value of Inflows			$2,287,900

That figure of $2,287,900 is the present value of the future cash inflows, which totaled $3,200,000. To calculate the net present value, you subtract the initial investment (the outflow) from the discounted inflows total:

Present Value of Inflows	$2,287,900
Minus Initial Investment	2,200,000
Net Present Value of investment	**$87,900**

Therefore, the investment will generate an additional $87,900 over the 10 percent discount rate you put on as a minimum requirement. The NPV is $87,900. That is the profit, expressed in the present value of the future cash flows.

Put another way, be advised that you should not consider the income on the project to be $3,200,000, which is the simple total of the projected cash flows for each of five years. Many untrained managers might simply add the five inflows and think that is their income, but the $3,200,000 figure does not take into consideration the time value of money. The actual value of that $3,200,000 spread over five years is $2,287,900.

NPV emphasizes that we already are considering the current cost of the initial outlay in determining an investment's value, and not just what the investment will return. The **Net Present Value Rule** states that an investment is worth making if it has a positive NPV, but if the NPV is negative, then the investment should be rejected.[67]

Internal rate of return

Abbreviated as IRR, the internal rate of return also considers the time value of money, but approaches it differently from NPV. If the internal rate of return on an investment exceeds the percentage rate required by the company on its investments, then the investment should be made. Otherwise, it should be rejected.

To determine IRR, you must discover what discount rate will make the future cash inflows equal the upfront cash outflow. The only way to find the IRR of a particular project is by trial and error, either by hand or preferably by using a financial calculator.

Using the NPV example, if we set up the same tables and applied a 12 percent discount rate, we would find a negative total of –$48,700, telling us that the IRR must be less than that. If we discounted using 11 percent, we would have a positive total of $18,100. Our conclusion, therefore, would be that the IRR must be slightly over 11 percent.[68]

You could figure both the NPV and the IRR very precisely and very quickly—and a whole lot easier—by using inexpensive hand-held financial calculators that work with the time value of money, including the Texas Instruments BAII Plus and the Hewlett Packard Business 10B.

Payback period

This is a very straight-forward calculation. It does not take into account the time value of money, which could be a severe shortcoming. Nevertheless, it is used frequently for relatively minor decisions over short periods of time.

If annual payments are the same for each year, the formula for the payback period is $P = I/C$, where P stands for payback period, I for the initial investment, and C for the annual cash flow (not discounted).[69]

However, most projects are complicated because they have irregular cash flows, as in the NPV example. The following type of visual aid can be drawn up, in this case showing an initial investment of $2,200 with the following cash flows for each of the next five months:[70]

Month 0	1	2	3	4	5
–2,200	200	500	700	800	1,000

By adding the cash flows as we go along, we will find that at the end of the fourth month we will have $2,200, the same amount as the investment. Therefore, that project's payback period is four months.

The simplicity of the payback period is an illusion, because the most difficult part of all of these analytical tools is coming up with accurate projections of future cash flows, discounted or not. The further out you need to project, the less likely your projections will be accurate.

Payback period calculations are not used by prudent managers for a project extending out several years. The effect of the time value of money would be too great. In fact, payback period calculations generally are not used if the project lasts more than several months or a year.

On short projects of a year or less, however, there usually is no compelling reason for anyone to consider the time value of money. While true that any amount of time influences the value of money, short periods are not going to have much effect unless the amounts of money being considered are huge.

Time value of money is usually ignored for short-term projects.

Some other terms you frequently hear in financial management are sunk costs and opportunity costs.

A **sunk cost** is money that's already been spent. Sunk costs should be ignored in deciding whether to accept or reject an investment project because they are not recoverable; they are spilled milk.[71] This term also came up in Chapter 5 as one of the hidden traps of decision-making.

As for the second term, there is a return anyone could earn on a sure-thing kind of investment, such as the relative security of buying a money market certificate. Foregoing the money you could have made by investing your cash there (or any other alternative available investment opportunity) is considered to be the **opportunity cost** of the investment.

The logic behind the concept is, if you can invest in a money market as one example and make 5 percent, why would you want to run the risk of pursuing any business investment that didn't return at least that percentage and probably higher? Put another way, if you can make 5 percent on a risk-free investment, you're not earning your keep as a financial manager unless you can come up with an investment that will return more than 5 percent—the more, the better.

CHAPTER 8

The never-ending conflict

BUDGETS ARE probably the most common flashpoint for conflicts between managers and their staffs. Because of the restraints of budgets that they are locked into implementing and enforcing, managers quickly learn they must often say "no" to all kinds of operational requests coming from staffers—from pay raises to expanding news coverage to allowing travel for news coverage.

The conflicts between the managers and the managed are unavoidable even in the most profitable and generous business. From the employees' standpoint, it is human nature to always want a little more than you already have. And from the manager's viewpoint, it is an executive's responsibility to protect the company's profits and build them higher.

A disadvantage for managers who want their viewpoint to be better known is that the writers they hire in their newsrooms tend to write a lot more articles and books than executives do.

And now the writers are even starting to cast media CEOs into the role of villain in novels. The latest example comes from mystery writer Carl Hiaasen, who also happens to be a columnist for the *Miami Herald*, a Knight Ridder newspaper. Hiaasen's 2002 mystery, *Basket Case*, depicts a soulless, profiteering young publisher named Race Maggad III who is ruining his newspaper for the sake of short-term big profits.[72] No less a light than Jim Naughton, then president of the Poynter Institute, thought he recognized Hiaasen's real-life boss, Tony Ridder, as the model for the fictional Race Maggad.[73]

It can be a thankless task to run and build a profitable company. Much of this book has been about how to work with employees and improve managerial skills in running a company. The next two chapters are devoted to building a company, of which there are only two ways: increased sales (including new product development), discussed in chapter 9, and expansion through acquisitions, discussed in chapter 10.

CASE STUDY — *Web Exercise on Making Changes to a Balance Sheet*

by DENNIS F. HERRICK
and BEN BERGER
University of New Mexico

For this exercise you will need Internet access and also a computer with Microsoft Excel software installed.

Go to <www.mediatextbook.com> and click on Balance Sheet Exercise. The directions for the exercise are located beside the sample of a balance sheet. The columns will add automatically as you enter each of the figures (be sure to include the comma for any number over a thousand). Click only once on a cell, and then type in the numbers specified in the exercise notes.

As you complete each of the four exercises, check the total on each side of the balance sheet. After putting in both numbers for each of the four exercises, each total always must equal the other. If not, check where your mistake is and do the exercise again until each side adds up the same.

AUTHORS:

Dennis F. Herrick teaches media management at the University of New Mexico and he is former publisher of a group of weekly papers. Ben Berger assisted with this Web exercise while a master's degree student in accounting at UNM's Anderson Schools of Management.

🖳 Suggested Web sites:

www.cribb.com/publish.html — U.S. newspaper sales from 1997 to 2003
www.bcfm.com — Broadcast/Cable Financial Management Association
www.veronissuhler.com/internetLib.asp — Media industry and financial information
www.bizmove.com/financial.htm — Financial management articles
www.teachmefinance.com — Web primer on basic financial facts
www.auburn.edu/~garriro/tam.htm — Time and money issues

Endnotes to Chapter 8:

[1] Bill Kovach, quoted in "Hot type: The best — and rest — of the press," *Editor & Publisher* (April 2, 2001): 29.

[2] Hugh Rawson and Margaret Miner, "Speaking of business," *American Heritage* (June 2001): 108.

[3] Fred S. Siebert with Theodore Peterson and Wilbur Schramm, *Four Theories of the Press* (Urbana: University of Illinois Press, 1963), 72.

[4] Milton Friedman, "The social responsibility of business is to increase profits," *New York Times Magazine*, September 13, 1970, 32.

[5] Merrill, John C., *Journalism Ethics: Philosophical Foundations for News Media* (New York: St. Martin's Press, 1997), 12–21.

[6] James K. Batten, "Press-Enterprise lecture," Riverside, Calif. (April 3, 1989).

[7] John Henry, "Buffet in Buffalo: His paper prints money. What else does it print?" *Columbia Journalism Review* (November–December 1998).

[8] Barry Diller, as quoted in *The New Yorker* (November 9, 1998): 34.

[9] Wendy Apkarian, "Are media mergers really good for journalism?" unpublished paper of April 30, 2002.

[10] Garden State Newspapers Inc., Form 10-K Annual Report 1998, Securities and Exchange Commission.

[11] Chuck Offenburger, interview with the author, October 20, 2000.

[12] John E. Flaherty, *Peter Drucker: Shaping the Managerial Mind* (San Francisco: Jossey-Bass, 1999), 84–87. Copyright © 1999, Jossey-Bass. Reprinted by permission of John Wiley & Sons, Inc.

[13] Herbert A. Simon, "Theories of decision-making in economics and behavioral science," in *Organizational Decision Making,* Marcus Alexis and Charles Z. Wilson, eds. (Englewood Cliffs, N.J.: Prentice-Hall, 1967) 208.

[14] Flaherty, *Peter Drucker: Shaping the Managerial Mind,* 90.

[15] Jim Willis, *Surviving in the Newspaper Business: Newspaper Management in Turbulent Times* (New York: Praeger, 1988), 1.

[16] Russ Parker, "A happy newsroom," *Columbia Journalism Review* (September–October 2001): 57.

[17] Geneva Overholser, "Our nose for news fails us when the smell is close to home," *Columbia Journalism Review* (September–October 2001): 56–57.

[18] Matthew Fogel, "Hard Times," *Columbia Journalism Review* (May–June 2001): 25.

[19] "Results of Continuing Operations," *Connecting . . . .* the 2001 Annual Report of Gannett Co. Inc., 21.

[20] Mike Freeman, "N. County Times to be sold: Lee Enterprises to buy Howard family holdings," *San Diego Union Tribune,* February 13, 2002, C1.

[21] George Benge, on John Morton's speech "Framing the Issues," presented to the National Association of Minority Media Executives, reported on NAMME Web site at <www.namme .org/conference2001_framing.asp>, accessed February 13, 2002.

[22] Delroy Alexander, of the *Chicago Tribune,* as published in "Enron case may alter accounting world," *Albuquerque Journal,* December 16, 2001, C1.

[23] Ibid., C2.

[24] David Croteau and William Hoynes, *The Business of Media* (Thousand Oaks, Calif.: Pine Forge Press), 2001, 8.

[25] Rick Edmonds, "Public companies no worse than private," at <www.poynter.org/content /content_view.asp?id=12122>, accessed January 6, 2003.

[26] James D. Squires, *Read All About It! The Corporate Takeover of America's Newspapers* (San Francisco, Calif.: Berrett-Koehler, 1994), xxi–xxii.

[27] Kirk Anderson, "Newspaper chain" cartoon ©Kirk Anderson and reprinted with permission.

[28] Kirk Anderson in personal e-mail to the author (May 8, 2003).

[29] William Pfaff, © 2000 Los Angeles Times Syndicate International, as published in "New economy's values are destructive to business," *Albuquerque Journal,* December 26, 2000, A11.

[30] Ibid.

[31] Frances Hesselbein with Marshall Goldsmith and Iain Somerville, eds, *Leading Beyond the Walls* (San Francisco: Jossey-Bass, 1999).

[32] William Pfaff, © 2002 Los Angeles Times Syndicate International, as published in "Bring back responsible capitalism," *Albuquerque Journal,* March 2, 2002, B3.

[33] Ibid.

[34] Greg Mitchell, "Poll finds profits rule: Most publishers and editors feel margins in error, and fear negative impact on industry," *Editor & Publisher* (April 9, 2001): 16.

[35] Keri Althoff, "The effect of the values-based concept on the ethical decision-making process in business," reporting Len Hadley's speech delivered November 4, 2000, at the Henry B. Tippie School of Business, unpublished paper of November 16, 2000.

[36] Ibid.

[37] "The 100 best corporate citizens," <www.business-ethics.com/100best.htm>, accessed December 26, 2000.

[38] Robert Hinkley, "How corporate law inhibits social responsibility," *Business Ethics* magazine, January–February 2002, and available at < www.business-ethics.com/constitEconDemoc .htm>, accessed August 12, 2003.

[39] Ibid.

[40] David Wessel, "American economy is a model that other nations envy, fear," *The Wall Street Journal,* January 18, 2001, 1.

[41] Ibid.

[42] Ibid.

[43] Scott Miller, "VW starts work on a new model: profits — Auto maker sets out to please investors as well as workers," and, Gregory L. White and Joseph B. White, "GM plans deep cuts in U.S. and Europe — Death of Oldsmobile brand may be overshadowed by big retreat overseas," both in *The Wall Street Journal,* December 13, 2000, A1.

[44] Peter F. Drucker, *Managing the Non-Profit Organization: Principles and Practices* (New York: HarperBusiness, 1992), 46.

[45] Michael Schlesinger, publisher of *Marshalltown (Iowa) Times-Republican,* in interview with author, February 5, 2000.

[46] Malcolm Forbes, as quoted by Steve Maller on Web site, "List of quotation authors," <www.maller.com/quotes/default.html?xauth=Malcom%20Forbes>, accessed January 12, 2001.

[47] James D. Squires, *Read All About It! The Corporate Takeover of America's Newspapers* (New York: Times Books, 1st paperback ed.,1994), 80–81.

[48] Balance sheet provided to author courtesy of Sterling Publications, Inc.

[49] Richard I. Levin and Virginia R. Travis. Reprinted by permission of *Harvard Business Review*. From "Small company finance: What the books don't say," (November–December 1987) 30. ©1987 by Harvard Business School Publishing Corporation, all rights reserved.

[50] Ibid.

[51] Income statement provided to author courtesy of Sterling Publications, Inc.

[52] Scott Clark, © 1999 HTC Group Syndicate, as published in, "What do all those ratios really mean?" Cedar Rapids, Iowa, *Gazette*, January 24, 1999.

[53] Stephen A. Ross, Randolph W. Westerfield, and Bradford D. Jordan, *Fundamentals of Corporate Finance* (Chicago: Irwin Custom Publishing, 3rd ed., 1995), 55.

[54] Clark, "What do all those ratios really mean?"

[55] "Avoiding cash flow problems," as detailed on <www.credit-to-cash.com /cash_flow/cash-flow-1.shtml>, accessed October 31, 2002.

[56] Ibid.

[57] Stephen A. Ross, Randolph W. Westerfield, and Jeffrey F. Jaffe, *Corporate Finance* (Burr Ridge, Ill.: Irwin, 3rd ed., 1993), 35.

[58] Ibid.

[59] Ibid., 33.

[60] A. Douglas Hillman, Richard F. Kochanek, and Noah P. Barsky, *Principles of Accounting: A Focus on Analysis and Interpretation* (Chicago: Thomson Learning, 2004), 3–2 to 3–4.

[61] Ross, et al., *Fundamentals of Corporate Finance*, 744–745.

[62] Ibid., 124.

[63] Ibid., 746–747.

[64] Ibid., 124.

[65] Ibid., 197.

[66] Tom Gorman, *The Complete Idiot's Guide to MBA Basics* (New York: Alpha Books, 1998), 167–168.

[67] Ross, et al., *Corporate Finance*, 68.

[68] Gorman, *The Complete Idiot's Guide to MBA Basics*, 169–170.

[69] Alexander H. Cornell, *The Decision Maker's Handbook* (Englewood Cliffs, N.J.: Prentice-Hall, 1980), 182.

[70] Ross, et al., *Fundamentals of Corporate Finance*, 200-201.

[71] Ross, et al., *Corporate Finance*, 186.

[72] Carl Hiaasen, *Basket Case* (New York: Alfred A. Knopf, 2002).

[73] Jim Naughton, "Mob Rule," *Poynter Report*, Summer 2002, 13.

CHAPTER 9

SALES, MARKETING

AND MARKET ANALYSIS

BURL OSBORNE, publisher of the *Dallas Morning News*, knows it can be difficult to convince newsroom staffers to consider the marketing aspects of the stories they write and edit. He summed up his efforts to turn reporters and editors into marketers, observing, "'Good journalists' say marketing (as if) they just bit into an apple and found half a worm."[1]

Kendra Oden, then a junior at the University of New Mexico, wrote in a paper that newspapers seem to be the last bastion holding out against the product marketing folks—or, at least the newsrooms of newspapers are. But she concluded that change is inevitable, and already evident all around us in recent years.

"As a solution to the constant technological threats and the competition against other media to obtain the reader's time for the newspaper, marketing has offered an answer—an answer, however, that many journalists feel goes against their ethics and what makes them journalists in the first place."[2]

Oden notes that Judy Pace Christie, editor of *The Times* in Shreveport, La., defends marketing techniques. Christie observes: "For those editors who wince at the idea of marketing the news, consider the role of headlines and above-the-fold promos. What do they do but grab the readers and sell stories?"[3]

Oden writes, "It is ironic to realize that newspapers have been using marketing techniques long before they became the controversial trend that they are today."[4]

As a daily newspaper reporter and later a weekly newspaper publisher, I can attest times are changing in the ways that news staffs and marketing staffs are willing to work together. I remember a protest by me and fellow reporters at *The Flint* (Mich.) *Journal* in the 1960s, successfully arguing that the advertising staff should write stories for an advertising supplement, not the news staff. But two decades later, when I was publisher of my own weekly newspaper in Iowa, I had my news staff writing stories for blatantly promotional supplements. Times had changed so much even by then in the newspaper business that I never considered my earlier purism nor my contradictory turn of philosophy.

Television broadcasters are masters (or slaves) of marketing because of the nature of their business. To determine advertising rates, the networks and local stations rate the sizes of their viewing audiences four times a year, in what has become known as the "sweeps" periods. The term comes from the early days of the ratings process, when the stations would be rated for audience size in the Eastern markets first, and then the process would "sweep" across the nation.

Newspaper executives, on the other hand, at least until recent times, have rarely been considered marketing geniuses. This is changing as a "be a marketer or be gone" realization settles over newsrooms, and advertising and financial executives are replacing editorial leaders in the key management positions at newspapers.

None less than the futurist Marshall McLuhan believes ads are more accurate than news in defining society anyway, predicting: "Historians and archeologists will one day discover that the ads of our time are the richest and most faithful daily reflections that any society ever made of its entire range of activities."[5]

Traditional wall between business and news

THE CONCEPT that the news and advertising sides should be separate and non-communicative entities for print and broadcast news organizations was dramatically altered overnight with what turned out to be the ill-fated arrival in the 1990s of professional marketer Mark Willes as CEO of the Times Mirror Company. Willes was written up in all of the trade journals, variously described as a brilliant visionary and as the devil incarnate, as he "cut costs and notoriously sought to remake the advertising-editorial relationship by breaching the wall between the two,"[6] as a biographer of Otis Chandler summarized Willes' efforts.

Willes was fired when the *Los Angeles Times* was purchased in 2000 by the corporate newspapering Chicagoans from the Tribune Co., but his legacy endures as more newspaper companies openly embrace the idea of no longer separating "church and state" in the uneasy co-existence inside companies of advertising/business and editorial missions.

In all fairness, the idea that business and editorial ever were clearly separated by even the great editors of the past is wrong.

Even the legendary editor William Allen White is said to have placed his desk at the *Emporia Gazette* in Kansas directly between the business office and the newsroom, with doorways opening into each.

Willes went a step farther, perhaps, in openly advocating greater influence—and in fact, greater authority—for the advertising department and business office over the newsroom. However, one of the oldest criticisms of newspapers and other media companies long before Willes is that news coverage has been unduly influenced by economic interests. And it has too often been a charge impossible to refute.

Willes remains the standard bearer for the concept, partly because he was so brazen about it and partly because it was he whom the trade journals turned into the best-known advocate for forcing the newsroom to work more closely with other departments of the newspaper. It remains a critical debating point whether this is an innovation that will be looked back on as the savior of at least the big city daily newspapers or as an abomination that further eroded public confidence in newspapers and further marginalized them as the source for information to the public. Was the revolution rightly or wrongly credited to Willes an innovation initiative, or a disastrous sidetrack?

But "it's not just in L.A.," to quote from an article by that title in the *Columbia Journalism Review,* "All around the country, at newspaper after newspaper, the walls between the newsroom and the business departments, once a sacred barrier, are being knocked down, and replaced by a commitment across all departments to the marketing mission of the newspaper—to sell ads, raise circulation, and promote itself."[7]

James D. Squires expressed with some regret that after nearly a decade as editor of the *Chicago Tribune* he had been instrumental in tearing down the walls between news and business at that paper. "And for the ease with which I let it happen," Squires said, "I can only offer the lamest of excuses, 'I really didn't know at the time what I was doing.'"[8] For better or worse, there has been a turn toward interdepartmental teamwork that was unheard of years earlier.

Today, nearly everyone in the executive ranks—and many in the newsroom as well—agree on the need for teamwork throughout any media company as a whole. Teamwork across all departments is being encouraged at nearly every newspaper and television station.

An example is the *Bradenton Herald* in Florida, where reporters and editors were placed on committees with staffers from circulation, advertising and other business departments to jointly produce marketing strategies. "We've changed the culture of this organization forever," commented the *Herald's* publisher, Craig Wells.[9]

Other "cross-divisional" teams have been established at a number of other papers, according to *CJR*, including the *Arizona Republic, Houston Chronicle, Austin American-Statesman* and *Fort Lauderdale Sun-Sentinel*. Several chains, including Knight Ridder and Gannett, have been pushing since the mid-1980s for "the open newsroom" in which all departments are expected to work together producing and promoting the paper.

The result indisputably has been a rise in creeping tabloidization in the worst instances.[10] For most others, there has been an increase in celebrity journalism and other forms of infotainment, and plain non-coverage of important news in both print and broadcast, that seems to draw more of a mass audience. Executives characterize this effect as giving the public what it wants, while many working journalists tend to consider it to be pandering to the public and skimping on serious news.

As for television, *The Business of Media* book observes, "Local television news, especially, has developed a reputation for featuring little hard news, almost no investigative news, and lots and lots of entertainment, poignant human interest, sports and weather."[11]

These "happy talk formats" are designed and dictated by national consulting firms such as Frank N. Magid Associates ("Action News"), McHugh & Hoffman ("Eyewitness News"), and others that have turned stations across the country into clones of sameness, all aiming more to please viewers than to inform them.

Many in newspaper and broadcast newsrooms, even the veterans who still recall the days of more independent and aggressive reporting, are going along with the new program. But many also are rebelling against the blurring of distinctions between the sometimes conflicting missions of the newsroom and the business side.

"Such reporters and editors also find it ironic that—despite all their talk about serving readers (and viewers)—the editors in many of these market-oriented newsrooms seem to be more concerned about offending advertisers," the *CJR* article noted, adding: "Despite more than a decade of pushing marketing solutions to newspaper problems, daily circulation is still stagnant or dropping . . . these marketing strategies simply don't seem to be paying off."[12]

The Audit Bureau of Circulations (ABC) report of Sept. 30, 2000, showed continuation of a trend over the last several years in which average daily circulation fell four-tenths of a percent and Sunday circulation fell seven-tenths of a percent over the six-month reporting period. In the next six-month report of March 31, daily circulation dropped nine-tenths of a percent and Sunday circulation sagged 1.7 percent.[13] This basic trend has held true since 1986.

Look over the chart of North America's 35 largest dailies and note how many of them suffered circulation declines in the recorded year.

35 largest North American daily newspapers

Circulation figures of September 30, 2001, compared with previous year.[14]

Rank	Newspaper	Daily	% ch.	Sunday	Rank
1.	USA TODAY	2,149,933	21.3	N/A	N/A
2.	The Wall Street Journal	1,780,605	1.0	N/A	N/A
3.	The New York Times	1,109,371	1.1	1,668,650	1
4.	Los Angeles Times	944,303	-9.4	1,369,066	2
5.	The Washington Post	759,864	-0.3	1,059,646	3
6.	New York Daily News	734,473	4.1	802,215	5
7.	Chicago Tribune	675,847	2.1	1,010,704	4
8.	Newsday	577,354	0.2	675,619	12
9.	Houston Chronicle	512,042	0.9	744,009	9
10.	New York Post	533,860	16.8	401,365	29
11.	San Francisco Chronicle	512,129	10.7	523,096	17
12.	Dallas Morning News	494,860	-0.1	766,387	7
13.	Chicago Sun-Times	480,920	2.1	393,196	30
14.	Boston Globe	471,199	1.4	704,852	11
15.	Toronto Star, Ontario	459,901	-0.2	456,946	22
16.	Arizona Republic	451,288	1.3	554,582	16
17.	Newark Star-Ledger	410,547	0.7	608,542	15
18.	Atlanta Journal-Constitution	396,464	21.5	640,292	14
19.	Detroit Free Press	371,261	1.5	**749,113	*8
20.	Philadelphia Inquirer	365,154	-9.6	732,412	10
21.	Cleveland Plain Dealer	359,978	-1.3	477,515	20
22.	Toronto Globe & Mail, Ontario	353,951	-4.2	N/A	N/A
23.	San Diego Union-Tribune	351,762	-5.3	433,495	24
24.	Portland Oregonian	351,303	0.8	430,551	25
25.	Minneapolis Star Tribune	340,445	1.2	671,359	13
26.	St. Petersburg Times	331,903	1.9	414,195	27
27.	Orange County Register	324,056	-10.7	378,934	33
28.	Miami Herald	317,690	-8.2	426,058	26
29.	Rocky Mountain News	309,938	-37.6	801,315	*6
30.	Toronto National Post, Ontario	308,808	-3.7	N/A	N/A
31.	Baltimore Sun	306,341	-2.9	474,230	21
32.	Denver Post	305,929	-37.3	801,315	*6
33.	St. Louis Post-Dispatch	290,615	-1.3	485,984	18
34.	Sacramento Bee	285,863	-6.2	344,791	40
35.	L.A. Investor's Business Daily	281,173	-8.0	N/A	N/A

* - Sunday combination of the Rocky Mountain News and the Denver Post
** - Sunday combination of the Detroit Free Press and the Detroit News

As newspaper analyst David M. Cole noted, the more troubling aspect of the circulation slide among daily newspapers is what he considers the "cumulative problem" that every year or so the average circulation drops another 1 percent.[15]

Squires maintains that sacrificing news for infotainment in newspapers and television has been counter-productive. "There is absolutely no evidence that the continual tinkering with the content of newspapers and broadcast news shows to make them more entertaining and consumer friendly has had the slightest positive impact," he asserts. "Newspaper penetration of households has continued to decline in the nineties, down to about 65 percent from 98 percent in 1970."[16]

Daily circulations spiked upward in ABC's report of Sept. 30, 2001.

But the trade magazine *Editor & Publisher* cooled any celebration by editorializing that new ABC rules allowing papers to include discounted copies in the top-line, paid-circulation category were the reason for the increase, not any ingenious marketing breakthrough by the publishers.[17]

Television viewership is suffering from the same problem. Individual local and national news shows all have been fighting a decline in viewers, steadily losing market share to cable/satellite television and the Internet. Both *Time* and *Newsweek* magazines are regularly outsold on newsstands by *Soap Opera Update*—at least until Sept. 11, 2001.[18]

The CEOs of the chains and networks maintain, however, that their declines would be even worse if not for the heavy emphasis in recent years on marketing all their programming, including news. What reporters and editors decry as trivializing and sensationalizing the news, the CEOs see as a salvation strategy that is minimizing their losses in the face of increasing media choices and preserving a potential of growth.

The CEOs and board members heading the chains believe it is the newsrooms, not them, who are out of touch with the needs of the day.

"There was a time," said William Dean Singleton, CEO of MediaNews Group, "when the editor had no interference from anybody, and he put out the kind of newspaper he thought he should put out. But as sophisticated publishers have used marketing research, it has become increasingly clear that a newspaper must be the brainchild of more than an editor—a marketing director and an advertising director. A newspaper must be produced by a management team. Some editors have a problem with that."[19]

Singleton's message is a typical viewpoint from the CEOs of modern media companies. It is simply a plain-spoken version of a traditional definition of marketing, as put forth in the eighth edition in 2000 of a well known book in its field, *Effective Public Relations*, which states, "Marketing is the management function that identifies human needs and wants, offers products and services to satisfy those demands, and causes transactions that deliver products and services in exchange for something of value to the provider."[20]

The 4 P's of marketing

TO CARRY OUT effective marketing requires research followed by a coordinated program encompassing the principles first described by E. Jerome McCarthy in 1960, and referred to ever since as the 4 P's of marketing: **Product, Price, Place, Promotion.**[21] Some would argue there's more to it than that, adding P words such as planning and packaging. (Some marketing experts think packaging is part of product, and some think it's part of promotion.) However, all of those elements and more still can be folded into what is universally known throughout the business world as the 4 P's, which is a useful mnemonic.

The marketing mix is the combination of elements, including public relations and advertising but not limited to them, that a company uses to build public awareness and achieve its business goals. The 4 P's are:

Product: What is it you are selling? Keep in mind that media companies are among the few "dual market" types of enterprises. The customers of media companies are (1) their readers, viewers or listeners, and (2) their advertisers. Media companies have come to believe that what they have to sell to advertisers is their access to consumers, and what they have to sell to consumers is whatever content interests them.

Price: After the product, price itself is the key element in the marketing mix. Again, media companies must concern themselves with one price for the consumer and another price for the advertisers, through the advertising rates. Consumers in either quality or quantity are needed to attract advertisers, who provide the greatest percentage of revenue by far in most cases. The five most common pricing strategies are (1) premium pricing (the highest price), (2) value pricing (based on the value that the customer perceives), (3) cost-plus pricing (cost plus profit), (4) competitive pricing (the lowest price), and (5) penetration pricing (for launching products).[22]

Place: In the marketing mix, "place" really means "distribution," but distribution doesn't start with a P, so everyone agrees to be a bit flexible in the use of place instead. Place is concerned with sales or distribution channels, which deliver the company's product to its customers. If the product is not delivered effectively and efficiently through whatever channels are available to it, then why are we all working so hard to put it together? For media companies, place (distribution) is becoming an increasingly confusing part of the marketing mix with the advent of low wattage radio, suburban weeklies, hundreds and perhaps soon even thousands of television channels, the Internet, and the rapidly developing world of wireless communications.

Promotion: Finally, we get to the roles of public relations, advertising and any other means at a company's disposal to get the word out about the company, its product, and where to buy or use it. Part of that effort includes product design and packaging. Every product needs a design and a package, even from media companies, which might be thought of more as service companies. A newspaper's package is its layout, use of color, and an interesting mix of stories, photos and ads. Television has the power of visual images and sound, blended into what seems to be a hypnotic effect for at least some people. Magazines have the same package as newspapers, but in a glitzier and more free-form format that leads them almost invariably to niche marketing. Each radio station strives for a certain kind of sound, an audio ambiance carefully designed to appeal to a particular audience segment. The Internet is the flashy new arrival, with each site competing for interactivity and outreach, whether dealing in porn and its accompanying vices or in providing actual useful information.

Proper use of the 4 P's should add up to an advantageous **product positioning** and more effective **branding.**

Product positioning is marketing lingo for the position of the product in relation to its competitors and in the minds of the prospects and customers. This doesn't necessarily mean that the product is the leading one of its kind (though it can mean that). Mainly, it refers to the consumer's motivation to buy the product, the consumer's perception of the product, the consumer's attitude that it needs or wants the product, and the ability of the product to become a "learned" part of the consumer's life—all as described by McCarthy.

Branding results from a marketing plan that is so effective that consumers identify your product when they have the desire or need for that product or any similar one. It means that you are instantly recognizable to consumers. The most effective branding in the world probably is done by Coca-Cola. Even in the remotest corners of the globe, it seems, Coca-Cola is a household name.

Research needs to commence even before the 4 P's of marketing. Research is not a first step in marketing. Instead, it is a preliminary step that must be completed before any marketing goals or strategies can be set. Prudent managers will conduct market research continuously. Specific types of research by different media companies include circulation (penetration), readership and/or viewership, and advertising cost and efficiency studies.

Research for any company seeks a better understanding of its customers and market. McCarthy's durable book, in its many editions over 40-plus years, emphasizes that market research is important because it is what builds a bridge from the company to the customers. He recommends a five-step market research process that is similar in its stages to the decision-making models discussed in Chapter 5.

His five steps are:[23]

(1) Defining the problem, which McCarthy maintains is the most important of the steps and could consume half or more of the total time in market research. McCarthy cautions market researchers not to confuse the problem with the symptoms.

(2) Analyzing the situation, which is when secondary data is obtained and a "big picture" is formed of the product's relationship to the market.

(3) Getting the problem-specific data through qualitative means, such as focus groups, and through quantitative means, such as surveys.

(4) Interpreting the data, accomplished through random sampling of the product in select markets, statistics, validity studies and managerial assessment.

(5) Solving the problem, by finding the most effective way to sell the product in the market.

At the end of market research is a decision on how to proceed. And as with most decisions, the final step, even if unspoken, is monitoring of the result to see if the decision is actually working. If it isn't, then a re-study of the original market research or perhaps a new market research project with new assumptions needs to be conducted.

In his market assessments, McCarthy takes Maslow's five-level Hierarchy of Needs, discussed in Chapter 3, and compresses it to four levels for purposes of marketing a product: physiological needs, safety needs, social needs and personal needs.

"Motivation theory suggests that we never reach a state of complete satisfaction," McCarthy says, summing up the desire-for-more engine that drives all successful advertising campaigns. "As soon as lower-level needs are reasonably satisfied, those at higher levels become more dominant."[24]

The basic characteristics most often studied in market research are **demographics** and **psychographics.**

Demographic characteristics include age, education, gender, marital status, occupation, income, number of children, race and housing. Most of that will come from secondary data gathered from census figures and other sources in the second step of market research, "analyzing the situation."

Psychographic characteristics are concerned with the individual's lifestyle preferences—their activities, interests and opinions, which marketers refer to as consumer AIOs. This information is more likely to come through the third step, "getting the problem-specific data," through direct research. Lifestyle analysis is undertaken because marketers will have a better chance of appealing to customers the better that they know them.

In the fourth step, "interpreting the data," market researchers try to understand the customers' motivations through their needs and desires; their perceptions whether logical or illogical; and their attitudes encompassing likes, dislikes, beliefs and personality.

Because all consumer behavior is learned,[25] the critical part of any marketing solution is to determine the best strategy on how to introduce the product, convince the potential customers to try the product and have a satisfactory reaction, and then reinforce the customers' natural inclination to stay with what they now know and continue to keep buying the product.

Consumer behavior also is changeable. "Consumers learn from their consumption decisions and adjust their expectations and behavior," notes the authors of *Marketing Management*. "As a result, a certain (advertising) approach that worked once does not necessarily keep on working."[26]

To monitor these dynamics of consumer behavior requires market research. The larger the company, and the more national in scope the marketing effort, the more expensive the market research project will be. Today's media conglomerates generally are constantly conducting market research for existing and anticipated products, especially as it becomes more difficult to attract consumers whose attention is becoming more fragmented as they are exposed to an increasing array of media alternatives.

Most newspapers and magazines once thought of themselves as vehicles for mass market audiences—until the proliferation of media outlet alternatives, from FM radio stations to cable and satellite TV and the Internet. As several general circulation magazines died, all of the establishment print media began to move toward aiming their marketing efforts like a rifle instead of a shotgun, trying to hit segments of the audience rather than be all things to all people. We seem to be near the beginning of the end for print to be considered a mass media except for shoppers, though TV still relies greatly on the mass media model.

Metro newspapers, many finding themselves trapped in the core of decaying cities encircled by prosperous suburbs, began switching their circulation strategies to attract the suburban readers with the demographic of high income, writing off the low-income inner-city residents. Total circulation numbers declined with this turn away from a mass audience effort, but the decision was gratifyingly encouraged and accepted by advertisers, paradoxically earning newspapers higher profits despite much less circulation.

Similarly, television rushed to programming aimed almost exclusively at the demographics of age and gender—audiences dominated by youth. In the words of Sandy Grushow, chairman of Fox Television Entertainment Group: "The only thing meaningful is the 18-to-49-year-old demographic, the 18-to-34, and the teen demographic. That's how we sell (to advertisers). That's how we make our money."[27]

Both of these examples in newspapers and broadcast are a manifestation of a marketing strategy known as **segmentation.** This strategy is the opposite of mass media and more akin to niche media, as media companies change their orientation on viewership or readership from trying to reach the most people to only trying to reach the people in whom advertisers are interested.

This is why the moves by all media companies to entertainment and infotainment are motivated directly by the will of the advertisers—and only indirectly by the consumers—in how many of the desired audience segments can be delivered to advertisers.

In the movie, "The Insider," cigarettes are described as just a vehicle for delivering nicotine to addicts. Media companies increasingly now see their product as just a vehicle for delivering consumers to advertisers.

Market research is conducted to find out what appeals to members of a desired demographic segment and how best to give them what they want. What they seem to want is infotainment, not serious perspectives and hard news, so that is what the media has been increasingly delivering.

The Business of Media reflects on this market orientation of the media, observing, "The argument that serving the public interest is elitist is often based on the assumption that our current media system is democratic in giving people what they want. But as we have already seen, media are giving *advertisers* what they want and responding to the interests of demographically 'desirable' audiences. If anything, this market oriented approach might itself be labeled elitist, because it favors those with more money . . . . The business dynamics of media usually limit audience choice to variations on a few profitable formulas developed to meet advertiser needs."[28]

Marketing should be thought of as bringing the company and its product to the attention of groups of people—as opposed to selling, which is done one-on-one by salespeople.

Market penetration and pricing

NO MEDIA EXECUTIVES would disagree with advertising executive Philip Dusenberry's characterization of advertising. "I have always believed that writing advertisements is the second most profitable form of writing," Dusenberry said. "The first of course is ransom notes."[29]

Media companies live or die by advertising. For that reason, it is vital for both print and broadcast companies to have ways to determine the numbers of customers reached for the benefit of advertisers, who in turn will reward media companies with increased advertising sales. The relationship between this market penetration and cost is a value called the **cost per thousand impressions (CPM).** The CPM is the measurement often used for reaching the desired market segment targeted by the advertiser. Presumably, from this CPM market penetration will come a measure of advertising efficiency in producing sales.

If the media company does not calculate CPM, you can be sure that major advertisers probably will conduct CPM research on their own. However, trying to compare the CPM for a newspaper with the CPMs for television, radio, billboards and other advertising outlets can be an exercise in futility.

Media companies have basic formulas for determining their own CPM for the benefit of advertisers, which they promote in their advertising rate cards. Most newspapers, for example, announce their CPM as the single column inch rate divided by their circulation. Magazines determine their CPM by dividing the cost of a full page ad by their circulation, while television and radio stations calculate their CPM by the cost of a 30-second commercial divided by the number of households they reach.[30]

Advertisers, especially those using more than one kind of medium, do not necessarily use the same formulas. Calculating the cost per thousand by the total contacts alone ignores whether those contacts actually represent buyers. Most advertisers are not interested in the total circulation or viewership. Instead they are interested in what number from that total actually represents the consumers they want to reach. Calculating CPM by the traditional media formulas also ignores the impact of one media outlet over another.[31]

Consequently, sophisticated advertisers compare their costs of advertising in different media by first determining the size of the ad or commercial they want (most don't want just a one-inch ad, for example, and they also might prefer some size other than a full page in a magazine or a 30-second TV or radio commercial). Also, they divide the cost for the size of the ad they want by the number of likely buyers in the desired demographic they are looking for that is reached by the newspaper, magazine or station—not by the total audience.[32]

Until advertisers began using this tactic, it always had been a given that newspapers and magazines attracted advertisers by large circulation, and broadcasters attracted advertising by having the largest number of viewers or listeners.

But as readers for newspapers and viewers for TV stations continue to decline in an increasingly fragmented market, this traditional mass media idea of pricing based on the CPM formulas is coming under attack. Although media advertising rate cards continue to be presented under a mass media business model, advertisers now are looking for niche demographic markets instead. The advertisers are forcing a major move away from the long-held mass media way of doing business and more into a business model that emphasizes reaching a high-income audience.

For broadcast, this has resulted in more ways than just CPM to measure a commercial's impact. Other terms are gross impressions (GI), based on the total number of people reached (used mostly in radio), and cost per point (CPP), reached by dividing the total cost of a commercial by the commercial's total gross rating points (GRPs). If an advertiser places six commercials on a program with an audience rating of 3.0, then 18 GRPs are accumulated.[33]

For newspapers, this means an effort to capture suburban readers and write off both their inner-city and their out-of-area customers, as discussed earlier. This in turn is exacerbating circulation declines but leading to revenue increases nevertheless, as the publishers charge advertisers more for what is presumed to be more profitable demographics.

But this tactic can backfire because the old mass media business model still remains more effective for some national and major local advertisers. As newspapers and magazines alike abandon their old mass market strategy, and household penetration consequently drops, some advertisers such as grocery stores, car dealers and big-box retailers are increasingly turning to direct mail so they can continue to reach every house in their market area.[34]

A Kansas City auto dealer told *The Wall Street Journal*, "Circulation is down so much that we don't get the results we used to (advertising in the *Kansas City Star*). And yet the *Star* keeps jacking up ad rates."[35]

He was referring to the fact that in the 1950s the *Star* said it reached 90 percent of local homes, but admits today to reaching only 40 percent, despite the fact that the newspaper continues to raise its ad rates every year.[36]

In a comment that could be written about nearly any newspaper or television market, *The Wall Street Journal* article observed, "During the 1990s economic boom, many advertisers accepted ad-rate increases unquestioningly. Now that the economy has weakened, however, some advertisers are starting to grumble at Knight Ridder's annual increases of 3 percent or more. It isn't lost on them that their own profit margins are nowhere near the 20 percent that (Tony) Ridder achieved at Knight Ridder, let alone the 25 percent that he vows to reach by the end of 2003."[37]

Rebellion is in the air. It remains to be seen whether a business model that has survived for many decades can continue at the nation's media companies, or what some new business model will be. Media managers of today and tomorrow must decide how to re-invent their companies and strategies to meet these often conflicting demands in conducting business.

Pricing and marketing decision tools

JUST AS analytical tools including Performance Evaluation and Review, Critical Path Method, and decision trees can help the manager in making decisions involving operations, there are other analytical tools especially useful in reaching sound decisions on the all-important issues of product pricing and marketing.

Marketing is essential, but price drives the marketing. Marketing battles fought over who has the lowest price are dangerous for everyone. "Price competition is the most savage and destructive form of business warfare," warn the authors of *Marketing Management*.[38]

The price-setting tools are break-even analysis, crossover analysis, and cost benefit analysis. The tools more aligned with marketing decisions are the law of diminishing returns, synergy and economies of scale, and diffusion of innovations.

None of these analytical tools is a substitute for managerial decision-making any more than the previously described PERT/CPM or decision trees. Instead, they are designed to help managers in the decision-making process by enabling them to "see" the process and alternatives more clearly.

Pricing analytical tools

BREAK–EVEN ANALYSIS: The break-even point for a product or service is when the total sales revenue for a particular product equals the total costs. In other words, how many units of a product do you need to sell at a certain price before you start making a profit?

You cannot start making a profit with the very first sale even on a kids lemonade stand because you have some investment of time, materials, overhead and possibly other costs that are incurred to make that first sale possible. Break-even analysis reveals how many sales you need to make before you finally attain an actual profit.

Break-even analysis is popular, but it also can be misleading. Can any product be sold indefinitely at the same price? A few can, but not most.[39] Break-even analysis is useful for determining when a profit can start being realized, but it is not as useful for determining future profits the further you go out in time after the break-even point.

Every business has a mix of fixed and variable costs.

Fixed costs are costs that remain the same regardless of the amount of product the company makes and sells. For example, the mortgage or rent on the company's building and its insurance remain the same, despite production or sales, and therefore are fixed. Some, but not all, fixed costs are considered overhead costs.

Variable costs are those costs that change depending on the company's production and sales volume. For instance, in publishing, printing more copies will require consumption of more rolls of newsprint and volumes of ink. In broadcasting, an increase in local news coverage will require more staff and probably more equipment.

Calculation of the break-even point takes up many pages in business texts and on-line business Web sites, so it is impossible to explain it thoroughly in this book. The most important fact for students to know is that the break-even point is reached when income from the number of units of product sold equal the fixed costs.

After the break-even point, you start making money.

Determining fixed and variable costs sounds more straightforward than it really is. Some costs might turn out to be surprisingly difficult to measure. In a multi-product firm, for example, costs being allocated among different products can make a determination of dollar amounts for fixed and variable costs problematic. Also, fixed costs remain fixed only over some range of production, and then they often change.[40]

The simplest break-even formula is to divide your total fixed costs by the price of the product minus its variable costs, which will tell you how many units you must sell before you will start making a profit.[41] A Google search of "break-even analysis" will turn up several detailed Web sites on the subject.

After the break–even point is reached, the money that is made becomes what is known as the company's operating profit, usually referred to as EBIT (Earnings Before Interest and Taxes).[42]

CROSSOVER ANALYSIS: This analytical tool can be used when comparing two or more comparable equipment options, as in trying to decide if you should buy or lease one copier or another. Each will have fixed and variable costs, which will differ from each other. The question is, which of the two seemingly equivalent copiers should you acquire?

What you must find is the point where the cost of the two alternatives equalizes, and one starts being more expensive than the other from that point on at a given rate of production or use. Crossover analysis will identify that point. The formula is:[43]

$$\text{Crossover units} = \frac{\text{Alt. \#2's fixed costs} - \text{Alt. \#1's fixed costs}}{\text{Alt. \#1's variable costs} - \text{Alt. \#2's variable costs}}$$

This will tell you at what level of production both machines are equal in cost. After that point, however, one is more most cost-efficient than the other. Then you can figure out the cost of each alternative below and above the crossover point, which will tell you which machine is cheaper to run below the crossover point and which is cheaper over that point.

This assumes that you as the manager can forecast the volume that you will be using with some accuracy. Just as important, crossover analysis does not take into consideration factors that might be of great importance, such as quality, reliability, etc. You probably are willing to pay more for better quality. Break-even and crossover analyses are just tools, and both often play a part in determining the cost benefit.

COST–BENEFIT ANALYSIS: Every product or service comes with a cost that, as we have seen, is made up of variable and fixed costs. This cost is measurable in dollars. Presumably every product—a successful one at least—also has a benefit, or it would not be accepted by consumers. This benefit also sometimes can be measured in dollars, but often it is at least partly qualitative and therefore difficult to measure.[44]

As the age-old business cliché states, you need to spend money to make money in business. But not every expenditure makes money, and some expenditures make more money than others.

To determine if an expenditure is worth making, a manager or owner might undertake some sort of formal or informal cost benefit analysis. Some people, through experience or instincts, seem to be able to make fairly quick decisions on whether some expenditures will result in a worthwhile return. Other times, they need to calculate what the benefit will be (for example, increased sales equaling some number) minus the expenditure required (such as extra electricity costs and staffing costs).

In its simplest form, determine cost–benefit by simply dividing the present value of benefits by the present value of costs.[45] If the value is greater than one, the project probably is worth doing.

You sometimes can simply subtract the cost from the benefits to get the net dollar gain. Even if there is a positive net gain in dollars, however, the total still might not be large enough to consider worth doing if there are mitigating factors, such an inconvenience, time away from family, danger, etc.

Marketing analytical tools

LAW OF DIMINISHING RETURNS: This is one of the best known business rules because it applies so much in anyone's personal life as well. Basically, the law says that if you keep adding more resources to increase sales or to accomplish other results, an improvement will be realized. But at some point, the benefit will begin tapering off, and as you put in more effort there will be some benefit realized, but less proportionately than at the beginning.

Estimating when returns will diminish is tricky because there are no formulas or rules of thumb to determine when the "law" will kick in. The law is an "empirical generalization"[46] that applies in real life but is hard to prove. All you can be sure is that, inevitably, there is a limit to what benefit can be realized without adding disproportionately more resources or different resources.

By the way, there also is a lesser-known Law of Diminishing Demand. It states that if the price is raised, then the demand will go down, and conversely, if the price is reduced then the demand will rise.[47] The law has a sense of real-life logic to it and certainly applies for routine products in a routine supply and demand economy. It is an articulation of **price elasticity of demand.**[48]

In other words, if price is reduced on some product, the usual result is that new buyers will be attracted and current loyal buyers might also buy the product in larger quantities. Though generally true, this law has its exceptions, because some products and services are more sensitive to price than others. For example, there are limits for media companies. George J. Stigler, author of the oft-reprinted book *The Theory of Price*, points out that a family still will buy only one copy of a newspaper even if the price is reduced.[49]

Similarly, even if an increase in price reduces sales, it does not necessarily follow that profit will go down, too. I was not the first publisher to discover this phenomenon. When I raised newsstand and subscription prices on my newspaper, sales would immediately slack off even if the increase was only a few cents per copy. However, I also could print fewer copies, which saved me more than the amount lost from the decreased sales. And as the public became more accustomed to the new price, sales would return to their previous levels but at the new, more profitable rate.

If the price–demand relationship in a product follows the Law of Diminishing Demand, than the demand is elastic. If total revenue decreases with a price reduction, however, or increases with a price hike, then the demand is inelastic.[50]

SYNERGY AND ECONOMIES OF SCALE: This concept explains why companies want to keep getting larger. Such economy of scale benefits as "volume discounts" and "market penetration" become possible through sheer size alone of business operations. Remember that the definition of fixed costs is that they stay the same regardless of the amount of product produced (to a point, at least). So the more a product is sold, the more a product is produced. If the fixed costs remain the same, they therefore are spread out over more units of product, thus lowering the average cost and resulting in economies of scale.

Economies of scale often are a major reason for the success of large operations or conglomerates. Not only will large competitors be able to operate at a lower cost per unit of product through economies of scale, they also can demand volume discounts from suppliers because of their massive market share. As media economist Robert G. Picard points out, "Firms with economies of scale can thus sell products and services at a lower price or retain greater profits than can firms with lower economies of scale."[51]

The only recourse for a small company facing dangerous economies of scale from a much larger competitor is to carve out a market niche. Those who continue to try to slug it out against a large competitor on the competitor's terms are doomed. As one small-town pharmacist explained to me, his wholesale price for some products is higher than the retail price charged by his "big box" competitors. So he developed a special niche in which to market his pharmacy.

Mergers and acquisitions not only add economies of scale but also typically provide synergies in which the blending of two companies or business operations can result in the strengths of one company or operation complementing the strengths of the other or the strengths of one offsetting the weaknesses of the other. Synergies are often the reason for centralizing company operations, and they are the driving force behind the media industries' constant efforts toward **vertical integration** and **horizontal integration**.

Only large companies are very much concerned with these concepts of organization, because small firms are usually concerned only with the core business. As companies develop to larger size and to more diverse activities through acquisition and growth, however, these terms become essential to understanding the power and reach of the conglomerates.

If a company is said to be vertically integrated, it means that it owns subsidiaries or is departmentalized within its organization to handle more than one primary function—i.e., it might own one or more of the production, distribution, marketing or research functions of its business line.

A horizontally integrated company is diversified by owning a number of different businesses, some of which might not seem related to each other, at least at first glance

Synergy can be positive or negative.[52] Synergy results when the combined parts of products, companies, staffs and anything else that can be combined have a more beneficial effect than could be obtained by just adding up the sum of their individual parts. Usually synergy refers to several businesses, all under one owner, reinforcing each other by cooperating in a complementary marketing effort.

There are plenty of other dynamics of human behavior and organizations that also apply, not the least of which is Murphy's Law that states that if anything can go wrong, it will. There also is its universal corollary, that everything takes longer than you think it will. Many other factors, including some with such esoteric titles as "spiral of silence" and "pluralistic ignorance," commonly interfere with the decision-making and judgment processes and thus further complicate marketing efforts by managers.

DIFFUSION OF INNOVATIONS: One of the key perspectives of marketing is the concept of dissemination or diffusion of innovations, which explains and measures the process of acceptance by the public of new products, services and ideas. Managers who want to introduce a new product or service need to understand this concept so their judgment is not compromised by overconfidence, impatience or ineffective marketing tactics.

The national model for product acceptance in the marketplace is the one researched and explained by Everett M. Rogers, a communication professor at the University of New Mexico. Now found in many textbooks dealing with marketing, Rogers' theory explains how any innovative development goes through stages of acceptance by the public, but with different speeds.

For example, the first commercial black-and-white television sets appeared on the American market in the late 1940s and quickly became the most quickly accepted new home appliance in the history of marketing. Only a little over a decade later, by 1960, an estimated 90 percent of American homes had a television set.[53] Products had always taken much longer to reach such overwhelming penetration previously. The telephone that we take so much for granted today was not in place in 50 percent of American homes until 1946, which was 70 years after its invention.[54]

But the World Wide Web is being accepted much faster, perhaps faster than even television. The Internet existed as an information-sharing technology between a select few research universities and the U.S. Department of Defense starting in 1969. It did not become accessible to the public until 1989, when British programmer Tim Berners-Lee ingeniously wrote software called Enquire Within About

Everything.[55] For the first time, it became possible for people outside the small defense research circle to access information being shared between networks and computers. Berners-Lee's accomplishment, which at first worked only on his computer, but quickly drew the attention of other programmers, led to development of the first public browser by computer engineering faculty and students at the University of Illinois in 1992. They named their browser Mosaic and made it available to other programmers. Later that year, there were 50 or so of the first non-defense commercial and individual sites on what became known as the World Wide Web.[56] The first commercial browser, Netscape, became available in 1994. Hundreds of millions of sites and users on the Web rushed to this new technological development in less than a decade.

Rogers says marketing an innovation is influenced by five key characteristics of the new idea or innovation.

The speed of adoption is determined by (1) the relative advantage of the innovation, that is, how much better it is than the idea it supersedes; (2) compatibility, measured by how it relates to the values and needs of the adopters; (3) complexity, or how simple the innovation is or appears to be; (4) observability, or how other people are able to see the innovation being used; and (5) trial-ability, in how easy it is to try the product through free samples, "light" versions of software, trial subscription periods and similar marketing exposures.[57]

Regardless of the speed, all innovations in the form of new products, services and ideas go through a similar "curve" of adoption, variously described as diffusion through the marketplace or acceptance by the public, in the manner described by Rogers.

"Innovators" are the venturesome customers who make up the first 2.5 percent of the market to adopt new ideas under Rogers' normal adopter distribution model. As the innovation earns public success, it is picked up by a larger number of "early adopters," representing 13.5 percent of the eventual market. Then it is picked up by most of the people who accept the innovation, made up of 34 percent of the "early majority" and 34 percent of the "late majority." Of course, there are always some folks—equal in number to a combination of the innovators and early adopters—who are known as the "laggards" and who only very late accept the new idea.[58] (People who never accept the new idea are not included in the model.)

Rogers' theory also can be applied toward individuals and how quickly they adopt, if they do at all, the new management challenges being posed by large media conglomerates. The innovators and early adopters will be the people who are picked for leadership. Ideally, they can change with the times without compromising principles.

Total market coverage

WITH THE possible exception of magazines, advertisers are the principal customer of all news-oriented U.S. media companies. The reader or viewer is considered a minor customer, if subscriptions are involved, but is primarily looked on as the consumer for whom the advertisements are sold. Many magazines historically have relied on subscriptions for the bulk of their income, but advertising typically provides about 80 to 85 percent of newspapers' income, while TV, radio and many Internet models derive virtually all of their income from advertising.

Broadcast competition is driven by ratings systems, whereby stations in the same market are ranked against each other by the numbers of households tuning in to a particular news or entertainment program, or to the station as a whole. Television stations are divided into 210 markets ranked by population across the United States, from the three largest metro markets of New York, Los Angeles and Chicago, to the three smallest of Alpena, Mich., North Platte, Neb., and Glendive, Mont.[59]

Because advertisers on TV and radio stations generally want to reach the largest audience per dollar expended, the ratings affect the advertising rates the stations can charge—the more households reached, the higher the ad rates can be.

The Nielsen ratings mentioned earlier in the text determine the prices that can be charged by stations as a whole and for specific programs. You can find the Nielsen ratings for each week's top 10 national TV programs at <www.broadcastingcable.com> and other sites. The ratings rank the programs by the number of viewers each have. The only alternatives available to broadcast stations to increase the number of viewers is to strengthen their signal (which is highly regulated) or to change programs in ways that draw viewers from on-air competitors.

Print media often employ a tactic known as **Total Market Coverage (TMC)** to reach more readers.

TMC is simply sending a copy of your publication free to every home in the area that you consider to be your geographic market. Some TMC publications are delivered by carriers, others by mail, and others by a combination of the two. Another kind of free distribution is putting copies in newsracks, but that should not be confused with TMC distribution, which although also free, is systematically designed to enter every single home.

Many large and small print advertisers still want mass media exposure and have been placing an increasing emphasis on the importance of reaching every household. The result is that free circulation papers and shoppers have been enjoying the greatest rate of growth for more than two decades.[60]

Existing daily and weekly newspapers usually accomplish TMC by having a free shopper distributed to every home, while the main paper with the same ads plus news goes to the subscribers. In the golden era of dailies, when many boasted household penetration of 90 percent or more, TMC was not a concern. But as the circulation of dailies began dropping in the 1980s, many of the national and local mass merchandising retailers began clamoring for a way to get their ads into as many homes as before. The solution was the TMC product, which usually is a shopper with no news.

The addition of TMC products marked the first major conflict between the news and the business sides in the 1980s. Many newspaper editors resisted starting up their own TMC products, standing on their beliefs that they were not to be concerned about selling ads.

In the small college town of Mount Vernon, Iowa, the publisher of the 110-year-old *Hawkeye* weekly newspaper refused to start a shopper. A new weekly, *The SUN*, started up against him in the late 1970s with a companion TMC shopper. Within weeks, the *Hawkeye* lost major advertising accounts and was forced to sell out. This scenario was repeated incessantly across the nation until publishers came to realize that creating a TMC was really about their own business survival.

A variation of TMC is **Non-Duplicating Coverage (NDC),** in which the shopper is sent only to the newspaper's nonsubscribers. This combination of subscription distribution by the newspaper and NDC distribution of the shopper ensures that every household receives the advertising.

Another delivery alternative for print media is **zoned coverage.** Putting out different editions of a day's newspaper is a decades-old practice, with the early edition(s) usually going to the suburban or state subscribers and the final edition into the city. Now, however, newspapers often publish zoned sections directed at individual communities, with separate ads and stories. To do so, they must pick up the costs of additional staffing and schedule valuable time on the presses. Magazines also now use zoned delivery with articles and advertisements varying on some pages, depending on the zip codes to which they are delivered.

The desire by many advertisers to attain total market coverage also led to **direct mail marketing,** in which advertising fliers are sent to a geographic market determined by the advertiser rather than a publisher. Advo is the largest of many national firms using direct mail to compete against news-oriented media companies. Direct mail companies have taken away a large volume of advertising from daily newspapers since the 1980s across the United States.

Market analysis

THE THREE TYPES of inter-related markets in which news-oriented media companies compete are **information, advertising** and **intellectual.**[61] The information and advertising markets reflect the dual products of nearly all media companies in capitalistic societies, selling news to readers and viewers and also selling that access to readers or viewers to the advertisers.

The intellectual market is more difficult to pin down because it is made up of the "marketplace of ideas" described by John Milton and John Stuart Mill, where individuals and groups seek information and ideas they want or need as citizens. It is the intellectual market (and the information market) that the First Amendment was specifically trying to shield from government interference. This is why journalists often say that newspapers especially, but also television and news magazines, are a "different" kind of business than other commercial enterprises.

Any attempt to discuss the information and advertising markets needs also to address the intellectual market—at least when dealing with media companies that provide news instead of only entertainment. Controversies over intellectual aspects of media company performance have erupted periodically ever since the first newspapers and fliers, and they seem to be coming up with even more frequency under the new business paradigm of conglomerate media companies reaching national and international size. Especially early on, outrage over what and how news was being disseminated was a concern mainly of government trying to control information. That government concern was reflected in laws pertaining to seditious libel and sedition that attempted to stop criticism of public officials and government policies in the 1800s and early 1900s. These days, such concern comes more from individuals upset with the coverage of what they see as trivia at the expense of more serious news.

The first law of marketing was expressed by marketing consultant George S. Day, who urged, "Love the customer more than the product."[62]

To make this work, one must understand the customer through market analysis. To begin the analysis of any market is to understand the nature of demand for a product or service in the marketplace.

Perfect competition exists in very few industries, but the economic theory behind perfect competition states that variations in demand are influenced by four factors:[63]

- The price of a commodity
- The prices of substitutes
- The income of the buyer (individual or family)
- The tastes or preferences of consumers.

The next step is to understand the way a market is organized. This market structure affects the way all media companies operate.

The concept of what constitutes a market often differs considerably between the producers, the marketers and the consumers. Producers and service providers tend to think of markets in physical terms, such as geographical or physical groupings of customers, or in terms of product category or the price charged for their product compared with the price charged by a competitor. This is another way of saying that those producing the product tend to think only of where customers they are trying to reach are located.[64]

Marketers, however, think of the market strictly in terms of customers and potential customers. They target these customers, trying to reach them by dividing the physical market into segments where the most likely buyers are to be found. And the two ways they segment the market are by consumer characteristics and consumer responses. These are explained in a popular textbook, *Marketing Management: Text and Cases,* as follows.

Consumer characteristics are based on who buys:[65]

- Geographic: region, urban vs. rural, etc.
- Demographic: age, gender, marital status, etc.
- Socioeconomic: income, social class, occupation, etc.
- Cultural: lifestyles, etc.

Consumer responses are based on what is bought:[66]

- Occasions.
- Usage frequency.
- Benefits from the product.
- Attitudes, including customer loyalty.

Peter Drucker maintains that the only reason for a company's existence is to attract and satisfy customers at a profit. E. Jerome McCarthy says simply, "The customer should be the target of all marketing efforts,"[67] while George S. Day declares that, "market-driven firms have a mission to find needs and fill them, not make products and sell them."[68]

The buyers and potential buyers of products might have very different ideas of what the market comprises. They might consider the market to simply be the city they live in, especially if it is a small town, or consider a newspaper to be one kind of market and a shopper and TV station as other kinds of markets. While the advertiser might think the customer is buying the product because of price, the customer might be buying the product for a totally different reason. "It behooves a supplier to know the true reasons because the promotional message often determines how the consumer perceives the product,"[69] the authors of *Marketing Management* point out.

Any producer of product or supplier of services needs to understand the nature of competitors—present and anticipated.

Competition is categorized in many ways, but the three most common are: **perfect competition,** where there are many companies producing many products that are so similar that they are comparable; **oligopoly,** where there are only a few sellers of similar products, perhaps as few as two; and **monopoly,** where one seller and its product serves the market.

As for the competitors themselves, the wise business owners and managers never take their eye off those who already are competing with them or who are likely to begin competing. The first category, the companies and people already in active competition against you, are obvious. The other category is much more difficult to identify, and it's never possible to eliminate all of the surprises. The potential future competitor might be a company that could move into your market by developing a similar product, or in the case of small businesses, it might be an individual who decides for whatever reason to start a new company and go into business against you.

The threat of a new competitive business starting up is always a concern for small businesses. Although the market power of an existing firm can be formidable, especially when combined with large size, small companies always exist in a state of relative vulnerability.

When others see your success, there are always some entrepreneurs who think they can either do it better than you or that there's enough to go around for one more entry in the field. In the 12 years I owned my newspapers and shopper, there were three attempts by other individuals to start up competing free-circulation advertising publications in my geographic market area.

Better that scenario, however, than the one where another company—especially if it is larger than yours—decides to move into your market and battle you for market share. The larger company with its economy of scale and ability to absorb operating losses for an extended period is the most dangerous threat to an existing company and its product or service. Large companies in some fields have reputations for letting a small firm do the work of building up traffic for a successful local business, and then moving into the same market area—maybe even across the street—and driving the smaller firm out of business.[70]

There always are **barriers to entry** for any enterprise, starting with the previously mentioned market power of an existing firm. Such power greatly increases the money and time required for a new company to succeed and, in fact, can make success all but impossible. This is why you rarely hear about a new daily newspaper starting up against an established daily. It is very difficult for any newcomer to get started against an established and well-run company unless the newcomer can exploit a specific weakness, such as poor reputation or high prices by the existing company. Even that can be fruitless, however, because the first reaction of the existing company's managers will be to correct the fault the newcomer is trying to exploit.

Another barrier is the requirement for sufficient capital to launch a new company in a competitive market. Because of expensive equipment, at one time starting a newspaper was a very capital intensive endeavor with high risk. However, with the desktop publishing capability, laser computers and centralized printing operations of today, weekly newspapers and shoppers can be started quickly and inexpensively.

A related barrier to entry can arise even after what appears to be a successful startup, when competition forces higher than expected fixed or variable costs that make long-term continuation for the new company too difficult.

A final barrier, especially in broadcast, can be government regulation. It is not possible to acquire a channel, for example, if none is available. Government also can block companies through various licensing requirements.

The constant competitive threat means managers need to market their business so they can serve customers better than any competitor, monitor their firm's market position, and quickly detect changes in the public's tastes and interests.

Market-driven journalism

IN HIS BOOK, *When MBAs Rule the Newsroom*, Doug Underwood notes that the rise of professional marketers and managers has been going on with newspapers since the early 1800s, but it is approaching its zenith now with the advent of **market-driven journalism.** He says it is manifested by editorial-business alliances, increasing news coverage of celebrities and other light infotainment, news coverage based on reader preference surveys, and very often sensationalism.[71]

"These marketplace pressures have led to the appearance of a new kind of editor," Underwood writes, "a cross between an editor and a marketing official," who is increasingly concerned with providing content that marketers say the public wants.

Underwood adds, "The new marketing-oriented editor is an outgrowth of a concept known as 'The Total Newspaper,' where newspaper executives are urged to coordinate the news and business departments (including circulation, advertising and financial) and work together to market the newspaper as a total product."[72]

The major premise behind the call for market-driven journalism has been to build print circulation or add broadcast viewers, which in turn will bring in more advertising dollars. But does market-driven journalism accomplish this goal? And even if it does work, should newspapers and broadcast outlets be doing market-driven journalism?

Many on the news side resent market-driven journalism because they believe it panders to the lowest common denominator in the public. They believe it therefore harms the quality and quantity of hard news and distorts judgments in what news should even be covered. In other words, they say, market-driven journalism slants the coverage toward what the masses want to know instead of what they need to know.

John H. McManus, in his book, *Market-Driven Journalism: Let the Citizen Beware?* dealing with both print and TV newsrooms, says forcibly, "For journalism purists, the trend toward letting the logic of the marketplace into the newsroom is defilement, a blasphemy."[73]

Anything can be overdone, of course. At least one study noted how newspapers are becoming more reader-oriented and market-driven, but it also concluded that this approach could remain consistent with public service goals of journalism if done in a prudent and responsible way.[74] A survey of newspapers across the country proves that many are finding an acceptable balance.

A recent study of daily newspapers, however, raises questions.

Randal A. Beam of Indiana University surveyed dailies across the country and was surprised by the results, reporting that his study "unexpectedly found no association between market orientation and the four circulation-based performance measures . . . . (despite) the emphasis the newspaper industry has put on becoming more reader focused to build circulation."[75]

Beam adds, "This does not necessarily mean that becoming market-oriented has been a waste of resources, however. It's still prudent for well-run businesses to strive to identify and meet their customers' wants and needs, even absent a clear short-term benefit from doing so. Perhaps the benefit will come in the long run."[76]

Market-driven journalism and the growing consolidation of ownership leading to large conglomerates have both undoubtedly been a boon for newspaper business managers as they have seen their influence grow markedly. "No more sitting in the basement counting beans," said Robert Kasabian, then executive director of the International Newspaper Financial Executives. "Financial officers are in the board rooms. We're in the publishers' offices, helping make decisions."[77]

Feelings are strong on both sides as leading media figures debate the uneven results of chain ownership, a major force behind market-driven journalism.

In 1988, C.K. McClatchy, publisher of a group of West Coast papers, told the American Society of Newspaper Editors he was concerned that newspapers were being compromised by big chains that seemed (as Oscar Wilde wrote in his definition of a cynic) to know the price of everything but the value of nothing.

"One can say that good newspapers are almost always run by good newspaper people," McClatchy wrote in the ASNE publication *The Next Newspapers*, but "they are almost never run by good bankers or good accountants . . . . American conglomerates have demonstrated special contempt for the press and its responsibility to inform the public. I fear it is just a matter of time before newspapers will be considered the same as any business, a fit prize for investment by interests that do not care about the principles of good journalism."[78]

Only a few years later, McClatchy's premonition was realized. All through the 1990s, several venture capital companies were formed to buy daily and weekly newspapers, as well as radio and television stations. These companies are headed not by journalists, but by investors and non-journalist business leaders lured only by the high profit margins of media companies. They are a particularly ruthless breed of entrepreneurs.

The first of these, the Journal Register Company, was formed in 1990 and now is America's 22nd largest newspaper chain. JRC is a harsh example of this new kind of media company—where venture capitalists pile on the debt to build the company through acquisitions to where it can convert to a stock-traded company. The investors then are paid back handsomely by the money received from selling stock.

Venture capitalists invest when they have in place an "exit strategy" for selling the company or taking it public in five to seven years, with as large a payoff as possible when they "harvest" the fruits of their investment. Therefore, investors' marketing and profit-taking strategies are short-term, and they tend to disregard a company's long-term financial viability.

In Mary Walton's chapter, "The selling of small-town America," in the book *Leaving Readers Behind*, she compares these nontraditional newspaper owners to "real estate speculators, buying properties, milking them for profits, and then auctioning them off."[79] Referring to JRC in a way that could apply to all or most of the highly leveraged venture-capital-backed chains, Walton notes, "On acquiring new properties, JRC typically whacks payrolls and merges operations with other papers to form a money-saving cluster (to be discussed in the next section). At the same time, it overhauls the format to fit the corporate model."[80]

Think of debt as resting on one end of a lever, with the other end under a rock of assets. A load of debt can pry the assets out of the ground and raise them up higher. This is what is referred to as "leveraging" a company. Debt is a proven engine of growth, but it also requires cutting costs, increasing revenues, or both, to pay the principal and interest incurred by the debt. The impact on the acquired company often is similar to Walton's scenario.

Reprinted by permission of Tribune Media Services

Newspaper comic strip reporter Brenda Starr expresses a lament.[81]

Journal Register Company received its original financing from Warburg, Pincus & Co., and the New York investment firm became the owner of three-fourths of JRC's stock after taking the company public in 1997.

Of the other venture-capital media companies, the largest and probably the best-known is Community Newspaper Holdings Inc. (CNHI), controlled and financed entirely by the $22 billion Alabama public employees pension fund. In less than five years, CNHI became America's 13th largest newspaper chain, owning 95 dailies in mid-2003.[82]

Another is Liberty Group Publishing, Inc., founded in 1997 with backing from the leveraged buyout company of Leonard Green & Partners and with financing also coming from the California, Michigan and Pennsylvania pension systems. Liberty tried to go public in 2003, but withdrew its $225 million Initial Public Offering (IPO) because of unfavorable market conditions.[83]

Other venture capital media companies include Westward, started by a Texas investment bank and now owned by Banc One Capital Partners of Columbus, Ohio, and Lionheart, which was bankrolled by Weiss, Peck & Greer Private Equity Group.[84]

Canada also has a new venture capital media firm, Osprey Media Group. Like its U.S. counterparts, it seemed to emerge in 2001 out of nowhere, funded in large part by the Ontario Teachers' Pension Fund. Osprey's ready access to a large pool of cash enabled it to acquire 22 dailies and more than 30 weeklies in Canada in less than two years.[85]

The power of the cluster

FORMATION OF THE venture capital firms since the 1990s led almost automatically to the economic strategy of **clustering** as they and other chains, burdened by acquisition debt loads, worked to find a way to make their loan payments by increasing profits.

Clustering is both a marketing tactic and a consolidation tactic, in a classic chicken-and-egg analogy. So it seems logical to place clustering at the end of this chapter on marketing as a jumping-off point for the next chapter on consolidation.

Though practiced for decades by some small media entrepreneurs, clustering is seen as a modern phenomenon because the conglomerates began emphasizing it only a few years ago. Since the early to mid-1990s, all newspaper chains have been buying both large and small newspapers in geographic proximity to one central printing plant. Similarly, broadcast giants are buying radio stations up to the legal limit in one city after another, big-city cable systems are buying out competitors in all the small towns around so they can group customers geographically, and television conglomerates are buying into nearby metropolitan markets.

Frequently in recent years media conglomerates that had been competing against each other—because each owned properties in two cities—have swapped properties so one could dominate one city while the other attained a dominance in the second city.

Clustering is a tactic not limited to just the giants.

As owner of a weekly newspaper, I bought another much smaller weekly in a town 12 miles away in 1987. I was able to make a profit on even a paper as small as it was because I could produce it entirely out of my larger paper's office with no increase in equipment, employees or overhead. I sold all of the smaller paper's equipment and stopped renting a building the smaller paper had been using. Then my existing staff took over all bookkeeping, ad sales, reporting and other functions. The smaller paper's only two full-time employees were the husband-and-wife owners. They left with the closing on the sale, of course, and there was no need to replace them. My own staff began producing both papers. Talk about economies of scale.

A freelance writer who lived in the smaller town attacked my purchase in an article in a statewide magazine. The writer lamented the sale of his hometown weekly to an out-of-town owner. Sound familiar? In a reference that would have brought guffaws if it had been read within the marbled halls of any publicly traded conglomerate, the writer even accusingly referred to my pip-squeak operation as "a chain."

So-called chains such as mine were run by weekly and small daily publishers across the country—publishers such as Mike Lyon, who owned his family's weekly in Mapleton, Iowa, as well as smaller papers in three nearby towns. Lyon is just one of many family newspaper publishers who ran clustered operations years before the concept ever occurred to hot-shot national media executives, though their motivation was more on saving the other papers, not in folding them into an empire.

Chain clustering has been a salvation for some newspapers and broadcast stations. For others, chain ownership has resulted in degrees of a lesser quality, infotainment journalism scathingly detailed in the 2001 book titled *Leaving Readers Behind: The Age of Corporate Newspapering*, edited by master newspaper editor Gene Roberts.[86]

Even the modest clustering that small town publishers practiced across the country resulted in incredible efficiencies and synergies—both in reducing costs and increasing revenues.

For example, the combination of clustering, consolidation and convergence enables publishers like Jerry Wiseman, who operates out of Armstrong, Iowa, to keep several nearby small-town weeklies alive that could not otherwise survive on their own.

In the hands of Wall Street buccaneers, however, the same clustering strategy used to save small papers results in economic plundering of papers and broadcast stations by chains financed through the stock market—or perhaps even more true, financed through venture capitalists who are planning to eventually issue stock through an IPO.

Clustering has changed the newspaper landscape, for better or worse. The Project on the State of the American Newspaper identified 125 regional clusters involving more than 400 daily newspapers and many times that number of weeklies.[87] Virtually all were formed in the 1990s.

With only a few exceptions, gone are the days when a newspaper company would own publications scattered across the nation, separated sometimes by hundreds of miles. The goal now is to cluster newspapers together, in geographic proximity. Some clusters are statewide in scope.

The economies of scale and the synergies that can be realized are the driving forces for creation of clusters.

The following illustration shows only a third of the clusters involving both dailies and weeklies in Iowa. Some clusters are owned by small family companies operating only in Iowa.

AT A GLANCE

The power of the cluster

Economies of scale and other economic efficiencies lead to large and small media companies "clustering" their newspaper holdings geographically or along highways, as shown here in Iowa

1A and 1B—Lee Enterprises	10—Community Media Group
2—Maquoketa Newspapers	11—Liberty Group
3—Woodward Communications	12—Mid-America Publishing
4—News Publishing Inc.	13A and 13B—Ogden Newspapers
5—Brehm Communications	14—Omaha World-Herald Co.
6—Inland Industries	15—Journal Publishing
7—Lancaster Publications	16—New Century Press
8A and 8B—CNHI	17—Concord Publishing House
9—Gannett	18—Lyon Publishing

Whatever effect it has on the reduction of newspaper quality, editorial voices and journalistic independence, it is indisputable that clustering also is a life saver for many struggling newspapers. "One of the beauties of clustering is that it takes papers standing on the brink and makes them very healthy," MediaNews Group CEO William Dean Singleton noted.[88]

Even critics need to concede that point. Clustering results in consolidation, but some newspapers cannot survive without clustering.

While clustering still is a driving force for newspapers, some second thoughts about its efficacy for radio stations started being expressed in 2003, even by people such as Mel Karmazin. As president and COO of media conglomerate Viacom, which owns CBS and the nation's third largest radio group, Infinity Broadcasting, Karmazin was one of the earliest advocates of clustering for the radio industry.

Karmazin and others are concluding that the overlapping of radio signals results in a different dynamic for radio stations than that for newspapers, which usually do not have overlapping circulations.

"There is an oligopoly in most markets (for radio)," Karmazin pointed out in *MediaWeek*. "In the past, there was a whole lot more individual station-selling and competition. Today there are clusters. I see no evidence that by combining eight stations under one marketing manager, that generates top-line revenue growth."[89]

In the same article, Emmis Communications CEO Jeff Smulgen noted, "Companies went to the financial markets and said that once you get five or six stations in a market that magic happens. But the reality is that you can't lump stations together to sell them. What works on Wall Street isn't what works on Main Street."[90]

Peter Smyth, CEO of radio group Greater Media, pointed out that "once you say 'cluster sales,' you say 'discount.'"[91]

It is important that U.S. consumers not lose perspective about the effects of clustering and consolidation. Newspaper ownership is even more concentrated in other Western democracies, such as Great Britain, Canada, France, Italy, Australia and Germany.[92]

It is indisputable that despite consolidation of U.S. media companies, new and developing technologies nevertheless have resulted in more choices than ever.[93]

It also needs to be pointed out that many of the chains are consistently praised for the quality of their journalism, including Advance Publications, Belo, Dow Jones & Co., McClatchy, the New York Times Co., Tribune Co. and the Washington Post Co.

Most chains show sparks of glory, such as in Gannett's promotion of women and minorities to editor and publisher positions and even to its board of directors, and Knight Ridder's domination of the Pulitzer Prizes until just recently. Several chains also have mounted vigorous legal defenses on behalf of their reporters and to gain public access to government records, readily accepting huge legal expenses that would be difficult to bear for many family-owned media companies. This is an advantage of large size that favors all of journalism.

CASE STUDY *Repositioning without Major Change*

by ROBERT G. PICARD, Ph.D.
Jönköping University

Radio 97 is a local radio station in a city with 100,000 population and a total population of 250,000 within its broadcast range. A second local station, Radio 105, also exists in the city.

Two national public service radio broadcasts (National 1 and National 2) and two national commercial stations (Hit Radio 100 and Classics 102) are also available in the market.

Radio 97 has been in operation for five years, and Radio 105 was established four years ago. Radio 97 is owned by Siècle Médias, a Luxembourg-based firm with stations in seven nations. The local newspaper, a local bank, and two private investors own Radio 105.

Both Radio 97 and Radio 105 use rock/pop formats designed to appeal to 13-to-35-year-old listeners. Radio 97 has the rights to broadcast matches of the local football team and the broadcasts produce excellent audiences and advertising because the city embraces football.

National 1 is a public service broadcaster that uses a variety format and is the nation's predominant source of radio news and public affairs programming. Its strongest audience is above 45 years of age, but its hourly newscasts receive a strong audience among those 25 years of age and above. National 2 is a secondary public service channel with a classic rock format that most appeals to persons in the 35-to-54-year-old age group. Classics 102 broadcasts light classical music that mostly attracts listeners from the 45-year-old-and-above age categories. Hit Radio 100 using a contemporary rock/pop format and is popular among persons between 13 to 35 years of age.

Average annual ratings

Station	3 Years Ago	2 Years Ago	Last Year	This Year
National 1	26	24	23	23
National 2	16	17	17	17
Classics 102	15	16	17	16
Hit Radio 100	13	14	14	15
Radio 97	20	17	16	15
Radio 105	10	12	13	14

Although Radio 97 remains the leading local station in the market, its dominance has been diminishing.

The management of Siècle Médias has been concerned about the diminishing ratings of Radio 97 and has commissioned audience research to determine the causes. The study has been completed and it reveals that:

• The music programming of Radio 97 is seen as desirable and similar to that of Radio 105.

• The disc jockeys are viewed equally at both stations.

• Radio 97 is perceived as being "less local" than Radio 105.

• The diminishing share is primarily occurring among 13-to-18-year-old age group.

• Diminishing share is mostly going to Radio 105 and Hit Radio 100.

During a strategy meeting with the operations manager for Siècle Médias, the research consultants, and managers for other company-owned stations, it is decided that operations of Radio 97 do not need radical programming changes. Instead, the station was directed to propose methods to fine-tune the way it positions itself in the market and to propose a promotional campaign with a budget of 100,000 Euros ($115,000) that will support those changes.

Radio 97's management committee is meeting to tackle the task. You are there to discuss the all or any of the questions, depending on time available:

• What are the strengths and weaknesses of Radio 97, Hit Radio 100, and Radio 105?

• Which of the competitors poses the most risk to Radio 97 and why?

• Should the Radio 97's management direct its efforts against only one, some, or all competitors?

• How can Radio 97 position itself differently in the market without significantly changing its format and programming?

• How can it change its position to appeal more to the 13-to-18-year-old listeners, without losing its strength in the 18-to-35-year-old age audience category?

• What kinds of programming or information can it add to its current broadcasts in an effort to counteract the ratings decline?

• What kinds of promotional efforts are most likely to appeal to the 13-to-18-year-old group?

• How should the promotion be integrated with other marketing activities of the station?

• How would you use the special promotion budget?

AUTHOR:

Robert G. Picard is Hamrin Professor of Media Economics and Director of the Media Management and Transformation Centre at Jönköping International Business School, Jönköping University, Sweden. He is the author of 16 books on media economics and management issues and is the editor of the Journal of Media Business Studies.

⌨ *Suggested Web sites:*

www.salesandmarketing.com—Sales and marketing issues
www.adage.com—*Advertising Age* magazine
www.prweekus.com—*PR Week* magazine
www.nielsenmedia.com—Nielsen Media Research
www.ctam.com—Cable & Telecommunications Association for Marketing

Endnotes to Chapter 9:

[1] Gene Goltz, "Reviving a romance with readers is the biggest challenge to many newspapers," *Presstime* (February 1988): 16–22.

[2] Kendra Oden, "Tradition, journalistic morale, and marketing: Can there be a middle ground?" unpublished paper of May 1, 2001.

[3] Judy Pace Christie, "Editors must lead the journalistic revolution," <www.poynterextra.org/centerpiece/jbv/pacechristie.htm >, accessed August 13, 2003.

[4] Oden, "Tradition, journalistic morale, and marketing: Can there be a middle ground?"

[5] Marshall McLuhan, *Understanding Media: The Extensions of Man* (New York: McGraw-Hill, 1st Paperback Ed., 1965), 232.

[6] Tim W. Ferguson, "From boosterism to big-time journalism . . . . And an uncertain future," *The Wall Street Journal* Interactive Edition (June 14, 2001), Rocket e-Book, 208.

[7] Doug Underwood, "It's not just in L.A.," *Columbia Journalism Review* (January–February 1998), 24.

[8] James D. Squires, *Read All About It! The Corporate Takeover of America's Newspapers* (New York: Times Books, 2nd ed., 1994), 73.

[9] Underwood, "It's not just in L.A.," 24.

[10] William A. Hachten, *The Troubles of Journalism: A Critical Look at What's Right and Wrong with the Press* (Mahwah, N.J.: Erlbaum, 2nd ed., 2001), 83. Hachten probably is not the first to use this term, but he's probably the first to use it as a subhead in a book.

[11] David Croteau and William Hoynes, *The Business of Media: Corporate Media and the Public Interest* (Thousand Oaks, Calif.: Pine Forge Press, 2001), 161.

[12] Underwood, "It's not just in L.A.," 26.

[13] Jon Fine, "Daily newspapers see circulation slide," *Advertising Age,* May 21, 2001, 37.

[14] "Top 100 daily newspapers in the United States according to circulation September 30, 2001," *Editor & Publisher International Yearbook* (New York: Editor & Publisher, 82nd ed., 2003), xi.

[15] Fine, "Daily newspapers see circulation slide."

[16] Squires, *Read All About It! The Corporate Takeover of America's Newspapers,* xv.

[17] "Retaining new readers: Post-Sept. 11 coverage has brought readers back to newspapers, but they will leave again if editors revert to the same old formulas," *Editor & Publisher* (November 5, 2001): 11.

[18] Jonathan Z. Larsen, "On the roller coaster," *Columbia Journalism Review* (October–December 2001).

[19] Jonathan Kwitny, "The high cost of high profits," *Washington Journalism Review* (June 1990): 29.

[20] Scott M. Cutlip with Allen H. Center and Glen M. Broom, *Effective Public Relations* (Upper Saddle River, N.J.: Prentice Hall, 8th ed., 2000), 7.

[21] E. Jerome McCarthy and William D. Perreault Jr., *Basic Marketing: A Managerial Approach* (Homewood, Ill.: Irwin, 9th ed., 1987), 37–38.

[22] Nancy Giddens, Joe Parcell and Melvin Brees, "Selecting an appropriate pricing strategy," at <www.muextension.missouri.edu/explore/agguides/agecon/g00649.htm>, accessed August 15, 2003.

[23] McCarthy and Perreault, *Basic Marketing: A Managerial Approach,* 129.

[24] Ibid., 174.

[25] Ibid., 179.

[26] Michael R. Czinkota, Masaaki Kotabe, and David Mercer, *Marketing Management: Text and Cases* (Cambridge, Mass.: Blackwell Business, 1997), 28.

[27] Ed Bark, of *The Dallas Morning News,* as published in "TV executives ignore viewers over 50," *Albuquerque Journal,* December 11, 2001, WSJ35.

[28] Croteau and Hoynes, *The Business of Media,* 152.

[29] BrainyQuote, <www.brainyquote.com/quotes/quotes/p/q103076.html>, accessed September 27, 2002, based on quote of Philip Dusenberry included in Eric Clarke's *The Want Makers: Inside the World of Advertising* (New York: Viking Penguin, 1990).

[30] Martyn P. Davis, *The Effective Use of Advertising Media* (London: Business Books, 1985), 108.

[31] Subhash C. Jain, *Marketing Planning & Strategy* (Cincinnati, Ohio: South-Western Publishing, 3rd ed., 1990), 564–565.

[32] Davis, *The Effective Use of Advertising Media,* 108.

[33] Alan B. Albarran, *Management of Electronic Media* (Belmont, Calif.: Wadsworth/Thomson Learning, 2nd ed., 2002), 221.

[34] Robert G. Picard, *The Economics and Financing of Media Companies* (New York: Fordham University Press, 2002), 136.

[35] Patricia Callahan and Kevin Helliker, "Knight Ridder has fewer readers but charges more to reach them," *Wall Street Journal* Interactive Edition, Rocket e-book, June 18, 2001, 120.

[36] Ibid., 122.

[37] Ibid., 126.

[38] Czinkota, et al., *Marketing Management: Text and Cases,* 351.

[39] McCarthy and Perreault, *Basic Marketing: A Managerial Approach,* 493-494.

[40] Ezra Solomon and John J. Pringle, *An Introduction to Financial Management* (Santa Monica, Calif.: Goodyear Publishing, 1977), 62.

[41] Ricky W. Griffin, Management (Boston: Houghton Mifflin, 4th ed., 1993), 237.

[42] Solomon and Pringle, *An Introduction to Financial Management,* 63–64.

[43] Tom Gorman, *The Complete Idiot's Guide to MBA Basics* (New York: Alpha Books, 1998), 100.

[44] Peter P. Schodervek, Richard A. Coser, and John C. Apler, Management (San Diego: Harcourt Brace Jovanovich, 2nd ed., 1991), 598.

[45] "Cost benefit analysis," at <http://faculty.washington.edu/bellas/cba/lecnote3.pdf>, accessed August 14, 2003.

[46] George J. Stigler, *The Theory of Price* (New York: Macmillan, 5th printing, 1968), 130.

[47] McCarthy and Perreault, *Basic Marketing: A Managerial Approach,* 51.

[48] Czinkota et al., *Marketing Management: Text and Cases,* 329.

[49] Stigler, *The Theory of Price,* 23.

[50] McCarthy and Perreault, *Basic Marketing: A Managerial Approach,* 54.

[51] Picard, *The Economics and Financing of Media Companies,* 73.

[52] Jain, *Marketing Planning & Strategy,* 204.

[53] Croteau and Hoynes, *The Business of Media,* 54.

[54] Benjamin M. Compaine, "Mergers, divestiture and the Internet: Is ownership of the media

industry becoming too concentrated?" Telecommunications Policy Research Conference (September 26, 1999) and recounted in summary of conclusion to *Who Owns the Media?* on <www. primushost.com/~bcompain/WOTM/ tprc99.htm>, accessed January 18, 2002.

[55] Kevin Maney, "Inventor of the Web weaves tale of its past, present, future," *USA TODAY*, October 20, 1999.

[56] Matter*form* Media Web site, <www.matterform.com>, accessed June 1, 2001.

[57] Everett M. Rogers, *Diffusion of Innovations* (New York: Free Press, 4th ed., 1995), 262.

[58] Rogers, *Diffusion of Innovations*, 262–266.

[59] Nielsen Media Research, "The sweeps—local market management," at <www.nielsenmedia .com>, accessed January 13, 2003.

[60] Robert G. Picard and Jeffrey H. Brody, *The Newspaper Publishing Industry* (Boston: Allyn and Bacon, 1997), 37.

[61] Stephen Lacy, "Understanding and serving readers: The problem of fuzzy market structure," 14, *Newspaper Research Journal* (Spring 1993): 55.

[62] George S. Day, *Market Driven Strategy: Processes for Creating Value* (New York: The Free Press, 1990), 357.

[63] Stigler, *The Theory of Price*, 43.

[64] Czinkota, et al., *Marketing Management: Text and Cases*, 202–203.

[65] Ibid., 207.

[66] Ibid.

[67] McCarthy and Perreault, *Basic Marketing: A Managerial Approach*, 38.

[68] Day, *Market Driven Strategy: Processes for Creating Value*, 357.

[69] Czinkota, et. al., *Marketing Management: Text and Cases*, 207.

[70] Alec Laughlin and Michael Howard, a manager and an owner respectively of a successful small coffee shop for many years in Santa Fe, N.M., in an interview September 10, 2002, talking about tactics routinely used by some large coffee shop operators, restaurateurs, book store chains, etc., in driving smaller locally-owned firms out of business. The strategy is applicable in small towns to media companies as well.

[71] Doug Underwood, *When MBAs Rule the Newsroom* (New York: Columbia University Press, 1993).

[72] Ibid., 15.

[73] John H. McManus, *Market-Driven Journalism: Let the Citizen Beware?* (Thousand Oaks, Calif.: Sage Publications, 1994), 1.

[74] Doug Underwood and Keith Stamm, "Balancing business with journalism: Newsroom policies at 12 West Coast newspapers," *Journalism Quarterly* (Summer 1992): 301–317.

[75] Randal A. Beam, "Does it pay to be a market-oriented daily newspaper?" *Journalism and Mass Communication Quarterly* (Autumn 2001): 477.

[76] Ibid., 479.

[77] Gene Goltz, "Financial executives," *Presstime* (January 1987): 32.

[78] *The Next Newspapers* (Washington, D.C.: American Society of Newspaper Editors, 1988), 44.

[79] Mary Walton, "The selling of small-town America," a chapter in, *Leaving Readers Behind*, Gene Roberts, editor in chief, and Thomas Kunkel and Charles Layton, general editors (Fayetteville, Ark.: University of Arkansas Press), 25.

[80] Ibid, 36.

[81] Brenda Starr comic strip panel, © 2003 Tribune Media Services Inc. All Rights Reserved. Reprinted with permission.

[82] Dori Perrucci, "Pumping and filling Community's chest," *Mediaweek* (August 24, 1998): 16.

[83] Mark Fitzgerald, "Liberty's IPO idea scrapped," *Editor & Publisher* (June 16, 2003): 8.

[84] Ibid, 20-27.

[85] Mark Fitzgerald, "The CNHI of Canada: Osprey Media Group didn't even exist two years

ago. Now it's the biggest daily chain in Ontario—and still growing," *Editor & Publisher* (May 19, 2003): 12.

[86] Roberts, Kunkel, and Layton, *Leaving Readers Behind: The Age of Corporate Newspapering.*

[87] Jack Bass, "Newspaper monopoly," a chapter in, *Leaving Readers Behind: The Age of Corporate Newspapers,* 106.

[88] Ibid., 115.

[89] Katy Bachman, "Karmazin changes clustering tune," *Mediaweek* (April 28, 2003): 6.

[90] Ibid., 7.

[91] Ibid.

[92] Hachten, *The Troubles of Journalism*, 72.

[93] Jim Rutenberg, "Fewer media owners, more media choices," *The New York Times,* December 2, 2002, C1.

CHAPTER 10
CONSOLIDATION AND CONVERGENCE

B EN H. BAGDIKIAN became concerned over the growing consolidation of media companies flying high on Wall Street's booster rocket as they began forming publicly traded, stockholder-driven companies in the 1960s. So he wrote a book in 1983, *The Media Monopoly.*

Early press critics, such as A.J. Liebling, George Seldes and H.L. Mencken, had assailed the irresponsibility of arrogant press barons running newspapers like personal empires. Bagdikian warned of a different kind of ownership problem. In that first edition of his landmark book, Bagdikian alerted America that its mass media were in a new kind of strangle grip, with more than half of all the media outlets owned by a mere 50 companies. Bagdikian expressed concern about the chilling effects of such consolidation on the media's ability and/or desire to serve the public's need to know the news. What's more, Bagdikian predicted, ownership was only going to become more concentrated.[1]

Mahatma Gandhi said any activist wishing to bring to light a social problem is at first ignored, then ridiculed, and then attacked. If the activist is right, however, the final stage of interaction between those who want change and those who resist change is to accept the activist's views as truth of a new order created by the conflict.

So seems to have been the stages for Bagdikian.

Ignored at first and even mocked by industry insiders, succeeding editions of his book over 18 years kept refreshening the debate, resulting in opponents describing Bagdikian as "alarmist" and dismissing him as an overwrought academic—from Berkeley, of all places. With his sixth edition in 2000, however, in which Bagdikian documents how the majority of America's media control now is reduced from 50 to only six firms in less than two decades, many are seeing him as having been right all along.

In the movie, "The War Between Men and Women," Jason Robards' character shakes his head wanly and bemoans, "It's all so clear to me now."[2] And that is the reaction of many former skeptics today to Bagdikian's early warnings.

"One of the most important critiques of the press ever written," declared the *St. Petersburg Times* about the book that is still a must-read nearly two decades later in many colleges and universities (despite the need for Bagdikian to update much of the research he cites in his book).

The effect of consolidation since 1920 on the numbers of America's independent daily newspapers can be seen in the adjacent graph produced by a special study, "The State of the American Newspaper," conducted by the Project for Excellence in Journalism and published during 1998 in *American Journalism Review*.[3]

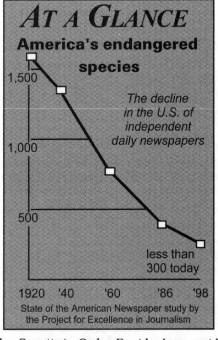

AT A GLANCE

America's endangered species

1,500

The decline in the U.S. of independent daily newspapers

1,000

500

less than 300 today

1920   '40   '60   '86   '98

State of the American Newspaper study by the Project for Excellence in Journalism

About three-fourths of the nation's dailies were privately owned at the end of World War II, but industry analyst John Morton reports that had slipped to about 18 percent by the late 1990s.[4] The percentage is still falling, continuing the slide depicted in the chart since the 1920s. The decline led one publisher to describe family-owned dailies as being "rare as whooping cranes."[5]

The pressure to sell to a chain is intense. Joe Hladky, a fourth-generation family owner of the *Gazette* in Cedar Rapids, Iowa, said his daily is not for sale but he receives telephone inquiries every week, usually from brokers who "have an interested buyer."[6]

Canada's concern over concentration of media ownership is even more intense than in the United States. Two committees studied media concentration in the 1970s and 1980s. The Davey Committee bluntly concluded that Canada "should no longer tolerate a situation where the public interest, in so vital a field as information, is dependent on the greed or good will of an extremely privileged group of businessmen."

The Davey Committee recommendations led to establishment of a Royal Commission on Corporate Concentration and press councils where citizens' complaints against media companies could be heard. The Kent Report used similarly strong language, issued in 1981 when only three chains (Quebecor, Gesca and Unimédia) owned 90 percent of French-language newspapers and three others (Southam, Thomson and the Sun group) owned two-thirds of the English-language circulation.[7]

It is difficult if not impossible for politicians to go up against concentrated media power. Few of the Davey Committee's recommendations were implemented, and even fewer of the Kent Report's. As in the United States, government policies in Canada have allowed media ownership to become even more concentrated since the 1980s.

The Media Monopoly maintains a strong presence with its sixth edition. Its pioneering revelation of media consolidation has been vindicated since by several books in recent years working that theme, including *When MBAs Rule the Newsroom* by Doug Underwood (1993), *Read All About It! The Corporate Takeover of America's Newspapers* by Jim Squires (1993), *Media Mergers* edited by Nancy J. Woodhull and Robert W. Snyder (1997), *Leaving Readers Behind: The Age of Corporate Newspapering* edited by Gene Roberts, *The Business of Media* by David Croteau and William Hoynes (2001), and *The News About the News* by Leonard Downie Jr. and Robert G. Kaiser (2002).

Bagdikian emphasizes that many of the parent firms of the six largest media conglomerates have their principal interests actually in other industries. Even since his last edition in 2000, the rankings have changed due to mergers.

Based on net U.S. revenue, *Advertising Age* magazines reports that the top six U.S. media companies in 2001 (taking mergers into consideration since then) were AOL Time Warner, Comcast–AT&T Broadband, Viacom, News Corp.–DirecTV, Walt Disney Co., and Cox Enterprises. The 2001 merger of AOL and Time Warner created a $350 billion company whose net revenue is nearly twice that of its closest rival. By 2003, the net U.S. revenues of these top six giants totaled more than the next 51 media companies combined.[8] (The biggest keep getting bigger. When Bagdikian did his list, the top six companies' revenue was "only" larger than the next 20 companies.)

Many of these six corporations also are represented in the Big 12 of television/entertainment ranked by 1996 revenues. Some of the Big 12 might be a surprise. They are Time Warner (even before the merger), the Walt Disney Co., News Corp., Viacom, TCI, Sony, General Electric, Gannett, General Motors, Comcast and Seagram.[9] (TCI and Seagram have since been swallowed by AT&T and Vivendi Universal, respectively.)

Between them, just this roomful of 12 CEOs, in 2000, owned all of the commercial broadcasting networks, at least 89 TV stations including the majority of stations in the Top Ten markets, 600 radio stations, two of three major news magazines, virtually all 24-hour news channels, more than 100 dailies (including most of the major ones), all of the major motion picture studios, virtually all of the producers of network entertainment, every cable channel that attracts more than one million viewers per week, more than half the nation's cable TV subscribers, more than half of the basic and pay channels on cable, 12 major trade book publishing companies, more than 60 magazines, and most of the recorded music in the United States. These 12 also own outright or control significant international holdings.[10]

"The immense size of the parent firms means that some of their crucial media subsidiaries, like news, have become remote within their complex tables of organization," Bagdikian writes. "That remoteness has contributed to the unprecedented degree to which the parent firms have pressed their news subsidiaries to cross ethical lines by selecting news that will promote the needs of the owning corporation rather than serve the traditional ethical striving of journalism."[11]

Bagdikian's point was that ABC represents less than 2 percent of Disney's profits, and NBC provides less than 2 percent of the profits at General Electric. Time Inc. contributes only a fraction of a percent of the profits of its conglomerate owner, AOL Time Warner.[12]

SYNERGY

Within months of the sixth edition of *The Media Monopoly*, Time Warner bulked itself up for its eventual AOL merger by paying about $475 million in October 2000 for the Times Mirror Co.'s niche sports magazines—an acquisition that ties down 25 percent of all the nation's magazine advertising to this one company.[13] There have been even more AOL Time Warner acquisitions since.

Mergers like this are desirable for conglomerates because of the benefits that result from synergy, in which the operations can become more efficient when combined, making the sum more valuable than either of the two parts alone. As executives like to define it, 2 plus 2 can equal 5, or even 6. Cartoonist Kirk Anderson's view of synergy looks at a different side.[14]

The AOL Time Warner merger, allowed by the federal government to go forward in early 2001, created such a diversified media behemoth that James Ledbetter, New York bureau chief of *Industry Standard* magazine, told *The Washington Post* that, "virtually every company they could possibly report on is now either a partner or a competitor."[15]

Media ethicist Rushworth M. Kidder believes AOL Time Warner's dominance and diversity in Internet, magazines, cable television, movies and niche publications will make it "almost institutionally incapable of providing information without the perception of bias . . . . Given its size, AOL Time Warner has the potential to degrade the core ingredient of the Information Age—information."[16]

But perhaps you can get too big. AOL founder Steve Case resigned as chairman of the mega-company in May 2003, lashed by stockholders and fellow executives as the price of AOL Time Warner stock plunged from $72 at the merger to $15 two years later. The collapse of the tech market was a large part of it, but a lack of synergy between the conglomerate's many businesses also was blamed.[17] After the merger, AOL's new media business was driving the much larger Time Warner's cable, film and magazine empire. By the time this book is available, Time Warner's executives are expected to be back in charge and AOL might be dropped altogether from the corporate name.

There's some safety in large size

MICHAEL WOLF of the international management consulting firm Booz-Allen & Hamilton writes in *The Wall Street Journal* that large size is necessary—at least in the television industry. He's been backed up by numerous others, from communication professor Robert McChesney's observation, "Media companies either get big or they get eaten,"[18] to a media industry stock analyst's concession stating, "I don't know if biggest is better, but big is better."[19]

Wolf writes about Rupert Murdoch's News Corp. recently acquiring Chris-Craft Industries and its 10 U.S. television stations, and he notes how that announcement "once again raises apparently uncomfortable questions: Will a few big companies control too much of what we get to see and hear? Are large companies making huge profits at the expense of the public good? And is broadcasting getting too consolidated?"[20]

Wolf asserts that the answer to each of these questions is no.

"Despite the recent wave of mergers, today's media environment is more competitive than ever," Wolf writes. "We have more programming choices, more outlets, more voices—including a wider spectrum of political voices—and more options than ever before. Technology and the marketplace will ensure that this trend will continue. Corporate consolidation has not automatically meant a concentration of editorial control. In fact, the marketplace has demanded, and received, diversity, and that diversity serves the public interest."[21]

Wolf emphasizes, as the media CEOs have done, that consolidation is the only chance of survival for many companies. The synergistic and economic advantages that a large company has over a small one enable it to afford expensive new technologies and other investments in the future. In television's case specifically, only the large companies can afford expensive experimenting with new programming and not be weakened.

Also driving the zeal to grow ever larger, Wolf says, is the increasing audience fragmentation taking place because of ever-intensifying battles for consumer attention for the small screen's offerings from cable, satellite, VHS and DVD, TiVo, Wi-Fi, WebTV (now known as MSNTV) and of course the Internet, to mention only a few.

"Those who worry about a concentration of power in the media often forget that consumers have free will and, more importantly, a remote-control," Wolf states, adding that conglomerates are bulking up in size, but it is more from a wish to survive, not necessarily to dominate the airwaves.[22]

This is much the same argument that is advanced by Federal Communications Commission chairman Michael Powell in urging an end to the cross-ownership ban, ownership lids and other regulations limiting further expansion by print and broadcast conglomerates. He believes competition is so intense that corporations need to grow larger just to survive.

Similarly, educators Eli M. Noam and Robert N. Freeman refer to media monopoly as a myth. They contend that advances in technology ensure there will be more competition in the future among U.S. media markets, not less.

"To evaluate all this," they write, "it is important to understand how the media world has evolved through stages . . . . Twenty years ago, we had limited media, with only three networks, one phone company, and one computer company. Today we are in the stage of multi-channel media, with many dozens of TV channels and with multiple phone networks. But this is still not the end of the story. The third stage, and the one we are entering now, is cyber-media. Cyber-text is already established. Cyber-audio is here. And cyber-telephony and cyber-video are emerging. In time, this will lead us to an entirely different system of mass media. Yet governments, media companies, and media critics are still looking backward to the good old days of scarcity."[23]

They refer to Bagdikian's figure of 10 dominant media firms in his fifth edition, noting that their research indicates "the combined share of the top 10 companies in the U.S. information industry declined from 59 percent in 1987 to 39 percent today. This is a totally different conclusion from those who claim that U.S media are now controlled by 10 firms."[24]

Monopoly, oligopoly and joint operating agreements

RELATED TO Wolf's argument that larger size is required of television companies is the economic theory advanced by some newspaper executives and politicians for several years. They contend that newspapers are a "natural monopoly"—that is, when two or more daily newspapers are in competition with each other, irrevocable laws of economics result in the strongest paper coming to dominate the market until competing dailies are killed off, creating a **monopoly.**[25]

A parallel in the television industry is the limited number of channels and network affiliations that are available, plus other entry barriers such as equipment. These limitations ensure that virtually every local TV station enjoys an **oligopoly,** in which only a few companies offer a similar product. For all of these reasons and more, TV stations face competition from other TV stations only to the extent that there is a capacity geographically determined by signal range and availability of licenses. Once the optimum number of stations is reached in a given market, it is impossible to start a new TV station. The few existing stations are left to fight among themselves in a kind of "forever war," to use the term coined by science fiction writer Joe Haldeman.[26]

The "natural monopoly" concept has been applied since the mid-1800s to businesses such as mining in considering natural resources, and to railroads and utilities when considering services to the consumer.

The concept is two-fold. First, it covers monopolies resulting from natural conditions, such as a limited supply of mining wealth; second, it is dictated by business characteristics that make competition too costly or impractical, such as in expensive duplication of services like rail lines and utility services.[27]

Tim A. Pilgrim, who frequently writes on newspaper management issues as a journalism educator at Western Washington University, recently reported how several studies have concluded that newspapers do not demonstrate the internal cost structures nor the external forces required for natural monopolies to exist among daily newspapers.

Nevertheless, he explained that monopolies do develop in newspaper markets, writing in a 1992 article, "As applied to the newspaper industry, the argument says dailies move inexorably toward natural monopoly status (because) natural monopoly means a larger newspaper can produce papers at a lower cost per issue. Such economies of scale are passed on to advertisers, who flock to the larger-circulating paper in order to send their advertising messages to a greater number of readers more inexpensively. Over time, the leading daily grows larger, while competition withers. Consequently, one by one, newspapers competing in a city are driven out of business until only one survives. Monopoly comes naturally to the survivor."[28]

Or, as one manager observed succinctly, "When you get 51 percent of the circulation, you get 70 percent of the advertising."[29]

In the late 19th and early 20th centuries, most American cities had at least two competing daily newspapers. By 2002, however, true competition between dailies owned by different publishers and not enhanced by sharing arrangements existed in only 22 markets (see following chart).[30]

A list of two-newspaper cities today should include the Minneapolis-St. Paul, Dallas-Ft. Worth, St. Petersburg-Tampa and Miami-Ft. Lauderdale metro areas because those cities have grown together, resulting in intense competition between dailies. Newspapers in many other cities also are starting to find themselves coming into competition with each other as their cities grow together, but those four are at least the major examples.

In 12 cities two dailies survive in a sharing arrangement called a **Joint Operating Agreement** (JOA). There also is sharing agreement similar to a JOA in Madison, Wis. Counting these sharing arrangements and the 22 two-newspaper markets, plus 12 cities where both dailies have the same owner but continue separate morning and afternoon editions, the number of American cities at the end of 2003 with at least two commercial daily newspapers totaled only 47. American cities with two or more dailies numbered 699 in 1910 and 334 in 1940.[31]

Even the total of 47 is higher than usually reported. Besides metro areas, many lists of two-daily towns also do not include JOAs and same-owner pairs on the assumption they are not true competitors.

Perhaps JOAs and same-owner pairs are not competitors in many aspects such as advertising, but even brothers and sisters in the same family still can and will compete fiercely in other areas. Even under a JOA or the same owner, those who work at such papers will tell you that competition thrives over circulation and news coverage. Editors of one

JOA rarely or never speak to their counterparts working for the JOA partner in the other newsroom, though they usually are only at opposite ends of the same building.

Cities in 2003 with at least two daily newspapers[32]
Not including university, ethnic or business dailies

Two or more dailies with two or more owners	Two dailies with same owner
Los Angeles, Calif.	Frederick, Md.
Pleasanton, Calif.	Hagerstown, Md.
San Diego, Calif.	Jefferson City, Mo.
San Francisco, Calif.	Ogdensburg, N.Y.
San Mateo, Calif.	Franklin-Oil City, Pa.
Aspen, Colo.	Lancaster, Pa.
Washington, D.C.	Philadelphia, Pa.
Miami-Ft. Lauderdale, Fla.	Reading, Pa.
St. Petersburg-Tampa, Fla.	Scranton, Pa.
Honolulu, Hawaii	Amarillo, Texas
Chicago, Ill.	Parkersburg, W.Va.
Boston, Mass.	Wheeling, W.Va.
Minneapolis-St. Paul, Minn.	
Trenton, N.H.	
New York, N.Y.	
Pittsburgh, Pa.	
Wilkes-Barre, Pa.	
Kingsport, Tenn.	
Dallas-Ft. Worth, Texas	
Manassas, Va.	
Clarksburg, W.Va.	
Green Bay, Wis.	
* - Madison, Wis.	

Two dailies in a Joint Operating Agreement

Birmingham, Ala.	Detroit, Mich.	York, Pa.
Tucson, Ariz.	Las Vegas, Nev.	Salt Lake City, Utah.
Denver, Colo.	Albuquerque, N.M.	Seattle, Wash.
Fort Wayne, Ind.	Cincinnati, Ohio	Charleston, W.Va.

* - A sharing arrangement, but not a JOA

About 75 university cities (including many cities in the preceding chart) also are, in theory at least, two-daily or even three-daily towns because of newspapers published by students. Many believe that university dailies do not pose real competition, but those who contend against the best of them often think otherwise.[33]

Many university dailies are like the *Daily 49er* or *The GW Hatchet*, published by students at California State University and George Washington University, respectively. Selling ads only to businesses targeting their students, circulated mainly on campus, and relying on campus news, they pose no economic threat to print media in Long Beach, Calif., or Washington, D.C.

However, in many university cities the student newspaper is more like the *Iowa State Daily*. At such papers, students write the news in and around their campus, as expected. But professional advertising staffers fan out across the city to sell a wide variety of advertising, while professional managers look for ways to increase public circulation of their university-subsidized papers. In Ames, those kinds of efforts—coupled with the fact that the local daily, *The Tribune*, was barred from selling to students on the Iowa State University campus—resulted in a months-long legal battle in 1997–1998. *The Tribune* is a Pulitzer Prize-winning commercial daily then edited by former NBC News president Michael G. Gartner. *The Tribune* sued the university and the student paper, charging them with unfair competition. *The Tribune* prevailed, forcing Iowa State University's publications board to scale back off-campus marketing activities, preventing the paper from being distributed outside the campus, while giving *The Tribune* more campus access.[34] The ironic result was that a respected daily was responsible for curbing students' First Amendment rights for a business advantage.[35]

Anyone would consider Ames, Iowa, as well as many others across the country, to be two-newspaper cities in terms of competition if one was not a so-called student newspaper.

The same is true of many other cities across the nation. However, it is difficult to get editors and publishers to comment publicly on their student-staffed and university-subsidized competition. On advice of their corporate lawyers, they almost inevitably respond that they can have no response.[36]

Except in Columbia, Mo., that is. There, the University of Missouri's student daily, the *Missourian*, operates as a university-subsidized community newspaper competing with the locally owned paper, the *Columbia Daily Tribune*. Jim Robertson, the *Daily Tribune's* managing editor and a Missouri alumnus, complained, "They've got the computer system, the new building from Knight Ridder, and they're taking food off my table."[37] Because the *Missourian* operates as if it were a community newspaper,[38] some list Columbia, Mo., as a two-daily city. This book does not because then it would also need to include many other university-subsidized dailies that are incorporated as independent businesses and circulate both on and off campus.

Also complicating the issue of multi-newspaper cities is the ethnic press discussed in Chapter 7, produced by several companies owned by African Americans, Asians, Hispanics, Native Americans and others.

Some large cities also have dailies that specialize in publishing government legal notices, court proceedings and business news, such as the 281,000-circulation *Investor's Business Daily* in Los Angeles.

As with university and ethnic dailies, these niche business dailies are not included in this book's chart of two-newspaper cities, though they are included in the lists compiled by some other publications. Even if they were included, the decline in two-daily towns still has been dramatic since the early 1900s.

However, even dailies that are said to have a monopoly in a city still face credible print competition—not from another daily, but from one or more aggressive weekly newspapers that might be more accepted by readers and some advertisers than the daily. Often these weeklies put out more pages in their once-a-week effort than the daily puts out on any given day. And sometimes they start up because the local daily is owned by a chain and residents feel they lost "their" paper. A good example is in Stevens Point, Wis., where the weekly *Portage County Gazette* started up after the daily *Stevens Point Journal* was sold to Thomson in 1997 and then sold again to Gannett. Many of the weekly's key editors and investors are former employees or shareholders of the daily.[39]

These weeklies can be so formidable, with groups of them sometimes circling the city in a stranglehold reaching in from the suburbs and nearby small towns, that they eventually are bought out by the daily's owner to bring an end to the threat they pose. Advance Publications, for example, became alarmed after an entrepreneur bought, over a period of several years, nine small-town weeklies ringing Flint, Mich. These weeklies were enjoying remarkable success together in attracting advertisers because their suburban demographics were more favorable than the city-based *Flint Journal*. They eventually were acquired by a chain of small dailies and weeklies in Michigan. If you can't beat 'em, buy 'em—which is what Advance finally did in the fall of 2002, though keeping only six of the weeklies' original 38 employees.[40]

Advance maximized the economies of scale and synergies it could realize by adding to the duties of existing *Journal* editors and reporters. Severance pay was given to the weeklies' employees not retained, but that was little consolation to people who lost jobs through no fault of their own.

Prosperous chains of weeklies around other large metro areas, condescendingly ignored for years by the large dailies in the city, now have grown into formidable competitors for advertising dollars in markets that include Chicago and Washington, D.C. Many, like at Flint, are being snapped up now by the conglomerates that own the dailies.

For such reasons, Pilgrim believes newspapers tend toward

monopolism but he insists they still are not natural monopolies. Papers face cutthroat competition, despite the precipitous decline of independently owned dailies and the increasing number of one-daily cities, all of which led to the Newspaper Preservation Act of 1970.

That law uniquely exempts daily newspapers from antitrust laws when they combine in a Joint Operating Agreement (JOA).

"Historically, communities had competing papers and benefited from the resulting diversity of ideas," Pilgrim wrote. "Only in the 20th century, after papers became even more oriented toward achieving business success and less toward providing citizens with news and ideas, have reduced profits and unforgiving tax structures thinned newspaper ranks."[41]

Perhaps surprisingly, sharing arrangements similar to JOAs predate the Newspaper Preservation Act. The law simply made JOAs less controversial and legitimized their existence.

The nation's first JOA was established in 1933 in New Mexico, and it still existed 70 years later. It is between the family-owned and dominant morning daily, the *Albuquerque Journal*, and the E.W. Scripps Co. afternoon daily, *The New Mexico State-Tribune* (now *The Albuquerque Tribune*). In those days, owners of two competing newspapers merely worked out details between themselves, usually bringing their papers into a single production plant and keeping the newsrooms separate while combining the advertising, circulation and business departments. All that was needed was "non-action" by the U.S. Department of Justice, which was usually not difficult to obtain.

There were newspapers in 22 cities in such mutually drawn agreements by 1969, when the U.S. Supreme Court ruled against a pact between the owners of the *Arizona Daily Star* and the *Tucson Citizen*. The court concluded that the Tucson JOA was a ruse for fixing prices, sharing markets and pooling profits.[42] (Though forced to be modified, the sharing arrangement at Tucson remains one of only 12 surviving JOAs.)

The Supreme Court noted, for example, that the two Tucson dailies together earned a profit of only $27,531 in 1940, when their JOA was implemented. By 1964, the last year for which records were available for the Court's review, combined profit had skyrocketed to $1.7 million.[43]

Alarmed publishers from some of the nation's largest chains immediately lobbied against the threat of the Supreme Court's 1969 ruling. A new law was introduced as the Failing Newspaper Act, with its name being changed on the advice of public relations consultants to the Newspaper Preservation Act of 1970. It was passed by Congress and signed into law by President Richard Nixon over the objection of his attorney general.

Joint Operating Agreements[44]
JOAs still in effect at the end of 2002

City	Term	Current Partners
Albuquerque, N.M.	1933–2022	Scripps/independent
Tucson, Ariz.	1940–2015	Pulitzer/Gannett
Fort Wayne, Ind.	1950–2033	Knight Ridder/independent
Birmingham, Ala.	1950–2015	Scripps/Advance
Salt Lake City, Utah	1952–2012	MediaNews/Mormon Church
Charleston, W.Va.	1958–2036	MediaNews/independent
Cincinnati, Ohio	1979–2007	Scripps/Gannett
Seattle, Wash.	1983–2083	Hearst/independent
Detroit, Mich.	1989–2086	Gannett/Knight Ridder
York, Pa.	1990–2090	MediaNews/Buckner
Las Vegas, Nev.	1990–2049	Stephens Media/independent
Denver, Col..	2001–2051	Media News/Scripps
* Madison, Wis.	since 1948	Lee/indepependent

* - Operates similar to a JOA, but not formally structured as one under the Act.

Former JOAs no longer in effect as of 2002[45]

City	History	Original Partners
El Paso, Tex.	1936–1997	Scripps/Gannett
Nashville, Tenn.	1937–1998	Gannett/indepependent
Evansville, Ind.	1938–1998	Scripps/indepependent
Tulsa, Okla.	1941–1992	Two independents
Chattanooga, Tenn.	1942–1966	Two independents
	1980–1999	
Shreveport, La.	1953–1991	Gannett/independent
* Franklin-Oil City, Pa.	1956–1985	Two independents
Knoxville, Tenn.	1957–1991	Scripps/independent
Columbus, Ohio	1959–1985	Scripps/independent
St. Louis, Mo.	1959–1983	Pulitzer/Advance
Pittsburgh, Pa.	1961–1992	Scripps/Block
* Honolulu, Hawaii	1962–2000	Gannett/independent
* San Francisco, Calif.	1965–2000	Two independents
Anchorage, Alaska	1965–1978	McClatchy/independent
Miami, Fla.	1966–1988	Knight Ridder/Cox

* - Denotes JOA dissolved, but both papers remain in existence as of 2003

Under a JOA as defined by the Newspaper Preservation Act, two dailies competing head-to-head are allowed to share their facilities as well as all operating departments except for news and editorial. The U.S. Department of Justice must approve a JOA.

It is debatable whether newspapers really need to go to the trouble of forming an official JOA under the Newspaper Preservation Act. One of many possible reasons the number of JOAs has declined in recent years is that competing newspapers can and do form joint operations even without the legalities of a JOA.[46]

The most similar sharing arrangement to a JOA—without actually being one—involves the two dailies in Madison, Wis. They compete under a sharing agreement dating back to 1948 that operates very similar to a JOA, maintaining separate newsrooms but combining most other functions. But their arrangement is not considered a true JOA subject to the Newspaper Preservation Act. The U.S. Department of Justice confirmed the legality of the Madison arrangement at the close of a Civil Investigative Review in the early 1990s.[47]

In 1999, and then in early 2003, two of America's largest newspaper chains—Gannett and MediaNews Group—took the sharing concept two revolutionary steps further. Until then, all JOAs and other sharing arrangements had been between dailies in the same city, which had been allowed antitrust exemption for the greater good of preserving a diversity of editorial voices in one community.

In California, however, Gannett, MediaNews Group and Stephens Media established a sharing arrangement between 21 dailies they own in 21 cities, forming the California Newspapers Partnership. It was the first sharing arrangement of its kind among dailies owned by three companies, allowing the three chains to cooperate on operations, cut costs, and share markets—without any objection from antitrust defenders.

Four years later, Gannett and MediaNews Group announced what they called the Texas–New Mexico Newspapers Partnership, but it actually was an agreement that handed Gannett operational control of MediaNews Group's five dailies and two weeklies in New Mexico. The arrangement centered on the Gannett-owned daily in El Paso, Texas, and five MediaNews Group dailies in New Mexico—including the Las Cruces daily just 35 miles from El Paso. In the two chains' joint press release, it was stated that Gannett would own "a 66 percent interest in the partnership."[48]

The Texas–New Mexico "partnership" was publicized as an arrangement sounding similar to a JOA, with Gannett and MediaNews Group news staffs to remain independent but to "share information," while the advertising and production departments operations were to be merged.[49]

The true nature of the arrangement became painfully clear less than two months later. The publisher, editor, production manager and others at MediaNews Group's *Las Cruces Sun-News* were fired, escorted out of the building, and replaced with executives appointed by Gannett. Printing of the Las Cruces paper was moved to El Paso. More executives also lost their jobs at other former MediaNews Group papers.[50]

Gannett was able to enter New Mexico under a subterfuge, and everyone would concede it was able to do so without fanfare. News coverage of the take-over was virtually non-existent. Even Gannett's Web site quickly listed the "partnership's" five New Mexican dailies as being owned by Gannett. The partnership-turned-sale left only eight states without at least one Gannett daily or TV station: Alaska, North Dakota, Wyoming, Nebraska, Kansas, New Hampshire, Massachusetts and Rhode Island.

Gannett reigns as the nation's largest newspaper company, and MediaNews Group is the seventh largest. Before the Texas–New Mexico Newspapers Partnership, Gannett owned 95 daily newspapers in the United States and 15 dailies in Great Britain, about 400 non-daily publications including the popular Sunday supplement *USA Today*, 22 television stations, a network of Internet sites, and a variety of companies dealing in advertising and media.[51] MediaNews Group owned 50 dailies and 121 non-daily papers across 12 states, a TV station, four radio stations, and 74 Internet sites.[52]

Afterward, Gannett owned 100 U.S. dailies, and MediaNews Group owned 45 dailies outright with only a one-third interest remaining in the five New Mexico dailies.

Gannett's firings of former long-time MediaNews Group executives are an instructive lesson for all managers and students. The acquiring company nearly always will fire the selling company's top managers, replacing them either with the acquiring company's executives or with other people who now realize that they owe their jobs to the new owner, not the former one. The difference is only in the degree of brutishness involved. The MediaNews Group executives were given no notice, and reportedly received two weeks severance pay.

The Texas–New Mexico partnership was a cover for an ownership change, while the California partnership was established between several dailies already enjoying sole-newspaper status in their cities.

However, both are only a step beyond sharing arrangements such as JOAs, which have been created for decades between dailies competing against each other in the same city. Those intra-city sharing arrangements have been allowed, though overseen by the federal government.

Publishers and their supporters in Congress maintain that JOAs and other sharing arrangements ensure that at least two newspaper voices will be preserved in a community—though the definition of what constitutes a community for other sharing arrangements now appears to be expanding to include ever-larger geographic regions involving several cities and even states.

While many kinds of sharing arrangements can simply be implemented, federal approval for an official JOA requires the newspapers' owners to prove that the weaker paper is doomed without such a synergistic blending of costs and revenues. While heading Gannett, Al Neuharth defended the JOA then proposed, and later approved, between Knight Ridder's *Detroit News* and Gannett's *Detroit Free Press*. "The fact is that the Detroit newspaper issue is very simple," Neuharth said. "Shall there be one daily newspaper or two?"[53]

Coleman Young, mayor of Detroit at the time, was skeptical. He noted that both dailies were pricing below market rates, leading him to conclude that the *Free Press* was deliberately losing money to qualify for the JOA and that it would raise prices as soon as the JOA was approved. If the *Free Press* and *News* both would just raise their prices at that time to market rates, Young said, they both would be making money.[54] Young oversimplified the business reality of such a unilateral move by either paper, but he was prescient in that both dailies raised newsstand and advertising rates shortly after approval in 1989.

Similarly, in 2001, when a JOA was approved between the *Denver Post* and the *Rocky Mountain News*, both papers immediately raised their advertising rates by so much that a Denver businessman sued them in an unsuccessful attempt to roll back the increases. And when MediaNews Group closed the *Houston Post*, Hearst Corp.'s *Houston Chronicle* exploited its newly won monopoly by hiking advertising rates by up to 40 percent.[55]

One of the 12 surviving JOAs became jeopardized in 2003. The family-controlled *Seattle Times* announced it intended to break its pact with the Hearst-owned *Seattle Post-Intelligencer*. The *Times* reportedly had lost money for three straight years. That could entitle the paper to end the JOA before the scheduled expiration in 2083, although Hearst promptly filed a lawsuit charging that the *Times'* losses were incurred on purpose as a ruse to end the JOA.[56]

Opponents of JOAs say the JOAs are being abused by giant corporations, who have turned a program originally intended to save struggling and independently owned newspapers in the same town into a safety net for rich chains. Opponents also say the result is a bold usurpation of laws that were intended to protect the public because JOAs hand over monopoly privilege and maximum profits to powerful and rich national conglomerates.

"These billionaire crybabies decided long ago that they don't want competition, and they brought in the government to license them (with a JOA)," complained Bruce B. Brugmann, publisher of the alternative *San Francisco Bay Guardian*, commenting on the break-up in 2000 of the San

Francisco JOA between the city's two dailies. "Now they can't even make it with a government-sanctioned monopoly! The minute they get into a position to do it, they kill the other paper."[57]

JOAs do in fact allow newspapers to engage in price-fixing, profit-pooling and market allocation with nary a single antitrust objection.

Conrad C. Fink of the University of Georgia asks, "When, in 1933, it began to succor failing newspapers, Congress didn't have to worry that television competitors would suffer if core city metros were aided. TV hadn't been launched yet. There was virtually no significant radio or suburban newspaper competition either. Has the newspaper competitive environment changed so radically that the end result of Congress' good intentions is changed?"[58]

Another good intention by government was the cross-ownership ban imposed in 1975 to prohibit newspapers and TV stations from owning both media outlets in the same market. The newspapers that already owned TV stations were allowed to keep them, but future mergers in the same city by a newspaper and a TV station were blocked for the next 28 years except for several waivers granted by the Federal Communications Commission (FCC).

The cross-ownership ban and other restrictions on media ownership affecting newspapers and TV and radio stations were removed or loosened in a predictable 3–2 vote in June 2003 by the FCC.

The removal of restrictions was expected to result in a wave of media mergers afterward, led by newspaper chains buying up TV stations in the cities in which they own papers. Al Tompkins of the Poynter Institute predicted that the practice of converging formerly separate news operations with each other also would start becoming common as more newspapers and TV stations come under common ownership.[59]

Already, joint operating agreements similar to newspaper JOAs have been placed into effect by many nonprofit organizations—including public TV broadcasters. For example, in 1999, two public TV stations in Indianapolis announced a merger of their program decision-making, fund-raising and master-control functions, while in Denver two public TV stations merged their master-control operations but kept separate their programming control functions.[60]

Combining forces and news roles

CONSOLIDATION and convergence are issues that go naturally together in media companies today—and not just because of alliteration. Basically, when we speak of consolidation, we are referring to a company owning several media outlets, which can all be of one type, such as television stations, or of several types, such as newspapers, TV stations and the Internet. When we speak of convergence, we are talking of how the talents or duties of employees are spread over some or all of the different kinds of media outlets a company owns.

"Media convergence is not a one-size-fits-all proposition," says an article in *Presstime*, the magazine for daily newspaper publishers belonging to the Newspaper Association of America. "It can be as elaborate as Media General's $40 million, state-of-the-art facility housing *The Tampa Tribune*, WFLA-TV and Tampa Bay Online. Or it can be as simple as a television news anchor reading morning headlines from the local newspaper."[61]

Though convergence usually is thought of as combining newsroom operations among outlets owned by the same company, Media General took convergence still another prophetic step forward by working out a precedent-setting convergence in 2002 with the Sarasota media owned by The New York Times Co., just a short way down Florida's Gulf Coast. Under the arrangement, stories will be shared between Media General's three Tampa news properties and the Times Co.'s *Sarasota Herald-Tribune*, SNN, Channel 6 and the heraldtribune.com Web site.[62]

The traditional convergence in Tampa, which then developed further with a two-company convergence, is pioneering a movement toward more such combined newsrooms. It is a movement that is sure to spread across the country. Different strategies will be explored, but combined newsrooms and multi-tasked reporters may become the rule. A database on newsroom and ad department convergence efforts is maintained at <www.americanpressinstitute.org/convergencetracker>.

Convergence strategies are being studied or implemented in those cities where a newspaper company owns other outlets, with some other joint broadcast-print newsrooms now being organized. One of the first after Tampa is in Lawrence, Kan. There, in the fall of 2001, a common newsroom was established to unite the news gathering operations of the *Journal-World* daily, its Web site and its cable TV channel.[63]

Even though there is no common newsroom in Dallas, Texas, Belo news executives have worked since 1997 to tear down competitive barriers there between Belo's own media companies. There is strong cooperation in news coverage between all of the Belo-owned media companies—the *Dallas Morning News* newspaper, ABC affiliate WFAA-TV, the statewide cable channel TXCN, and several of Belo's Web sites across the state. Now they are working with Belo's other TV stations in Houston, San Antonio and Austin as well. *Morning News* reporters appear on TV, while WFAA writers and producers have bylines in the newspaper.[64]

A less obtrusive variety of convergence began shaping up in 2002 at *The Albuquerque Tribune* in New Mexico. A Scripps executive met with reporters, telling them they would need to start writing television and online stories in addition to their newspaper stories. A digital video camera from KRQE Channel 13 was placed in the *Tribune's* newsroom in a furthering of a cooperative arrangement between the newspaper and the separately owned TV station.[65]

Similarly, print reporters for *The St. Paul (Minn.) Pioneer Press* are expected to write a Web site story of any event they cover within 30 minutes, before they write their newspaper version.[66]

Howard Kurtz of *The Washington Post* echoed the feelings of many in the newsroom who feel convergence is more about money than it is about journalism. Kurtz observed, "As the journalistic precincts of cyberspace turn increasingly competitive, newspapers are transforming themselves into 24-hour news machines, in part by asking their print reporters to do double duty."[67]

Most media company leaders see it another way. William Dean Singleton, whose MediaNews Group owns broadcast stations and daily newspapers in the West, cites the synergies that can be realized by a combined newsroom.

AT A GLANCE

U.S. magazine circulation
Larger than largest newspapers

	Avg. Circ. (millions)
NRTA/AARP Bulletin	21.5
Modern Maturity	18.4
Reader's Digest	12.6
TV Guide	9.3
National Geographic	7.7
Better Homes & Gardens	7.6
Taste of Home*	5.0
Family Circle	4.9
Good Housekeeping	4.5
Woman's Day	4.2
Time	4.1

Source: *Advertising Age*, September 13, 2002.
* - Not verified by Audit Bureau of Circulation

"When you take a local market that has a newspaper and Internet operation and add to it a TV station and a couple of radio properties," he said, "and then you consolidate operations into one newsroom, one sales department, one accounting department—one everything—you can leverage your news coverage across several platforms."[68]

A pioneer in using convergence, economies of scale, clustering and synergy to produce his newspapers, Singleton notes that "the sum of all revenue is dramatically increased" over what each newspaper could have produced alone, adding, "Technology and the convergence revolution fits small papers just as well—perhaps better than large newspapers."[69]

The savings realized through convergence has been one of the driving forces behind publishers and broadcasters lobbying for an end to the cross-ownership ban so more can own newspapers, radio stations, TV stations and Web sites in the same market.

One of the few publishers opposing repeal of the cross-ownership ban is Frank A. Blethen, CEO and publisher of *The Seattle Times.* Blethen believes repeal of the ban would lead to more convergence newsrooms and a new form of "monopolistic market control."[70]

Blethen explained, "From a purely business perspective, we would love to own a TV station in Seattle. And, yes, it would significantly increase the value of our company. But we don't believe we need it to survive and compete. Indeed, we believe it would be bad public policy if we were allowed to do so."[71]

A repeal of the cross-ownership ban undoubtedly would spark increased acquisitions by media companies. Of course, consolidation will continue aggressively even without that encouragement.

AT A GLANCE

U.S. magazine revenue

Fueled by advertising dollars

	Revenue (millions)
People	$1,119.9
TV Guide	955.7
Time	843.0
Sports Illustrated	841.7
Better Homes & Gardens	641.8
Reader's Digest	580.5
Parade	570.5
Business Week	454.8
Good Housekeeping	414.3
Fortune	389.6

Source: *Advertising Age,* September 13, 2002.

The chart at the beginning of this chapter showing the decline in independently owned newspapers shows what has been taking place throughout the 20th century and into the 21st.

Similar consolidation, though more recent in time, also has been taking place in radio, television, magazines, book publishing, movie studios, advertising and public relations. Even weekly newspapers and small dailies began getting snapped up in the late 1990s by two new chains, Community Newspaper Holdings Inc. and Liberty Group Publishing, both financed by pension fund investors.

Consolidation of daily newspapers has been probably the best documented, and a great deal of the public awareness about newspapers has been due to the serial publishing of six editions from 1983 to 2000 of Bagdikian's book. Some predictions of his first edition of *The Media Monopoly* misfired. (He wrote, "If mergers, acquisitions and takeovers continue at the present rate, one massive firm will be in virtual control of all major media by the 1990s."[72]) However, in fairness, Bagdikian put his emphasis instead on one analyst's prediction of six corporations by 2000, which was right on the mark. Bagdikian has focused public attention on how media companies are quickly getting larger by swallowing their rivals and diversifying into several media fields.

The newspaper merger mania continued unabated until the 2001 recession, when newspaper acquisitions came to a near dead halt. Transactions for 2001 totaled about $400 million, barely 3 percent of the $14.2 billion in the sales of more than 100 dailies the previous year.[73] As just one example of the slow-down imposed by the recession, Liberty Group Publishing had purchased 170 newspapers in just two years, for a total of 330, but the company bought none in 2001.[74]

Major consolidation has been true throughout all kinds of media companies in recent years, with radio joining the consolidation movement just since the Telecommunications Act of 1996, which removed most limits on radio ownership.

Media analyst Patricia Aufderheide reported on the astonishing rapidity with which both TV and radio consolidation took place, writing, "Total TV and station sales almost doubled between 1995 and 1996. The biggest short-range prize was radio, where national concentration limits had been lifted entirely. Virtually overnight, an industry marked by relative diversity of ownership and formats, and low advertising rates, became highly concentrated. Within a year and a half, more than a quarter of U.S. radio stations had been sold at least once. Radio stock prices rose 80 percent in 1997, reflecting the new market power of group owners."[75]

AT A GLANCE

Top 10 U.S. TV Owners

Many also own radio stations

	Stations	House-hold %
Fox (News Corp.)	34	40.7
CBS, UPN (Viacom)	38	40.1
Paxson	69	34.8
Tribune Co.	23	30.5
NBC (G.E.)	13	26.6
ABC (Disney)	10	23.8
Univision	25	18.6
Gannett	22	17.3
Hearst-Argyle	33	15.8
Sinclair	62	14.6

Percentage of households reached in 2001, reported by *Columbia Journalism Review*

The buy-out frenzy that followed the Telecommunications Act of 1996 reduced the number of commercial radio owners by 2001 from 5,100 to 3,800 and the number of commercial TV station owners from 543 to 360.[76]

Broadcast companies that were modest entities or that did not even exist a decade ago now own hundreds of radio stations across the nation, often up to eight in a given market,[77] which is the maximum allowed. Clear Channel alone owned 1,238 stations in 47 of the top 50 markets in mid-2003, growing from being only a 36-station chain when the Telecommunications Act of 1996 was passed. The second largest radio group was Cumulus Media, with about 270 stations, and third was Viacom's Infinity Broadcasting with about 180. This is a mind-boggling change from less than a decade earlier, when a big radio operator was anyone owning up to what was then the legal limit of 40 stations.

Consolidation races on with TV broadcasting, too. All of the nation's television networks changed hands in the 1980s and 1990s (ABC and CBS were sold twice), and all now are wholly owned subsidiaries of much larger conglomerates whose main revenues, in most cases, are made outside of media. The current lineup at press time: ABC is owned by the Walt Disney Company (1995), CBS is owned by Viacom (1999), NBC is owned by General Electric (1985), the Fox network was created and still is owned by News Corp. (1985), and CNN is owned by AOL Time Warner (1996). There also are several network wanna-bes on the rise, including UPN, which also is owned by Viacom, and Telemundo, whose ownership is traced through a series of ever-larger companies until ultimately belonging also to General Electric.[78]

In a compilation of just the billion-dollar-plus deals since 1985, sociologists David Croteau and William Hoynes document mergers and acquisitions among media companies totaling $653.3 billion in constant 2000 dollars over the past 15 years.[79]

Their book was published with this round-up in early 2001, but it was quickly made out-of-date by other big deals. Some of the largest examples announced since their book are: (1) In October 2001, NBC announced it was buying Telemundo Communications Group in a deal valued at $2.7 billion;[80] (2) in December, AT&T Broadband agreed to be purchased by Comcast for $72 billion by the end of 2002, to create the nation's largest cable television operator with 22.3 million subscribers;[81] (3) at the end of 2001 EchoStar (Dish Network) announced its intention to buy its main competitor—Hughes Electronics (DirecTV)—for $26 billion, which would give it 90 percent of the U.S. digital satellite TV market with more than 19 million subscribers.[82]

The EchoStar–DirecTV deal soon foundered, however, on anti-trust concerns that even the merger-loving Federal Communications Commission could not ignore. The FCC voted 4–0 in the fall of 2002 to reject the deal, killing its chances.[83]

That was the first time in 30 years the FCC had voted to block a proposed merger.[84]

The deal rejection led to Hughes' parent, General Motors, again contacting Rupert Murdoch to see if News Corp., which was outbid earlier by EchoStar, might still be interested in buying DirecTV.[85] He was. In April 2003, News Corp, agreed to purchase a controlling interest in DirecTV for $6.6 billion in cash and stock, pending FCC approval, giving Murdoch the largest U.S. satellite provider as an outlet for his global satellite television network.[86]

A month after rejecting the EchoStar-DirecTV merger, the FCC voted 3–1 to approve the merger of Comcast and AT&T Broadband. Because of stock market decline, the deal had dropped in value by more than half to $29.2 billion. The new company controls 29 percent of the nation's cable TV market, reaching twice as many homes as its nearest competitor, AOL Time Warner.[87]

Just eight months after NBC's purchase of Telemundo was announced, the largest Spanish-language TV group, Univision, said it was buying the largest Spanish-language radio group, Hispanic Broadcasting, for $3.5 billion in stock. Univision had to outbid NBC's corporate parent General Electric to put the deal together,[88] and was motivated by self-defense to block its main competitor from gobbling up even more of the Hispanic market. Hispanics have been the nation's fastest growing segment for the past decade, became the nation's largest minority in 2002, and are expected to make up 25 percent of the nation's population by 2050.[89]

AT A GLANCE

Largest U.S. paper chains
Many also own TV and/or radio

	2001 net (millions)
Gannett	$4,909
Tribune Co.	3,844
Knight Ridder	2,858
New York Times Co.	2,826
Advance Publications	2,025
Dow Jones & Co.	1,455
Cox Enterprises	1,350
Hearst Corp.	1,323
McClatchy Co.	1,040
MediaNews Group	977

Source: *Advertising Age,* August 19, 2002.

In the first major newspaper acquisition since pre-recession 2000, and one that further illustrates the escalating consolidation of media companies, publicly traded Lee Enterprises Inc. announced its intention in 2002 to buy privately owned Howard Publications, with its 16 mid-sized dailies across the country and other interests, for $694 million.[90] Lee had plenty of cash for the deal, sitting on $560 million received when it sold its TV group in October 2000 so it could focus on newspapers.[91]

One massive merger possibility arose in late 2002 involving CNN and ABC News. Merger of any two networks is one of the worst-case scenarios most feared by those media analysts who think there already is too little diversity in media voices. Through much of 2002, AOL Time Warner's CNN and Disney's ABC News investigated the possibility of merging into a joint venture news operation.[92]

In a revealing insight into the corporate mind, the merger was being sought by both corporations just to make profitable operations even more profitable. CNN reportedly had pre-tax profits of $200 million on $1.6 billion in sales,[93] while ABC News posted about $60 million in pre-tax profits on its annual sales of $600 million.[94]

Jeffrey Chester, director of the Center for Digital Democracy, immediately announced opposition to any CNN-ABC merger. "The loss of independence by both CNN and ABC News, in order to help shore up sagging stock prices of Disney and AOL, is too high a price for the American viewing public to pay," Chester said.[95]

AOL Time Warner withdrew from the talks with the Walt Disney Company in early 2003, its executives explaining that they did not have time to pursue a CNN-ABC merger because they had too many other problems to worry about, especially a massive write-down in the corporation's value because of its ailing AOL division.[96] However, over the previous 20 years, CNN has explored the possibility of mergers with NBC, CBS and ABC,[97] so a joint venture or merger with one of those networks can be expected to be discussed again some day.

Advertising and public relations firms also have been buying each other out or taking other moves to combine forces to, as a media investment analyst pointed out, "catch up to what the media and clients already have done."[98] In a $3.5 billion deal in early 2002, three already giant advertising agencies in Chicago, Paris and Tokyo (Bcom3, Publicis and Dentsu) agreed to merge into an ad powerhouse that would move The Publicis Groupe up from the world's fifth largest ad agency to the fourth largest, with $4 billion in annual revenue.[99]

Those agencies' incentive to combine was attributed by *The New York Times* to a need to serve clients that in turn are growing ever larger and international in scope.

"As the world's marketers, which spend almost $500 billion annually on advertising, grow ever larger, they seek to work with agencies that also are large," *The Times* observed in reporting the Publicis deal. "They want agencies that can work in many countries to create campaigns that will appear in many media, from television to the Internet and signs in stores. At the same time, the ownership of the media is being concentrated in fewer hands, so agencies want to bulk up to gain more power in buying space and time for clients' campaigns from huge companies like AOL Time Warner, the News Corporation, Viacom and Vivendi Universal."[100]

Croteau and Hoynes cite four major developments in recent years that have profoundly affected the structure, size, influence and character of the giant media conglomerates:[101]

(1) GROWTH: Mergers and buyouts have made media corporations bigger than ever.

(2) INTEGRATION: The new media giants have integrated either horizontally by moving into multiple forms of media such as film, publishing, radio and so on, or vertically by owning several stages of production and distribution—or both.

(3) GLOBALIZATION: To varying degrees, the major media conglomerates have become global entities, marketing their wares worldwide.

(4) CONCENTRATION OF OWNERSHIP: As major players acquire more media holdings, the ownership of mainstream media has become increasingly concentrated.

A fifth development seems appropriate to add to the list: the rise of intense intermedia competition.

Companies no longer are staying in their own back yards. The competition among existing media companies to go after each others' business through intermedia competition also has led to a fragmentation of audiences for all media companies. Many media companies are discovering that they are now competitors of companies and products they never had considered before.

As late as just before World War II, news was for all practical purposes a monopoly of a 17th century invention—the newspaper.

The first intermedia competition really began in the late 1800s with the telegraph, and the early 1900s with radio, but newspapers still were by far the only widespread way for news and information to be delivered. In the mid-1900s, both newspapers and radio faced new competition from the development of television. And by the late 1900s, intermedia competition intensified for everyone with the emergence of new media platforms such as cell phones, the Internet, satellite broadcasting, wireless, and a host of other communication breakthroughs resulting from rapid improvements in digital technology, as well as a strengthening of magazine and book publishing.

Research findings are mixed on the effects of this intensifying inter-media competition.[102] However, the one conclusion driving larger size for all media companies is expressed by researcher David Demers, "News-papers (and other media companies) that acquire the characteristics of the corporate form of organization (as opposed to family-owned) will be in a better position to survive in the post-industrial age."[103]

Going international

THE TREND TOWARD international influence is well underway. Of the dominant six media firms Bagdikian listed in *Media Monopoly*, Bertelsmann is based in Germany while News Corp. started in Australia, and the four U.S.-based media firms are all moving to a greater reliance on overseas revenues.

This new development by media conglomerates toward international domination is causing concern among those who recognized it early on. Bagdikian frets about "the dominant corporations' increasing global scale"[104] in his latest edition. Richard A. Gershon, author of *The Transnational Media Corporation*, presented a study of these global media companies in 2000 in the *Journal of Media Economics.*

"As today's media companies continue to grow and expand," Gershon observed, "the challenges of staying globally competitive become increasingly difficult. Such competition has engendered a new competitive spirit that cuts across nationality and economic class . . . . characterized by a belief that size (and complementary strengths) is crucial to business survival."[105]

Going international, however, carries unexpected perils for American companies because they are not nearly as familiar with the politics and policies of foreign nations as they are of their own.

While U.S. regulators give their blessings to super-mergers such as General Electric's proposed purchase of Honeywell for $43 billion, Mario Monti has not been so easily swayed.

Monti, head of the European Union's competition commission, vetoed the GE-Honeywell deal in 2001. The year earlier he also scuttled the MCI Worldcom merger with Sprint. *CFO* magazine predicts Monti also will take a hard line against Microsoft when he reviews its competitive practices in Europe, despite Microsoft's settlement with U.S. officials.[106]

The international business component has become so vital to U.S.-based conglomerates of all kinds, media or otherwise, that U.S. approval is becoming no longer enough. If European anti-trust officials refuse to go along, merger deals die.

Jack Welch, considered the masterful CEO when he headed NBC's parent, General Electric, could not save the Honeywell deal after going mano-a-mano with Monti.[107]

It remains to be seen what this European skepticism about American big business will mean for media companies as they become more dependent on international sales and therefore more vulnerable to international regulatory approval.

Nevertheless, the drive to grow ever larger, and to go international, is fueled by a fear about business survival that is real and palpable among even the most successful and powerful business moguls. Its influence on the aggressive take-no-prisoners attitude of media industry CEOs in their relentless quest to improve stock prices and, therefore, increase corporate value should not be under-estimated.

A Poynter Institute study of 14 leading print and broadcast CEOs in 1997 found every one of them focused overwhelmingly on the need to increase stock prices, market their products, build their brands, and attract readers and viewers. Unlike publishers and broadcasters of the past, all were exploring other possible revenue-producers outside their main fields, looking into new media, Internet, each others' business lines and any number of new products—all in a determination to be one of the survivors in the technological and managerial upheavals of the 21st century.[108]

Even Bill Gates feels the fear at Microsoft. He wrote of it in 1999, closing with one of his more memorable lines:

"Companies fail when they become complacent and imagine they will always be successful. That's even more dangerous in a world that is changing faster than ever, especially technologically. So we are always challenging ourselves: Are we making what the customers want and working on the products and technologies they'll want in the future? Are we staying ahead of our competitors? What don't our customers like about what we do, and what are we doing about it? Are we organized most efficiently to achieve our goals? Even the most successful companies must constantly re-invent themselves."[109]

Fragmentation of media markets

CONSOLIDATION, CONVERGENCE, clustering, profit maximization, stockholder ownership of media companies on the stock market, layoffs dictated by slow times or Wall Street analysts, stratospheric buy-outs and mergers, international expansion, and market-driven journalism such as infotainment and sensationalism in the news to attract ever larger and younger audiences . . . . Whew, what a litany of what many would consider media sins.

It is no coincidence that all of these trends either originated or dramatically intensified with the fragmentation of markets brought on by new media technologies since 1985.

Readership of daily newspapers in the United States continues to decline at an average of about 1 percent a year despite a growing population, and surveys show that only about a fourth of Americans under age 30 read a daily the previous day.[110] Younger news consumers might read a Sunday paper, but they tend to turn to Internet news sites and cable news during the week. U.S. dailies circulation peaked at 62.8 million in 1985 (the year America On Line was founded—coincidence?), but has declined every year since then to only 55.6 million by 2001—a decline of nearly 11 percent in 12 years.[111] Conversely, from 1985 to 2000, weekly newspapers' circulation increased from 49 million to 71 million,[112] which is a 45 percent increase, and still another competitive factor in the decline of dailies.

Even more devastating for dailies is the industry's plummeting share of total advertising. U.S. dailies' share fell to 20 percent in 2001, compared with 29 percent in the late 1970s.[113]

Television viewership overall is keeping pace with population growth, but the fragmentation brought on by hundreds of new cable channels has brought devastating declines to the audience share of the original three major networks: ABC, NBC and CBS. For example, cable viewership rose another 11 percent in 2001,[114] but the original networks have half as many viewers as in 1985.

"It is fragmentation that is bringing increased pressure on us," said Tribune Co. executive Jack Fuller. "Not a bunch of greedy, Dickensian corporate bean counters . . . . It is in every serious journalist's interest to help figure out how to beat these new competitors."[115]

15 largest media conglomerates in revenue
Based on annual reports and other diverse sources[116]

Rank	Company	2002 revenue (in $ billions)	Major holdings
1.	AOL Time Warner	41.0	Time, AOL, movies, CNN
2.	Walt Disney Company	25.3	ABC, film, entertainment
3.	Viacom	24.6	CBS, entertainment, movies
4.	*Bertelsmann	15.8	Books, magazines
5.	^ Vivendi Universal	15.6	Books, film, music, cable, etc.
6.	News Corp.	15.2	Books, newspapers, TV stations, cable
7.	Comcast	12.5	Cable
8.	^Sony	11.9	Film, music, entertainment, etc.
9.	Clear Channel	8.4	Radio
10.	Cox Communications	8.0	Cable, Internet, newspapers, TV, radio
11.	Thomson Corp.	7.8	On-line, textbooks, magazines
12.	Gannett	6.4	Newspapers, TV stations
13.	Tribune Company	5.4	Newspapers, TV, radio
14.	Reed Elsevier	5.0	Book publishing
15.	^ NBC	4.8	TV network

* - Privately owned German company, so its finances are an estimate.
^ - Includes only income from media holdings; parent companies are much larger.

CASE STUDY   *Where Will We Put*
              the Billiards Table?

by ROBERT G. PICARD, Ph.D.
Jönköping University

The owners of two advertising agencies, Mullins, Nugent & White
(MN&W) and Digital Image Advertising (DIA), have agreed to merge and
the final financial transactions to complete the merger will be concluded
shortly.

The merger follows the death of Philip Nugent, who was one of the
founders of MN&W 30 years ago. In order to meet the estate needs of his
family, his interests in the firm are being withdrawn. The remaining
partners began efforts to restructure the firm when they were
approached by DIA about a possible merger. After analyzing their
operations and finances, a deal was made to bring the two firms together.

Digital Image Advertising specializes in campaigns for computer-
related hardware and software designed for the consumer market. It was
established 10 years ago. MN&W focuses its efforts on health care
electronic diagnostic and treatment equipment. The management of both
firms believes the merger will position the expanded company well in the
high-technology advertising market and that the competencies and
clients of the two firms complement each other.

Managers of both firms found the business segments they serve as
providing advantages to a merged firm. The demand for advertising
services for the health care electronics field is growing slowly, but the
number of producers and consumers is relatively stable. Services
provided in this sector were seen as providing a stable foundation for the
merged company. Demand for advertising services for the computer-
related field is growing rapidly because of the rapid proliferation of
products and services provided by a growing number of producers and
an increasing number of users. Services provided in this sector were seen
as providing the potential for growth of the merged company.

MN&W has a staff of 33 and an annual payroll and benefits cost of
$2.4 million. DIA has a permanent staff of 20 and is employing an
additional 16 persons as temporary workers and contract employees. Its
payroll and benefits costs are $1.8 million annually.

MN&W is a well-established firm with stable billings. Its clients tend to be firms with long histories in health care electronics. The average client has been with MN&W for nine years.

DIA is a maturing firm whose clients produce products that change every two years, whose clients often use different advertising agencies for different product lines, and whose clients review advertising contracts relatively often. Its average client has been with DIA for three years.

Billings (in $ millions)

	5 Years Ago	4 Years Ago	3 Years Ago	2 Years Ago	Last Year
MN&W	30.2	31.0	31.8	32.7	33.5
DIA	22.4	23.1	31.8	28.8	30.0

Operating Expenses (in $ millions)

	5 Years Ago	4 Years Ago	3 Years Ago	2 Years Ago	Last Year
MN&W	4.3	4.4	4.5	4.6	4.7
DIA	2.5	2.6	2.3	3.3	3.4

Integration Issues

Now that the merger is being completed, the managers of the pre-existing firms must integrate the operations of the two firms. As part of the merger, a strategic decision was made by the owners to fully combine the two firms and not to operate them as separate divisions of a holding company. After a review of the merger and the operations of the two firms, managers have raised a number of issues.

One issue is the name of the new firm. Mullins, Nugent & White was a well-recognized name among its target advertisers, but with the withdrawal of Nugent's financial interests his name will not stay on the firm. MN&W managers, however, believe that keeping Mullins and White in the name will be beneficial. Digital Image Advertising's managers argue that their firm's name is known among its potential clients in the fast growing computer electronics area and that the firm should keep that name because it will be helpful in client acquisition.

A concern of many employees is differences in compensation plans between the two firms. Although benefits are roughly equivalent, MN&W has a traditional salary structure, while employees in DIA receive about 15 percent less in actual salary but can gain performance-based annual bonuses. The bonus plan means that DIA employees have the opportunity to obtain annual compensation about 10 percent higher than MN&W workers receive. During the last five years, about 70 percent of the employees have received performance bonuses each year. When the merger is implemented, a single compensation scheme will cover all employees. Employees at MN&W view the DIA plan as a reduction in their pay and entailing a good deal of risk. DIA employees view the MN&W salaries as reasonable but dislike the idea of giving up incentive bonuses.

Employees in the two firms differ. MN&W employees have an average age of 39, while DIA employees average 28 years of age. MN&W has a conservative culture in which business dress is the norm and office space is traditionally decorated. DIA's culture has no dress code, except for meetings with clients, and employees are permitted a great deal of latitude in furnishing and decorating their offices.

Both firms have operated relatively conservatively in fiscal and account management activities, but have differed in creative aspects of advertising. MN&W has typically produced traditional and rather conservative advertising campaigns and materials, while DIA has often offered clients more contemporary, innovative, and cutting edge advertising campaigns and materials.

Because both firms bring with them existing clients, it has been determined that the emerging firm will need to keep all existing personnel in account management and copywriting. However, a duplication of functions and personnel in the accounting, traffic, and art departments will warrant reductions. A brief initial review has determined that three persons will be eliminated from accounting, two from traffic and five from art departments.

The office building in which MN&W now occupies the fifth floor will have vacant space on the sixth floor when its current tenant vacates in eight months. The merged firm will acquire that space and move the DIA employees into the office building. The space is slightly smaller than current facilities, leading some DIA employees to wonder where the billiards table and video games now located in their existing office will be relocated.

Working in teams, decide the following questions as time allows:

• How should management handle the question of the name change?

• How should management deal with the issues of employee compensation?

• How will the differences in company cultures be expected to affect personnel and what can managers do about potential conflicts that may occur?

• How will the differences in type and styles of advertising campaigns affect the new firm's ability to integrate its workforce?

• What is the appropriate way to handle the reduction in redundant personnel in the new firm?

• How should the company handle the movement of DIA employees to the new offices?

• How will the differences in the stability of the revenue and expenses of the merging firms affect the operations of the new firm?

• What will the employment differences in the two merging companies (DIA uses flexible employment; MN&W uses traditional employment) mean to employees in the new firm? How might the management handle the issue?

• How will the differences in clients and client longevity of the two firms affect the merged firm?

AUTHOR:

Robert G. Picard is Hamrin Professor of Media Economics and director of the Media Management and Transformation Centre at Jönköping International Business School, Jönköping University, Sweden. He is the author of 16 books on media economics and management issues and is editor of the Journal of Media Business Studies.

CASE STUDY *Expanding and Consolidating*

by HUGH S. FULLERTON, Ph.D.
Sam Houston State University

(Fourth in a series of five related case studies)

The *Jamestown Call* has become established under Jerry's owner-ship. Jerry has owned the paper for three years. Profits have risen so he can easily make expenses, including his monthly payments to the former owner, and take out a salary adequate for his family to live on in a small community. They do not have a lot of luxuries, but they are doing okay. Jerry's wife was readily employed in the local school system, and his children seem like their small town.

His business is secure and profitable, and he is no longer working 80-hour weeks as he did for the first year or so. After three years, however, Jerry has learned enough to realize *The Call* is not likely to have much growth, and he has maxed out any improvement due to efficiency. The only chance for growth appears to be if he buys another paper.

An opportunity presents itself. The *Village Venture*, another small weekly located 30 miles away, is for sale because the owner is ready to retire. Jerry and the owner have become friends, and the owner suggests to Jerry that he buy it. The asking price seems reasonable, based on Jerry's experience in operating small newspapers.

If Jerry does not buy the *Venture*, the owner will put it on the open market. An outsider might buy the *Venture* and be in a similar position to Jerry three years earlier. Or a larger chain might buy it, which could represent some threat to *The Call*, since the papers' circulation areas overlap a bit. Jerry has managed to pay down the principal from *The Call* purchase, so his credit is good, and he might be able to come up with a down payment if the owner is willing to finance most of the purchase.

What does Jerry need to ask—about the *Venture* itself as well as his ability to manage a second paper—before he goes ahead with the purchase? Should he buy it?

AUTHOR:

Hugh S. Fullerton was a reporter at daily newspapers and also was publisher of a group of weekly newspapers in Michigan for several years. He an associate professor of journalism at Sam Houston State University in Huntsville, Texas.

🖥 Suggested Web sites:

www.cjr.org/owners—"Who Owns What?"
www.ajr.newslink.org/special—AJR site on business issues
www.naa.org/info/facts02/index.html—Newspaper Association of America statistics
www.magazine.org—News of the magazine industry
www.americanpressinstitute.org/convergencetracker—Database on convergence programs
www.ajr.org/News_Wire_Services.asp?MediaType=10—Media companies
www.democraticmedia.com—Center for Digital Democracy
www.journalism.org/resources/research/reports/ownership/deregulation2.asp—Media ownership and deregulation

Endnotes to Chapter 10:

[1] Ben H. Bagdikian, *The Media Monopoly* (Boston: Beacon Press, 6th ed. 2000).

[2] "The War Between Men and Women," dir. Melville Shavelson, 110 min., National General Pictures, 1972. Videocassette.

[3] James V. Risser, "Endangered species: State of the American newspaper," *American Journalism Review* (June 1998), 29. Article also is available at <www.ajr.org/article.asp?id=1534>, accessed August 12, 2003.

[4] Rick Romell, "Front page identity crisis: Stevens Point remains divided over newspaper's sale to chains," *Milwaukee Journal Sentinel*, November 25, 2001.

[5] Risser, "Endangered species: State of the American newspaper," 20.

[6] Joe Hladky, e-mail to author, June 26, 2003.

[7] Media Studies, "Concentration of newspaper ownership," at <www.pch.gc.ca/progs/ac-ca/ [progs/esm-ms/prob4_e.cfm>, accessed May 14, 2003.

[8] "23rd annual 100 leading media companies," *Advertising Age*, August 19, 2002, S1-2.

[9] William Baker and George Dessert, "The road ahead," *Television Quarterly* (Spring 2000): 2.

[10] Ibid.

[11] Bagdikian, *The Media Monopoly*, xi.

[12] Bill Kovach and Tom Rosenstiel, *The Elements of Journalism* (New York: Crown Publishers, 2001), 32.

[13] Matthew Rose and Nikhil Deogun, "Time Warner to pay $474 million for Times Mirror magazines," *Wall Street Journal*, October 20, 2000.

[14] Kirk Anderson, "Synergy" cartoon © Kirk Anderson, reprinted with permission.

[15] Rushworth M. Kidder, "Can media ethics survive the AOL-Time Warner merger?" Institute for Global Ethics, February 7, 2001.

[16] Ibid.

[17] Peter Svensson of the Associated Press, as published in "AOL chairman to quit," *Albuquerque Journal*, January 13, 2003, A5.

[18] Mark Fitzgerald, "Chain reactions," *Editor & Publisher* (January 1, 2001): 20.

[19] Stuart Elliott, quoting Michael J. Russell Jr. of Morgan Stanley Dean Witter in "3 ad competitors unite to conquer: Publicis will become No. 4 among the agency companies," *The New York Times*, March 8, 2002, C20.

[20] Michael Wolf, "Manager's Journal: In TV land, bigger is better," *The Wall Street Journal*, August 21, 2000, A18.

[21] Ibid.

[22] Ibid.

[23] Eli M. Noam and Robert N. Freeman, "The media monopoly and other myths," *Taking Sides: Mass Media and Society* (Guilford, Conn.: McGraw Hill-Dushkin, 6th ed., 2001), 270.

[24] Ibid., 271.

[25] Tim A. Pilgrim, "Newspapers as natural monopolies: Some historical considerations," 18, *Journalism History* (1992): 3.

[26] Joe Haldeman, *The Forever War* (New York: Avon Books, 1974, 1975, 1997).

[27] *McGraw-Hill Dictionary of Modern Economics* (New York: McGraw-Hill, 3rd ed., 1983).

[28] Pilgrim, "Newspapers as natural monopolies: Some historical considerations," 3.

[29] Jim Willis, quoting a financier in *Surviving in the Newspaper Business* (New York: Praeger, 1988), 79.

[30] Paul Farhi, "The death of the JOA," *American Journalism Review* (September 1999): 53. Article also is available at <www.ajr.org/Article.asp?id=317>, accessed August 12, 2003.

[31] Michael Emery and Edwin Emery, *The Press and America: An Interpretive History of the Mass Media* (Englewood Cliffs, N.J.: Prentice-Hall, 5th ed., 1984), 399, 676.

[32] Numerous sources, including *Editor & Publisher International Yearbook* (New York: Editor & Publisher, 82nd ed., 2003), xix; "Daily newspapers," *American Journalism Review*, <www.newslink.org/daynews.html>, accessed October 23, 2001; "Who owns what?", *Columbia Journalism Review*, <www.cjr.org/owners>, accessed October 23, 2001; and Benjamin Compaine and Douglas Gomery, *Who Owns the Media? Competition and Concentration in the Mass Media Industry* (Mahwah, N.J.: Lawrence Erlbaum Associates, 3rd ed., 2000), 9.

[33] Interviews with some publishers in university cities who did not want to be quoted on the record.

[34] "Read all about it: Why Iowa State's newspaper had to scale back its use of professional advertising salespeople," formerly at <www.universitybusiness.com/9905 /update.html>, accessed October 25, 2001. Site is no longer available on the Web.

[35] Thomas L. Beell, associate professor of journalism at Iowa State University, in e-mail to Iowa State Press and the author (December 27, 2002).

[36] Daily newspaper editor who requested anonymity, in personal e-mail to the author (December 28, 2001).

[37] "Read all about it: Why Iowa State's newspaper had to scale back its use of professional advertising salespeople."

[38] Mark Fitzgerald, "Missouri paper refutes report," *Editor & Publisher* (December 16, 2002).

[39] Romell, *Milwaukee Journal Sentinel*.

[40] Jim Rosenberg, "8 weeklies, 2 weeks: Flint Journal redesigns and produces eight Michigan community pubs soon after Advance acquisition of Heritage group's papers," *Editor & Publisher* (October 28, 2002): 26–28.

[41] Pilgrim, "Newspapers as natural monopolies: Some historical considerations," 3.

[42] "JOA: A 50-year record of newspaper life-saving," *Editor & Publisher* (March 13, 1982): 14.

[43] Ibid.

[44] Numerous sources, including Newspaper Association of America, "Facts about newspapers, 2000," Table 30, at <www.naa.org/info/facts00>, accessed October 23, 2001; Newspaper Association of America, "Newspaper joint operating agreements," Table 17, at <www.naa.org/info/facts02/17_facts2002.html>, accessed January 5, 2003; Ron Larson, library director at Madison Newspapers, e-mail to author (October 30, 2001); and Dan Hayes, of Lee Enterprises, e-mail to author (October 31, 2001).

[45] Numerous sources, including David M. Cole, *NewsInc.*, "Death in Honolulu means more than just one paper," <www.colegroup.com/ newsinc/990927SA.html>, accessed October 23, 2001; Newspaper Association of America, "Facts about newspapers, 2000," Table 30, at <www.naa.org/info/facts00>, accessed October 23, 2001; and "San Francisco, Honolulu JOAs dissolved; papers didn't," *Detroit Free Press* at <www.freep.com/jobspage/links/joa.htm>, accessed October 23, 2001.

[46] John C. Busterna, "Newspaper Preservation Act: To be or not to be—that is irrelevant!" *Newspaper Research Journal* (Summer–Fall 1993): 2

[47] Hayes, e-mail to author.

[48] "Gannett Co., Inc. and MediaNews Group announce new partnership," joint press release from the two corporations by Tara Connell of Gannett and Joseph J. Lodovic IV of MediaNews Group, March 17, 2003.

[49] Chris Roberts, The Associated Press, as published in "N.M., El Paso newspapers to share," *Albuquerque Journal,* March 18, 2003, C6.

[50] The firings and take-over by Gannett were a main topic of discussion a few days later, on May 16, 2003, among editors and publishers gathering in Albuquerque to conduct committee meetings for the New Mexico Press Association. They said they were were shocked, but not surprised, by Gannett's brutal treatment of their friends at Las Cruces.

[51] "Gannett Co., Inc. and MediaNews Group announce new partnership."

[52] Ibid.

[53] Al Neuharth, "Mackinac straight talk: How dailies survive," *Detroit News*, June 1, 1986, 23A.

[54] Mark Fitzgerald, "Detroit JOA sparks protests, requests for hearing," *Editor & Publisher* (June 7, 1986): 20.

[55] Eileen Davis Hudson and Mark Fitzgerald, "Houston has power to survive shocks," *Editor & Publisher* (October 8, 2001): 16A.

[56] Joe Strupp, "RIP for the JOA?" *Editor & Publisher* (January 27, 2003): 7.

[57] Farhi, "The death of the JOA," 51.

[58] Conrad C. Fink, *Media Ethics: In the Newsroom and Beyond* (New York: McGraw-Hill, 1988).

[59] "Kansas company converges newsrooms," *Quill* (January–February 2002): 7–8.

[60] "Once wary stations take their vows in Indianapolis," *Current* (August 30, 1999).

[61] Lisa Rabasca, "Benefits, costs and convergence," *Presstime* (June 2001), full text at <www.naa.org/presstime/0106/convergence.html>, accessed June 12, 2001.

[62] "Tampa, Sarasota create news-sharing agreement," *Quill* (March 2002): 8.

[63] "Kansas company converges newsrooms," 7–8.

[64] Jeremy Murphy, "Hard news for hard times," *Mediaweek (*April 18, 2002): 22.

[65] Rick A. Maese, reporter for *The Albuquerque Tribune,* in interview with the author on April 9, 2002.

[66] Brian S. Brooks with George Kennedy, Daryl R. Moen, and Don Ranly, *News Reporting and Writing* (Boston: Bedford/St. Martin's, 7th ed., 2002), 429.

[67] Ibid.

[68] Mark Fitzgerald and Lucia Moses, "Putting it together," *Editor & Publisher* (February 18, 2002): 11.

[69] William Dean Singleton, in keynote address at the state convention of the New Mexico Press Association, November 2, 2002.

[70] Frank A. Blethen, "A 'dangerous step,'" *Editor & Publisher* (March 18, 2002): 30, and also on the Web as "A voice in the wilderness" at <www.editorandpublisher.com/editorandpublisher/headlines/article_display.jsp? vnu_content_id=1430591>, accessed August 13, 2003.

[71] Ibid.

[72] Bagdikian, *The Media Monopoly.*

[73] Mark Fitzgerald, "Newspapers hold values despite dearth of deals," *Editor & Publisher* (October 29, 2001): 9.

[74] "Liberty readies for opening bell: A $225 million IPO in the offing," *Editor & Publisher* (June 10, 2002): 6.

[75] Patricia Aufderheide, *Communications Policy and the Public Interest* (New York: Guilford Press, 1999).

[76] Bill McConnell, "The National Acquirers," *Broadcasting & Cable,* December 10, 2001, 26.

[77] "Commercial radio now," *Columbia Journalism Review* (November–December 2001): 123.

[78] David Croteau and William Hoynes, *The Business of Media* (Thousand Oaks, Calif.: Pine Forge Press, 2001), 75–79.

[79] Ibid., 73–74.

[80] Seth Sutel, of The Associated Press, as published in "NBC purchasing Telemundo," *Albuquerque Journal*, October 12, 2001, B7.

[81] "Comcast now No. 1 in cable oligopoly," *Albuquerque Journal*, December 23, 2001, B2; and "Merger won't shave bill: Analysts see no savings for Comcast customers," *Albuquerque Journal*, December 25, 2001, C4.

[82] Robert Gehrke, of the Associated Press, as printed in "Western lawmakers urge rejection of EchoStar, DirecTV merger, *Arizona Daily Sun*, January 6, 2002, A4.

[83] Paul Davidson, "EchoStar-DirecTV deal rejected," *USA TODAY,* October 11, 2002, B1.

[84] Yochi J. Dreazen and Andy Pasztor, "FCC rejects proposed deal between EchoStar, Hughes," *The Wall Street Journal* Interactive Edition, Rocket e-book, October 11, 2002, 143.

[85] Ibid.

[86] Paul Chavez of The Associated Press, as published in "Murdoch gains U.S. TV outlet," *Albuquerque Journal,* April 11, 2003, B7.

[87] David Ho of The Associated Press, as published in "AT&T, Comcast can join: Feds approver merger that will create a cable TV giant," *Albuquerque Journal*, November 14, 2002, Outlook 5.

[88] Frank Ahrens, "Univision, Hispanic Broadcasting Merge: $3.5 billion deal creates Spanish-language giant," *The Washington Post,* June 13, 2002, E1, E4.

[89] Ibid., E4.

[90] Mike Freeman, "N. County Times to be sold: Lee Enterprises to buy Howard family holdings," *San Diego Union Tribune*, February 13, 2002, C1.

[91] Lucia Moses, "Lee may cast wider net in wake of Howard buy," *Editor & Publisher* (February 18, 2002): 4.

[92] Kirkpatrick and Carter, "AOL Time Warner and Disney revive talks on news venture," C1.

[93] Ibid.

[94] Joe Flint, Martin Peters and Emily Nelson, "ABC News, CNN heat up talks about a merger," *The Wall Street Journal*, September 25, 2002, B1.

[95] Jeffrey Chester, "An AOL Time Warner and ABC News combination would reduce diversity of voices, harm the public interest," on <www.democraticmedia.org/news/marketwatch/aolCNN.html>, accessed September 26, 2002.

[96] "CNN and ABC end talks of merger," *The Albuquerque Tribune*, February 13, 2003.

[97] David D. Kirkpatrick and Bill Carter, "AOL Time Warner and Disney revive talks on news venture," *The New York Times,* September 25, 2002, C1; also Joe Flint, Martin Peters and Emily Nelson, "ABC News, CNN heat up talks about a merger," *The Wall Street Journal,* September 25, 2002, B1.

[98] Elliott, "3 ad competitors unite to conquer: Publicis will become No. 4 among the agency companies," C20.

[99] Ibid, C8.

[100] Ibid.

[101] Croteau and Hoynes, *The Business of Media,* 73–74.

[102] David Demers, *The Menace of the Corporate Newspaper: Fact or Fiction?* (Ames: Iowa State University Press, 1996), 134–137.

[103] Ibid., 323.

[104] Bagdikian, *The Media Monopoly*, xxi.

[105] Richard A. Gershon, "The transnational media corporation: Environmental scanning and strategy formulation," 13, *Journal of Media Economics* (2000): 82.

[106] Stephen Barr, "Deal breaker of the year," *CFO Magazine* (January 2002): 23.

[107] Ibid.

[108] Marty Linsky, *The View From The Top* (The Poynter Papers: No. 10, St. Petersburg, Fla.: The Poynter Institute for Media Studies, 1997), 1–44.

[109] William Gates, "Remaking Microsoft," *Business Week* (May 17, 1999): 106.

[110] David Moore, *Media Life Magazine*, "Dramatic slide in newspaper reading: Key 35-49 demographic sees greatest dip in daily habit," at <www.medialifemagazine.com/news2002/jun02/jun10/5_fri/news2friday.html>, accessed January 7, 2003.

[111] Newspaper Association of America, "U.S. daily newspaper circulation," at <www.naa.org/info/facts02/14_facts2002.html>, accessed January 5, 2003.

[112] Newspaper Association of America, "Total of U.S. non-daily newspapers," at <www. naa. org/info/facts02/13_facts2002.html>, accessed January 7, 2003.

[113] Lucia Moses, "Profits still speak to the faithful," *Editor & Publisher* (January 6, 2003): 16.

[114] *Broadcasting & Cable* magazine, "Cable viewership on the rise" (January 3, 2003).

[115] Taken from a 2002 speech to editors given by Jack Fuller that included many elements from his book *News Values*.

[116] John V. Pavlik and Shawn McIntosh, *Converging Media: An Introduction to Mass Communication* (Boston: Allyn & Bacon, 2004), 54–55; Benjamin M. Compaine and Douglas Gomery, *Who Owns the Media?* (Mahwah, N.J.: Lawrence Erlbaum Associates, 3rd ed., 2001), 560; and the on-line annual reports of the corporations.

CHAPTER 11

ENTREPRENEURSHIP

JUST ABOUT EVERYONE who has ever (successfully) run his or her own business will tell you the same thing: It's hard to even consider working for someone else once you have been your own boss, in your own business.

One of the most predictable bad endings is when someone sells a business and then is kept on to continue running the company for someone else. Almost inevitably it results in the previous owner getting fired by the new owner.

And most persons who have owned a business know of friends and acquaintances who tried to have it both ways only to endure an ignominious and often embarrassing termination at the hands of their buyer. Newspaper brokers routinely warn sellers not to try to stay on after the sale, and nearly every time that their advice is ignored the situation ends up badly within a year.

In his book on weekly newspapering, *The Hard Way*, Alexander B. Brook tells the woeful tale of what typically happens to owners who stay on after the sale.[1]

Ted Turner has said his biggest business regret was in selling Turner Broadcasting Systems to Time Warner in 1996, because he ended up being fired by Time Warner's then CEO, Gerald M. Levin. If he had just bought Time Warner instead of selling to it, he said, he would have had the pleasure of firing Levin instead.

"I never thought in my wildest dreams I would lose my job," Turner said afterward. He warned young entrepreneurs that, if they sell their company, they should leave on their own terms at the sale rather than be booted out afterward.[2] Turner was able to return to Time Warner only because Levin retired soon after firing him, but the point had been made.

The reason former business owners find it so difficult to transition into a position where they are taking orders as someone else's employee is that most of them are independent cusses—that's why they bought or started their own business in the first place. That's also why, no matter how competent they are, they usually end up being fired by the people to whom they sold their business. And it's why other employers often don't want to hire them.

The other reason they find it difficult to transition to another business and to work for someone else is because they know this: Entrepreneurship leading to ownership can be the most financially rewarding of all endeavors, even when building equity just through a small company such as a weekly newspaper, radio station, public relations consultancy or advertising firm. Building equity in a business while also paying yourself a salary is a potent wealth-building combination.

Entrepreneurs and managers

OFTEN A GREAT entrepreneur turns out to be a poor manager once a new business becomes successful. Likewise, professional managers often flinch from the risk-taking decisions entrepreneurs seem to relish that are essential for a business to grow and progress. In this chapter, we will discuss how the qualities of managers and entrepreneurs can differ, and so might require two roles.

Interestingly, entrepreneurs often thrive on disorder, friction and malperformance—perceiving those dysfunctional consequences of non-management or poor management as proof that a new approach, or a new product, or a whole new business is needed.

Both entrepreneurs and managers need to call on leadership abilities to change the status quo, as represented by the problems they face. The entrepreneur might create change by creating a new company, while a manager will tend to create change by tackling problems head-on and revising procedures. But both still are in their different ways attempting to change the status quo in which they perceive problems, and both are working to move into the future.

Leadership, as we have seen, involves setting a direction based on the leader's vision of the future, aligning people with the vision, and motivating them to achieve it.[3]

Managers, on the other hand, lead by solving or avoiding problems within their existing organization, using leadership and authority to win cooperation from employees, and using the manager's tools of expertise, planning, budgeting and monitoring to accomplish their goals.

Entrepreneurs and managers often are set apart from each other by these important and basic differences in how they perceive a challenge and in how they react to it.

On the other hand, crossover between the two is very common. Entrepreneurs often become managers through changes in circumstance and through an ability to shift gears from envisioning and starting a company to actually running it day by day. From the other side, managers (and employees) are the perennial seeds for the entrepreneurial process, becoming entrepreneurs themselves when they see that problematic situations should be abandoned rather than simply fixed again.

Mary Quass is an excellent example of an employee working her way up to manager, becoming an entrepreneur, transitioning back into being a manager again after selling her company, and then becoming an entrepreneur once more.

Quass began her career in 1977 selling advertising time for KHAK radio in Cedar Rapids, Iowa, thinking it would be a temporary job, but later moving up to station manager.[4] Then in 1988 she saw an oppor-

tunity to found her own radio company and buy KHAK, primarily by managing to borrow a few million dollars and obtaining some seller-financing by the previous owner. (The process of putting this financing together could be the subject of an entire book.) She went on to buy more local radio stations while also managing all of her new acquisitions as her company's president. Her management role became accentuated in 1997 when, like so many other radio entrepreneurs, she sold her stations to one of the largest radio groups in America and ended up heading a 50-station division at Capstar Broadcasting.[5]

Mary Quass

Quass noted that the Telecommunications Act of 1996 "changed the entire direction of our (radio) business" by instantly creating an environment in which large national radio corporations could be formed by individuals and companies with access to vast amounts of capital. Until then, she said, a "large" radio operator might own 10 or so stations, but within a year large conglomerates had taken over the radio industry.[6] Then as now, the largest is Clear Channel Communications Inc. In 1996, Clear Channel owned only 36 radio stations, but by mid-2003 it owned 1,238—nearly all acquired in the first five years after deregulation through a dizzying series of ever larger acquisitions,[7] which included KHAK being sold four times in that same period.

"The Telecommunications Act has made it harder for entrepreneurs because now it's big business," Quass said in 1999 to a University of Iowa journalism class.[8]

In a way, she switched from entrepreneur to manager out of necessity, although she already had worked through much of that transition in operating her own company.

Quass enjoyed both of her roles as an entrepreneur and as a manager, but her highest pride is reserved for her risk-taking, independent, adventurous periods as an entrepreneur accountable to no one but herself.

Those qualities often are what appeal most to entrepreneurs, even more greatly than the money as a matter of fact. Once they've savored the freedom of entrepreneurship and owning their own company, most such people find it very difficult to ever consider working for someone else again, even, sometimes, as a manager.

Quass sees opportunity rather than discouragement in the rapidly changing conditions of her industry, radio. She is ready to start all over again. She will never give up. She is optimistic.

"None of us has been through it, everything is new," she said of the radio industry. "Change is the way we're going to live our lives. We're at a very critical time, when radio needs to change and adapt to our listeners."[9]

Leaders of that adaptation apparently will include Quass. She explored the possibilities of Internet radio in 2001, and by 2002 she had formed a new corporation, NewRadio Group LLC, and purchased 22 radio stations in Wisconsin and Illinois for $19 million.[10] Stay tuned.

Traits of an entrepreneur

ENTREPRENEURS are a special breed of confident and daring contrarians who often are challenged, rather than discouraged, by nay-sayers and the glib experts of conventional wisdom.

Entrepreneurs lead by going outside the "system" with pioneering concepts.

They are people like Roy Reiman, who confounded all conventional wisdom by starting up 11 highly unusual magazines. Unlike every other magazine, none of Reiman's publications accept advertising in their pages. The great bulk of their income comes from subscriptions—$300 million worth of subscriptions in 2000, built on a combined paid circulation of about 16 million. Despite his success, you might never have heard of his magazines, which are targeted toward rural America with titles such as *Taste of Home* (the nation's sixth best-selling consumer magazine, which with 5 million subscribers, comes in just below the much better known *Better Homes & Gardens*). Reiman's other magazines include *Country Woman, Bird & Blooms, Farm & Ranch Living* and *Reminisce*.[11]

A freelance writer in 1970, Reiman noticed that two farming

magazines had eliminated their "women's features," so he started a publication he called *Farm Wife News* and sent out a test mailing of 40,000 copies. His ad-free formula and homespun writing were so appealing that his early prototype evolved into *Country Woman*, which today has a paid circulation of 1.8 million—which is more than *Vogue*, a magazine with which most of us are familiar.[12] Entrepreneurship pays: Reiman sold a controlling interest in his magazine empire in 1998 for $633 million to a Chicago investment company.[13]

And of course there was Turner, who founded CNN in 1980 and thereby proved wrong all the experts who had insisted there was no room for another network besides ABC, CBS and NBC.

Everyone also knows you cannot start a new daily newspaper in America, right? It's too expensive, and the big conglomerates will eat you alive. People have been telling that to Dave Danforth for more than 20 years, but he has started up seven daily papers, beginning with the *Aspen* (Colo.) *Daily News* in 1978 and including his most recent, the *Santa Monica* (Calif.) *Daily Press* in 2001. They are totally unconventional, popping up in cities where previous publishers have sold out or been forced out by big chain competitors. Called "micro-dailies," they defy all the daily newspaper models by borrowing something from some weeklies in that they are distributed free and supported only by advertising.[14]

The fastest growing new media concept is that of a free commuter daily, which was dreamed up by two Swedish reporters, Pelle Anderson and Robert Braunerhielm.[15] The first *Metro* was introduced in Stockholm in 1995. The tabloid, distributed free to transit commuters, came to the United States with *Metro* tabloids established in Philadelphia in 2000 and in Boston in 2001. There also is a Montreal *Metro*. As of early 2003, there were 25 *Metro* editions in 16 countries and 14 languages, making London-based Metro International the world's fourth largest newspaper company in only eight years.[16] In 2001, Metro International began making the entire content of Stockholm *Metro* available to 486,000 Scandinavian subscribers of Viasat's digital television cable service, making it the world's first digital TV newspaper.[17]

Alarmed by the rapid success of *Metro* dailies across the world, the Philadelphia *Metro* was greeted by lawsuits filed by Knight Ridder, Gannett and the New York Times Co., but as of early 2003 the lawsuits had resulted in nothing except massive publicity for *Metro*. A different tack was taken by the *New York Daily News*, which started its own free commuter daily in 2001 called the *Daily News Express*.[18] The worldwide success of *Metro* is one of international journalism's least covered business stories.

A more traditional daily newspaper hit the streets for the first time in the competitive nightmare of New York City, when investors who include Canadian publisher Conrad Black and some venture capitalists used the revered name of the old *New York Sun* for a multi-million dollar start-up venture in spring 2002.[19]

Continually, some entrepreneur somewhere responds to dissatisfaction with the status quo by starting up a new newspaper, Internet site, low-wattage radio station, newsletter, magazine, or some other media business.

They can't help it. Buoyed by confidence, optimism and maybe even a dash of adventure, they know they can do something better, and they can become obsessed with proving it. Very often they are right, and it is from such daring people that change comes.

Promotion or ownership?

THERE IS A POINT in every person's career when he or she decides on whether to continue climbing the corporate ladder or to promote themselves overnight to the top by starting or buying their own company. It was Harvey McKay's opinion that, "Owning 1 percent of something is worth more than managing 100 percent of anything."[20]

William Dean Singleton was one of many who believed in the power of owning rather than managing, and he prepared himself for eventual ownership by learning the newspaper business working for others, eventually rising to become publisher of the *Trenton Times* in New Jersey. But even as the top executive at Trenton, where one of his first decisions was to fire a fourth of the staff,[21] he still was not his own boss. He was an employee of someone else's chain.

In these days of lavish pay and perks for super-CEOs, it certainly is possible to acquire wealth through promotion to the top of a major corporation. A far more satisfying route, however, and perhaps even easier in some ways, is ownership.

It would be great if ownership involved only skill, nerve and opportunity, but it takes money, too. A friend at a newspaper recalled how, as a young man about to graduate from college, he approached a publisher at a convention and asked for a job. The publisher, probably toting one drink too many, garrulously replied that the way to make money in newspapers was to own one, not work for one.[22]

In 1983, Singleton became one of those who has made the fateful decision to strike out on his own. At age 32, he found an investor willing to provide seed money. He founded MediaNews Group, starting with a part-interest in the daily in Woodbury, N.J. By 2002 his company owned a stake or owned outright 55 dailies, some TV stations and numerous weeklies, making MediaNews Group the seventh largest chain in America in less than 20 years,[23] and still privately owned.

Before you make any decision to buy or start up your own media company, you need to ask if you are mentally tough enough. Owners must be willing to put the long-range "greater good" of the company's success over the immediate jobs of some individuals, as hard and unpleasant as that can be.

For example, Singleton gained a reputation of being a "ruthless manager" as he built his chain, repeating his Trenton episode at many of the other papers he acquired, such as when he fired 20 percent of the staff at the *Long Beach* (Calif.) *Press-Telegram* and cut the salaries of the survivors. His response is that he could only afford to buy failing newspapers in the beginning, and the usual crippling reasons included staffs that were inefficient and too large. The only sensible solution was to cut payrolls.[24]

Trying repeatedly is what brings 'luck'

THIS SECTION was inspired by what might be the slimmest business volume ever written, Dale Dauten's *The Max Strategy*.[25] Dauten is referred to often in this book through his syndicated newspaper columns on business. *The Max Strategy* is just a little more than 100 pages long and takes an hour or less to read. Its theme is that success is a matter of constantly experimenting and failing and being alert to opportunities when you do stumble across them as a result of always trying something new.

"If you aren't smart and hardworking and all that, you're going to fail ten times out of ten," Dauten notes. "But if you do all the right things, guess what? You fail (only) nine times out of ten."[26]

Dauten continues: "Keep experimenting, which is a trial-and-error, bump around, muddle-through, random, messy business . . . . Given enough chances, chance is your friend."[27]

Maybe your great breakthrough or invention will even be what other less imaginative people would think was a mistake. The 3M Company spends about a billion dollars a year on research and development. However, some of 3M's most profitable products resulted from blunders, including Post-It Notes from a failed glue and Scotchgard from a beaker of liquid dropped on a lab's floor. "When we put together a batch of product development stories, we were embarrassed," a 3M executive told Dauten. "It made us look like a bunch of klutzes."[28] Numerous books have been written on the phenomenon of accidental inventions.

Luck certainly is a factor in business. Sometimes you really are in the right place at the right time, get "discovered" by the right person, stumble across a breakthrough product, accidentally discover a formula for what becomes a multi-million-dollar market.

But, reminiscent of what Dauten says, Mark Twain was the first of many who observed that the harder they worked, the luckier they got. Add to that the well-known old folk saying that luck is a lazy person's explanation for a hard-working person's success. You need to be out there actively looking for luck if luck is going to have the best chance of finding you.

Success in business often is a combination of a great idea, luck, and perseverance.

Tips for entrepreneurs

FOLLOWING ARE some tips for those who aspire to be entrepreneurs. Though slanted toward the specific media business of weekly newspapers, their general points could apply to any media business.

On the entrepreneurship track, the sure way to achieve management status is to start or buy your own business. A word of caution, however, on going into business for yourself. You should have worked for some other company in that field first to give yourself the best possible chance of success once you strike out on your own.

In your own business, even without employees, you must learn to become very disciplined in the management of yourself. That can be difficult for some people. With employees, of course, proper management of others becomes a far more serious prospect than just the promotability of some employed manager. Proper management by a small business owner very often is the difference between life or death of the entire company.

You will never work harder in your life than the couple of years after you start or buy your own business. Ownership is not for the faint-hearted, the indecisive, or the lover of steady pay and generous fringe benefits. Modest or extreme wealth can be the final result, but usually not in the earliest years.

Today's biggest challenge to buying a business is the fact that everyone fears change. Journalism salaries have been rising in recent years, everyone has valuable fringe benefits, and journalism job security seems to be getting more reasonable, now that the 2001 recession is behind us. It can seem safe and comfortable in the corporate cocoon.

But here's something to ponder: You'll never be able to build much wealth by just drawing a salary from someone else.

Now is the best time to start considering the possibility of buying or starting your own newspaper, radio station, or other media firm. The 30s and 40s are the age range when such ambitions are realized—or set aside forever. Once past their mid-40s, few people will become a first-time buyer, though start-ups can continue with people into their 60s.

There must be an entrepreneurial zeal in you as a buyer or start-up, plus a level of self-confidence that can accept calculated risk. Think of a skydiving analogy: A person must be willing to risk free-falling for a while.

The rewards are great. Entrepreneurs can do things their way, pay themselves what they think they are worth, and be building equity all at the same time.

The greatest ownership risk lies in one's ability to manage operational assets, sales and people. Inability to manage either of the first two can be fatal. Inability to manage people can be fatal, too, but usually it will just make your life miserable.

Of course, there is that problem of money.

Even the smallest five-day dailies will sell for over $1 million. A mid-sized radio station will sell for nearly that much. That's quite an entry barrier for most first-time individual buyers.

That's why most first-time buyers look to small and mid-sized weeklies as their best chance to become publishers. It is fortunate there is such a wonderful opportunity in newspapering. Along with some dot-com companies, advertising firms and public relations offices, weekly newspapers are among the only kinds of media companies still affordable enough for an individual to buy or start. Radio stations used to be affordable, but not since they attracted the attention of the conglomerates in 1996.

You will be expected to come up with a down payment of one-fourth to one-third of the purchase price, with the remainder financed.

Be forewarned, however. Most banks are stubbornly reluctant to lend to first-time business buyers, with or without a Small Business Administration (SBA) guarantee of the loan. Your best bet is to begin saving toward a down payment as soon as possible, and look to seller-financing and other sources for the rest. Banks will be happy to pick you up as a customer later—after you've succeeded with your first paper.

Make sure you see three years of financials before you buy, and run them by a CPA. After you take out what's needed to service your debt and pay taxes, make sure there's enough left to pay you. If so, this might be the time to take the big step forward and buy your own company.

Starting up a business

SEE A NEED? Then fill it. That's about as simply and directly as you can describe the motivation for an entrepreneur to begin a new company or a new product. New companies start up by the tens of thousands each year in the United States, the land of capitalistic opportunity and American ingenuity.

Most fail, unfortunately, and they fail because of poor management skills far more often than because of a faulty product.

It's been proven time and again that the superior product idea often fails in the market against an inferior product if it's the latter that has the benefit of better management.

In hindsight, most would agree that the Tucker Torpedo auto was far safer and more innovative than any General Motors or Ford model of 1948; the Betamax was a superior technology in the 1970s to the VHS video player; and the 1984 Macintosh operating system was much easier to use and vastly more reliable than Microsoft's MS-DOS (which was based on QDOS, an acronym meaning "Quick and Dirty Operating System," which Microsoft bought from another developer for $50,000).

But we all know who won those competitions. What we might not realize is that the winning companies won not on the basis of product, but because they did a better job of mastering critical management skills to enable their products to succeed in the marketplace. Superior management and, in turn superior marketing, were the keys to victory—not superior product.

The importance of good management is rated so highly by venture capital companies that they often will be willing to finance a company with an outstanding management team even if they have lingering doubts about the company's product. William Hearst III recalled venture capitalist John Doerr telling him that, in evaluating an investment, Doerr would consider whether he trusted the leadership enough that he would be willing to get into trouble with them, because he knew that sooner or later he probably would.[29]

How important is leadership? Business researchers such as Warren Bennis and Fred E. Fiedler go so far as to say that leadership is the most important factor in a company's performance.

"If I have learned anything from my research, it is this," Bennis wrote. "The factor that empowers the workforce and ultimately determines which organizations succeed or fail is the leadership of those organizations. When strategies, processes or cultures change, the key to improvement remains leadership."[30]

Similarly, Fiedler observed, "The success or failure of an organization depends on the quality of its management."[31]

Perhaps you are determined to become this most important person, the organization's leader. If you make a conscious effort to develop the qualities of leadership referred to in this book, then the opportunity to run your own company is opened up to you.

Probably little else has greater allure in America's capitalist society than the dream many people have of starting their own company, being their own boss and, of course, becoming rich.

The five-year success rate is dismal, but you can improve your odds greatly by doing one thing that an astonishingly high number of people trying to start their own business do not do—conduct extensive preliminary research and planning.

One of the best resources available (maybe the best for the price—it's free) is the U.S. Small Business Administration. The SBA is well known for its 90-percent guarantees of bank loans to help small businesses. It also has tremendous advice resources as well, including a mentoring program for new entrepreneurs in many cities where experienced business retirees will take you by the hand and guide you through the critical early days, months and years.

Despite all of this book's talk of conglomerates and stifling competitive pressures, there still are a large number of entrepreneurial opportunities among media companies. Individuals constantly are starting up or buying small business operations in weeklies and niche publications, shoppers, radio and TV stations, advertising and public relations firms, and the Internet.

Starting up a company is the least expensive option to owning your own business, though I believe it is usually the most risky.

There are those who certainly disagree. Entrepreneur Norm Brodsky warns in *Inc.* magazine that first-time buyers of businesses often are so unsophisticated and impulsive that they pay too much for a business or buy a dying enterprise. Thus, he maintains they would be better off to start a business instead.[32]

What he says is true for anyone acting unwisely. It is certainly true that many businesses are put up for sale because they are on the brink of ruin, and it is the seller's hope that a buyer will come along who is reckless enough to make an ill-advised purchase. Such sellers want you to go broke instead of them.

What Brodsky doesn't acknowledge is that it is also very common for someone to start up a business and use such bad judgment that the new business is doomed to failure. He ignores the fact that numerous studies show that most start-ups fail.

Follow the advice in this chapter's opening essays, research the target business intelligently, and rely on professional advice from others more experienced than you such as lawyers, accountants, former business owners, and lenders. If you do, it is far more likely you will succeed by buying an established business with a verified marketplace position, product and cash flow than you usually will by starting up a business with no record of achievement.

To succeed in a start-up or a business purchase, you need to have a business plan and cash, or access to cash. First, consider the business plan, and then the need for cash.

Seeking success with a business plan

IMPROVE YOUR chance for success by taking the time up front to explore and evaluate your business and personal goals. Then use this information to build a comprehensive and well-thought-out business plan that will help you reach these goals.

The following information is taken from the SBA's "How to Start a Small Business" Web site by following the <www.sba.gov/> main page address.

Starting and managing a business takes motivation, desire and talent. It also takes research and planning. Like a chess game, success in small business starts with decisive and correct opening moves. And although initial mistakes usually are not fatal, it takes skill, discipline and hard work to regain the advantage.

The process of developing a business plan will help you think through some important issues that you may not have considered. Your plan will become a valuable tool as you set out to raise money for your business. It should also provide milestones to gauge your success.

1. Getting Started—Before starting out, list your reasons for wanting to go into business. Some of the most common reasons for starting a business are:

• You want to be your own boss.

• You want financial independence.

- You want creative freedom.
- You want to fully use your skills and knowledge.

2. Next, you need to determine what business is "right for you." Ask yourself these questions:

- What do I like to do with my time?
- What technical skills have I learned or developed?
- What do others say I am good at?
- Will I have the support of my family?
- How much time do I have to run a successful business?
- Do I have any hobbies or interests that are marketable?

3. Then you should identify the niche your business will fill. Conduct the necessary research to answer these questions:

- What business am I interested in starting?
- What services or products will I sell?
- Is my idea practical, and will it fill a need?
- What is my competition?
- What is my business advantage over existing firms?
- Can I deliver a better quality service?
- Can I create a demand for my business?

4. The final step before developing your plan is the pre-business checklist. You should answer these questions:

- What skills and experience do I bring to the business?
- What will be my legal structure?
- How will my company's business records be maintained?
- What insurance coverage will be needed?
- What equipment or supplies will I need?
- How will I compensate myself?
- What are my resources?
- What financing will I need?
- Where will my business be located?
- What will I name my business?[33]

Your answers will help you create a focused, well-researched business plan. It should serve as a operational blueprint. It should detail how the business will be managed and capitalized.

One of the most important cornerstones of starting a business is this business plan. SBA offers you a tutorial on preparing a solid plan with all its essential ingredients on its Web site. Once you have completed your business plan, review it with a business mentor. When you feel comfortable with the content and structure, make an appointment to review and discuss it with your banker. The business plan is a flexible document that should change as your business grows.

This business plan is probably the most important single document an entrepreneur can prepare before starting a business. Try to be as objective as possible in writing it, with realistic budget and marketing projections based on research and your own truly best guess. It should take you days, or even weeks or months to prepare if you do it right. An excellent outline for a business plan is at <www.sba.gov/starting/indexbusplans.html>, and many others also are on the Web.

The necessity of money

C ASH. You'll need some if you want to start up or buy a business, so the best advice is to start saving now. Loans and other forms of other people's money are extremely important, but in the end you still need your own cash if you want to have a successful long-term business instead of a flash in the pan.

In buying any kind of business, you will need to come up with enough capital to pay a fourth to a third of the purchase price up front. Wilbur M. Yegge, an experienced business broker, puts it succinctly in his book on how to buy a business when he declares, "It is quite difficult to acquire business property with less than a 25 percent *cash* down payment."[34] That's Yegge's own emphasis on the word "cash."

He puts the life of an entrepreneur in perspective. "In purchasing (or starting) a small, closely-held business," he notes, "we traditionally leave the world of working for others and become self-employed. Regardless of the business type, and its ability to meet cash needs, we are, in no small sense, buying a job."[35]

That is why banks and credit unions are reluctant to lend money to a first-time business. If you are buying a $300,000 house, it is easy for the lender to determine if you have enough income from your job to pay back the principal plus interest on a loan. The collateral also is easy to evaluate. If you want to borrow $300,000 to buy or start a business, however, you will have little or no other income as a rule, and so the lender must decide if there will be adequate cash flow from that business to pay off the loan. If the lender knows nothing about your business acumen, your loan is a much riskier proposition.

Yegge gives the following criteria on how a lender determines interest or disinterest in financing a purchase (or, in a modified sense, a start-up) of a business. It's an excellent checklist for the entrepreneur as well. Taken from his book, Yegge says a lender will consider:[36]

- Overall marketplace appeal of the business, its products, and/or services;

- Realism of cash down payment and other terms of sale;

- Realism of debt load to cash flow;

- Stability of historic cash flow;

- Predictable longevity of business;

- Economic, environmental factors outside direct influence of business or owner;

- Extent of "displacement" or lost marketing effort caused by the retiring owner;

- Ability of owner to fill retiring owner's shoes; and

- Technical knowledge required to run a business (lenders evaluate this risk in terms of buyer failure, foreclosure, and the ability to resell their collateral).

Yegge lists one more point, motivation of the seller, and it is the single most important point to keep in mind when trying to buy a business. Make sure your contract gives you some recourse in case they resort to outright lies to convince you to buy their business. Others want to sell a business because they are burned out, they have family difficulties, they want to try something else, or they want to retire.

Business broker Robert F. Klueger's all-important observation on this point about motivation is this: "Why does the seller want to sell the business? If you don't know the answer to this question with reasonable certainty, you don't know anything."[37]

If you are without a track record in running a business, most lenders simply will not loan you money. I cannot say it any more directly than that. Even if you qualify for an SBA guarantee, it probably will be extremely difficult for you to obtain traditional financing on the start-up or purchase of a first business. Even a profitable business can be quickly ruined by an incompetent new owner, and all lenders have seen it happen too many times.

This huge obstacle to first-time financing is what drives many entrepreneurs to use the "easy money" available through maxing out their credit card. You hear about the few successes who created their company by loading up their credit cards. What you don't hear about is the vast majority who do it and end up badly, even bankrupt. I urge the strongest caution before you take on 18 percent-plus financing from any source, but especially from credit cards. If it's too easy, as in using a credit card, then it's probably the wrong way to go.

There are other sources for the miracle of cash. Your savings account is the obvious one, but these days—again, largely because of credit cards—many people do not have much in savings.

If you want to be an entrepreneur, however, you will have some money saved. Frankly, a savings account is a sound indicator of your financial discipline and of how successful you will be in business. Spendthrifts rarely survive in small business. Lack of adequate personal savings is a death blow to any hopes for other financing.

But even a savings account can fall short of what you need for a cash down payment on a business costing, say, $100,000 or more. That size of a company is about as small as you can buy and still expect to get a return that is worth the work you will be putting into this new job you just bought. Do the math on the cash flow expected from any business before you buy. Is it enough for you?

Beware of promises of financial help from friends. Dear old mom and dad usually can be relied upon to carry through with their promise. But no matter how enthusiastic they sound, other people generally will disappoint you when it comes time to pony up the money. By the way, lenders often look askance at money borrowed from family and friends anyway, and might actually hold it against you in considering whether to approve your loan for all or some of the remainder.

One source of cash that many do not realize exists lies in your life insurance policy. Most insurance companies will allow you to borrow the "cash value" of your policy at a low interest rate. Many companies do not even require you to pay it back (what a great loan!); they just reduce your death benefit proportionately. The longer you have had the policy, the larger the cash value, which can total thousands of dollars. Talk to a financial adviser first.

If you have stocks, you can sell them. That goes for other assets as well. Do you really need that second car or adult toys like the motorcycle and boat you own? If not, sell.

You might be surprised at how much cash you can generate from your own assets if you really set your mind to it. You also might be dismayed to realize how deep you might need to dig to do it.

Save some of your money to buy at least one or two books written by experts on how to buy or start up a business. The few paragraphs on financing alternatives that this book provides are expanded on greatly in business books such as *A Basic Guide for Buying and Selling a Business*, by Yegge, and *How to Buy a Business,* by Richard A. Joseph, along with a lot of other information you need to know.

The latter book makes a strong point about savings by noting that other people—such as lenders and business partners—will measure your credibility by how much of your own money you are willing to risk. "If (the entrepreneur) contributes capital, the investment will seem more credible to the other participants and it may, therefore, be easier to raise money," the book points out.[38]

But why are we even talking about banks or credit unions? Even with the SBA guarantee, most lenders still are reluctant to provide money for an unproven entrepreneur.

To emphasize the point, the major source of financing for most business acquisitions is the seller.

According to *The Business Broker* newsletter, about three-fourths of business sales involve seller-financing, as it is called, often for the full amount after down payment.

Knowing this fact, which you might not realize if you didn't take any business classes, can help you get off to an early start on owning your own business. People think they cannot afford to buy a business. Now you know that for a business priced at $100,000, for example, you only need about $25,000 to $35,000. Maybe less. That's still a lot of money, but it's not $100,000.

One caution on seller-financing is that the terms are anything the buyer and seller agree on. There are no set rules, as there are in institutional lending.

When sellers finally concede they need to carry three-fourths or so of the price to sell the business, most will try to make the amount they are financing due as soon as possible through a "balloon payment." Typically, a seller will try to reassure the buyer that by then financing will be available through the local bank. Well, maybe it will be and maybe it won't.

Most seller-financing contracts are for at least five years, and frequently they go out to ten years or more. For a lot of reasons, Yegge points out in his book, "Notes calling for balloon principal payments being made in less than five years demand utmost scrutiny, for sellers to get paid without continuing stress and for buyers who want to survive the financing ordeal."[39]

Seller-financing requires a lawyer to draw up a Purchase Contract between the buyer and the seller. Examples of such agreements can be found on the Internet and in books such as those cited in the endnotes at the end of this chapter.

A full guide on how to buy or start up a business is not possible in this one chapter. But there is one more basic point encountered in nearly every business purchase. That question is whether you should buy the assets of the company, or the company itself. If you buy a sole proprietorship, you are buying the whole business, but you can buy just the assets if the business is a partnership or corporation.

The seller will want you to buy the full business because of tax advantages to the seller and because it is the easiest. If the business is a corporation, for example, the seller simply endorses the stock certificate to the buyer and the deal, for all practical purposes, is accomplished if the financing already is arranged.

Generally speaking, it is best from a buyer's perspective to purchase only the assets, including the business name.

If you buy the entire business instead of just the assets, as one example, you become liable for any lawsuit brought against the company for past actions even before you were the owner—such as from libel or sexual discrimination committed under the previous ownership. This unexpected eventuality could ruin an otherwise sound business.

There are a few situations when you might need to buy an entire corporation because a valuable asset cannot be transferred. A radio station's broadcast license might be owned by the corporation and not be capable of being transferred. In that case, there is no choice but to buy the entire business structure instead of just the assets.[40]

If you do buy the entire business, however, include a contract provision whereby the seller indemnifies you against anything that didn't happen on your watch.

A final warning: Entrepreneurs who think they can start or buy a small business, and then relax on a beach or hammock while their employees do all the work, will be in for a nasty shock. Many small companies fail because of lazy owners.

In his aptly named book, *How to Buy a Newspaper and Succeed,* James J. Brodell states, "Newspaper ownership (or any kind of media company ownership) requires a rare combination of skill, guts and intuition found only in a few persons. You have to have the heart for the job. The long hours are not all compensated by money. There is an intangible pride that goes a long way towards paying back the owner-publisher . . . . Ask anyone who has done it. Each will tell you the work was hard, sometimes very frustrating, but generally the best times of his or her life."[41]

When should you buy a small media company?

Well, consider Malcolm Forbes Sr., who went on to become a famous magazine publisher. Forbes wrote his senior thesis at Princeton University in 1941 on weekly newspapers. He bought his first weekly two days after graduation.[42]

Ten secrets of entrepreneurial success

(1) First, there are no secrets. Understand the fundamentals of business before you get involved in starting, owning or managing a business. Those fundamentals include but certainly are not limited to the competence of experience, the need for lots of sweat equity, the time value of money, the four P's of marketing, the hidden traps of decision-making, rules for leadership and management skills, and the happiness of a positive cash flow.

(2) A business idea is not necessarily a business opportunity. Be as sure as is reasonable that you're right before you commit financially. But remember, make that decision before you're 100 percent sure or you'll be too late.

(3) There is no such thing as no competition. If you have a business idea no one else has thought of, be assured that competition will appear as soon as others see your success. Be prepared.

(4) Maintain a positive attitude; strive for optimistic realism.

(5) Business success is a human process and not totally a financial or technological process. You can make a difference.

(6) Treat people fairly. That includes yourself and your family, as well as your employees, customers and all other stakeholders.

(7) Do sweat the small stuff—at least when it comes to financial management. Even one small unnecessary cost in the budget repeated day after day adds up, and up, and up.

(8) Marketing and financial mismanagement can quickly and sometimes even silently destroy a company. Personnel mismanagement might not ruin your company, but it can make your life hell. Remember that no single management style works for everyone.

(9) Unless you win the lottery (and the odds are extreme that you won't), success is neither quick nor painless. Hard work, perseverance and constant attention to customers are what count in business.

(10) Never, ever run out of cash.

CASE STUDY   Taking that Big Step:
                   Buying a Business

by HUGH S. FULLERTON, Ph.D.
Sam Houston State University

(Fifth in a series of five related case studies)

Jerry has decided to look further into the purchase of *The Call*. He has seen the P&L and balance sheet of Jamestown Call Inc., parent company of *The Call*, and they show a company that has been moderately profitable over the past five years. The current owner is taking out a modest salary to support himself and his wife, who also works in the business.

The financial information has been put together by a CPA, so Jerry is reasonably confident that the information is accurate. Besides, he rather likes the owner, and can see himself living a similar lifestyle in a small community.

Jerry is not one to take things on faith, however. His reporting background tells him he needs to get a lot more information before he makes such an important decision. He mentally categorizes the information he needs into three broad areas:

• The company. Is it being run efficiently? Can he squeeze more profit out of it to make the monthly payments to the seller?

• The community. What is the potential for maintaining and increasing advertising and circulation?

• Being a newsman, Jerry thinks a lot about news. How might a small town differ from a medium size city in its news preferences? Will the readers like the way that Jerry pursues news?

What specific information should Jerry try to get before proceeding with the deal?

AUTHOR:

Hugh S. Fullerton was a reporter at daily newspapers and also was publisher of a group of weekly newspapers in Michigan for several years. He is an associate professor of journalism at Sam Houston State University in Huntsville, Texas.

🖳 Suggested Web sites:

www.sba.gov/starting/indexsteps.html — SBA site on starting a business
www.sba.gov/starting/indexbusplans.html — SBA site on business plans
www.bizmove.com — Articles on business entrepreneurship
www.youngentrepreneur.com — Young Entrepreneur Web site

Endnotes to Chapter 11:

[1] Alexander B. Brook, *The Hard Way: The Odyssey of a Weekly Newspaper Editor* (Bridgehampton, N.Y.: Bridge Works Publishing, 1993).

[2] Lynn Elber, The Associated Press, as published in "Turner recalls empire not purchased," *Albuquerque Journal*, November 30, 2001, D5.

[3] "Short-term wins: The linchpin of a change initiative," *Harvard Management Update* (August 1999): 2.

[4] Jim Jacobson, "Cedar Rapids woman named broadcaster of the year," Cedar Rapids, Iowa, *Gazette*, February 12, 1999.

[5] Mary Quass, remarks to media management class at the University of Iowa, September 9, 1999.

[6] Ibid.

[7] Jeff Leeds, for the *Los Angeles Times*, "Numbers give big clout to radio: Clear Channel's growth prompts allegations of bullying," as published in the *Albuquerque Journal*, March 3, 2002, C-1, and in "Radio broadcast merger completed," Cedar Rapids, Iowa, *Gazette*, August 30, 2000.

[8] Quass, remarks of September 9, 1999.

[9] Quass, remarks of September 9, 1999.

[10] Quass, interview with author, August 25, 2000.

[11] Paulette Thomas, "A magazine publisher finds fertile ground for profits," *The Wall Street Journal* Interactive Edition (August 23, 2000): Rocket e-book, 128–129.

[12] Ibid., 133–134.

[13] Ibid., 143.

[14] Hilary E. MacGregor , "The inside scoop from outsiders: Sure, they may have a formula for success, but Santa Monica isn't the easiest place to launch a daily newspaper," *Los Angeles Times* (January 9, 2002) at<www.latimes.com/features/lifestyle/la010902smpapers.story?coll=la %2Dheadlines%2Dliving>, accessed January 13, 2002.

[15] John Fischer, "Metro launch causes media frenzy," at <www.philadelphia.about.com/library/ weekly/blmetro.com.htm>, accessed January 12, 2003.

[16] Metro International S.A., at <www.metro.lu>, accessed January 12, 2003.

[17] Charlie White, "Sweden launches first DTV newspaper," at <www.dtvprofessional.com/ 2001/08_aug/news/cw_metro_dtv_news.htm>, accessed January 12, 2003.

[18] Gabriel Spitzer, "A year old, Metro has yet to wow Philadelphia," at <www.medialife magazine.com/news2001/feb01/feb12/5_fri/news3Friday.html>, accessed January 12, 2003.

[19] Lucia Moses, "'Sun': It shines for some," *Editor & Publisher* (January 21, 2002): 12.

[20] Harvey Mackay, *Swim with the Sharks without Being Eaten Alive* (New York: William Morrow & Co., 1988), 183.

[21] Benjamin M. Compaine and Douglas Gomery, *Who Owns the Media? Competition and Concentration in the Mass Media Industry* (Mahwah, N.J.: Lawrence Erlbaum Associates, 3rd ed., 2000), 24.

[22] Jim A. Frost, assistant design editor at the *Albuquerque Journal,* in interview with author, November 18, 2002.

[23] William Dean Singleton, in keynote address at the state convention of the New Mexico Press Association, November 2, 2002.

[24] Compaine and Gomery, *Who Owns the Media?* 24.

[25] Dale Dauten, *The Max Strategy: How a Businessman Got Stuck at an Airport and Learned to Make His Career Take Off* (New York: William Morrow and Company, 1996).

[26] Ibid., 27.

[27] Ibid.

[28] Ibid., 72.

[29] Shelby Coffey III, *Best Practices: The Art of Leadership in News Organizations* (Arlington, Va.: Freedom Forum, 2002), 57.

[30] Warren Bennis, "The 4 competencies of leadership," *Training & Development Journal* (August 1984): 16.

[31] Fred E. Fiedler. Reprinted by permission of *Harvard Business Review.* From "Engineer the job to fit the manager," 43 (1965): 115. © 1965 by Harvard Business School Publishing Corporation, all rights reserved.

[32] Norm Brodsky, "Caveat emptor," *Inc.* magazine (August 1998): 31–32.

[33] "How to Start a Small Business," as presented by the U.S. Small Business Administration at <www.sba.gov/starting/indexsteps.html>, accessed December 23, 2001.

[34] Wilbur M. Yegge, *A Basic Guide for Buying and Selling a Company* (New York: John Wiley & Sons Inc., 1996), 13.

[35] Ibid., 12.

[36] Ibid., 131–132.

[37] Robert F. Klueger, *Buying and Selling a Business: A Step by Step Guide* (New York: John Wiley & Sons Inc., 1988), 10.

[38] Richard A. Joseph, with Anna M. Nekoranec and Carl H. Steffens, *How to Buy a Business* (Chicago: Enterprise•Dearborn, 1993), 127.

[39] Yegge, 82–83.

[40] Ibid., 105–106.

[41] James J. Brodell, *How to Purchase a Newspaper and Succeed* (Grand Junction, Colo.: Mountain West Publishing Co., 1982), 1.

[42] "Weekly Almanac," *NewsInc.* magazine (November 1991): 8.

CHAPTER 12
TECHNOLOGY CREATES NEW MEDIA

ROGER F. FIDLER, in his forward-looking 1997 book *Media-morphosis*,[1] wrote of the social, political and economic forces that have resulted in profound cultural changes in the United States since the end of World War II, and how they have made an impact on present-day technology.

Fidler wrote, "Historians and sociologists generally agree that our culture has been shaped in the past five decades by the convergence of three momentous postwar developments: (1) The Cold War and the United States' emergence as the world's dominant economic, political and military superpower; (2) the explosive rise in birth rates immediately following World War II that produced a great baby boom; (3) the rapid diffusion of television and other electronic media throughout all social and economic strata of society."[2]

That diffusion of electronic innovation continues at a rapid pace throughout all of the media industry. In fact, the adoption of technological breakthroughs in both print and broadcast have come at a dizzying pace since the emergence of desktop computers pioneered in the early 1980s by Atari, Commodore and Apple.

The world has never seen such a quick and wholesale adoption of new technology. Even today's commonplace television sets did not catch on as quickly as desktop computers and the accompanying digital communications technology of the Internet.

In 1982, a crude thermal imaging facsimile machine was still considered a rarely encountered and expensive use of telephone lines, electric typewriters were state-of-the-art word processing for almost everyone, and desktop computers were marketed more as toys than business machines. Computers for business use were mostly seen only in the largest corporate settings.

In those not-so-long-ago days, a system of electronic storage and retrieval of information between computers over telephone connections, known as ARPANET, existed only inside the military and a few university research institutions. It was starting to be called the Internet, but only a few high-tech, computer-savvy people could access it. Most of us had never heard of it in the early to mid-1980s.

No one could have imagined where we would arrive less than 20 years later. "This decade's (the 1990s) big puzzle is new media," said former FCC Chairman Alfred C. Sykes. "What is it, people and companies ask . . . . What kind of shape will it take? Can new media businesses be built and, if so, how long will it take? The questions go on and on."[3]

And yet, there were some prophets, a few who saw more clearly than others into a near future of possibilities even though they could not guess at the specifics.

Journalism educator Benjamin M. Compaine seems downright prescient today when we realize he wrote in that year of 1982, "The technology that transformed the internal methods for producing the newspaper in the 1970s, i.e., computers and video display terminals, was threatening to reach out to the world of the consumer. Systems were being put into place to create what might be called the electronic newspaper, videotext or data-base publishing. Whatever the term, the promise was that the consumer would be able to get all or much of the content of the newspaper delivered via some electronic highway. Telephone lines were one route. The cable that brought in video was another. Over the air, via broadcasting, was yet a third pathway."[4]

This was published two years before Apple began marketing its desktop laser printer in 1984; three years before America On Line was founded in 1985; seven years before Tim Berners-Lee wrote the first information retrieval software in 1989 to begin accessing ARPANET's resources; and a full decade before students and software developers at the University of Illinois developed a "user-friendly" graphical user interface (GUI) browser in 1992, which allowed the World Wide Web to burst upon the scene a year later with a few hundred Web sites.

Consumer-affordable scanners, digital cameras, satellite television, Internet radio, satellite radio, hand-held computing devices, desktop computers more powerful than the first room-sized military computer ENIAC, and a host of other electronic technologies have burst upon us with astounding rapidity in recent years, accompanied by billions of Web pages and hundreds of millions of Internet users around the globe. For all of his vision, not even Compaine could have ever foreseen such wondrous technology materializing in less than two decades.

The challenge—both life-sustaining and life-threatening—that faces all media companies is how to best exploit all of the technological developments of the present and future so as to re-invent themselves as new media companies.

Technology and the new media resulting from it are transforming journalism in four major ways, according to journalism educator John V. Pavlik.[5]

First, the content of the media is changing because of the new technology being brought to bear in the practice of journalism, including interactive news with audience involvement, omnidirectional cameras, increased pressure to cover news stories fast, and the ability to customize and personalize news for individuals.

Second, the way journalists do their work is being rethought in the digital age. Media sites are moving from "shovelware," where stories simply are placed online with little or no change from the original source, be it a newspaper story or a TV story, to the creation of original content for the Web. A third stage is being entered where the content not only is original but is written specifically for Web or Web-like interactivity.

Third, the physical structure of the newsroom is undergoing major change as many newspapers, TV stations, and even magazines are being remodeled to accommodate convergence strategies that combine more than one outlet in a newsroom. Various concepts for mobile journalist workstations are being developed that strap onto the reporter a variety of equipment such as digital cameras, a GPS receiver, telephone, a head-mounted display, wireless computer access, etc.

Fourth, new media are realigning news organizations, journalists and the consumers of media. New ethics questions are posed by much of the new technology, such as the omnicamera that is filming you even when it is pointed in a different direction, remote controlled flying cameras, Sony's new infrared camcorder that can see through clothes, and satellite photography from miles up in space. There are also privacy concerns brought on by the Web.

In *Management Challenges for the 21st Century*, Peter F. Drucker notes that we are now in what he calls the Fourth Information Revolution. The first one was the invention of writing in present-day Iraq more than 5,000 years ago. The second revolution was the written book, first produced in China about 1300 B.C. And the third revolution was the invention of the printing press and movable type in about 1450.[6]

Just as Fidler reported three great changes changing society after World War II, Drucker also has a mix of technological and social changes that he believes are going to profoundly affect society in the 21st century.

The great baby boom changed society in the last 50 years of the 20th century, but Drucker said the ironic difference for the foreseeable future is the totally unexpected collapse of the birth rate now going on in all the industrialized nations. He calls population decline the "most important new certainty" of the new century because birth rates have fallen below population sustainability in the developed nations of the North American, European and Asian continents.

"In Japan and in Southern Europe, population is already peaking, as it is in Germany," Drucker said. "In the United States it will still grow for another 20 to 25 years (thanks to new immigrants), though the entire growth after the year 2015 will be in people 55 years and older."[7]

Even more significant than the declining population is the age distribution, he said, as an increasingly larger proportion of the total population becomes more than 60 years old, thus skewing the familiar balance between those who are working and those who are retired.

This change will have enormous implications no one can do more than guess at for now about immigration, retirement policy, political stability, social norms and economics—and very definitely in the way business is conducted.

How that big picture will affect our little picture of media companies and the increasing technological changes in our industry is still to be seen, but change is already here, and more change is coming.

In a 2002 speech to the New Mexico Press Association, MediaNews Group CEO William Dean Singleton said technology will be the newspaper industry's largest challenge in the coming years, but he emphasized that technology also will be newspapering's savior.[8]

Managers will need all of the insight and leadership they can muster as the walls come tumbling down between the news department and all of the other business-oriented departments of today's market-driven media companies. The general marketing of a media company as a business—with all that entails in terms of market penetration, segmentation, image-building, sales, research and marketing—plus the reliance for revenue on that most peculiar commodity of the media, advertising, is sure to lead to natural conflicts with the news role. To appeal to an increasingly aging and in some cases diminishing population, media companies might adopt new strategies of competition or intensify the current efforts.

The challenge of today's generation is to adapt to the inevitable while preserving the core values of responsible journalism. It will not be easy.

Newspapers and technology

FIDLER IS best known for his research and efforts to develop a portable tablet newspaper. He spearheaded an early project by Knight Ridder to develop a tablet newspaper. For four years, Fidler led a Knight Ridder tablet newspaper research team until Knight Ridder executives scuttled the project in 1995 out of concern they were too far ahead of their time.[9]

He went on to continue his work developing tablet newspapers and other digital-based communications technologies at Kent State University as director of its Institute for CyberInformation.

Finally, in late October 2002, at the annual meeting of the Inland Press Association, Fidler demonstrated an electronic newspaper on a Tablet PC that had downloaded 210 PDF (portable document format) pages of the *Los Angeles Times* over the Internet. The Tablet PC is 8.25 by 10.7 inches, about one inch thick, weighs three pounds and features color clarity, audio and video capabilities.[11]

The electronic tablet newspaper, introduced in 2002 after two decades of research by Roger Fidler.[10]

It hit the stores in early 2003 for the hefty price of about $2,500, which is expected to come down as it gains acceptance.

The Tablet PC with the newspaper software is being referred to by Fidler's two-decade-ago term as the tablet newspaper (not to be confused with an alternative print weekly by that name in Seattle).

The tablet newspaper was made possible by two technologies converging in 2002 into a single platform. Fidler devised a prototype electronic newspaper in 1991, the first year that Fujitsu produced the first of what has turned out to be 18 generations of tablet computers.[12]

All that was needed was wireless technology, high capacity hard drives, screen resolution, the Internet and fast connections, handwriting recognition, and a few dozen other high-tech achievements to all catch up with the original pair of ideas.

Several manufacturers began producing different versions of the wireless Tablet PC in 2002, powered by the Windows XP Tablet PC operating system from Microsoft.

One of those models, the Compaq, was the first to combine PDF software from Adobe Systems Inc., a pioneering effort from the *Los Angeles Times*, and a newspaper template called the Kent format to create the first tablet newspaper.

"The Kent format blends contemporary newspaper layouts with Web-like interactive hypermedia in a magazine-like page layout," Fidler explained.[13]

The abilities of the 2002 tablet newspaper are remarkably similar to the prototype he was working on at the Knight Ridder lab, which was featured in a 1994 video titled "The Tablet Newspaper: A Vision for the Future." The accuracy of that vision was especially remarkable taking into consideration that the Internet was just barely available that year through public browsers.

So the vision of the future now has arrived, with an accomplishment that could have been Knight Ridder's passing instead to Kent State.

"The debate now," Fidler noted, "is whether 20 years from now newspapers will be on paper."[14] The same thing could be said in large part for books and magazines.

But until the tablet newspaper's price comes down, the main newspaper strategy for digital delivery in 2003 remained Web sites and beyond that online downloads to wireless phones, personal digital assistants, pagers, desktop computers, and even audible editions that read the news to you while you are driving.

All agree now that digital delivery, increasingly wireless, is how newspapers and many other print products will be delivered in the near future, saving the lives of millions of trees every year.

The first small steps in this race to digital delivery already are being taken. Since 1999, for example, digital subscriptions to *The Wall Street Journal* and a few magazines have been available for downloading to handheld electronic readers such as the Rocket eBook and SoftBook. The downloads are digitized versions of leading articles in each issue, but do not include every article. The great advantage of these small devices is their portability, as they are the size of a paperback book.

Like hundreds of other dailies, weeklies, magazines and even some books, the *Times* has been available free on the Web for the past few years. Like all other online publications, however, including sites delivering downloads to the Rocket eBook and SoftBook devices, only a few articles from any issue are available over the Web—and they reflect the selective judgment and taste of editors, not necessarily those of the readers.

Then, on Oct. 24, 2001, *The New York Times* went a step beyond the limited-text option of the handheld devices and Web downloads when it debuted its Electronic Edition, which is an "exact digital replica" of every page of each issue of the newspaper. Downloading to a desktop computer through the Web was made available at an introductory equivalent of 65 cents a day.[15]

Since then, many other newspapers around the world have begun offering electronic editions using the same NewsStand software, which displays photographic images of the actual news pages. It is similar to PDF files that can be downloaded from the Web and read by Adobe's Acrobat Reader.

Now, *Times* readers have the options of subscribing to the print edition, reading selected Web site articles online for free, or subscribing to NewsStand's digital replica of the *Times*.

Chip Scanlan of the Poynter Institute began subscribing to the *New York Times* Electronic Edition on the first day. He sees an advantage to having all three over-the-Web possibilities offered to readers.

In an early review, he wrote, "Why couldn't there be multiple opportunities for online consumption? One for a generation that has grown up reading news on a computer screen, and another for aging baby boomers like me who spent our formative years rattling pages of ink-stained newsprint."[16]

He said the experience of reading the Electronic Edition is similar to the print version, with the added advantages of its computer platform, thanks to the capabilities built in by the NewsStand software. "With the click of a mouse," he noted, "I can move from page to page, follow jump lines, and scan for interesting stories, photos, charts, the ads, even the fine print, whether or not I'm on-line . . . . I can magnify the page, providing relief for my middle-aged presbyopia. Other features include word search, zoom in and out, browsing by page, section, or article, including hyperlinks that make the leap from story jumps faster than clicking Next online."[17]

The holdback for some people will be that a broadband connection is needed. But that problem is diminishing daily as more cable modems and DSL lines are installed. Within two years, NewsStand's offerings had increased to 40 newspapers from the United States, Canada, Latin America, Europe and Asia, plus 12 magazines including *Harvard Business Review*, and a Consumer Reports newsletter. These electronic full-page editions could be ordered over the Web and then delivered to your computer no matter where you traveled.

Actually, by 2003 there were a total of six digital ways to read the *Times*. Besides the three just mentioned, the *Times* also makes a fax edition available on letter-sized paper to subscribers who cannot receive same-day delivery of the printed paper. The fax edition is often provided to American hotel guests in other countries, such as in the Caribbean, where I read one every day while vacationing.

Other digital delivery methods for newspapers began in 2002 when a few magazines and newspapers, including *Salon, The Wall Street Journal*,

The Washington Times, The Provo (Utah) Daily Herald, and *The New York Times* began offering free download subscriptions for the Palm personal digital assistant.

The *Times* and more than 170 other newspapers from around the world also are available through a digital service delivered via satellite link called NewspaperDirect, established in 1999 in Canada. The service allows pages of the newspapers to be printed upon order onto 11-by-17-inch pages for guests at away-from-home locations such as hotels, cruise ships, resorts, libraries and corporate offices.

In addition, about 120 newspapers from 47 countries are globally available through what might be the newspaper vending machine of the future—an electronic print-out delivery system from Satellite Newspapers. Based in the Netherlands, Satellite Newspapers was founded in 1999 as PEPC Worldwide. Satellite Newspapers operates through self-service kiosks at locations for travelers such as hotels and airports, providing what is in effect an electronic, digitally printed vending machine that accepts payment from credit cards or a proprietary Satellite Newspapers card instead of coins. A newspaper can be downloaded, printed and stapled within two minutes.

As of 2003, you still could not get *The New York Times* from Satellite Newspapers, but you could get *The Washington Post, USA Today, the Miami Herald, El Nuevo Herald, Atlanta Journal & Constitution, The Christian Science Monitor, The Philadelphia Inquirer, Los Angeles Times, San Francisco Chronicle* and *The Washington Times.*

Oh, you also could still buy newspapers printed with ink on newsprint through subscriptions, mechanical vending machines and wire racks at stores—but that's so low tech and old-fashioned, isn't it?

Meanwhile, we have two bold insights to ponder about the future of print journalism, both uttered in 2001:

• Dick Brass, Microsoft's vice president of technology while showing off the company's prototype 122-dpi Tablet PC: "In 20 years, the broadsheet newspaper will be dead."[18]

• Bruce Chizen, Adobe president and CEO, while discussing what he called his company's network publishing initiative: "It is no longer just about paper, no longer just about browsers on desktops. It's about getting information anywhere, anytime on any device."[19]

Fidler sees the future just as strongly in a chapter he wrote for an American Press Institute book, *2020: Visions of the Newspaper of the Future.* In the book, Fidler predicts most newspapers will no longer publish weekday editions on paper by 2020 and that they will be in a life-or-death struggle with digital competitors such as Microsoft Corp.,

CNN and AT&T, as well as with nontraditional publishing companies such as eBay and Amazon.com, fighting for a share of audiences and advertising dollars.[20]

Fidler concludes, "If established newspaper publishers are to survive in the next century, they must be prepared to abandon the last vestiges of industrial age publishing—printing presses and delivery trucks. Their only viable option is to make a full conversion to cyberage publishing within the next two decades."[21]

A combination of the Internet and wireless communications will make electronic delivery of publications feasible. Newspapers are mostly ignored by children, but some who can barely read already are avid users of the Internet. An Internet study group reports that 10 million children under the age of 12 were on-line by 1998, and it estimates that 45 million children will be online by 2002.[22] Those kids include, by the way, my oldest grandson who began surfing the Web for sites about dinosaurs when he was 6. At least he also reads the comics in the newspaper.

Television and technology

ANALOG TECHNOLOGY has been quickly put out of its misery. The analog mobile telephone is following the rotary phone into oblivion as the FCC plans to allow wireless carriers to shut down all analog networks by 2007.[23]

In the television industry, the only game in town now is digital technology. Television executives are notifying journalism educators that students who are not acquainted with digital technology once they leave college or the university are not truly prepared for the real world.[24]

Digital cameras, both still and for motion, have revolutionized the news business.

Sometimes the change has not been for the better. For example, it always was possible to alter photographs or film to make things seem different than they really were, but at least it took a real darkroom pro to pull it off. Today, with digital photography and filming, anyone can make the camera lie. Now John Wayne can promote products in realistic filmed advertisements of products that were never invented until years after he died. One network can replace a rival's logo on the side of a building with its own, and the only people who will know any different are the ones who were physically present—the TV audience will see a different logo altogether. One magazine can seamlessly put Oprah Winfrey's head on Ann-Margret's body, and another can shade O.J. Simpson's face and subtly change facial characteristics to make him look as sinister as possible. There are the fantastically real special effects that digital technology has brought to the movies and that can spill over into TV news on a more modest scale through such devices as re-enactments of broadcast stories and placing anchors on the scene of a news story even when they are many miles or even a continent away.

All of these possibilities have ramifications for television and the World Wide Web, of course. Just as the Internet was undreamed of a couple of decades ago, so perhaps we are blind now to the possibility of moving pictures and sound on our tablet newspapers in 2020, or of holograms replacing TV in our living rooms by then.

"Nearly everyone, it seems, has an opinion about TV's future," Fidler wrote in his book. "At one extreme is the belief that it is doomed and will not survive much beyond the end of this decade. At the other extreme are those who argue that 'high definition' and 'interactive' technologies will completely revitalize the medium and lead it to a new golden age.["25]

Fidler seems to believe the latter. Just as he sees a digital future of subscribers' tablet newspapers with their stories downloaded at electronic newsstands or by radio waves, so too does he see an incredible future of change for an interactive vision media.[26]

Others, like futurist George Gilder who believes TV will become irrelevant, think so only because today's TV technology will seem so primitive by comparison in a few years. "Whether offering 500 channels or thousands," Gilder said, "TV will be irrelevant in a world where you can always order exactly what you want when you want it, and where every terminal commands the communication power of a broadcast station today."[27]

Ever higher-definition TV, narrow-casting, broadband, personal channels, off-line services, broadcasting on the Web, interactive home theaters and commercial holographic theaters are all seen as widely accepted possibilities in the near term.

One thing is for certain: Those media executives and media companies that do not stay abreast of new technology will be doomed. "Once a new technology rolls over you, if you're not part of the steamroller, you're part of the road,["28] noted Stewart Brand, author of *The Media Lab: Inventing the Future at MIT*.

Earlier it was noted that newspapers are losing customers to the Web, but that kind of loss also is happening with television.

Pavlik reports, "For the first time in history, television usage dropped among children in 1997, and much of that drop is directly attributable to Internet and other new media consumption."[29] A 2003 CBS MarketWatch study showed that 13-to-24-year-olds were on-line 16.7 hours per week, not including e-mail, compared with 13.6 hours per week watching television, 12 hours listening to the radio, and 7.7 hours talking on the telephone. So the battle for a share of a market increasingly fragmented by the Internet is not just a problem for newspapers, but for television and all other traditional media as well.

Media business and new technology

CHANGES WROUGHT by digital technology already are coming so rapidly that it is understandable why media executives fear that they will be left behind if they do not run faster, adapt more quickly, and get richer and bigger so they can be ready for anything. New technologies will force massive adaptations in the media companies, create still more incredible opportunities in business, and transform the society we know in unimaginable ways.

It is estimated there were nearly 360 million users worldwide of the Internet in September 2000.[30] In 1995, the United States claimed 90 percent of all Internet users, but by late 2000 about 60 percent of Internet users lived outside the United States. The United States Information Agency reported that all of but 40 of the world's 247 nations had some form of Internet connection by 2000.[31]

The growth of the Internet can only get larger. As Pavlik points out, even with 360 million people on-line that still leaves about 94 percent of the world's 6 billion people off-line, about half of whom have never even made or received a phone call.[32]

The traditional media are scrambling to not get left behind.

Fidler believes that media companies and journalists face a big challenge in learning how to create, manage and deliver print, audio, video and interactive content in a convenient and user-friendly way.

"In the rush to cash in on emerging forms of digital communication," he wrote, "media companies and professionals should not lose sight of their implicit responsibility to keep people informed about social developments, government activities, and community affairs, regardless of their race, gender, age, education, financial status, or level of technical skills. The mainstream media must continue to serve as community builders and forums for public expression as well as marketplaces for businesses and individuals."[33]

Technology can have several types of impact: desirable or undesirable, direct or indirect, anticipated or unanticipated.[34] Notice how the dynamics of each pair can cancel out each other. That is why new technology can bring complications as well as solutions to a business and its manager. The change brought by technology can be pleasant or an ordeal. Frustration and confusion can sometimes seem to be winning out over enhanced efficiency and effectiveness as managers and employees struggle to master any new technology.

Internally, technology changes managers' style of management by raising challenges in the way managers work and in the control managers have. Employees can become more knowledgeable than managers about key functions of the organization.[35]

Externally, technology is viewed by managers as a tool to produce a positive change in the market and enhance the company's competitive positioning and profits. Technologies that do not accomplish these kinds of goals are not pursued. But again, remembering both sides of the pairs of consequences mentioned earlier, the change can take various forms.

For example, technology can expand or diminish competition.[36] The ability to digitally compress broadcast signals, squeezing more bits-per-signal capability into a signal, allowed the wireless cable TV industry and network television to "jam" more channels into allocated bandwidth and thus compete more effectively against wired cable TV. Wired cable operators slow to invest for acquiring the digital signal were quickly placed at a competitive disadvantage, at least in the short term.

The Internet has proven to be a double-edged sword for nearly everyone.

In San Francisco, both the *Examiner* and the *Chronicle* have on-line versions of their print editions on the Web, opening up a new revenue stream and adding another dimension in which they can build their businesses. However, the Internet also has forced a redefinition of geographic limits for a market area by, for example, opening up the opportunity for Taiwanese-based newspapers to provide electronic versions of their papers to compete with San Francisco papers for the Chinese-American audience there.[37]

Technology also can blur market boundaries and create new markets, thus creating both new competitive pressures and the promise at least of new revenue streams.[38]

The Internet is an excellent example of the impact of new technology. "There is always one moment . . . when the door opens and lets the future in," observed author Graham Greene,[39] and that seems to be a dramatically apt description of the sudden arrival of the Internet and its immediate impact around the world.

The Internet is the first medium that can provide transmission of written, audio, pictorial and video depictions of news events in real time. Depending on how it is done and on the site, the Internet can combine in one Web location all of the strengths of newspapers, magazines, radio, television, cable, movies and even libraries from both mainstream and alternative media sources.

Research into electronic paper and digital ink combined with computer power promises to give a similar ability to tablet newspapers, where viewers could click on a story and have it read to them, or click on a still photograph and have it immediately convert into a movie clip of at least several seconds.[40]

While tablet newspapers probably will have the ability to read stories audibly to you in the future, the *San Francisco Chronicle* launched a service in the fall of 2002 that already enables commuters to have that paper's stories read to them. Subscribers download a file of stories for that day's issue from the Internet, burn them onto a CD, and hear an audio of that day's columns and top news stories while driving to work.[41] Skeptics say it will never work, but they might be underestimating the number of CD burners that serious newspaper readers already own or are willing to buy. You can download shows from radio stations to transfer to your iPod for listening anywhere.

Wireless transmissions already are transforming the cable television and telephone industries, eliminating old distinctions and causing each to become interested in the business of the other. (AT&T is the world's largest telephone company and also was the world's largest cable television provider until selling its broadband division to Comcast.) Publishers still worry about the potential of AT&T putting its Yellow Pages on-line, thereby threatening newspapers' profitable classified advertising base. On the other hand, telephone companies, including AT&T, see an Internet threat in Voice Over Internet Protocol (VoIP), which might end up replacing the conventional long distance telephone call because it is so inexpensive and the quality is rapidly improving.[42]

The print media of newspapers, magazines and newsletters are in a transition stage, many producing both print and Web versions of their publications. At first, several tried to turn Web users into subscribers for their sites. Virtually all publications that tried to implement a subscription fee for their electronic versions later recanted, however, and now host free sites. From 1996 to 2000, the only newspaper charging for Web subscriptions was *The Wall Street Journal*. It remains by far the most successful, claiming 664,000 Web subscribers by 2003, which is about 150 times more than the next best effort.[43]

The move by other newspapers back to charging Web subscriptions for non-print customers is slowly starting, led at first by pioneering small dailies. The *Chanute* (Kan.) *Tribune* began charging for Web subscriptions in April 1999, followed by *The Daily News Journal* of Murfreesboro,

Tenn., in January 2000; the *Lewiston* (Idaho) *Morning Tribune* in December 2000; and the *Daily American* of Somerset, Pa., the *Post Register* of Idaho Falls, Idaho, and *The Daily Astorian* of Astoria, Ore., all in January 2001. The first large dailies to venture forth were the *Tulsa* (Okla.) *World,* the *Albuquerque Journal,* the *Gazette* of Cedar Rapids, Iowa, and the *Arkansas Democrat-Gazette* of Little Rock, Ark., all during 2001.[44] Others have gone to subscription since then.

Another model is one allowing access if the reader first records a free registration, such as at *The New York Times* among others, in what is seen as a precursor to charging for Web access. Some media Web sites began reporting slim profits in the late 1990s.[45]

New technology changes consumption habits, which also affects advertising and promotion strategies.[46]

Examples are the VCR, which allows people to tape their programs and then fast-forward through commercial messages, and TiVo, which can zap the commercials. This has caused at least some advertisers to alter their messages, creating, as an example, shorter and more appealing messages that have a better chance of attracting and holding the viewers' attention before they decide to fast-forward, or to construct commercials in such a way that a theme gets across even when fast-forwarded if consumers are at least watching the screen.

The use of "cookies" and related Web technologies lets Web publishers deliver a more personalized Web experience, right down to the advertisements. Returning visitors are recognized automatically and see advertising messages based on their previous purchases, browsing history and responses to innocent-seeming surveys.

Some consumers oppose cookies and advertisements. They can turn off cookies as an option in most browsers, and they also have begun buying software that blocks Web advertisements, which is every bit as ominous a development for Web publishing as TiVo and manual fast-forwarding. Apple's new browser, Safari, has a menu command that allows the user to block all pop-up windows on any visited site. As such capability becomes widespread, it will bring new worries and uncertainties to the still-developing model for Web publishers to sell ads to support their Web business.

Finally, every manager knows that technology often develops faster than attempts to control it.[47] We all know this instinctively, based on the fact that every time we purchase a new state-of-the-art computer it is invariably so far out of date a few weeks later that we often succumb to buyer's remorse for purchasing it when we did, even though we might very well have needed it and are still able to do what we originally wanted to do.

21st century electronic and digital media

ELECTRONIC INK, E-paper, "newspapers" transmitted to your home by radio signals instead of by carriers, floppy computer screens, telepathic mail, digital tablets combining the best of newsprint, radio, television and the Internet—and we're not even going to discuss holograms in your living room,

What does the future hold? These are just some of the technological breakthroughs already in the invention stages in laboratories. They will transform the media industry during the careers of most of you who are reading this book.

All of this and more will, of course, be wireless.

In the 1967 movie, "The Graduate," the young and newly graduated Dustin Hoffman is advised by a businessman on where all the action will be for the future—a whole career encapsulated in just one word, "plastics." If that same movie were to be remade today, the word probably would be "wireless."

The presence of high-tech digital innovations re-inventing the mass media seems common now. But it was not too long ago that newspapers, television and radio were thought to be already fully developed, mature industries.

When I took my first full-time journalism job in 1965, the newspaper was produced with Linotype machines, molten lead, manual and electric typewriters, and letterpress composing rooms and presses.

Now I must show photos of Linotype machines to students who have never heard of such a mechanical contraption, let alone ever seen one.

Back in early 1965, color televisions were just starting to catch on, and there were only three television networks to watch, AM radio was king, and slide rules still were used by engineers because pocket calculators had not yet been invented. A car phone was practically unheard of. Computers were a technology limited to the military, research universities and the largest corporations. Laser printers would not be invented for two more decades. Vacuum tubes were still the dominant electronic technology, and Bill Gates was just a 9-year-old kid.

It is sobering to realize that in its first five years, the Internet reached 50 million people—an accomplishment that took the telephone 70 years, the radio 40 years, and the television 15 years to achieve.[48] And by 2002, just about every American adult either owned a desktop or laptop computer or had relatively easy access to the use of one at a school, library or community center.

We are accelerating into a brave new world of still unimagined technology—just as the technology we take for granted could never have been guessed at only a few years ago. Much of what is so common today is relatively new technology, as can be seen in the Technological Milestones chart at the end of this chapter.

Monumental changes are inevitable for media companies.

Imagine the positive impact on the environment, and the negative impact on the national economies of logging areas, if newspapers begin transmitting their editions electronically to computerized tablets instead of publishing on newsprint. To give you some idea of the scale with one example, *The New York Times* typically requires about 63,000 trees to make the newsprint just for its Sunday edition of about 1.7 million copies.[49]

The 1994 Knight Ridder film on the tablet newspaper, mentioned earlier, did such an excellent job of looking into the future that it still remains relevant today.

The Knight Ridder vision, or perhaps more accurately Roger Fidler's vision while he was with Knight Ridder, was of a tablet newspaper whose daily content from your favorite newspaper could be downloaded at kiosks that are as conveniently located as soft drink machines. The tablet newspaper's technology enabled it to (1) present text and photos like newspapers, (2) turn photos into short film clips with sound like television, (3) read any story aloud like radio, and (4) provide in-depth detail behind the main story by clicking a link, and also order products from ads, as can be done today on the Internet. All features were accessible by touching the screen with a stylus.[50]

Most futurists predict that whatever form the mass media take in the future, the model will be something like Fidler's tablet, at least in the ability to merge the features of newspapers, television, radio and the Internet—and probably the telephone as well—all into one microprocessor-driven, portable and wireless electronic platform. You can see it beginning to happen now, as many newsletters are discontinuing their print versions and becoming published only on the Web.

The invention of the desktop computer and laser printer in the 1980s resulted in such tremendous savings that many weeklies in small towns were given a longer and more profitable life. They were further helped in the 1990s with the advent of digital cameras and photo scanners, enabling them to discontinue expensive photo-processing. Similarly, many weeklies in small communities facing extinction in the early years of the 21st century might be able to survive and continue serving their small towns by converting their printed papers to on-line publishing.

"I think it is economics that will ultimately drive newspapers to become electronic," Fidler said. "That doesn't mean we're talking about the death of newspapers. We're talking about the transformation of papers into a different medium."[51]

Arthur O. Sulzberger Jr., publisher of *The New York Times*, believes, like Fidler, that large newspapers will benefit just like small papers from the increasing acceptance of the Web as a source for publications. "The marriage of newspapers and the Internet will happen," Sulzberger said. "It makes sense. We are faced with the need to adapt to a new and very unproven business model."[52]

David Neuman, president of Digital Entertainment Network, declared flatly, "This amazing, revolutionary medium (the Internet) is going to blow everything else away in the long run."[53]

Here are some other visions of the future already under development by engineers, scientists and various research-and-development folks at high-tech companies.

• "E-mail was fine for a while, but being tied to a stationary PC was so limiting. Laptops and wireless palm units provided freedom, but the problem with such handheld devices is simply that: you have to hold them. What a chore. Coming soon is microdisplay, a technology that can provide PC-quality images from a device so small it could fit into a pair of eyeglasses, allowing us to roam, hands-free, while still being plugged into the world of news and information."—Howard Saltz, media editor of *The Denver Post.*[54]

• "A million Americans can access the Internet through their cell phones (in 2000) . . . . Internet cell phone service available in this country (since only about 1999) has the potential to supplant the personal computer as the preferred means of using the net . . . . John Patrick, IBM's vice president of Internet technology, predicts that between 40 percent and 50 percent of all Web access may eventually occur via wireless phone."—Chris Cobbs of the *Orlando Sentinel.*[55]

• "Portable, handheld digital tablets that download and enable the reading of books on a screen are currently used primarily for electronic books. But they promise to do so much more—including one day becoming a popular medium for reading news . . . . Eventually most of the e-book readers will have wireless connectivity to the Internet, so that users at any time will be able to download the latest news or editions of a publication."—Steve Outing of *E&P Interactive.*[56]

• "A team of Xerox engineers in Palo Alto has toiled in virtual secrecy (on e-paper called Gyricon) since 1991 . . . . It's a rubberized, reflective substance made entirely of microscopic beads that are half-black, half-white. The Gyricon material is laminated between two sheets of plastic or glass and has the thickness of about four sheets of traditional paper . . . .

CHAPTER 12

When an electronic charge is applied through a computer or a wireless radio wave, the beads rotate into place. Some turn black side up, others black side down. A pattern emerges and words appear."—Sam Bruchey in *Upside* magazine.[57]

• "(In 1999) E-Ink (Corp.) mounted a 6-foot-long, 3-millimeter-thick digital sign . . . . The sign, which weighs 8.7 pounds, flashes a different digital message every 10 seconds. Messages can be changed from any location using a pager, but last indefinitely if not changed . . . . It is the first digital display to run on a wireless impulse, creating an image as clear and permanent as if it were written in ink. E-Ink's technology, Immedia, is similar to Gyricon."—Sam Bruchey in *Upside* magazine.[58]

• "Imagine a publisher dispensing with ink, newsprint, press, trucks and local deliverers, while a subscriber does without toner, paper, printers and computer. Where's the newspaper? On the breakfast table each morning—freshly imaged, up to date, and dependent upon no visible means of delivery or printing. No wires, no machines, no consumables. What's more, the same piece of 'paper' is re-imaged every night with the next day's edition . . . . The technology to accomplish this feat exists."—Jim Rosenberg in *Editor & Publisher* magazine.[59]

• "Electronic ink, which is under development at the Massachusetts Institute of Technology's Media Lab, would be energy efficient. It would print in black on fiberglass-reinforced white (electronic) paper, simulating the way newspapers now appear.—The Associated Press.[60]

• "Phillips Electronics NV said (Sept. 5, 2000) that its researchers have created a soft plastic computer display that could result in floppy electronic newspapers."—The Associated Press.[61]

• "'Urban Jungle Pack' . . . is the name given to the mobile journalist's work station of the future, a wearable set of computers that stream audio, video and text from the field reporter back to the newsroom. The first UJP was deployed in Berlin (in July 1999) by a consortium of European television producers . . . . The package features a head-mounted video camera . . . (and it) includes a Global Positioning System . . . UJP-equipped reporters can watch the outgoing video through a head-mounted Sony Glasstron display, a translucent image through which he or she also can see the actual event."—Adam Clayton Powell III.[62]

• "Electronic paper (is) a high-contrast, low-cost, read/write/erase medium. By binding these pulplike, electronic leaves, lo and behold—you have an electronic book. These are quite literally pages onto which you can download words, in any type, in any size. For the 15 million Americans who want large-print books, this will be a gift from heaven . . . . This is the likely future of books."—Nicholas Negroponte of the MIT Media Lab.[63]

• "'You're going to see television evolve to become more like the Internet,' says Bran Ferren of Imagineering . . . . World News Tonight with Peter Jennings could be enhanced. You could have the option of changing camera angles. If you wanted, you could pause what a correspondent is saying and go back to Peter Jennings . . . . A menu would appear . . . . If you are watching a cooking show, for example, you can print the recipe or even pause the show and buy the ingredients . . . . While you're watching a commercial, you can click on it and have the option to buy the clothes the actors are wearing."—Jack Smith of ABC News.[64]

In one possible transition to "electronic delivery," some newspapers already are experimenting with what has been dubbed "clicks and mortar" business by publishing only on the Web. The *Orem (Utah) Daily Journal* discontinued its traditional newsprint product and began appearing only on the Web in 1999.[65] The following year a daily was started up as an Internet publication—making Vero Beach, Fla., a most unusual "two-newspaper" town in challenging the traditionally printed Scripps paper there.[66] Regardless of the eventual fates of these individual efforts, such "virtual" newspapers are pioneering an inevitable move to some kind of electronic digital delivery for all media.

In a 1998 article titled "Future 'scary' for media bosses," *Editor & Publisher* columnist Marc Wilson summed up concerns of media managers that remain as valid today as then.

"It's scary to think about the monumental challenges facing the next generation of media managers," Wilson wrote. "Not since the invention of the telegraph have there been more changes in gathering and dispersing information then there will be as the Internet becomes ubiquitous."[67]

He quotes Peter Leyden of *Wired* magazine who had declared, even at that relatively early stage of the Internet's development: "Historians will look back on our times, the 40-year span between 1980 and 2020, and classify it among the handful of historical moments when humans reorganized their civilization around a new tool, a new idea. . . ."[68]

In *The News About the News,* authors Leonard Downie Jr. and Robert G. Kaiser summed up the rapid changes taking place in the media today and in the near future, stating, "The expansion of the country's network of fiber-optic cable will bring nearly infinite capacity to transmit sound, pictures and words by land lines into America's homes. Soon millions of consumers will combine television, Internet and telephone service in a single box. Advances in wireless communications are putting cordless Internet-connected computers into briefcases, handbags, pockets and mobile phones . . . . Free news on the Internet . . . .

The audience for television news is splintering among over-the-air broadcasting, cable (and satellite), and the Internet.

"Advertising . . . provides most of the profits for all news organizations, (and) is sloshing around these media unpredictably, destabilizing their business models."[69]

Young managers and today's college and university students are the lucky ones. Not only will they be part of this exciting and changeable future, they will shape and direct it.

Technological Milestones of the Computer Era[70]

Year and Invention

1939: What is believed to have been the first digital electronic computer is built by John V. Atanasoff and graduate student Clifford Berry at Iowa State University.

1946: U.S. military and the University of Pennsylvania build ENIAC, a super-calculating electronic computer. It contains 18,000 vacuum tubes and weighs 30 tons.

1948: Bell Laboratories announces the invention of the transistor, which many today still consider the greatest invention of the 20th century.

1954: RCA begins selling the first color TV sets.

1954: Modem is invented, allowing computers to communicate over phone lines.

1957: Russia launches the first space satellite, Sputnik.

1958: The microchip is invented by Jack Kilby of Texas Instruments.

1963: Douglas C. Engelbart invents the computer mouse.

1964: IBM releases OS/360, which is to become the first widely used computer operating system.

1969: The U.S. military and research universities establish ARPANET (Advanced Research Projects Agency Network), sharing defense-related information over computers linked by telephone lines in what would eventually evolve into the Internet.

1969: Theodor H. Nelson coins the terms "hypertext" and "hypermedia."

1970: Texas Instruments introduces first electronic pocket calculator. It costs $400.

1971: The first microprocessor, the 4004, is invented by Marcian "Ted" Hoff of Intel, which had been founded by Robert Noyce three years earlier. The 4004 could perform 60,000 transactions per second. (Today's microprocessors perform several hundred million transactions per second.)

1975: Microsoft Corp. is founded by Bill Gates, 19, and Paul Allen, 22.

1975: The MITS Altair 8800 is the first mass-produced personal computer.

1976: Apple Computer is founded by Steve Wozniak, 26, and Steve Jobs, 22.

1977: The Apple II goes on the market as the first user-friendly desktop computer, using a TV set for a monitor and audiocassette tapes for data storage.

1978: The first commercial cellular phone operation begins in Chicago, five years after the cell phone had been invented by Martin Cooper, formerly of Motorola.

1981: IBM introduces its first desktop computer, which uses the MS-DOS operating system provided by Microsoft Corp.

1983: Canon invents the laser printer.

1985: America On Line starts as a computer bulletin board service by Steve Case.

1989: Tim Berners-Lee creates HTTP (hypertext transfer protocol) and URL (Uniform Resource Locater) for a global hypertext project he calls the "World Wide Web."

1992: Palm Inc. is founded, ushering in the age of handheld computers.

1993: Marc Andreeson and others at the University of Illinois release Mosaic, the first Web browser for the public. By June there are 130 sites on the World Wide Web, according to Web researcher Robert H. Zakon.

1994: Netscape Communications is founded and becomes the dominant Web browser. Interest in the Internet takes off, with Zakon reporting more than 10,000 sites on the World Wide Web by the end of 1994.

1995: Though expensive digital cameras had been used for years by large media companies, the first digital cameras priced under $1,000 for consumer and small company use are introduced — Kodak's dc40 and Apple's QuickTake 100.

2002: Internet expert Sreenath Sreenivasan of Columbia University estimates there are about 3 billion Web pages from several tens of millions of Web sites. He reports that every month an additional 2 million Americans go online.

CHAPTER 12

CASE STUDY   *Improving the Web Site*
So It Is Worth Doing

by WILLIAM KOVARIK, Ph.D.
Radford University

Your newspaper has supported a weak companion Web site for a few years. All it does is republish the same news and pictures that are in the newspaper. Now the time has come to integrate it with other operations and better serve communities of readers. The site needs to rise to its potential.

A committee is put together to see what can be done. It consists of a news editor, the Web site manager, the circulation manager, the advertising manager, and representatives from an affiliated local TV station.

The Web site is not profitable, and that worries the publisher, but she steadfastly maintains a view that the paper must stay with its Web site for the long haul. There are four overall goals: (1) serve various regional communities in new and effective ways, (2) encourage a serious interest among young people in news and public affairs, (3) bring in more paper subscribers (eventually), and (4) develop new sources of income.

The current budget consists of about $10,000 in overhead along with two mid-level salaries ($60K each) and two entry-level assistants ($30K each). The site generates about $90,000 in ad sales, mostly through local computer and technology stores who don't usually advertise in the newspaper.

One of the Web assistants sells advertising for the site directly to existing customers. She has suggested integrating the Web advertising with display and classified advertising, which seems like a good idea to the advertising managers. Advertising needs to hammer out a policy that builds in incentives for regular display advertising customers to try Web advertising. This would be an expense in the beginning if advertisers wanted motion banner ads, but production costs for special ads could be charged to the customer.

The circulation manager wants the Web site to help with circulation and worries that free news is eroding the print circulation base. The Web site manager says that other papers have found it is impractical to charge for Web access. Possibly other incentives would help. The circulation manager believes print subscribers might be given free access to the database of news articles, or special forums. Also, a form allowing suspension of newspaper delivery during vacations would be nice, but could it be secure?

The news editor wants to use the Web to appeal to different segments of the community in a sort of psycho-graphics zoned edition. Young professionals, Gen-Xers, sports fans, kids doing homework, teens who need to express themselves—every virtual community should be served by the paper's Web site. The question is, how? Some reporter resources can be devoted to the project, but could community members make their own contributions?

The TV and radio folks have seen some TV stations that put scripts on the air and think its just a peachy idea. (For example, see Roanoke, Va. CBS affiliate at <www.wdbj7.com/scripts/6.htm>) But they would like quick links from their nightly news scripts to the newspaper's stories. They also want to create sites for promotions but need better design services.

ASSIGNMENT:

1. In groups of five, one participant each is designated to be from the Web manager, news, circulation, advertising departments and affiliated TV station.

2. Who are the communities that an expanded Web site might serve better? What kinds of forums, on-line charity auctions and hobbyist/enthusiast exchanges could be created and promoted?

3. What ideas can advertising, circulation and news cooperate on to promote the Web site to younger people?

4. Is it enough to put TV scripts on the Web site? What other dynamic content could draw viewers/readers to the site?

5. Considering the broadest possible horizon, several decades down the road, with ultra-broadband and highly portable communication, what long term vision will best serve the regions communities and carry on the newspaper and TV station's public service mission?

AUTHOR:

William Kovarik teaches technology courses for journalism students at Radford University, in Radford, Va. He is author of Web Design for the Mass Media, *published in 2002 by A.B. Longman <www.wdmm.net>.*

🖥 *Suggested Web sites:*

www.reznetnews.org—Example of a purely on-line newspaper
www.digitaljournalist.org—The Digital Journalist site
www.handheldmagazine.com—Photojournalism site
www.maxmon.com/history.htm—History of computers
www.worldtechnews.com—Technology news
www.wired.com—Internet news
www.futureprint.kent.edu—Future of Print Media site
www.cptech.org—Consumer Project on Technology
www.newsandtech.com—*Newspapers & Technology* magazine
www.newsstand.com/index.cfm?fuseaction=main—NewsStand home page
www.newspaperdirect.com/defaultDial.asp—NewspaperDirect home page
www.satellitenewspapers.com—Satellite Newspapers home page

Endnotes to Chapter 12:

[1] Roger F. Fidler, *Mediamorphosis* (Thousand Oaks, Calif.: Pine Forge Press, 1997).

[2] Ibid., 109.

[3] Alfred C. Sykes, in the foreword to *Mediamorphosis* by Roger F. Fidler.

[4] Benjamin M. Compaine, *Who Owns the Media? The Concentration of Ownership in the Mass Communications Industry* (White Plains, N.Y.: Butterworth-Heinemann, 2nd ed., 1982), 27.

[5] John V. Pavlik, *Journalism and New Media* (New York: Columbia University Press, 2001), xiii.

[6] Peter F. Drucker, *Management Challenges for the 21st Century* (New York: HarperCollins Publishers Inc., 2001), Rocket e-book edition v. 1, 2002, 213.

[7] Ibid., 98–99.

[8] William Dean Singleton, in keynote address of November 2, 2002, at the state convention of the New Mexico Press Association.

[9] Kent State University biography of Roger Fidler at <www.ici.kent.edu/fidler.htm>, accessed January 14, 2002.

[10] Photograph courtesy of Roger Fidler of Kent State University.

[11] Mark Fitzgerald, "Take one e-tablet and read it in the morning," *Editor & Publisher* (November 4, 2002): 5.

[12] Jim Rosenberg, "A 12-MB daily dose of news in a tablet," *Editor & Publisher* (December 16, 2002): 28.

[13] Marcelo Duran, "Tablet PCs hard to swallow for newspapers," *Newspapers & Technology* (February 2003), <www.newsandtech.com/issues/2003/02-03/ot/02-03_tablet.htm>, accessed June 12, 2003.

[14] Paul Colford, "Going digital," *Editor & Publisher* (May 8, 2000): N35.

[15] Chip Scanlan, "The virtual newspaper arrives; The New York Times Electronic Edition: A consumer's view," <www.poynter.org/centerpiece/103101nytimes.htm>, accessed November 5, 2001.

[16] Ibid.

[17] Ibid.

[18] Kelly Lunsford, "Publishing's future: Paper or plastic?" *MacWorld* (April 11, 2001) and its Web site at <www.macworld.com/2001/04/bc/11future>.

[19] Ibid.

[20] Roger F. Fidler, in his chapter for *2020: Visions of the Newspaper of the Future* (Reston, Va.: American Press Institute, 2002), 127.

[21] Ibid., 124.

[22] "FIND/SVP internet usage study," <www.worldtechnews.com>, as reported in Pavlik's *Journalism and New Media,* 139.

[23] Paul Davidson, "Analog phones could hang it up; FCC expected to OK system shutdown," *USA TODAY,* August 8, 2002, 3B.

[24] Professor Richard Schaefer of the University of New Mexico in remarks to the author, December 3, 2001.

[25] Fidler, *Mediamorphosis,* 196–197.

[26] Ibid., 195–196.

[27] George Gilder, *Life After Television: The Coming Transformation of Media and American Life* (New York: Norton, 1994), 52–70.

[28] Stewart Brand, as quoted by Katherine Fulton in "Future tense: The Anxious Journey of a Technophobe," *Columbia Journalism Review* (November–December 1993), 29.

[29] Pavlik, *Journalism and New Media,* 139.

[30] Ibid., 138.

[31] Ibid.

[32] Ibid., 142.

[33] Fidler, *Mediamorphosis,* 264–265.

[34] Everett M. Rogers, *Communication technology: The new media in society* (New York: The Free Press, 1986), 162.

[35] Ardyth Broadrick Sohn with Jan LeBlanc Wicks, Stephen Lacy and George Sylvie, *Media Management: A Casebook Approach* (Mahwah, N.J.: Lawrence Erlbaum Associates, 2nd ed., 1999), 125–136.

[36] Ibid., 130.

[37] H.I. Chyi and G. Sylvie, "Competing with whom? Where? And how? A structural analysis of the electronic newspaper market," 11, *Journal of Media Economics* (1988): 1–18.

[38] Sohn, et al., *Media Management,* 131–132.

[39] Graham Greene, as quoted in "Electronic innovations liberate newsgatherers," by Jules S. Tewlow, 14, *Newspaper Research Journal* (Spring 1993): 31.

[40] "The Tablet Newspaper: A vision for the future," Knight Ridder Information Design Lab, 1994. Videocassette.

[41] Elisa Batista, "All the news that's fit to burn," *San Francisco Chronicle,* September 13, 2002, at <www.wired.com/news/business/0,1367,55094,00.html>, accessed on September 13, 2002.

[42] Brian Bergstein, The Associated Press, as published in "Net phone no longer two cans and a string," *Albuquerque Journal,* September 15, 2002, C4.

[43] "Pay-to-play newspaper Web sites," *Editor & Publisher* (January 20, 2003): 22.

[44] Ibid.

[45] Pavlik, *Journalism and New Media,* 150.

[46] Sohn, et al., *Media Management,* 133–134.

[47] Ibid., 135.

[48] Ravi Kalakota and Marcia M. Robinson, *E-Business: Roadmap for Success* (New York: Addison-Wesley, 1999).

[49] Isaac Asimov, *Isaac Asimov's Book of Facts* (New York: Wings Books, 1979), 414.

[50] "The Tablet Newspaper: A vision for the future." 1994.

[51] The Associated Press, "IBM now developing electronic newspaper," as published in *Editor & Publisher* (September 15, 1999): 3.

[52] Barton Crockett of MSNBC, "Old media bash new media at conference," formerly at <www.msnbc .com>, accessed March 10, 1998. Article is no longer available on the Web.

[53] Jack Smith, "TV of the future: Interactive TV will empower the viewer," <www.abcnews .go.com/onair/CloserLook/wnt_000204_CL_InteractiveTV_feature.html>, accessed July 23, 2002.

[54] Howard Saltz, "T-mail messaging," *Editor & Publisher* (August 28, 2000): 30.

[55] Chris Cobbs, as published in "The Web is going wireless," Cedar Rapids, Iowa, *Gazette,* October 23, 2000, 8D.

[56] Steve Outing, "Sizing up the future: Take two tablets to cure news ache," *Editor & Publisher* (July 10, 2000): 12.

[57] Sam Bruchey, "The paper chase," *Upside* (August 2000): 290.

[58] Ibid.

[59] Jim Rosenberg, "Electronic ink on a paper screen," *Editor & Publisher* (August 9, 1997): 20.

[60] The Associated Press, as published in "IBM now developing electronic newspaper," *Editor & Publisher* (September 15, 1999): 2.

[61] The Associated Press, as published in "Phillips creates plastic PC screen," Cedar Rapids, Iowa, *Gazette*, September 6, 2000, 6B.

[62] Adam Clayton Powell III, "Reporter's 'work station of the future' debuts in Europe, reported on <www.freedomforum.org>, accessed August 29, 1999.

[63] Nicholas Negroponte, "The future of books," formerly at <www.web.media.mit.edu/ ~nicholas/Wired/WIRED4-02.html>, accessed July 23, 2002. Article is no longer available on the Web.

[64] Jack Smith, "TV of the future: Interactive TV will empower the viewer."

[65] "Orem Daily Journal abandons print, moves to the Web," *Confidential Bulletin* of the Iowa Newspaper Association, September 1, 1999, 5.

[66] David Noack, "Pulling in the net at a beach," *Editor & Publisher* (July 10, 2000): 29.

[67] Marc Wilson, "Future 'scary' for media bosses," *Editor & Publisher* (January 24, 1998): 56.

[68] Ibid.

[69] Leonard Downie Jr. and Robert G. Kaiser, *The News About the News: American Journalism in Peril* (New York: Alfred A. Knopf, 2002), 11–12.

[70] Several sources, many located through <www.ask.com> with key sites being <www.zakon .org/robert/internet/timeline> maintained by Robert H. Zakon and <www.inventors.about.com/ library/weekly/aa010500a.htm> maintained by Mary Bellis, all accessed July 19, 2002; <www.maxmon .com/history.htm>, "The history of computers," accessed June 15, 2003; as well as the book by Everett M. Rogers, *Communication Technology: The New Media in Society* (New York: The Free Press, 1986), 25–26.

INDEX

1001 Ways to Reward Employees, 114
15 largest media conglomerates in revenue, 330
2002 net profit margins of leading corporations, 191
35 largest North American daily newspapers, 267
4 P's of marketing, 268, 270
5-P Rule, 127

ABC, 9, 46, 20, 196, 197, 306, 320, 323, 324, 325, 326, 330, 345, 381
accrual basis accounting, 251
Adams, J. Stacy, 95
Adams, Scott, 125, 126
Adelstein, Jonathan S., 10
Adobe Systems Inc., 368
Advance Publications, 29, 74, 76, 77, 92, 193, 194, 212, 295, 313, 315, 325
Advertising Age, 47, 172, 173, 174, 305
advertising budget, 249
Advo, 284
Afghanistan, 75
AFL-CIO, 70, 71
Akron (Ohio) Beacon Journal, 89
Albuquerque Journal, 7, 111, 195, 314
Albuquerque Tribune, 314, 321
Allen, Woody, 42
Althoff, Kari, 235
America On Line, 330, 364, 383
America's endangered species, 304
American Journalism Review, 18, 79, 207
American Newspaper Publishers Association, 74
American Society of Newspaper Editors, 14, 48, 79, 290
anchoring trap, 154, 155
Anderson, Kirk, 233, 306, 307
Anderson, Pelle, 345
Annenberg Public Policy Center, 46
Anniston Star, 205
AOL Time Warner, 20, 305, 306, 307, 326, 330, 341
Apkarian, Wendy, 229
Apple, 155, 191, 363, 364, 376, 383
approved contradiction, 193, 195
Arizona Daily Star, 314
Arizona Republic, 265, 267
Arkansas Democrat-Gazette, 376
ARPANET, 363, 364, 383
Arthur, John, 19
Ashe, Reid, 189
Associated Press, 28, 44, 173, 182, 380
AT&T Broadband, 305, 324, 325
Atlanta Journal & Constitution, x, 267, 370
Audit Bureau of Circulations, 266
Aufderheide, 323
Austin American–Statesman, 265

Ayers, H. Brandt, 205

Babcock, William (case study), 99
Bagdikian, Ben H., 10, 11, 303, 304, 305, 306, 309, 322, 328
Bakersfield Californian, 46
balance sheet, 240, 241, 242, 243, 244, 245, 247
Baldesty, Gerald, 125
Baltimore Sun, 267
bankruptcy, 181
Barnard, Chester I., 88, 139
barriers to entry, 287
basic decision tool, 145
Basic Guide for Buying and Selling a Business, 357
Batten, James, 228
BBC, 9
Bcom3, 326
Beam, Randal A., 289
Beell, Thomas L. (case study), x, 61
Belker, Loren, 49
Bellows, Jim, 12
Belo, 8, 29, 175, 191, 220, 295, 320
Bennis, Warren, 39, 108, 116, 117, 351
Benton Foundation, 9
Berger, Ben, 190, 259
Berners-Lee, Tim, 282, 364, 383
Bertelsmann, 328, 330
Better Homes & Gardens, 321, 322, 344
Bezanson, Randall, 10
Bill of Rights. *See* First Amendment
Black, Cathleen, 46
Black, Conrad, 21, 201, 208, 346
Black Entertainment Television, 45
Blair, Jayson, 183, 184, 185
Blethen, Frank, 322
Block Communications, 8, 29, 315
Blum, Ken, 54
Boccardi, Lou, 44, 46
Bodenwein, Theodore, 205
Bolitho, Thomas C., 23
Booth Newspapers, 6
Boston Gazette, 192
Boston Globe, 20
Boyd, Gerald, 99, 184
Bradenton Herald, 265
Brand, Stewart, 372
branding, 270
Brass, Dick, 370
Braunerhielm, Robert, 345
break-even analysis, 276
Brehm Communications, 294
Brewer, Kelly, 46
Brill's, 3
Broadcasting & Cable, 47
Brodell, James J., 358
Brodsky, Norm, 351, 352

Brook, Alexander B., 341
Broun, Heywood, 70
Bruchey, Sam, 380
Brugmann, Bruce B., 318
Buckner News Alliance, 315
Buffalo News, 229
Buffet, Warren, 23
bureaucratic principles of structure, 218
Burnham, James, 193
Bush, President George W., 60, 68, 121,
    172, 173, 174, 175, 176
Business Broker newsletter, 357
Business Ethics, 199
Business of Media, 172, 266, 273, 305
business plan, 352, 354
Business Week, 168, 322

C corporation, 213
calculated risk, 56, 109, 110, 127, 152
California Newspapers Partnership, 204, 316
Campbell, Cole C., 189, 191
Canada, 22, 71, 78, 81, 154, 207, 221, 291,
    295, 304, 369, 370
Canadian Heritage, 78
Capstar Broadcasting, 343
Carroll, Lewis, 93
Case, Steve, 307, 383
cash flow, 238, 240, 244, 247
CBS, 20, 31, 32, 42, 218, 295, 323, 324,
    326, 330, 345, 385
celebrity journalism, 190, 266
Center for Digital Democracy, 326
Center for Media Education, 174
centralcasting, 198, 204
Central Newspapers, 220
Chandler, Otis, 212, 264
Chanute (Kan.) *Tribune*, 376
Chapman, Alvah H., 201
Cherokee Phoenix, 208
Chester, Jeff, 88, 139, 174, 326
Chicago Defender, 208
Chicago Sun-Times, 22, 267
Chicago Tribune, 4, 20, 126, 198, 232, 239,
    265, 267
child labor, 179
Chinese Daily News, 71
Chinigo, Marajen Stevick, 205
Chizen, Bruce, 370
Chris-Craft Industries, 307
Christian Science Monitor, 100, 370
Christians, Clifford G., 201
Christie, Judy Pace, 263
Chronicle of Higher Education, 15
cities in 2003 with at least two daily
    newspapers, 311
CJR, 265, 266
Clark, Scott, 247
Clear Channel Communications, Inc., 22,
    191, 198, 324, 330, 343
Cleveland Plain Dealer, 267
Clinton, President Bill, 121, 175
Cloud, Barbara, 5
clustering, 292, 293, 294, 295, 321, 329
CNBC, 8, 45

CNN, 8, 17, 20, 44, 324, 325, 326, 330, 345,
    371
Cobbs, Chris, 379
Cole, David M., 189, 267
collective bargaining, 73, 74, 177, 207
Columbia Daily Tribune, 312
Columbia Journalism Review, 11, 14, 17,
    79, 106, 124, 207, 265
Columbus Dispatch, 179
Comcast, 305, 324, 325, 330, 375
Committee of Concerned Journalists, 79,
    227
common sense, 108, 109, 195
Communication Workers of America, 12, 71
Community Media Group, 294
Community Newspaper Holdings Inc., 16,
    21, 29, 291, 294, 322
commuter daily, 345
Compaine, Benjamin, 19, 20, 21, 364
competencies of leadership, 116, 117, 118
Complete Idiot's Guide to MBA Basics, 214
compounded interest, 253, 254
computer spreadsheet, 152, 153
Concord Publishing House, 294
Confessions of an S.O.B, 43
confirming evidence trap, 156
Connell, Tara, 175
consolidation, 5, 8, 9, 13, 16, 23, 26, 172,
    174, 192, 193, 289, 292, 293, 294, 295,
    303, 304, 305, 308, 319, 322, 323, 325
Consumer Federation of America, 174
contract, 27, 54, 72, 74, 81, 82, 177, 178,
    181, 331, 355, 358
convergence, 23, 24, 31, 204, 303, 320
cookies, 376
Coolidge, President Calvin, 59
Copley Press, 29, 212
Copps, Michael J., 9, 10
corporation, 22, 210, 214, 328
corrections, 182
cost per thousand (CPM), 274, 276
cost-benefit analysis, 278
Country Woman, 344, 345
Cox, 8, 29, 175, 212, 305, 315, 325, 330
Cranberg, Gilbert, 10
Cronkite, Walter, 197
critical path method (CPM), 144, 145, 146,
    147, 148, 149, 157,
crossover analysis, 277
cross-ownership, 6, 7, 8, 10, 173, 174, 175,
    204, 308, 319, 322
Croteau, David, 232
Cumulus Media, 324
Curley, John, 232
Cutraro, Andy, 25
cyber-media, 308

Daily 49er, 311
Daily American, 376
Daily Astorian, 376
Daily Home, 205
Daily Iowan, 4
Daily News, 98, 206, 208, 267, 345, 376
Daily News Express, 345

Daily News-Miner, Fairbanks, Alaska, 206
Dale, Francis, 57, 121, 347
Dallas Morning News, 263, 267, 320
Danforth, Dave, 345
Dauten, Dale, 121, 128, 128, 347, 348
Davey Committee, ix, 78, 304
Day, George S., 285, 286
debt loads, the effects of, 14, 22, 292, 355
De Pree, Max, 119
death spiral of local TV news, 196, 198, 204
Decision Tree, 144, 145, 149, 150, 151
decision-making steps, 138
Demers, David, 19, 20, 193, 194, 327
demographics, 271, 272, 275, 313
Dentsu, 326
Denver Post, 20, 98, 267, 318, 379
departmentalization, 219
depreciation, 244
deregulation, 6, 22, 173, 174, 175, 343
Des Moines Register, 5, 17, 212
Deseret Morning News, 20, 207
Detroit Free Press, 20, 98, 267, 318
Detroit News, 19, 20, 98, 267, 318
Diario Las Americanas, 208
diffusion of innovations, 281
digital cameras, 371
Dilbert Principle, 125, 126
direct mail marketing, 284
DirecTV, 8, 305, 324, 325
Dispatch Printing Co., 8
divine right of capital, 199
Dixon, Lisa, 81
Doerr, John, 351
Dow Jones & Co., 6, 8, 29, 46, 72, 98, 191, 212, 220, 295, 325
Downie Jr., Leonard, 305, 381
Downs, Hugh, 9, 197
Drucker, Peter F., 14, 39, 40, 41, 52, 53, 73, 86, 92, 93, 94, 108, 109, 125, 126, 127, 136, 138, 139, 140, 141, 142, 144, 156, 203, 286, 365, 366
Dubuque Leader, 206
Dumas, Alexandre, 69
Dunne, Finley Peter, 74
Dusenberry, Philip, 273
Dyer, Carolyn Stewart, viii

E&P Interactive, 380
E.W. Scripps Co., 8, 29, 191, 212, 220, 230, 232, 315
Eagle-Tribune of Lawrence, Mass., 28
Eat That Frog! 54
EBIT, 277
EBITDA, 190
Eccentric, 81
EchoStar, 324, 325
Economics and Financing of Media Companies, 21
economies of scale, 20, 21, 276, 279, 280, 287, 292, 293, 310, 313, 321
Editor & Publisher, 4, 9, 19, 46, 47, 76, 174, 179, 196, 235, 268, 380, 381
Edrington, Mary, 121
Effective Executive, 53

Effective Public Relations, 268
eight required survival objectives, 230
E-Ink, 380
El Nuevo Herald, 208, 370
electronic ink, 380
electronic paper, 381
Emerson, Ralph Waldo, vii
Emmis Communications, 295
employee stock ownership plan, 206, 212
employment-at-will, 82, 177
Emporia (Kan.) *Gazette*, 26, 265
e-paper, 380
equity, 95, 96, 248, 291
Erie Times-News, 111
Employee Stock Ownership Plan (ESOP), 206, 212
Estes, Ralph W., 199
estimating and forecasting traps, 157
Evening News, 206
Exodus 18:21, 219
expense budgets, 238

Fair Labor Standards Act, 179
Family Circle, 321
Fang, Ted and Florence, 60
Farm Wife News, 345
Farson, Richard, 112
Federal Communications Commission (FCC) , 6, 7, 8, 9, 10, 31, 46, 172, 173, 174, 175, 308, 319, 324, 325, 364, 371
Ferren, Brian, 381
Fidler, Roger F., 363, 365, 366, 367, 368, 371, 372, 373, 378, 379
fiduciary responsibility, 78, 201, 217
Fiedler, Fred E., 351
firing of employees, 82, 83
Fink, Conrad, 69, 319
First Amendment, 14, 26, 27, 28, 123, 124, 167, 172, 193, 202, 204, 285, 312
First-Time Manager, 49
fixed costs, 277
Flaherty, John E., 40, 52, 74, 108, 125
Flint (Mich.) *Journal*, 263, 313
Forbes, Malcolm, 52, 359
Ford Foundation, 4
Fort Lauderdale Sun-Sentinel, 265
Fortune magazine, 46, 322
Fox TV, 7, 20, 323
fragmentation, 203, 308, 327, 329, 330
framing trap, 156
Frank N. Magid Associates, 266
Franklin, Benjamin, 108, 119, 120, 253
Freedom Communications, 8, 22, 29, 212
Freedom Forum, 164, 170, 185
Freeman, Robert N., 308
Friedman, Milton, 227, 228, 233
Fuller, Jack, 44, 198, 330
Fullerton, Hugh S. (case studies), 63, 129, 186, 335, 360
full-time equivalents (FTEs), 97
functional parts of a business, 214

Gadsden (Ala.) *Times*, 204

Galbraith, 193, 194, 195, 200
Galvin, Christopher B., 60
Gandhi, Mahatma, 303
Gannett, x, 4, 6, 8, 17, 20, 22, 28, 29, 43, 46,
    47, 69, 72, 92, 109, 115, 141, 175, 190,
    191, 193, 194, 195, 212, 220, 265, 293,
    294, 295, 305, 313, 315, 316, 317, 318,
    323, 325, 330, 345
Gantt chart, 240, 241
Ganzi, Victor, 196
Garner, John, 18
Gartner, Michael G., 312
Gassaway, Bob, 67
Gates, Bill, 209, 329, 377, 383
Gazette, Cedar Rapids, Iowa, 4, 8, 206, 376
General Electric, 20, 191, 305, 306, 323,
    324, 325, 328
General Motors, 236
Gershon, Richard A., 328
Ghiglione, Loren, vii
Gilder, George, 372
Giles, Robert H., 19, 50, 51, 89, 137
Gingrich, Newt, 209
Goldman, Debbie, 12
Good Housekeeping, 321, 322
Gorman, Tom, 54, 149, 254
Gover, Raymond L., xi, 77
Grady School, 11
Graphic Communications International
    Union, 71
Gray Television, 8
Greater Media, 295
Green Bay (Wis.) News-Chronicle, 72
Greene, Graham, 16, 375
Griffin, Ricky W., 138, 141
group decision-making styles, 159
groupthink, 159, 160
Grove, Andrew S., 51, 52
Grushow, Sandy, 272
Guild, 70, 71, 74, 81, 97. See Newspaper
    Guild.
Gup, Ted, 168
GW Hatchet, 311

Ha, Louisa (case study), 130
Hadley, Leonard A., 235
Haile, L. John, 24
Haldeman, Joe, 309
Hamilton, William P., 227, 228
Harari, Oren, 68, 122, 137
Harris, Jay T., 13, 45, 79, 194, 231
Harris Enterprises, 13
Harris, Doug, 118
Harvard Business Review, 51, 52, 111, 143,
    154, 369
Hawkeye, 284
Hawthorne Effect, 86, 87, 88
Hearst Corp., 8, 29, 196, 204, 315, 318, 325
Hearst III, William, 43, 350
Hearst–Argyle, 191, 323
Henley, W.E., 40
Henry, Neil, 15, 16
Hernandez, Macarena, 183
Herrera, Dan, 113

Herrick, Dennis F. (case study), 259
heuristics, 153
Hiaasen, Carl, 258
Hickey, Neil, 230
hidden traps of decision-making, 153
Hileman, Richard A., 178
Hinkley, Robert, 235
Hladky, Joe, 304
Hollinger International Inc., 21, 22, 29, 220
Hollings, Senator Ernest, 174
horizontal integration, 280
Houston Chronicle, 204, 265, 267, 318
How to Buy a Business, 357
How to Buy a Newspaper and Succeed, 358
*How to Succeed in Business without Really
    Trying*, 125
Howard Publications, 325
Howell, Deborah, 124
Hoynes, William, 232
Hughes, Cathy, 45, 324
Human Side of Enterprise, 88
humanistic (or behaviorist) management, 86
humor, 41, 83, 120, 171, 216
Hutchins Commission, 193, 228
Hyman, Mark, 198

Inc. magazine, 352
income statement, 240, 245, 247
Independent Association of Publishers'
    Employees, 72
independent contractor, 179
Independent Newspapers, Inc., 204
Indian Country Today, 208
individual decision-making styles, 158
Industry Standard, 307
Infinity Broadcasting, 295, 324
information revolution, 365
infotainment, 13, 16, 50, 190, 204, 266, 267,
    273, 288, 293, 329, 330
institutional investors, 6, 12, 29, 77, 194,
    212, 231
Intel, 51, 191, 383
intellectual watchdog, 143
intermedia competition, 327
internal rate of return (IRR), 254, 256
Internal Revenue Service, 179
International Association of Machinists, 71
International Brotherhood of Electrical
    Workers, 71
International Brotherhood of Teamsters, 71
International Newspaper Financial
    Executives, 289
International Typographical Union, 70
Internet, 3, 18, 21, 24, 25, 33, 58, 122, 155,
    163, 169, 174, 175, 193, 217, 232, 236,
    259, 266, 268, 269, 270, 272, 281, 283,
    307, 308, 317, 320, 321, 326, 327, 329,
    330, 344, 346, 351, 358, 363, 364, 367,
    368, 371, 372, 373, 374, 375, 377, 378,
    379, 381, 382, 383
Iowa City Gazette, 4
Iowa City Press-Citizen, 4
Iowa Co-Operative Publishing Co., 206
Iowa State Daily, 312

Iraq, 16, 25, 75, 183, 365
irreversible decision, 141
Ivins, Molly, 172, 190

Jackson, Beverly, 46
Jameson, Barclay, 47, 182
Janis, Irving I., 159, 160
Jaske, John B., 69, 71
Jennings, Peter, 381
jerks, 128
Jersey Journal, 77
Jerusalem Post, 22
Jobs, Steve, 383
Johnson, Robert, 45
Johnson, Tom, 17, 44, 47, 130
Joint Operating Agreement (JOA), 5, 204, 310, 311, 314, 315, 316, 318
Jones, Alex, 17
Joseph, Richard A., 4, 357
Journal of Communications, 8, 206
Journal of Media Economics, 20, 328
Journal Publishing, 294
Journal Register Company (JRC), 29, 220, 290, 291
Journal Star, 212
Journalism History, 5
Journal-World, 320
Junck, Mary E., 46

Kaiser, Robert G., 305, 381
Kamen, Charles, 74
Kansas City Star, 275
Kanter, Rosabeth Moss, 105, 113
Karmazin, Mel, 295
Kasabian, Robert, 289
Kay, Linda (case study), 221
Kelleher, Herb, 105, 112, 113
Kelly, Marjorie, 46, 145, 199, 200
Kent format, 368
Kent Report, ix, 304
Ketter, William, 14
Keyes, Ralph, 112
Kezziah, Bill (case study), xi, 30
KHAK, 343
Kidder, Rushworth M., 307
Kildee, Representative Dale E., 166
Klueger, Robert F., 355
Knight Ridder, 20, 29, 46, 60, 79, 80, 115, 118, 124, 191, 194, 201, 212, 220, 228, 230, 231, 233, 258, 265, 275, 295, 315, 325, 367, 378
Korda, Michael, 122
Korean Times, 208
Kouzes, James M., 109, 110, 113, 115, 120
Kovach, Bill, 227
Kovarik, William (case study), 384
Kramer, Roderick M., 52
KRQE, 321
KTNN-AM, 20, 207
Kurtz, Howard, 183, 321
Kwitny, Jonathan, 192
KWRK, 208

Lacy, Stephen, 80, 196

Lambeth, Edmund, 80, 195
Lancaster Publications, 294
Landmark Communications, 8, 29
largest U.S. chains, 325
laser printer, invention of, 383
Las Cruces Sun-News, 316
Laventhol, David, 79
Lavine, John, 13, 69
law of diminishing returns, 278
layoffs of employees, 75, 81, 82
Leadership Challenge, 109
Leadership is an Art. See Max De Pree
Leadership practices, 109–114
Leading Your Team to Excellence, 161
Leaving Readers Behind, 290, 293, 305
Ledbetter, James, 307
Lee Enterprises, 29, 46, 191, 220, 294, 315, 325
Lelyveld, Joseph, 4, 14, 184
LePatner, Barry, 118
leverage ratios, 248
Levin, Gerald M., 341
Lewiston (Idaho) *Morning Tribune*, 376
Leyden, Peter, 381
Liberty Group Publishing, 29, 291, 294, 322, 323
Liebling, A.J., ix, 3, 14, 26, 50, 74, 303
Linsky, Marty, 122, 123, 167
Lionheart, 291
liquidity ratios, 247
LLC corporation, 214
Lloyd, Robert, 112, 120, 135
Loeb, William and Nackey, 205
Long Beach (Calif.) *Press-Telegram*, 347
Lopez, Steve, 60
Los Angeles Investor's Business Daily, 267, 313
Los Angeles Herald Examiner, 12, 57
Los Angeles Times, 6, 19, 20, 44, 60, 169, 212, 264, 267, 367, 368, 370
Lowe, Ken, 232
Lyon, Mike, 293
Lyon Publishing, 294

Machiavellian ethics, 169
Mackay, Harvey, 67, 111, 114, 116
macroeconomics, 137
Madigan, John, 119
Management and the Worker, 87
Management by Objectives (MBO), 92, 93, 94, 95
Management Challenges for the 21st Century, 203, 365
Management of Organizational Behavior, 106
Management of the Electronic Media, 83
Managing Media Organizations, 69
market-driven journalism, 13, 228, 288, 289, 290, 329
Marketing Management, 272, 276, 286, 287
Martin, Hugh J., 80
Mascle, Deanna, 51
Maslow, Abraham H., 90, 91, 92, 271
Maslow's Hierarchy of Needs, 90, 91

Maquoketa Newspapers, 294
Mayo, Elton, 86, 87, 88
MBA, 49, 58, 145
McCain, Senator John, 174
McCarthy, E. Jerome, 268, 270, 271, 286
McCaw, Wendy P., 23
McChesney, Robert, 74, 307
McClatchy, C.K., 290
McClatchy Company, 29, 77, 191, 212, 220, 295, 315
McCord, Richard, xi, 28
McCorkindale, Douglas, 194
McCormick, Robert R., 126, 198
McDermott, Larry, 77
McFarlin, Diane, 46
McGregor, Douglas, 88, 89
McHugh & Hoffman, 266
McLean, George A., 29, 205
McLuhan, Marshall, 264
McManus, John, 13, 289
Media General, 8, 29, 220, 320
Media Management Center, 13, 58
Media Mergers, 305
MediaNews Group, 8, 16, 20, 29, 46, 74, 110, 268, 294, 315, 316, 317, 318, 321, 325, 346, 366
MediaWeek, 47, 295
Mencken, H.L., 303
Mercury News, 45, 79, 80
Meredith Corp., 191
Merrill, John C., 169, 196
Metcalfe, Robert, 112
Metro, 272, 345
Meyer, Eugene, 171
Meyer, Philip, 80, 196, 197
Mid–America Publishing, 294
Miami Herald, 112, 258, 267, 370
micro-dailies, 345
Microsoft, 175, 190, 191, 259, 328, 329, 350, 367, 370, 371, 383
milestone, 240, 241
Miller, Edward D., 3
Milwaukee Journal Sentinel, 206
Minneapolis Star Tribune, 267
Missourian, 312
MIT Media Lab, 381
Mitchell, Lawrence E., 197
MMC, 13
mobile journalist, 24, 25, 365, 380
Modern Maturity, 321
monopoly, 21, 31, 175, 287, 308, 309, 310, 313, 318, 319, 327
Monti, Mario, 328
Moon, Sun Myung, 207
Moore, Ann, 46
Moorhouse, Virginia F., 46
Mormon Church, 8, 315
Morris Communications Corp., 29
Morton, John, 230, 231
Mosaic, 282, 383
Motorola, 60, 383
MSNTV, 308
Mt. Sterling (Ky.) *Advocate*, 51
Munsey, Frank, 26, 27, 190
Murdoch, Lachlan, 60

Murdoch, Rupert, 60, 194, 208, 307, 325
Murphy, Tom, 228
Murphy's Law, 140, 148, 281
Murrow, Edward R., 27, 29

Nagel, Roger C., 195
nanny state, 236
Nanus, Burt, 108
National Association of Broadcast Employees and Technicians, 71
National Association of Broadcasters, 173
National Geographic, 321
National Labor Relations Act, 72
National Post, 22, 267
National Public Radio (NPR), 10, 17, 208
natural monopoly, 310
Naughton, Jim, 79, 258
Navajo Nation, 20, 207
Navajo Times, 208
NBC, 20, 306, 312, 323, 324, 325, 326, 328, 330, 345
Negroponte, 381
Ness, Susan, 46
net present value (NPR), 254, 255, 256, 257
net profit, 18, 190, 191, 246
Netscape, 282, 383
Neuharth, Al, 43, 109, 115, 318
Neuman, David, 379
Newark Star-Ledger, 267
New Century Press, 294
New England Weekly Journal, 192
New London (Conn.) *Day*, 205
Newsday, 267
New York Daily News, 267
New York Observer, 184
New York Post, 20, 60, 173, 267
New York Sun, 22, 346
New York Times, 3, 6, 8, 11, 14, 20, 23, 26, 28, 29, 46, 60, 98, 139, 169, 170, 171, 180, 183, 184, 191, 212, 220, 267, 295, 320, 325, 326, 345, 368, 369, 370, 376, 378, 379
Newhouse, Donald and Samuel I., 76, 77, 194
NewRadio Group LLC, 344
News Corp., 7, 8, 20, 21, 60, 173, 174, 194, 208, 305, 307, 323, 324, 325, 326, 328, 330
NewsHour, 195
Newspaper Associates, x
Newspaper Association of America, 173, 175, 320
newspaper carriers, 179
Newspaper Guild, 33, 70, 74, 80, 81, 98
Newspaper Preservation Act, 5, 172, 314, 315, 316
Newspaper Research Journal, 20
NewspaperDirect, 370
News Publishing, Inc., 294
Newsroom Management, 50, 95
NewsStand, 369
Newsweek, 8, 20, 184, 268
Nidey, Frank J., 118
Nielsen ratings, 50, 283

Nieman Foundation, 19
Nixon, President Richard M., 5, 314
Noam, Eli, 308
non-compete covenant, 177, 178
non-duplicating coverage, 284
non-programmed decision, 143, 144
NRTA/AARP Bulletin, 321

Oden, Kendra, 263
Ogden Newspapers, Inc., 29, 294
Ogilvy, David, 121
oligopoly, 287, 295, 309
Omaha World-Herald, 206, 294
Omaha World-Herald Co., 29, 229
Only the Paranoid Survive, 51
operating profit, 18, 190
operating ratios, 248
opportunity cost, 257
optimism, 119, 120, 123, 346
Orange County Register, 267
Orem (Utah) Daily Journal, 381
Orlando Sentinel, 379
Osborne, Burl, 263
Osprey Media Group, 291, 292
Ottaway Newspapers, 8, 29, 46
Ouchi, William G., 89, 90
Outing, 380
Overholser, Geneva, v, 5, 17, 79, 92, 230
owners equity, 243, 248

Packard, Vance, 114
Paley, William, 42, 218
Parade, 322
Parkinson, C. Northcote, 125, 127
Parkinson's Law, 125, 127
Parsons, Richard, 45
partnership, 8, 209, 210, 211, 213, 316, 317, 358
Patriot-News, Harrisburg, Pa., 77, 97
Pavlik, John V., 365, 373
payback period, 254, 256, 257
pay-off matrix, 145, 151
Paxson Communications, 323
People magazine, 322
perfect competition, 285, 287
performance ratios, 248
Performance Evaluation and Review Technique (PERT), 144, 145, 146, 147, 148, 149, 157, 276
Peter Principle, 126
Pfaff, William, 195
Philadelphia Daily News, 45
Philadelphia Inquirer, 115, 267, 370
Picard, Robert G., 12, 21, 196, 280, 296, 298, 331, 334
Pilgrim, Tim, 309, 313, 314
Pittsburgh Press, 71
point and counterpoint, 143
Porter, Jill, 168
Portland Oregonian, 267
Posner, Barry Z., 109, 110, 113, 115, 120
Post Register, 376
Post-Standard, 111
Powell, Colin L., 68, 114, 122, 137, 173,

174, 380
Powell, Michael, 173, 174, 308
power of the cluster, 294
Poynter Institute, 48, 58, 79, 97, 122, 167, 189, 192, 201, 205, 258, 319, 329, 369
Poynter, Nelson, 206
Practice of Management, 93, 138
Presstime, 49, 320
price elasticity of demand, 279
principles of authority, 218
product positioning, 270
profit and loss statement, 240, 245, 247
profit-maximization, 227, 228, 237
programmed decision, 144
progressive discipline, 82
Project for Excellence in Journalism, 97, 189, 304
Project on the State of the American Newspaper, 293, 304
protected category, 176
Provo (Utah) Daily Herald, 370
Pruitt, Gary, 77
psychographics, 271
Public Broadcasting System (PBS), 10, 208, 192, 208
Publicis Groupe, 326
Publishers' Auxiliary, 54
Puerto Rico, 71, 81, 98, 99
Pulitzer Newspapers, Inc., 29, 315
Pyramid Climbers, 114

quality of work life, 90
Quass, Mary, 343, 344
Quebecor, 304
Quill magazine, 24
Quinn, Terry, 12, 18

Radio One, 45
Radio-Television News Directors Association, 48
Raines, Howell, 184
reactive or proactive decision, 141
Read All About It! The Corporate Takeover of America's Newspapers, 232, 305
Reader's Digest, 321, 322
Record Searchlight, Redding, Calif., 46
Redmond, James, 49
Reed Elsevier, 191, 330
Reed, Mike, 16
Reider, Rem, 79
Reiman, Roy, 344
restraint of trade, 181
retained earnings, 242, 244
return on assets, 244
Rich Media, Poor Democracy, 74
Ridder, Tony, 60, 79, 194, 258, 275
right to work, 177
RMA Annual Statement Studies, 249
Roberts, Gene, 116, 293, 305
Robertson, Jim, 312
Robinson, Janet, 46
Rockefeller, John D., 48
Rocket eBook, 368
Rocky Mountain News, 267, 318

Roosevelt, President Franklin D., ix
Rogers, Everett M., 77, 156, 281, 282
Rosenberg, Jim, 380
Rosenstiel, Tom, 189
Rosenthal, Abe, 3
routine decision, 141
rules of the road, 170, 171

S corporation, 214
Sacramento Bee, 267
Safari, 376
sales budgets, 238
Salon, 370
salaries for graduates, 41
Saltz, Howard, 379
San Antonio Express-News, 183
San Diego Union-Tribune, 267
San Francisco Bay Guardian, 318
San Francisco Chronicle, 267, 370, 375
San Francisco Examiner, 60
Santa Barbara News-Press, 23
Santa Monica (Calif.) *Daily Press,* 345
Sarasota Herald-Tribune, 46, 320
Satellite Newspapers, 370
Sault Ste. Marie (Mich.) *Evening News,* 70
Sawyer, Ron, 51
Schwarzkopf, H. Norman, 117
scientific (or classical) management, 84
Seagram, 305
Seattle Post-Intelligencer, 71, 98, 318
Seattle Times, 29, 98, 318, 322
Securities and Exchange Commission
    (SEC), 231, 260
segmentation, 13, 273, 366
Seldes, George, ix, 3, 14, 303
September 11, 2001, 16, 268
Serrin, William, 12
sexual harassment, 179, 181
shovelware, 365
Shreveport Times, 263
Simon, Herbert A., 136, 138, 143, 144
Sinclair Broadcasting, 198
Sinclair, Upton, ix
Sing Tao Daily, 208
Singer, Jane, (case study) 24, 31, 34
Singleton, William Dean, 16, 111, 232, 268,
    294, 321, 346, 347, 366
Sloan, Alfred P., 142
Small Business Administration (SBA), 350,
    351, 352, 354, 355, 357
Smiddy, Deborah, 46
Smith, Jack, 381
Smith, Terence, 195, 219
Smulgen, Jeff, 295
Smyth, Peter, 295
Smythe, Joe, 204
Soap Opera Update, 268
*Social Problems of an Industrial
    Civilization,* 87, 88
Society of Professional Journalists, 29, 100
SoftBook, 368
Sohn, Ardyth B., 67, 138
sole proprietorship, 209, 210, 213, 358
Soloski, John, 10, 11, 12

Sony, 191, 305, 330, 365, 380
sources of power, 105, 106, 108
Southam, 304
span of control, 218
Spartanburg (S.C.) *Herald-Journal,* 204
Sports Illustrated, 322
Squires, James D., 232, 233, 239
St. Louis Post-Dispatch, 25, 267
St. Paul Pioneer Press, 124, 196, 233, 321
St. Petersburg Times, 205, 206, 230, 267,
    304
Standard Oil Company, 48
Starck, Kenneth A., 91
Starr, Brenda, 291
status-quo trap, 155
Steffens, Lincoln, 5
Stengel, Casey, 115
Stephens Media Group, 29, 315
Stevens Point Journal, 313
Stier, Mary P., 46
Stone, Gerald, 20
Strategic Newspaper Management, 69
Sulentic, Joe, 55, 56, 59
Sun group, 304
sunk cost, 257
sunk-cost trap, 156
Sulzberger, Arthur Hays, 60
Sulzberger Jr., Arthur O., 11, 26, 43, 139,
    170, 379
Sulzberger, Arthur Ochs, 60, 184
Survival of a Free, Competitive Press, ix
Sweeney, Anne, 46
S.W.O.T. analysis, 162
Sykes, Alfred C., 364
synergy or synergies, 276, 280, 281, 293,
    306, 313, 321

tablet newspaper, 366, 367, 368, 378
Tablet PC, 367, 370
tabloidization, 266
Tacitus, 105
Taft-Hartley Act, 73
*Taking Stock: Journalism and the Publicly
    Traded Newspaper Company,* 10, 11,
    202, 220
Tampa Bay Online, 320
Tampa Tribune, 189, 320
Taste of Home, 321, 344
tax payments, 180
Taylor, Frederick W., 84, 85, 86
TCI, 305
teamwork, 56, 76, 87, 88, 93, 94, 112, 113,
    143
technological milestones of the computer
    era, 383
Telecommunications Act, 6, 7, 22, 172, 197,
    323, 324, 343
Telegraph, of London, 22
Telemundo, 20, 324, 325
Texas–New Mexico Newspapers
    Partnership, 316, 317
The Business of Journalism, 12
The Business of Media, 232
The Max Strategy, 347

The Media Lab: Inventing the Future at MIT, 372
The Media Monopoly, 10, 11, 16, 303, 305, 306, 322
The News About the News, 305, 381
The SUN, Mount Vernon, Iowa, 284
The Transnational Media Corporation, 328
The Tribune, Ames, Iowa, 312
Theory of Social and Economic Organization, 106
Theory X, 88, 89, 107
Theory Y, 88, 89
Theory Z, 88, 90
Thomas-Graham, Pamela, 45
Thomson Newspapers, 12, 18, 22, 80, 250
Thornton, Leslie-Jean (case studies), x, 163, 183
Time, 14, 20, 46, 321, 322
time management, 54, 55
time value of money, 238, 251, 252, 253, 254, 256, 257, 359
Time Warner, 306, 307, 341
time and money, 137
Time, Inc., 46
Times Mirror Co., 220, 264, 306
TiVo, 308, 376
total market coverage (TMC), 283, 284
to-do list, 55
top minimum wage, 97, 98
top 10 U.S. TV owners, 323
Toronto Globe & Mail, 267
Toronto National Post, 267
Toronto Star, 267
total turnover rate, 96
Townsend, Robert, 112, 114
Tracy, Brian 54
Trager, Robert, 49
Trenton Times, 346
Trever, John, 7
Tribune Co., 8, 20, 24, 29, 44, 175, 191, 220, 264, 295, 323, 325, 330
Tucson Citizen, 314
Tucker, Cynthia, x
Tulsa (Okla.) *World*, 376
Turner, Ted, 341, 345
Turner Broadcasting Systems, 341
Tuscaloosa (Ala.) *News*, 51, 204
TV Guide, 321, 322
Twain, Mark, 348
Tyranny of the Bottom Line, 199

Underwood, Doug, 124, 125, 167, 288, 305
Unimédia, 304
Union Leader, 205
United Auto Workers, 70, 207
Univision, 323, 325
Up the Organization, 111, 114
UPN, 173, 198, 323, 324
Upside magazine, 380
USA Today, 20, 317, 370
U.S. magazine circulation, 321

U.S. magazine revenue, 322

Valley News Today, Shenandoah, Iowa, 229
Vanderbilt, William H., 227
Van Noord, Roger, xi
variable costs, 277
venture capital, 124, 290, 291, 292, 350
vertical integration, 280
Viacom, 7, 45, 173, 191, 198, 295, 305, 323, 324, 326, 330
Viasat, 345
Vivendi Universal, 22, 305, 326, 330
Vogue, 345
VoIP, 375
Volkswagen, 236

Wackman, Daniel B., 69
Wall Street Journal, 72, 125, 179, 190, 192, 200, 267, 275, 307, 368, 370, 375
Walt Disney Co., 20, 212, 305, 306, 323, 324, 326, 330
Walton, Mary, 290, 291
Washington Post, xi, 5, 6, 8, 20, 28, 29, 71, 171, 183, 212, 220, 267, 295, 307, 321, 370
Washington Star, 12
Washington Times, 207, 370
Weaver, Al, 120
Weaver, Janet, 46
Weber, Max, 106, 194
Wehco Media, 29
Welch, Jack, 328
Western Electric Company, 86
Westin, Av, 196, 197
Westward, 291
WFAA-TV, 320
WFLA-TV, 320
When MBAs Rule the Newsroom, 124, 288, 305
White, William Allen, 26, 190, 264
who's really in charge? 220
Wi-Fi, 308
Willes, Mark, 264, 265
Wilson, Marc, 381
Wiseman, Jerry , 293
Woman's Day, 321
Wolf, Michael, 307, 308, 309
Wood, Frank, 72
Woodward Communications, 294
work specialization, 219
World Company, 8
World Journal, 208
World Wide Web, 281, 364, 372, 383
Writers Guild of America, 71

Yegge, Wilbur M., 354, 355, 35

zoned coverage, 284